122458

Limited Classical Reprint Library

THE

FOOTSTEPS OF ST PETER:

BEING

𝔗𝔥𝔢 𝔏𝔦𝔣𝔢 𝔞𝔫𝔡 𝔗𝔦𝔪𝔢𝔰 𝔬𝔣 𝔱𝔥𝔢 𝔄𝔭𝔬𝔰𝔱𝔩𝔢.

BY

J. R. MACDUFF, D.D.

Foreword by
Dr. Cyril J. Barber

Klock & Klock Christian Publishers, Inc.
2527 Girard Avenue North
Minneapolis, Minnesota 55411

Originally published by
James Nisbet & Co.
London, 1876

ISBN: 0-86524-149-X

Printed by Klock & Klock in the U.S.A.
1982 Reprint

FOREWORD

Charles Churchill, when discussing the difficulties involved in writing well, stated:

Little do such men know the toil, the pains,
The daily, nightly racking of the brains,
To range the thoughts, the matter to digest,
To cull fit phrases, and reject the rest
(*Gotham*, II,i,11).

Writing a book is not an easy task. To write a good book demands the painstaking skill and perseverence of one whose innate creativity cries out for expression. To write a book which will retain its merit to succeeding generations requires that solitary toil and skillful expression which only a few possess.

A writer worthy of repeated reading is John Ross Macduff (1818-1895). He was an eloquent Scot whose pulpit ministry endeared him to an ever-widening circle. When he "retired" in 1870, Dr. MacDuff devoted himself to a literary ministry. The books which he wrote during this period of his life sold literally hundreds of thousands of copies and were a blessing to people throughout the English-speaking world.

Dr. MacDuff possessed the ability to vividly describe the human element in the Scriptures. As a result, he became famous for his Bible character studies. Among his most popular works were *Elijah, the Prophet of Fire, The Footsteps of St. Paul,* a later work dealing with the last days of Paul in Rome, numerous studies of incidents in the gospels, and the work presently before the reader.

Dr. MacDuff travelled widely, mainly in the Near East. The cultural and climate of the countries surrounding the Mediterranean had changed little since the time of Christ and the Apostles. This enabled Dr. MacDuff to observe details and describe scenes which he later used to enliven historical passages of Scripture. The result to readers of Dr. MacDuff's books is the enhancement of the biblical narrative.

The content of *The Footsteps of St. Peter,* however, contains more than the random reminiscences of a world traveller. There is evident on every page a thoroughness of research, a precision in dealing with historical details, and an accuracy in treating the inspired record, that gives proof of the writer's long exposure to the events which helped mold, and the circumstances which gave impetus to, Peter's ministry.

While some may find J. R. MacDuff a trifle loquacious, let it be remembered that he was one of the finest products of his age. He was adept at culling the right phrase and painting on the canvas of the mind vivid recreations of biblical events. We, therefore, continue to stand in his debt.

Cyril J. Barber
Author, *The Minister's Library*

31681

PREFACE.

——◆◆——

THE Author accomplishes in the subsequent pages
a long-cherished purpose of writing a companion
volume to " THE FOOTSTEPS OF ST PAUL."

The Great Apostle of the Gentiles will always
occupy his own pre-eminent pedestal in the Church
as the grandest *ideal* of the Christian Teacher, whom
Chrysostom, in one of his golden epithets, truly calls
" the Heart of the World." But second only in
interest to him is his ' Brother of the Circumcision :' in some respects indeed more interesting, as
the personal follower and friend of his Divine Lord ;
whereas the other was, " as one born out of due
time." While the life of St Paul, moreover, is more
diversified in what may be called dramatic incident,
yet, as Dean Alford observes, " there is no one of the
leading characters in the Gospel History who makes
so deep an impression (as St Peter) on the heart and
affections."

While the Writer trusts he is warranted in what follows, to lay some humble yet substantial claim to independent research,—perhaps flattering himself too, that circumstances have given him exceptional advantages in treating the theme, he has not scrupled to glean, as in the companion volume alluded to, any available help from other works to which he has had access ;—" things new and old," bearing alike on the Apostle's life and on the Apostolic age. Moreover, instead of borrowing at secondhand the thoughts and suggestions of others, and incorporating them with his own, he has in most instances deemed it better, by extracts longer and shorter, to let these authors speak for themselves in their own graphic way. This from no unworthy expedient of abbreviating labour ; for he can truthfully aver that on no book he has written has he bestowed more time and pains, but simply from the desire of making the Volume as full and instructive as he could. The obligation thus referred to, extends not only to writers on contemporary history, but to the works of observant travellers who have indirectly by ' reflected lights ' aided the endeavour to present a faithful portraiture. It will thus be seen that he has considered it well not to limit himself strictly to the biography of St Peter, but so to broaden his canvas, as to include the Apostle's " times and surroundings : "—in other

words, whatever in political event, or local association or human companionship, tended, along with
higher influences and impulses, to mould his character.

A liberty of a more personal kind scarcely requires
apology. In one or two of the earlier chapters, the
Writer has ventured to transfer, but always either in
an abridged or expanded form, descriptive extracts
from some of his own former Volumes, especially in
connection with events associated with the Sea of
Galilee. These might indeed have been entirely
recast, but it is with an Author as with an Artist,
the freshness and vigour of a first sketch is often lost
by reproduction.

While he does not hesitate to avow that he has
had considerably in view the Sunday-reading of
thoughtful youth, he has also desired to furnish what
would not be unacceptable to those of maturer years
and riper attainments. It is almost unnecessary to
say, that there is no attempt made at 'practical
lessons' or 'reflections.' These would be foreign to
the design and intention of the Volume.

In conclusion, he trusts that a personal familiarity
with many, indeed most of the scenes intimately
connected with the 'footsteps of St Peter,' may
serve to impart additional interest and fidelity to
what he has written. A few of the illustrations which

head the chapters were hastily sketched on the spot, and may help to vivify the localities described. The design on the title-page—forming the central portion of Raphael's comparatively little known but great painting of 'St Peter in prison,' in the Stanze of the Vatican, is from a photograph of the original picture obtained in a recent visit to Italy.

CONTENTS.

———◆◆———

CHAPTER I.

CHAPTER II.

CHAPTER III.

CHAPTER IV.

CHAPTER X.

CHAPTER XI.

CHAPTER XII.

CHAPTER XIII.

CHAPTER XIV.

CHAPTER XV.

CHAPTER XVI.

CHAPTER XVII.

CHAPTER XVIII.

CHAPTER XIX.

CHAPTER XX.

CHAPTER XXI.

CONTENTS.

LIST OF WOODCUTS.

FULL-PAGE ILLUSTRATIONS.

VIGNETTE ILLUSTRATIONS.

(22 *of the Woodcuts are engraved by Mr Pearson of Bolt Court,*
Fleet Street.)

CHAPTER I.

Introductory.

BIRTHPLACE, BIRTH, PARENTAGE, AND CALLING.   REMARKS ON
CONTEMPORARY JEWISH HISTORY.

" Judea now, and all the promised land,
Reduced a province under Roman yoke,
Obeys Tiberius : nor is always ruled
With temperate sway.   Oft have they violated
The Temple, oft the Law with foul affronts,
Abominations rather, as did once
Antiochus."
—Paradise Regained, Book III.

" It is fit men should be taught who they were, who were
willing at so dear a rate to plant Christianity in the world ; what
was that piety and that patience, that charity and that zeal, which
made them to be reverenced while they lived, and their memories,
ever since, to be honourably celebrated through the world ;
infinitely beyond the glories of Alexander and the triumphs of
Pompey and Cæsar."*—Dr Cave's Lives of the Apostles*, 1662.

" The land of Zabulon, and the land of Nephthalim, by the
way of the sea, beyond Jordan, Galilee of the Gentiles ; the
people which sat in darkness saw great light ; and to them which
sat in the region and shadow of death light is sprung up."
—Matt. iv. 15, 16.

T HE 30th of March and two following days will always retain their place
in the mind of the writer, as pleasant
anniversaries of a visit to the LAKE OF GENNESARET: of
the many hallowed memories of a pilgrimage to Palestine perhaps the most hallowed. Above all other
sacred localities (not even Jerusalem excepted) this
now lonely inland sea possesses the undying interest
of being the most frequent and familiar resort of the
Divine Redeemer during the period of His earthly
ministry. Every green hill and valley and thorny
brake—every spire of grass and lily of the field—every
sheltered nook of its winding shore—every tributary
stream and fountain—every wave that ripples and
murmurs on its pearly beach—either recall His words
or are suggestive of His presence. If there be inspira-

tion in dumb scenery, it is surely here.   No region on
earth lifts one so near all that is great and holy.   I felt
gigantic Baalbec or Egyptian Pyramid, Athenian Par-
thenon or Roman Coliseum, to be piles of cold magnificence compared with the sanctuaries of sacred thought
which crowd in imagination these now desolate shores.
In other famous spots in the land of Israel, the solemnity
of feeling is often rudely disturbed by the guesses and
uncertainties of traditionary "holy places."   On the
shores of Tiberias doubt gives way to assurance.   You
can traverse the ruined courts of this Great Temple of
Nature with the cherished conviction, ' Here lived and
walked and taught the Son of the Eternal God ! Words
and deeds which *have* lived and *will* live for ages, were
here first spoken and performed.   These are the waters
which bore Him in calm and in storm.   These mountains are the midnight oratories from which moon and
stars listened to their Maker's voice : and where, as the
Great Intercessor, He pled for a perishing world."

It may truthfully be added, that with the exception
of thus tracing the footsteps of HIM who gave to that
region its highest consecration, no place was looked for
with greater interest than the supposed site of *Bethsaida*
—the village home of PETER and his fellow-disciples,
—the special eyewitnesses of that Incarnate Glory.
Although the locality of " the House of Fish," as Bethsaida means,[1] cannot positively be identified, it does not
at all events share the same amount of doubt which
surrounds many others sacred in Gospel Story.   It

---

1 " The lake, probably from the numerous streams, including the Jordan
itself, which discharge their produce into its waters, abounds in fish of all
kinds, which there increase and multiply, as certainly as in the Salt Sea
they are cast up dead upon the shore.   From the earliest times—so said the
Rabbinical legends—the lake had been so renowned in this respect, that

might be enough, indeed, to know that *somewhere* on that north-west shore, the child first saw the light whose manhood and history are to occupy our attention in the succeeding pages. But in pointing to the modern village of El-Tabijah as possessing the strongest claim to the honour, I am fortified by having the warrant and authority of nearly all the most reliable of Eastern travellers.[1]

It was on a Monday morning when, after resting on the Sabbath "according to commandment," we sailed from Tiberias in company with two Jewish boatmen across the northern portion of the lake, to explore the ruins of Tel Hum. "Roman galleys and pleasure barges had, in former days, floated on these waters; but even could they have been still procured, more pleasing far was the thought that we were sailing on Gennesaret in a rude fishing-boat, similar probably to the craft of Zebedee and his fishermen sons; similar rather, to that in which, with the omnipotence of Godhead, He who rules the raging of the sea rebuked the winds and waves; or when, stretched on the bare planks, exhausted nature asserted its claims on repose, and yielding to the innocent infirmities and needs of a common humanity, He fell asleep."[2] In returning to meet our horses and dragoman at Khan Minyeh on the Damascus road, we skirted the shore, and had a

one of the ten fundamental laws laid down by Joshua on the division of the country was, that any one might fish with a hook in the Sea of Galilee, so that they did not interfere with the free passage of boats."—*Sinai and Palestine*, p. 370. We partook of the fish as we "dined on the shore" where our tent was pitched. They seemed to resemble our "perch" in appearance and flavour.

[1] The reader is referred among other authorities to Dr Robinson and Dr Porter.

[2] Preface to "Memories of Gennesaret."

full view of the hills behind, rising in a succession of
swells which may be said to terminate only with the
heights of Safed, the latter perched like an eagle on its
lofty rocky nest,—the reputed " City set on an hill."
The land which at Tel Hum is comparatively flat, here
becomes bold and even mountainous.   The home of
the apostle fishermen, if we can thus speak confidently
of El-Tabijah,[1] nestles in a natural recess or bay of fine
pearly sand and shells, formed by the encircling hills,—
a natural breakwater ; "just such a place," as has been
well observed, " where fishermen would like to ground
their boats."[2]   Had time permitted us to land we might
have explored the ruins of an aqueduct or aqueducts,
as well as some remarkable streams, some of them hot
and brackish, which burst from the hill above amid
thickets of nabk and agnus castus.   Closer to the shore
is a water basin enclosed with a circular stone wall, and
bearing the name of 'Ain Eyûb, " Job's fountain."[3]
An enterprising traveller[4] who moored his slender craft
in the bay, while he describes it as " admirably suited
for boats, shelving gradually, the anchorage good, and
where boats can be safely beached ;" speaks also of
" boulders of great rocks projecting from the shore into
the waves ; while verdure most profuse teems over
them, and long streamers of maidenhair and richest
grasses and ferns and briers and moss wave in the
breeze and pendant trail upon the water ;" adding, that
" the place soon asserted its right to the name Bethsaida by the exceeding abundance of the fish seen
tumbling about."   Amid a fringe of oleanders and

---

1 See the frontispiece sketched from the boat on the lake, the moonlight
effect added by the artist.

2 Porter's Hand-Book in Palestine, ii. 49.   3 Ib., ii. 429.

4 Rob Roy on the Jordan, p. 342-44.

brambles we saw the combined streams rushing down by a mill erected near the beach, and which gives a picturesqueness, perhaps I should rather say a home look, to the scene : " the sound of rivulets and cascades and the musical dripping of water from the long pointed stalactites in the caverns beside us, and the low, rumbling, splashing, tremulous beat of the mill wheels working unseen, blend a mixed harmony round the sunny little cove." [1] In early spring (the season we visited it), here and there the black goats-hair tent of the wandering Arab may be noted occupying the spot where the old fishermen of Galilee spread their nets or reared their huts. [2]

Though the birthplace can be thus fixed with tolerable certainty, we can only approximate the precise year in which the infant fisherman was born. We cannot be far wrong in making his nativity ten years preceding that of the more illustrious Child of Bethlehem. So that we may afterwards think of him, when he became an apostle, as about forty years of age : a decade the senior of his divine Lord, perhaps, too, the senior of most of his brother apostles.

Before farther describing his childhood and its surroundings, it may be well to note the era of his birth in Hebrew history, in connection with any contemporary events that would be more likely to leave their impress

[1] Rob Roy on the Jordan, p. 343.

[2] The most competent and reliable of recent authorities, from the advantage alike of scholarship and long residence, asks, " What do you make of this Tabijah ? It was the grand manufacturing suburb of Capernaum, and hence the fountains took their name from the city. Here were the mills, not only for it, but for all the neighbourhood, as is now the case. So also the potteries, tanneries, and other operations of that sort, would be clustered round the great fountains."—*Dr Thomson's Land and Book, in loc.*

on his youthful feelings and imagination.   During these
years of his infancy and boyhood, Herod (falsely distinguished as the Great) ruled with almost despotic power
in Palestine.   In him and his family " a kingdom of
the world was established, which in its external splendour
recalled the traditional magnificence of Solomon." [1]   He
had reared for himself a new palace on Mount Zion.
He had strengthened the city with gates, walls, and
towers.   The large importation of skilled artisans from
Greece had enabled him to replace the baser architecture of Hebrew craftsmen with piles of surpassing
beauty and costliness.   More especially was this true
in the case of the latest and grandest monument of his
munificence, one so flattering also to the pride of those
whom he ruled—the wonderful Temple, of which in a
subsequent chapter we shall come more appropriately
to speak—with its successive terraces and colonnades
crowned by the Holy fane ; its walls of white marble,
its gilded roof and costly wrought gates ; above all, its
succession of cloisters with which even the boasted
Loggie of the Roman Vatican, or the noble porticoes of
Bernini in the Piazza of St Peter's, can hold no comparison.   It has been remarked as " scarcely a figure of
speech to say, that he rebuilt Zion, as Nero after him
rebuilt Rome, leaving a city of marble where he had
found one of mud and lime."   Herod's jurisdiction
extended to Galilee as well as to Judea.   The young
boatman's imagination, therefore, could not fail to be
filled and awed with the stories of those cruelties, unlike
Solomon's reign of peace, which had rendered the
present sovereign's name a terror throughout the land.
He had done all he could to render his rule hated and

himself obnoxious. He offended the religious scruples of the Jews by offering, on his elevation to the throne, sacrifices to Capitoline Jupiter, and afterwards by placing a large golden eagle over the gate of the Temple. The massacre of the Innocents in Bethlehem, though the best known and remembered, was only one of many incidents in his " reign of terror." He committed a series of savageries almost unparalleled in the annals of human crime. Neither youth, nor sex, nor old age, nor relationship were proof against his passionate thirst for blood. His pastime was the shriek of tortured victims. His own favourite wife, Mariamne, with her two sons, Alexander and Aristobulus, and their aged grandmother Alexandra, were put to a violent death ; the last act of his life was when, on the verge of seventy, the dreams of ambition were fading away and the tiger ferocity of his nature was goaded and stimulated by his own bodily sufferings, he commanded his attendants to raise him in bed in order to sign the mandate for the execution of another son. This, it was said, had been preceded by an injunction to his sister Salome, to make his death the signal for a butchery of the chief families in Judea. They were to be shut up in the Hippodrome among the palm groves and balsam gardens of Jericho, and murdered by his guards in cold blood ; so that a universal mourning might, by this horrible artifice, be secured throughout the land.[1] He must have ended his infamous career during Peter's early years ; and his son Herod-Antipas—who, with greater weakness and cunning, inherited much of the wicked and wanton cruelty and ambition of his father —succeeded as Tetrarch of Galilee.

[1] See Milman's History of the Jews.

Another political occurrence during the period of
Simon's youth, and one which agitated the entire nation,
took place immediately after Herod's death, and could
not fail, as any such stirring event among ourselves
would have done, to form an absorbing theme of conversation in the fishermen's homes on shore, or in their
boats on the lonely sea, as well as in Greek villas or
Roman barracks. An insurrection was originated and
headed by a warlike spirit, who made in the first
instance the district round Bethsaida and Tiberias the
main scene of his exploits. Although, indeed, called
"Judas of Galilee," his birthplace, according to Josephus,
seems to have been in Gamala, on the other side of
Jordan ; the same wild district—the " Palestine Highlands "—which had reared more than one hero-Prophet
and warrior in earlier ages, such as Jephthah the Gilead-
ite and Elijah the Tishbite. This man combined the
frenzy of the Jewish devotee and zealot, the austerity
of the ascetic, and the rigid sectarianism of the Pharisee,
with the wild, brigand, freebooter life and nature of the
Arab. Stung to the quick with the wrongs of his
country under Roman subjugation, he roused the people
to a religious crusade, espousing as their watchword, in
imitation of the war-cry of the Maccabees, " We have no
lord nor master but God." With the fiery eloquence
with which Peter the Martyr stirred the religious enthusiasm of the Middle Ages, Judas, according to
Origen, drew thousands around his standard, who welcomed him as an inspired deliverer, or rather as the
predicted Messiah of his race. He had communicated
his own reckless daring to his followers. They carried
fire and sword first through the province, and then
through the entire land, laying waste indiscriminately

cities and homesteads, vineyards and corn-fields. Ico-
noclasts of their day, they specially let loose unsparing
vengeance on groves and images. Every imported
symbol of Pagan idolatry, whether of Greece, Phœnicia,
or Rome, was hurled from niche and pedestal. They
regarded with stoical indifference individual torture
and suffering, animated with the one mastering thought
of vindicating their God-given national rights, driving
the usurping Cæsar from the theocratic soil, and restoring the sceptre of Judah to its legitimate owners. The
shepherds and vinedressers on the hills of Galilee, the
fishermen and craftsmen on the lake and from the
adjacent towns, caught the general infection. Perhaps
if Peter had reached the maturity of youth, he might
have been among the first to be carried away with the
popular enthusiasm, thus forfeiting his future place
under a far different Master, and in a more noble cause :
probably he might have perished in battle. The number as well as trained discipline of the Roman troops
proved too much for the rudely-armed insurrectionists.
On a bloody field they encountered the soldiers of
Cyrenius. After a desperate engagement the rebellious
bands were utterly routed ; Judas was slain, and the
villages of Galilee—probably Bethsaida among the
number—were either made receptacles for the wounded,
or echoed with wailing for the dead. Could the son of
Jonas, with a nature such as we shall find his to have
been, have listened unmoved to the story of these wild,
ruthless adventurers ? or rather, could he have seen unmoved the visible traces, all around, of the greatest Holy
War since the days of Judas Maccabeus ? He may even
have shared in the deep sympathies which we know not
only were kindled, but which survived in the bosoms

of thousands on thousands for a cause apparently lost, but which had struck its roots deep among the masses of the nation, and was only extirpated with the destruction of Jerusalem itself.

The true secret of the popularity and partial success of Judas and his followers suggests yet one other grand national "idea;" or rather, a great expectation and pervading thought, which could not fail to have its marvellous influence on these ripening years of the future apostle, as well as on every true Israelite whether old or young on the shores of Galilee. I allude to the universal, the growing conviction, inspired by their ancient prophets and deepened by the signs of the times,—a conviction, moreover, which we are told by Tacitus had spread over the entire East among the astrologers of Persia and disciples of Zoroaster,—that the Great Messiah Deliverer, the Conqueror of Judea and of the world, was about to appear.[1] True, the Jews had entirely misread their holy books. The intolerant despotism of their foreign rulers had goaded them on to a purely carnal interpretation. The spiritual element in Messiah's reign was lost in the thought of the great warrior who was " to gird His sword upon His thigh ;" whose " arrows were to be sharp in the heart of His enemies," and whose " right hand was to teach Him terrible things." With the death of Judas of Gamala on that fated field, the wild, extravagant hopes of many may have been dashed to the ground for the moment ; but the hope itself of a Messiah yet to come, and soon to come, remained unextinguished. Can we

[1] To the same effect Suetonius says, " There had been circulating throughout the East an ancient and constant opinion, that a person or persons were destined to appear at this time in Judea, who should obtain the government of the world."

suppose that the fishermen of Bethsaida were exceptions to the bright dream which haunted and inflamed the waking and sleeping thoughts of their countrymen ?— of One clothed in 'raiment of byssus,' "glorious in His apparel," travelling in the greatness of His strength, "mighty to save," heading a victorious army on the way to the Throne of David and the Palace of Zion? Rather, can we suppose that they failed to share the truer and nobler aspiration of others ; that the long-drawn sigh and prayer of humanity, wearied with the atrocities and crimes of the darkest of ages, was soon to be answered :—that the Great Physician would ere long appear to heal all wounds and redress all wrongs ; that the Great Sun of Righteousness would speedily arise on a benighted world?

Ere we pass from the political and religious "situation" of Peter's early days, a few words may be needful to put the reader in possession of the complex social influences which surrounded him, and which, so far also, must have moulded his mind and character. Galilee, far more than Southern Palestine, was no longer exclusively or even mainly a Jewish province. The old Hebrew race, indeed, still preponderated among the agricultural and sea-faring population. Jewish husbandmen tilled the land and tended the vineyards and oliveyards. Jewish fishermen moored their boats on the beach where teemed the fishing hamlets of the Sea of Tiberias. Jewish artisans still swarmed in the unwalled cities of the province. But a vast crowd of foreigners were found, mingling with the children of Abraham, from the shores of Greece and Phœnicia—from Antioch and Alexandria—from the banks of the Nile and the Ganges—the Euphrates and Barrada—

from Crete and Cyprus; and above all, from Imperial Rome :—a strange medley of material that refused in any shape to fuse or coalesce with the Jewish element, retaining their separate national customs—speaking their own languages—and worshipping their own divinities. The Roman had imported his riches—his luxuries—his vices—his pride of power and dominion—his love of pomp and show : he had his baths and theatres—his chariot races and gladiatorial combats—his athletes and actors—his slaves and courtesans. The Athenian and Macedonian craftsmen—cunning workmen in gold and silver, brass and stone, bronze and marble—were attracted in thousands to minister to the tastes of these Imperial rulers and their retainers. From the shores of Attica they had transplanted the worship of temple and grove into the region of Palestine which, in natural configuration and wealth of production, most nearly resembled their own climate and soil. Crowds of other foreigners had not missed the golden opportunity thus presented. The wharfs and bazaars of the walled towns were crowded with costly merchandise. Wares and dried fruits from the manufactories and orchards of Damascus—bales of embroidery from the looms of India and Persia—cosmetics and unguents from the forests and balsam groves of Arabia. While in strange contrast with these children of civilisation, were to be found the roving sons of the desert, marauding Arabs from beyond Jordan, in dress and bearing much as they were in the old days of Gideon, much as they are seen at the present hour on Sharon and Esdraelon, with gay, brilliant-coloured caftan and fillet, sword and lance. " Men who still dwelt under their black tents, driving their flocks and herds from valley to valley, coming with the verdure, going with the dearth, and owning no allegiance to either Cæsar or to his tributary kings." [1]

But to return. Of Peter's father we know nothing, save that his name was Jonah or Jonas : while tradition tells us his mother was called Johanna.[2] He himself received the appellation common among the Jews of *Simeon* or *Simon*, a word which means "hearing," and which was frequently bestowed, as has been supposed, by grateful parents in acknowledgment of their prayers being heard in the birth of a son. He had at all events one brother Andrew. We are permitted to think in imagination of a fisherman's home ; parents and children members of that sturdy, fearless, independent race which, whether on the shores of Tiberias or of Britain, have a character peculiarly their own ; moulded much by the life of peril and adventure to which they are habituated. A fisherman occupying one of the adjoining hamlets, and doubtless a familiar acquaintance of Jonas or partner in the same craft, was Zebedee, and his wife Salome. They also had two children. One of these would be but an infant when Peter was already a sturdy boy able to handle the tackle or to ply the oar. This infant of the neighbouring cottage was in a distant future to become the most intimate friend and companion of the son of Jonas, and to be known to the end of time, by the endearing name, " The disciple whom Jesus loved."

" Some," says an interesting writer,[3] " have been dis-

---

1 See the entire description in Mr Hepworth Dixon's Holy Land, p. 120.
2 See note, Smith's Bib. Dic.
3 Life and Writings of St Peter, by author of "Essays on the Church," p. 267. An excellent and suggestive volume, to which I am under frequent obligation in future pages.

posed to regard Peter as one raised above the indigence
which is commonly the lot of an ordinary fisherman. We
are told, it is said, of his house, of his wife and his
wife's mother ; of his 'partners' and of their 'hired
servants ;' and Peter's own language in Matt. xix. 27,
seems to imply, that he had made some sacrifice in
resolving to follow a Master who 'had not where to lay
His head.' But all these circumstances, when examined, will be found to do little towards elevating
Peter, before his call, to any position differing from that
of the ordinary fisherman, who is, and who always has
been, a man whose life is one of severe toil, and
poverty, and privation. Wherever a seashore is found,
and a population exists, there we are sure to find fishermen. They have dwellings and neighbours, wives
and children, like other men ; and they employ boys as
learners, as apprentices, or hired servants, to help them
in their labour. Also as a fishing boat in rough
weather often needs three or four hands, they form
partnerships or agreements. 'Do you go with me
to-day, and I will go with you to-morrow.' All these
are the ordinary surroundings and daily events of a
fisherman's life. He builds, or rents, a cottage or hut,
near the shore. He owns a boat, often old and patched,
descending from father to son. This, with its sails and
fishing-nets, constitutes his chief worldly possession.
In this boat, if the weather permits, he puts forth, each
evening, and often ' toils all the night, taking nothing '
(Luke v. 5 ; John xxi. 3). Then, returning home
empty, he subsists on the remains of yesterday's food,
takes some sleep, and returns to the boat to mend his
nets (Mark i. 19). Sometimes success attends him,
and a good night's work gives him a supply for several

following days. The sale of the best of the fish replenishes his store of bread, and enables him to purchase some article of clothing. Such is a fisherman's life everywhere. A thriving neighbourhood and a good market (as in England) help to raise his condition ; just as a scanty and poor population lowers it." [1]

We have no reason, therefore, to picture Jonas and his young boys otherwise than as hardy, rough, bronzed toilers, accustomed to the capricious storms that swept their lake :—night after night out at their often unsuccessful labour—waited for in the morning, at times, by anxious inmates of their homes, who had listened to the roar of the hurricane coming down the gorges of the hills behind, and converting what was a placid surface the night before, into a sheet of crested foam[2]—

" For not upon a tranquil lake
Our pleasant task we ply,
Where all along our glistening wake
The softest moonbeams lie :

" When rippling wave and dashing oar
Our midnight chant attend,
Or whispering palm-leaves from the shore
With midnight silence bend.

" Full many a dreary, anxious hour
We watch our nets alone,
In drenching spray, and driving shower,
And hear the night-bird's moan." [3]

---

[1] "They were of the lower, though perhaps not quite the lowest, class of Galilean peasants."—*Milman's History of Christianity.*

[2] The name Gennesaret is supposed by some to be derived from the Hebrew word signifying "harp"—and to have been called so from its harp-like shape. "Sure the high winds," says quaint Fuller, "sometimes made but bad music to the ear of the mariners when playing thereupon."

[3] The converse, however, is an equally truthful delineation given by one who understands well how to describe pictorially the surroundings of this

gospel picture, however inadequately and unworthily he deals with its nobler inner meaning. " The beautiful climate of Galilee," says M. Renan, "made the life of these honest fishermen a perpetual delight. They truly preluded the kingdom of God,—simple, good, happy, rocked gently on their delightful little sea, or at night sleeping on its shores. We do not realise to ourselves the intoxication of a life which thus glides away in the face of heaven; the sweet, yet strong love which this perpetual contact with nature gives, and the dreams of these nights passed in the brightness of the stars, under an azure dome of infinite expanse."

CHAPTER II.

Boyhood.

HIS EDUCATION.   THE SURROUNDINGS AND OCCUPATIONS OF HIS
EARLY HOME.

> " Now upon Syria's land of roses
> Softly the light of eve reposes,
> And, like a glory, the broad sun
> Hangs over sainted Lebanon;
> Whose head in wintry grandeur towers,
> And whitens with eternal sleet,
> While Summer, in a vale of flowers,
> Is sleeping rosy at his feet."

"It was on the shores of the Lake of Gennesareth, under the humble roof of poor, ignorant fishermen, that the expectation of the Messiah had been preserved in greatest purity.   There the voice of ancient prophets retained its power in the midst of that grand serenity of nature; there the piety of mothers kindled that of sons; there grew up those who were to become subsequently St Peter and St Paul."—*Pressensé.*

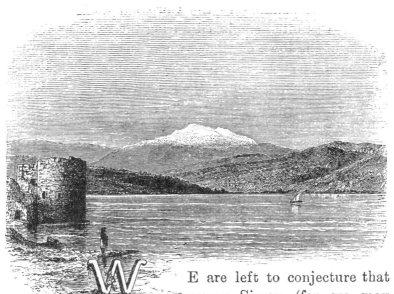

E are left to conjecture that young Simon (for we may adhere for the present to his original name) would receive the elementary education common in his time and humble position, and which by legal enactment was compulsory on all Jewish youths. Schools in great towns had been founded seventy years before by Simon Ben Shelach, one of the great leaders of the Pharisees under the Asmonean princes.[1] A school was generally connected, too, with every synagogue; and if Bethsaida was not of such importance as to be possessed of either of these, we can picture the fisherman boy, in company with a group of Bethsaidans of similar age, pursuing the road by the lake-side to the adjoining city of Capernaum, attired in red *caftan* or cloak, with perhaps the striped *abbâ*

1 See Jost, quoted in Bib. Dic.

either girded or ungirded, and the white *keffieh* protecting his head.   The chazzân of the synagogue, an
official corresponding to the Christian deacon or sub-
deacon, was often employed during the week as school-
master of the town or village where the synagogue was.[1]
We have good reason, however, to infer that Peter's
early education was more than elementary.   From the
conversation he held with Cornelius at a long subsequent period, it is evident he must have mastered the
Greek language, and the same conclusion must be
drawn from the style of his Epistles.[2]   Nor must we
adopt a different impression from the phrase afterwards
applied to Peter and John, that they were "unlearned
and ignorant men."   In the words of Dr Kitto, "This
simply means that they had not received what was considered a high theological education, which added to
the common education a *critical* knowledge of Hebrew,
an acquaintance with the law and the traditions of the
Fathers : and whoever had not received this education
in the schools was regarded as an uneducated man by
the arrogant Pharisees of that day, whatever other knowledge he might possess."[3]

If the child be the father of the man, we can with

1 See art. " Synagogue," Smith's Dic.
2 See art. " Peter," Bib. Dic.
3 "Daily Readings," vol. i. p. 280.   Similarly, also, it will be remembered,
the question was asked by the hostile Pharisees regarding our blessed Lord,
" How knoweth this man letters, having never learned ? " (John vii. 15,) by
which they did not mean to insinuate that He was devoid of the usual
education of the mass of the people, which was considerably above the
standard of other nations ; but how comes He to have this erudition, quali-
fying Him to speak so authoritatively on religious subjects, when He has
sat at the feet of no learned Rabbi, or been initiated into what formed the
great test of Jewish culture—a knowledge of the oral law and oral traditions.
Those who had not made these oral laws and traditions their study were
considered by these "wise " (as they deemed and called themselves), "unlearned and ignorant men."

safety venture to draw a mental portrait of the son of
Jonas in these youthful years, as open, artless, impulsive, rash, ambitious. Very probably, if we may use a
modern phrase, the leader of the playground; tempted
at times, perhaps, to lord it over his playmates ; though
with a strange mixture, too, of pusillanimity and courage : involved ever and anon in boyhood troubles with
his Hebrew pedagogue, who, however, in his turn, would
not be severe on the ardent nature of his young charge,
when he saw that his rashness and outspokenness were
counterbalanced by openness and frankness, generosity
and gratitude. May we not think of him as foremost
in every perilous adventure that had a charm to boy-
nature then, as now; whether with his father out amid
the familiar waves, "launching forth into the deep"
under the stars of an Eastern heaven ; or when a longer
day's holiday beguiled him to daring deeds in the
Valley of Pigeons, rising at early morn and brushing
the dew from the spangled carpet of poppies, daisies,
and anemones spread on his way ; ascending among
the rocky retreats of the conies, half hid with the caper
plant ; climbing to the nests perched on the top of pine
and terebinth ; or penetrating the robber haunts which
had only a few years previously been cleared of their
ruffian tenants by Herod, and still bore evidence of the
perilous struggle.[1]   At another time his expertness in
swimming (with which we are familiar at a later date),
prompting him to some rash feat under the bluff gorges

[1] This Valley of Doves or Pigeons—Wady Haymân or Hamâm—must have
been a familiar one to Peter in after years, during the Saviour's ministry.
"We are just entering the throat of this tremendous gorge.   It is called
Hamâm from the clouds of pigeons which flock to their windows in these
rocks.   Look up now to that cliff on the left.   It is more than a thousand
feet high, and a large part is absolutely perpendicular.   It is perforated by
a multitude of caverns, holes, and narrow passages, the chosen resort of

of Gadara, to the east of the lake. Or yet again, venturing, it may be, amid the shouting and wrangling of
the caravans in the public thoroughfare,—Arabs from the
desert on their swift horses, Egyptian traders with their
camel-loads of spices and balm, Phœnician merchants
with earrings and bracelets, caftans and abbâs from the
bazaars of Damascus ; may we not picture young Simon,
thus mingling, close to his home, with the motley multitude around the immemorial halting-place of the modern
Ain et Tin, the perennial "spring of the fig ; " for,
though its present rim of mossy verdure, aquatic plants,
and noble guardian tree may have been then unknown,
the precious fountain itself must have been a frequent
and familiar resort.   Or, yet once more, if we picture
these early years of boyhood under the domestic roof,
we can think of him as aiding his mother in her smaller
household cares—trimming the lamps of red clay,
bruising the parched corn, watching the boiling pot-
tage of lentiles, or preparing the fish of the lake on the
glowing charcoal embers ; sweeping the floor, and readjusting the mats for the frugal meal alongside the
baked bread or oil and honey cakes, the earthen jars
of *leban* and occasional wine-flagons of fig *sherbet.*   At
other times shaking the olives, carrying water from the
stream that tumbled into the lake ; or, it may be,
spreading the maize and hemp to dry on the roof-top in
the summer sun, ready for the distaff to beguile the
long autumn and winter hours, while the seafarers

robbers in former days. . . . . Josephus has a graphic description of the
capture of these caves by Herod the Great.   After various expeditions to
expel them had failed, he let boxes filled with soldiers down the face of the
precipice, and landed them at the entrance of the caverns.   By fire and
sword the robbers were exterminated."—*Dr Thomson's Land and Book,*
p. 423.

were still out at their precarious and protracted toils on the lake.

> "Fair boy ! the wanderings of thy way
> It is not mine to trace,
> Through buoyant youth's exulting day,
> Or manhood's bolder race.

> "What discipline thy heart may need,
> What clouds may veil thy sun,
> The eye of God alone can read,
> And let His will be done." [1]

We have just spoken of Simon's *ordinary* education : the *religious* knowledge imparted to him, like that of all Jewish youths, would, in accordance with the strict injunctions of the Mosaic law, be communicated by his parents, saving perhaps some simple instruction by the *Sopherîm,* or other attendants of the synagogue. We may transfer to the Galilean boy what has been so well said regarding the early life of one who will come often to be associated with him in future chapters—young Saul of Tarsus :—"The rules respecting the diligent education

---

[1] The following recent description of a modern home at Nazareth may be appropriated with equal fidelity to one of the old lake homes of Bethsaida. It is all the more graphic and interesting as having been seen by the narrator : "Nothing can be plainer than those houses, with the doves sunning themselves on the white roofs, and the vines wreathing about them. The mats or carpets are laid loose along the walls; shoes and sandals are taken off at the threshold ; from the centre hangs a lamp, which forms the only ornament of the room; in some recess in the wall is placed the wooden chest, painted with bright colours, which contains the books or other possessions of the family ; on a ledge that runs round the wall, within easy reach, are neatly rolled up the gay-coloured quilts, which serve as beds, and on the same ledge are ranged the earthen vessels for daily use ; near the door stand the large common water jars of red clay with a few twigs and green leaves, often of aromatic shrubs, thrust into their orifices to keep the water cool. At meal-time a painted wooden stool is placed in the centre of the apartment, a large tray is put upon it, and in the middle of the tray stands the dish of rice and meat, or libbân, or stewed fruits, from which all help themselves in common. Both before and after the meal, the servant, or the youngest member of the family, pours water over the hands from a brazen ewer into a brass bowl."—*Dr Farrar's Life of Christ,* vol. i. 61, 62.

of children, which were laid down by Moses in the 6th and 11th chapters of Deuteronomy, were doubtless carefully observed ; and he was trained in that peculiarly *historical* instruction spoken of in the 78th Psalm, which implies the continuance of a chosen people, with glorious recollections of the past, and great anticipations for the future : ' The Lord made a covenant with Jacob, and gave Israel a law, which He commanded our forefathers to teach their children ; that their posterity might know it, and the children which were yet unborn ; to the intent that when they came up, they might show their children the same : that they might put their trust in God, and not to forget the works of the Lord, but to keep His commandments' (vers. 5–7).   The histories of Abraham and Isaac, of Jacob and his twelve sons, of Moses among the bulrushes, of Joshua and Samuel, Elijah, Daniel, and the Maccabees, were the stories of his childhood.   The destruction of Pharaoh in the Red Sea, the thunders of Mount Sinai, the dreary journeys in the wilderness, the land that flowed with milk and honey—this was the earliest imagery presented to his opening mind.   The triumphant songs of Zion, the lamentations by the waters of Babylon, the prophetic praises of the Messiah, were the songs around his cradle." [1]   Besides this, he would hear the law read and expounded on the Sabbath-day in the synagogue probably of Capernaum.   He was doubtless devoid of the culture of his great contemporary just mentioned, who had been brought up at the feet of the learned Gamaliel. It must be remembered, that the native peasantry of Galilee, compared even with the other inhabitants of Palestine, were reputed boorish and half civilised—a

[1] Howson and Conybeare's St Paul, p. 46.

turbulent race—inhabiting a frontier land on which heathen shadows rested—" Galilee of the *Gentiles*." Far removed from the intellectual influences of the capital, their language was a coarse *patois*, " a harsh and guttural dialect of the Syro-Chaldaic ; " [1] the old Hebrew language being only spoken, and that in a corrupted form, by learned Pharisees and doctors of the law. We shall find afterwards, in the case of Peter, that this very harshness of speech (what we should call " vulgar pronunciation "), perhaps mingled with a burr, betrayed his origin. It convicted him in the palace of Caiaphas of being a Galilean accomplice of his Lord— "Thou art a Galilean ;" " Thy speech bewrayeth thee." [2]

But if Peter was deficient in high intellectual training, and in the refinement which accompanies it, yet, judging from his subsequent powers as a preacher and writer, [3]

[1] Milman, p. 122.

[2] Mark xiv. 70 ; Matt. xxvi. 73.

[3] Peter's pictorial power—in other words, his vivid perception of the details of outer Nature—which escape the other Evangelists, is conspicuous in various places in St Mark's Gospel. And it may be well in this note, without cumbering the narrative, to advert shortly to the certain connection which he had in the composition of this record of the second Evangelist. The latter is spoken of as the ἑρμηνευτής or Interpreter of the former, writing down at his dictation ("Secretary"). Tertullian's words regarding this connection are "Cujus interpres Marcus." Irenæus and Papias speak of Mark, the one as "Interpres," the other as " Interpres et Sectator Petri." Jerome still more explicitly affirms the relation of the two : " Petro narrante et illo scribente." Eusebius to the same effect represents Mark, on the authority of Clement of Alexandria, as writing his Gospel with Peter's express sanction, and that Gospel, as the Apostle's narrative, being recognised and read in the churches. Many commentators have noted these pictorial touches above referred to. I may give a few of them in the words of a recent discriminating writer : " In Mark iv. 38 the description given of the storm and the Saviour asleep differs from that given by St Matthew (viii. 24), and that given by St Luke (viii. 23), by the introduction of such a little detail as only an eyewitness, and an eyewitness who was apt to regard such details, could have suggested. St Mark says (in contrast to the other Evangelists, who merely mention that He was sleeping), ' And He was *in the*

we can imagine that, as he passed from youth to manhood, his natural gifts made him abundantly capable of
appreciating the varied loveliness of that wondrous picture in outer Nature which was constantly unfolded to

hinder part of the ship, asleep *on a pillow.*' In the description of the
feeding of the five thousand, St Matthew says (xiv. 19), 'And He commanded the multitude to sit down on the grass,' &c. St Luke (ix. 15) remarks, 'And they made them all sit down.' St Mark's words are (vi. 39),
'And He commanded them to make all sit down *by companies* upon the
green grass.' Surely that is the description of one on whom the actual sight
of those groups, clad in white and variegated garments, dotted over the
bright green grass, had made an impression from the picturesqueness of the
scene. St Matthew and St Luke both narrate at length the details of our
Lord's temptation, but St Mark alone (with the appreciation of one who regarded intensely the natural aspects of a scene) adds (i. 13), 'And He was
there in the wilderness forty days, tempted of Satan, *and was with the wild
beasts.*' This is the more remarkable, as St Mark does not give—beyond
the mere mention of it—any record of the Temptation; and yet he gives that
one suggestion which an appreciator of Nature would be struck with, of the
complete loneliness and awfulness of those forty days. St Mark, in describing the finding of the colt, on which Christ was to make His triumphal
entry into Jerusalem, gives a little detail unnoticed by the other Evangelists
—that the animal was found 'without, in a place where two ways met.'
'And they said among themselves, Who shall roll away the stone from the
door of the sepulchre? And when they looked, they saw the stone was rolled
away, *for it was very great,*' &c. &c." See the entire article in "Bible Educator," "Contrasts of Scripture," p. 161. Among other examples, there has
also been noted the minute description of the demoniac of Gadara. A most
discerning eyewitness, with the natural aptitude of a pre-Raphaelite painter
for grasping minute details, must have either penned or dictated the following: "Who had his dwelling among the tombs; and no man could bind
him, no, not with chains; because that he had been often bound with fetters
and chains, and the chains had been plucked asunder by him, and the fetters
broken in pieces: neither could any man tame him. And always, night and
day, he was in the mountains, and in the tombs, crying, and cutting himself
with stones. But when he saw Jesus afar off, he ran and worshipped Him"
(Mark v. 3–6). Bishop Wordsworth further observes, that "The author of
this Gospel makes use of the *present tense* more frequently than any of the
Evangelists, and appears to realise the transactions described, as actually
before his own eyes. . . . . He recites more often than any of the Evangelists the very *words of Christ*, not in Greek, the language in which he
was writing, but in the original *Syro-Chaldaic* uttered by Christ, as if the
sound of that Divine voice was still ringing in his ears; and he notices
more frequently the expression of Christ's aspect and look, as if the
features of that blessed countenance were indelibly engraven on his
memory."—*Wordsworth's Greek Test.*, p. 113. "Is it not to him," remarks

his eye. An eloquent writer has said : "If Christianity was to be the offspring of mere beauty of Nature, it might assuredly have found a more enchanting birthplace, such as the golden shores of Ionia, or those magic isles which rise out of a sea of azure on the shores of Asia Minor."[1] And yet, at the age in which Peter lived —not certainly in Palestine—we question if in many places out of it, could a scene alike more unique and diversified be witnessed than around the Sea of Galilee. *Gennesaret*—almost unknown in Old Testament times— (the Chinnereth of Joshua) (xii. 3), or memorable only as the spot where the first Amorite shepherds pitched their tents, had become, in the reign and mainly through the munificence and luxury of the Herodian Court, the most populous and fashionable district of the kingdom. The lake was girdled with at all events nine proud cities and their varied palatial homes, recalling to many a Roman the sumptuous villas, temples,

Bishop Ellicott, "that we owe the last touch, as it were, to that affecting picture of our Lord's tenderness and love, when He *took up* the young children *in His arms*, and put His hands upon them, and blessed them"? (p. 25). Nor is it unworthy of (note in confirmation of the opinion of the early Fathers of the Church referred to at the commencement of this note) that the sacred art of the Middle Ages has in the same way associated St Mark and Peter as apostle and amanuensis. The authoress of "Sacred and Legendary Art" mentions, that in the Treasury of the Duomo of St Mark's, Venice, is preserved a golden reliquary of a square form, containing, it is said, a fragment of the original Gospel in the handwriting of St Mark. A figure of Peter is on the chased cover, while the Evangelist is in a kneeling attitude at his feet writing from his dictation. The same authority refers, among other examples, to two beautiful pictures, one in the Florentine Gallery, by Angelico da Fiesole, in which St Peter is represented in a pulpit, and St Mark below, similarly occupied as his disciple and scribe ; another, by Bonvicino, in the Brera Gallery of Milan, in which the two apostles are standing together, St Mark holding a scroll and inkhorn ; while St Peter is reading the Gospel he has just submitted to him for his approval and confirmation. (See "Sacred and Legendary Art," p. 149, 195.) We shall in a subsequent chapter advert more particularly to St Mark's personal relation to Peter.

[1] Pressensé's Life of Christ.

baths, and theatres which crowded their favourite Lucrine lake or the shores of Baiæ. Nigh to Peter's native hamlet, unchanged to this hour, was the great thoroughfare from the East to the South, paved like the Roman *Via Sacra.* As we have already noted, often doubtless must he have seen the long file of camels and horses, caravan on caravan, on the road from Damascus to the markets and bazaars of Tiberias and Jerusalem, Cæsarea and Alexandria.

We may try for a moment to embody in word-painting the view, which, day after day, would meet the gaze of the youthful fisherman, either as he was preparing his nets on the beach for the night of toil, or, shall we rather say (realising in thought the season when all secular work was suspended), on the Jewish Sabbath-eve, when, seated with his parents and companion brother in the green alcove on the top of his flat-roofed dwelling, he had leisure in Nature's " still, golden hour" to drink in the wonders of the prospect.[1] Nigh at hand, though possibly half-hidden by a rugged promontory to the left, the waves of the lake would lave what are now piles of ruin, but which were then the edifices of proud Capernaum, with its barracks and wharfs,—the gleaming marble of its white synagogue doubly luminous under such a sky :—a city with which Simon was afterwards to be sacredly associated, not only as his own adopted home, where he lived with his wife's mother, but where most of the miracles of his Divine Master, of which he himself was most generally spectator, were performed. It was, moreover, the only settled residence which the Homeless One claimed,—

---

[1] See accompanying ideal view of "Gennesaret Restored," from the hills above Bethsaida.

" His own city." [1] On the disputed question of its site
it would be out of place here to enter. In wandering,
not many years ago, among the marble fragments which
stud the desolate jungle at Tel Hum, I have elsewhere
stated the grounds for the very strong belief that we
were treading the relics and memorials of that city of
the Gospel age ; and that in the columns and entabla-
tures which strew the ground were beheld fragments
(probably) of that old monument of the munificence of
a Roman soldier, who, stranger as he was to Jewish
customs, and an alien to the Jewish race, still "loved
their nation, and built them a synagogue" (Luke vii. 5).
Vain, I need not say, was the question, Where, in
this voiceless desolation, was the dwelling of Peter,
"the Home of Jesus"? Enough to feel, that somewhere near, that hallowed habitation, in all likelihood,
had been ; that, from its vine-festooned lattice or open
roof, the Eye of Incarnate Godhead must have gazed on
the very scene spread before us, blighted and blasted
truly, yet, like the skeleton leaves of a flower, " beautiful
in death." [2]

But, to return to our ideal picture, farther east would
rise before the eye of the young spectator the edifices
of Chorazin, all the brighter, too, in the setting of
black basalt rocks around. In front, to the right, where
now is a miserable, battered village with a solitary palm,
he would have before him the town of Magdala, which

---

[1] Matthew ix. 1.

[2] I was struck with what Dr Thomson specially mentions, " heaps of lava
which encumber the shores and the fields." The marble of the white synagogue was, according to the same, "cut from the mountains to the north-west,
where it is seen in place and very abundant" (p. 350). The name Capernaum indicates a humbler commencement to the great city of apostolic
times, meaning, as it does, "The village of comfort," or "The lovely village." See Milman's History of Christianity.

in future he would associate with a touching story of
Divine goodness and grace ; while other two miles in
advance, and occupying the more commanding situation,
were fast rising, if not already built, the stately towers
and imperial edifices of Tiberias, " flinging far into the
lake the reflections of its marble lions and sculptured
architraves ; " a city built by Herod Antipas in honour
of his master, on the site whereon Jerome tells us once
stood a city called Chinneroth.[1] Humbler fishing huts
fringed the lake, and teeming villages climbed the
mountain-sides.   Nor had Nature left what was attractive to art and man.   The setting, in this case, was
beautiful as the jewel.   Not inaptly has it been called
" The Zug of Palestine, wrapped in the arms of a circle

---

[1] This principal city of the region, at all events in the days of Peter's
early manhood, and with whose outer magnificence he must have been very
familiar, may merit fuller description. I give it in the words of a vivid
writer : " Herod's plan was laid at the base of a steep hill, around the waters
of a hot spring, among the ruins of a nameless town and the graves of a
forgotten race. A great builder, like all the princes of his line, Antipas
could now indulge his taste for temples, palaces, and public baths, conceived in a Roman spirit and executed on a Roman scale, while flattering
that capricious master who might any day send him to die, as his brother
was dying, in a distant land. The new city grew apace. A castle crowned
the hill. High walls ran down from the heights into the sea. Streets and
temples covered the low ground which lay between these walls. A gorgeous
palace rose high above the rest of the public works ; a palace for the prince
and court, having a roof of gold, from which circumstance it came to be
known as ' the golden house.' A port was formed ; a pier thrown out ; a
water-gate built ; and a fleet of war-ships and pleasure-boats danced on the
sparkling wave. Towers protected and gates adorned a city which Antipas
dedicated to his master, inscribed on his coins, and made the capital of his
province, the residence of his court. This new city, though ruled by a
Jewish prince, and seated in the midst of Pharisaic hamlets, was in no sense
a Jewish town. It was a Syrian Syracuse ; a city of pleasure, a refuge of
intelligence, of toleration, and of force ; in which all the strangers of the
earth could assemble in peace and safety, bringing with them, as into an
open market and a common forum, their speech, their customs, and their
idols. In fact, under the Herodian prince, the city of Tiberias was a Roman
fortress, held by a Syro-Macedonian army, and governed by an Asiatic
court."—*Dixon's Holy Land*, pp. 268–270.

of tiny Alps," and yet with greater truth has another said, " The features of the scene are neither górgeous nor colossal ; there is nothing here of the mountain gloom or the mountain glory ; nothing of that ' dread magnificence ' which overawes us as we gaze on the fiery dome of tropical volcanoes or the icy precipices of northern hills." [1] It is a well-known saying of the Talmud, " Of all the seven seas God created, He made choice of none but the Lake of Gennesaret." That re- markable basin, 650 feet below the level of the Mediter- ranean, enjoyed a tropical climate. Flowers and shrubs that would have drooped on Olivet, Bethlehem, or Sa- maria, grew in exuberant luxuriance there, and made it— what it was called—a terrestrial Paradise. As Josephus says, " Nature brought thither trees of all climates." The oleander, with its luscious blossoms,[2] the vine, the pomegranate, the orange, the tamarisk, the lotus, the fig, the agnus castus, not forgetting the now unfamiliar palm—all had a home in this clime of the sun. Well may " the smiling district " be designated by a well- known French author as " the true home of the Song of Songs." The extreme edge of some of the upper portions of the lake would be fringed, as they are now, with colossal reeds, meadow grass, and rushes,—a safe retreat alike for the pelican, the blue-and-white-winged jay, the little bright-eyed tortoise, or for the stately heron that more rarely made a solitary excursion from the Jordan jungle and the sedges of Lake Merom. The same picturesque writer, just referred to, adds to the

[1] Dr Farrar's Life of Christ, vol. i. p. 174.

[2] " Nowhere else will you see such magnificent oleanders as at the head of this lake. I saw clumps of them here twenty feet high and a hundred in circumference—one mass of rosy-red flowers—a blushing pyramid of exqui- site loveliness."—*Land and Book*, p. 351.

number "delicate and lively turtle-doves, blue birds so
light that they rest on a blade of grass without bending
it, crested larks which venture almost under the feet
of the traveller, storks with grave and modest mien,
which, laying aside all timidity, allow man to come
quite near them, and seem almost to invite his approach." The blue lupin and salvia, the purple hya-
cinth, the yellow and white crocus, would combine their
modest tints with the louder tones of the scarlet poppy
and gladiolus, or the luscious masses of the flowering
almond ; while the crimson and pink anemone, the
"lilies of the field," familiar still at every turn, which
were afterwards pointed to as excelling the glories of
Solomon—weaving a richer mantle than any Syrian loom
—would mingle their brilliant hues with the green turf,
and the ebbing and flowing waves lapping this silver,
shell-strewn strand.

> "What went ye out to see
>   O'er the rude, sandy lea,
> Where stately Jordan flows by many a palm,
>   Or where Gennesaret's wave
>   Delights the flowers to lave,
> That o'er her western slope breathe airs of balm?
>
> "All through the summer night,
>   These blossoms red and white
> Spread their soft breasts unheeding to the breeze,
>   Like hermits watching still,
>   Around the sacred hill,
> Where erst our Saviour watched upon His knees."
>   —*Keble.*

The wide "Plain of Gennesaret"—the "El-Ghuweir,"
or Little Ghor, as the Arabs now call it—formed by a
recess in the limestone crags, would be seen almost close
by, teeming with vegetable life, and irrigated by plen-

teous streams. In this richest portion of the lake-side, familiar to the eye of young Simon would be ' the sower ' in early spring scattering his handfuls of grain on the bounteous soil, birds from lake and mountain screaming around his head, and picking up the stray grains which the harrow had missed, or which had been tossed on the hardened footroad :—a future fertile text for Divine lips, " Behold, a sower went forth to sow."[1] The Horns of Hattin, already alluded to, near which the crusaders under the Great Saladin of a future age sustained their last fatal defeat, but which was to have a different association to the future Apostle as " the Mount of Beatitudes," formed, along with the Betharbel of Hosea and its fortified caverns, the prominent object in the right of this panorama ; while rugged cliffs of limestone, more varied in outline than the other hills of the district, terminated above the houses of Magdala. " Nature had invited man by her own true signs to dwell on the western banks of this lake, where she had smoothed her gentle slopes and hidden her refreshing springs ; bright little towns and villages crowded upon each other, as in our own day villas and hamlets sparkle around the shores of Como and Geneva. On every patch of loam, in every rift of rock, on every gentle knoll, sprung a cluster of stone sheds, the homes of reapers and fishermen, each hamlet having its bit of uneven cornfield, its narrow ledge of vines, and its tiny beach of sand. Some of the neighbouring peaks being

[1] I can attest from personal recollection the truth of Dr Thomson's observation : " Gennesaret is now pre-eminently fruitful in thorns. They grow up among the grain, or the grain among them, and the reaper must 'pick the harvest out of the thorns' (Job v. 1) ; the same prickly shrub common in Palestine, which is said to have formed the Redeemer's crown of thorns (*ziziphus spina Christi*), 'armed with small, sharp spines.'"

volcanic, huge masses of basaltic rock lay tumbled along the shore."[1]   In the distance, as far as the eye could reach, the gleaming waters of the lake itself contracted to a point.   From one of the higher eminences behind his native village, the beholder would be able to note where the Jordan issued forth in a sheet of foam from this great northern basin on its way through the Ghor, hastening down its rocky gorges to lose itself in the Sea of Death.   If we imagine him climbing higher still, he would obtain in that clear atmosphere towards the right a view of the wooded crest of Tabor, and the green top of Gilboa : while far north the prospect was bounded by what gave peerless glory to the whole scene—the crest of Hermon, Jebel-es-Sheikh, the " kingly mountain," with its crown of everlasting snows. Even the hills around his native village would seem (from the near view I obtained) not to be without their own interest and beauty.   Too steep and undulating to admit well of human habitations, his eye would ramble over grassy plateaus and slopes, interlaced with hollows and " becks," studded with the grisly nâbk ; while the scene familiar now, might have been as familiar then, the shepherd, followed by his flock, coming down from the hills to fold them for the night, and water them at the copious fountains,—occasionally perhaps returning

1 Dixon's Holy Land, pp. 26, 27.   I have thus elsewhere recorded my own impressions in relation to familiar scenery at home.   " They reminded one less of the northern Highlands of Scotland than of the peculiar pastoral hills in Ettrick and Yarrow in the South, or in Cumberland and Westmoreland ; while in the upper end of the lake, as they recede to girdle in the fertile 'Plain of Gennesaret,' they display here and there bold, rocky cliffs, beginning above the now ruined Magdala ; more broken and not so continuous, yet those who are familiar with Salisbury Crags at Edinburgh may have a tolerable impression conveyed to them of their peculiar character and contour."

from a distance bearing in his arms some truant from the thorny brake. "Far higher above the lake than Ain et Tin and Mudawara," says Mr Macgregor, describing the heights behind El-Tabijah, "a perennial stream comes from a great round fountain, also girded by walls which are at least twenty feet high. Some part of the masonry is very ancient; and fig-trees, bursting through it, clamber down the sides, and hang their white-barked, hoary limbs over a hot, sullen pool below."[1] A similar observant traveller, with a keen eye for the picturesque, thus describes those higher hills behind Bethsaida on which the youthful feet of Simon must have wandered : "The path wound down a steep ravine, with ever-changing views of the lake; while from every crevice between the broken rocks bloomed an infinite number of giant pink cyclamens and purple auriculas. . . . . Turning round the west hill, we looked down upon a Bedoueen encampment of black tents, with large herds of cattle ; and further on we found a delicious valley of nâbk trees, where scores of graceful camels with their young ones were feeding. A lovely scene it was, increasing in beauty as we reached the shores of that lake."[2] Nor to the youthful fisherman would the eastern shore—the inheritance of Manasseh, doubtless in every way less interesting and picturesque than the western side—be without its weird grandeur, at all events in evening light, the last flush of sunset. As the purple shadows fell, there would be brought out in bold relief the blue cliffs and seamed crevasses of the Gadara mountains, some of the latter rising 900 feet above the lake, the last ramparts and outliers of Hermon, guarding

1 Rob Roy on the Jordan, p. 371.
2 Miss Beaufort's Syrian Shrines, p. 37.

the ancient kingdom of Bashan. This ideal picture would be incomplete without including the bosom of the lake itself, spoken of enthusiastically by Jewish writers as "beloved of God above all the waters of Canaan." Simon and his fellow-adventurers would have it, doubtless, much to themselves in the lonely night watches, only now and then would they note the glistening wake of some friendly craft in the clear moonlight or starlight. But by day, or in the cool of the evening, the whole expanse would be alive and furrowed with pleasure-boats, sumptuous barges, galleys, and pinnaces, gay as the Venetian gondolas of a later age ; while vessels of heavier tonnage would be seen plying between the ports of Bethsaida-Julias and Capernaum, or moored in the busy wharves filled with merchandise, where officials, like the future Apostle Matthew, would be seen sitting at the receipt of custom to collect the impost.

Amid, then, such surroundings as these, the Fisherman boy was trained for the great work of the future ; a befitting school surely for his subsequent varied labours. The rough life of adventurous toil, the heats of summer and storms of winter, which braced his physical frame, would nerve and inure him to cope with sterner difficulties. He had doubtless no thought in these his earlier years, save of living an unobtrusive life, and of dying an unnoted death by the Galilean lake. But the God of his fathers had a nobler destiny in store for him. Like his spiritual brother of Tarsus, he was yet to be made a " chosen vessel." Nets and toils and buffeting elements undreamt of by the sailor of Bethsaida, were to supersede his homely occupations. The modest name of the village on the Sea of Tiberias was ere long to take its place among the memorable spots of earth; as memorable, though for a very different reason, as either Rome or Athens. In a sense which the great prophet of the nation never imagined his words to convey, it might be said of that whole region, alike with regard to the bounties of Nature and of grace, " O Naphthali, satisfied with favour, and full with the blessing of the Lord." [1]

One other reflection occurs in connection with the early life of Simon. While he was plying his oar in the midnight sea, or mending his nets by day on the shore, there was growing up in a remote village in Galilee, not many miles from Bethsaida, a mysterious Child, his junior in years, but whom he was by-and-by to feel honoured in calling Lord and Master. When the youth of the Gennesaret villager had merged into early manhood, he would probably, in the lovely spring season of Palestine, as was the general wont, form one of the caravan of pilgrims to the Paschal feast of Jerusalem. We have in a passage in St John's Gospel an indirect intimation that Capernaum formed a rendezvous for those coming from North Galilee. If they took—as we know they frequently did—the western itinerary rather than that of the Jordan valley, who knows but possibly in passing Nazareth, with its circuit of green hills, they may have been joined, before crossing the plain of Esdraelon, by a lowly carpenter, his wife and Son, " twelve years of age,"—the latter going up for the first time to the city of solemnities with the multitude that kept holiday; who knows but these two youths, afterwards to be linked in so holy a relation,

[1] Deut. xxxiii. 23.

might have pitched their tents together in that sacred
cavalcade ?—sometimes travelling in company in early
morning and cool evening—sometimes, as was the custom, by night, to avoid the sultry heat of day.   Who
knows but that, under these clear, starlit heavens, the
Master and the subsequent disciple may have, unknown
to each other, blended lip and voice in singing the songs
of Zion ? the young boatman little dreaming that many
of these were to the praise of the wondrous Being who
in human form walked by his side !   " The pilgrimage
was a sweet solemnity for the provincial Jews.   Entire
series of psalms were consecrated to celebrate the happiness of thus journeying in family companionship
during several days in the spring across the hills and
valleys, each one having in prospect the splendours of
Jerusalem, the solemnities of the sacred courts, and the
joy of brethren dwelling together in unity.   The route
in these journeys was that which is followed to this
day, through Ginæa and Shechem.   *Ain-el-Haramie*,
the last halting-place, is a charming and melancholy
spot, and few impressions equal that experienced on
encamping there for the night.   The valley is narrow
and sombre, and a dark stream issues from the rocks,
full of tombs, which form its bank.   It is, I think, ' the
Valley of tears,' or of dropping waters, which is described
as one of the stations on the way in the delightful 84th
Psalm, and which became the emblem of life for the sad
and sweet mysticism of the Middle Ages." [1]   The ima-
ginary journey, in relation to the divine, youthful Pilgrim
of Nazareth, has thus been beautifully sketched ; but,
with hardly the change of a word, we may apply it with
equal truth, so far as regards the localities, to His future

1 Renan, p. 77.

apostle. "As the Passover falls at the end of April and
the beginning of May, the country would be wearing its
brightest, greenest, loveliest aspect, and the edges of
the vast corn-fields on either side of the road through
the vast plain would be woven, like the high-priest's
robe, with the blue and purple and scarlet of innumerable flowers. Over the streams of that ancient river—
the river Kishon—past Shunem, recalling memories of
Elisha as it lay nestling on the southern slopes of Little
Hermon—past royal Jezreel, with the sculptured sarcophagi that alone bore witness to its departed splendour
—past the picturesque outline of bare and dewless Gilboa—past sandy Taanach, with its memories of Sisera
and Barak—past Megiddo, ... the road would lie
to En-Gannim, where, beside the fountains and amid
the shady and lovely gardens which still mark the spot,
they would probably have halted for their first night's
rest. Next day they would begin to ascend the mountains of Manasseh, and crossing the 'Drowning Mea-
dows,' as it is now called, and winding through the rich
fig-yards and olive-groves that fill the valleys round El-
Jîb, they would leave upon the right the hills which,
in their glorious beauty, formed the ' crown of pride ' of
which Samaria boasted, but which, as the prophet foretold, should be as a 'fading flower.' Their second
encampment would probably be near Jacob's well, in
the beautiful and fertile valley between Ebal and Gerizim, and not far from the ancient Shechem. A third
day's journey would take them past Shiloh and Gibeah
of Saul and Bethel to Beeroth ; and from the pleasant
springs by which they would then encamp, a short and
easy stage would bring them in sight of the towers of
Jerusalem. The profane plumage of the eagle-wings

of Rome was already overshadowing the city; but, towering above its walls, still glittered the great temple, with its gilded roofs and marble colonnades, and it was still the Jerusalem of which royal David sang, and for which the exiles by the waters of Babylon had yearned with such deep emotion, when they took their harps from the willows to wail the remorseful dirge that they would remember her until their right hands forgot their cunning. Who shall fathom the unspeakable emotion with which the boy Jesus " (and we may add, the young man Simon) " gazed on that memorable and never-to-be-forgotten scene ? " [1]

It may not be out of place, in closing this chapter, to note, that if we may believe the description which Nicephorus gives of his outer appearance, the apostle-fisherman was " of middle size, his complexion pale, his hair thick and curled, his eyes black, his eyebrows thin, his nose large but not sharp." And though in this we are anticipating, yet, to complete these references to the youth and opening manhood of the son of Jonas, we may add, that it is specially mentioned by a reliable authority (Clement of Alexandria), in recording very ancient traditions, that in early life Simon was married to one called Perpetua. Her name was not inappropriate, as the same authority accredits her with the willing abandonment of her earthly all, for the sake of the common Master they came to serve.

[1] Dr Farrar's Life of Christ, vol. i. pp. 70, 71.

CHAPTER III.

The Momentous Interview.

" Like an arrow from the quiver
    To the sad and lone Dead Sea,
Thou art rushing, rapid river,
    Swift and strong and silently.

" Through the dark-green foliage stealing,
    Like a silver ray of light,
Who can tell the pilgrim's feeling
    When thy waters meet his sight?"
                    —Anderson.

" Let others tell of the early genius and precocious talents of those whose history they narrate ; to the Evangelist, the point alone from which the narrative becomes worthy of his pen, is the hour which beholds the subject of his history brought to an acquaintance with the Saviour of the world."
                    —Blunt's Lectures on St Peter.

"Such a '*Eureka!*' never before was uttered by man. He was found, for whom the world had waited forty centuries."
                    —Bengel.

**IMON** emerges from the seclusion of his life at Bethsaida, on the banks of the Jordan.

As he and his fellow-fishermen were occupied with their wonted callings on the Sea of Tiberias, we may imagine the conversation turning on the all-engrossing topic of the day—at least what was so among the earnest-minded of the Jewish people—the Great Revival Prophet, the son of Zecharias a priest, who had risen in Judea, and whose thunder-tones, far more than the warlike appeals of Judas, were stirring society to its depths. Never since Elijah's age had bolder words been uttered ; never had a more vehement shaking taken place amid the dry bones of the degenerate nation. Leaving his child-hood's dwelling amid the sunny vineyards of Hebron and Eschol,[1] he makes his adopted home the scathed and blasted deserts around the Dead Sea shores and the Ghor of the Jordan. " That one Voice crying in the wilderness," says a writer, " touched the deep religious romance of every patriotic heart. It was like the olden time. So had the great prophets done. Even one of less greatness than John would have had a tumultuous reception. But John was profoundly in earnest. It was his good fortune to have no restraints or commitments. He had no philosophy to shape or balance, no sect whose tenets he must respect, no reputation to guard, and no deluding vanity of an influence to be either won or kept. He listened to the word of God in his own soul, and spake right on. When such a one speaks, the hearts of men are targets, his words are arrows, and multitudes will fall down wounded." " He was like a burning torch," says Lange, " his public life was quite an earthquake : the whole man was a sermon." May he not possibly (was the thought and the wish of not a few hearts) be the Kingly One for whom all true souls are longing :—the Mighty Prince who is to expel the usurper from the throne—chase his legions into the sea, and restore the kingdom of Dávid to its pristine unity and glory ? Alas ! his was the passing splendour of the meteor, soon to be eclipsed in a cruel death. " Like Moses," is the beautiful remark of Pressensé, " he dies on the border-land of promise. He sows in tears and hears not the joyous song of the reapers." The passover, to which I have already alluded, will ere long be at hand. Meanwhile the proposal is made among these Bethsaidans,

---

[1] There is a Jewish legend that he made a miraculous escape, in the arms of his mother Elizabeth, from the massacre at Bethlehem.

that before going to the city of solemnities they would
undertake a special journey to the "fords of Jordan,"
in order with their own ears to hear the burning words
of this new messenger from heaven; who, in addition
to the interest which had gathered around his own person, had announced himself the herald of a Greater,—
the "voice of one crying in the wilderness, ' Prepare ye
the way of the Lord, make His paths straight.' "

The land was beginning at least to be clothed with
verdure. Those flowers, spoken of at the close of last
chapter, so impressive to every Palestine traveller, would
tinge valley and mountain-side with their first flush of
beauty. "No sooner," says a recent writer, well
able to speak of the flora of Palestine past and present,
"have the heavy rains of January and February fallen,
than the soil of the plains and valleys, baked hard by
eight months' exposure to a cloudless sky, burst forth
into a sudden green, whose vividness seems all the
greater by contrast with their previous bareness. A
thousand brilliant flowers, chiefly of bulbous plants,
convert the uniform drab-coloured livery of the country,
during its long dry season, into a gaudy carpet, as varied
as the patterns of a kaleidoscope." [1] Outer Nature
would thus seem to be in harmony with the remarkable revival of spiritual life. What a singular scene
must have met the eye of Simon and his brethren when
crossing the sacred river at Bethabara (or Bethany),[2]

---

[1] Preface to Mrs Zeller's " Wild Flowers of the Holy Land."

[2] "*Bethany*" (though not of course the Bethany which was the home of
Lazarus and his sisters) is the reading in the best MS. See Ellicott's "Life
of our Lord," and Tischendorf, *in loc.* The former inclines to the more
southern ford near Jericho, "to which the multitudes that flocked to the
Baptist from Judea and Jerusalem would have found a speedier and more
convenient access."

near Succoth ! At the great ford they found themselves
in the midst of a motley multitude. The whole country,
from the passes of Lebanon to the pastures of Beer-
sheba, seemed to have caught up the sacred enthusiasm,
—flocking to this wild natural Sanctuary in East Palestine, to listen to the strange ambassador of heaven—with
his unshaven locks, clothed in rough camel-hide fastened
with leathern zone, reminding of the fiery Tishbite ;
living in a cave by night, and, after satisfying hunger
with wild desert fare, coming forth by day to deliver his
faithful fearless message. There were Pharisees from
Jerusalem, publicans from Jericho, Gilead freebooters,
Bashan shepherds bringing their sheep and lambs
across the river for Temple sacrifices, Galilean fishermen, Samaritan vinedressers and husbandmen, soldiers
from the barracks of Cæsarea, Tiberias, and Jerusalem ;
mothers with infants in their arms, old men leaning on
their staff for very age, bereaved ones with dimmed
eyes and broken hearts, profligates sated with guilty
pleasure, rich men whose gold had failed to answer the
question, "Who will show us any good?" poor men,
hanging in the rags of want, driven to despair by the
unkindness and cruelty and selfishness of others. "The
tall 'reeds' or canes of the jungle waved, shaken by the
wind : the pebbles of the bare clay hills lay around, to
which the Baptist pointed, as capable of being transformed into the children of Abraham : at their feet
rushed the refreshing stream of the never-failing river." [1]
All are seen gathered listening with arrested ears to the
spare, worn, sunbrowned, ascetic man, whose words are
evidently bringing tears to eyes that never wept before,
and sending swift arrows home to hardened hearts, as

[1] Sinai and Palestine, p. 311.

he calls upon all without distinction of age, or sex, or history, to " flee from the wrath to come." " What a contrast," says Pressensé, " was there between him and the doctors of Jerusalem, puffed up with their virtues and knowledge, wearing ostentatiously their long robes and broad phylacteries ! Habited like the simplest shepherd of the mountains, the Baptist tramples under foot all the idle prejudices, all the evil passions, all the vices of his nation. He carries truly in his hand that axe which is to be laid at the root of every corrupt tree, for his unsparing speech strikes at the very foundation of evil." [1]

In common with others of his associates, the impressible nature of the son of Jonas had been touched with the fervid appeals of the desert preacher. He felt the stirrings within him of a new and nobler life, as he listened to the trumpet-call, " Repent ! for the kingdom of Heaven is at hand." New thoughts and aspirations had broken in upon the monotony of his life of toil and the gains of the Bethsaida fishery. That bold prophet had not only flashed upon him a sense of his guilt,—" made him possess the iniquities of his youth," —but, more than all, had he stirred within him intense longings to see the great " Consolation of Israel," whose advent was declared to be imminent—" the true Light which lighteth every man that cometh into the world."

One day as this remarkable man was addressing the thronging multitudes, a Figure is seen in the distance,

[1] The same writer notes that the year in which the Baptist left the desert was a Sabbatical year—a time of universal rest, when a pause was made in all the occupations of common life. This accounts for the extraordinary concourse of men gathered round the Forerunner.

D

alone and unattended, as if immersed in pensive thought.
Nothing in His external appearance denotes superiority.
He wears the garb of an ordinary native of Galilee.
That solitary One walking along the margin of the
Jordan, and in which a few weeks previously He had
been baptized, is none other than the promised MESSIAH
—"the Hope of Israel and the Saviour thereof." He
is just returning from the scene of the forty days'
temptation among the caverns and lairs of wild animals
in the desert, wherever that was,—whether in the traditional locality—the bare, blighted Quarantania with
its rocks of precipitous limestone near to Jericho,
stretching north from the old valley of Achor ; or as
others suppose, among the unexplored mountains of
Nebo, from whose heights Moses surveyed the distant
land of promise, and from whose recesses Elijah was
borne to heaven in a whirlwind. The eye of the Baptist instantly caught sight of the Divine Conqueror
returning from fierce spiritual conflict. It is the
Morning Star owning the presence of the Great Sun of
Righteousness ! He stops suddenly in his discourse,
and, lifting his finger in the direction of the Stranger
—his voice subdued into a tone of reverend emotion—
he exclaims, "Behold the Lamb of God, which taketh
away the sin of the world ! "

None of the Galilee fishermen seem to have been
present on this first occasion. But the next day the
same sight gives rise to the same exclamation.[1]
Andrew, and John the son of Zebedee, heard it. They
listened, they beheld, they believed, they rejoiced !
Taking, moreover, the words—as they were doubtless

---

[1] The Baptist looked with an intent, arrested gaze (as the word in the
original means) on the Divine Stranger ($\epsilon\mu\beta\lambda\epsilon\psi\alpha\varsigma$).

intended to be—an encouragement to approach the mysterious Personage Himself, " they followed Jesus."

" What seek ye ? " was the first question asked, when, turning round, He saw them advancing behind, perhaps with misgiving footstep.

But His look and demeanour reassured them.   They need fear no chilling repulse ; and gathering confidence, they venture on the modest request—" Rabbi " (a title significant of distinction and greatness on His part, and of honour and respect on theirs), " where dwellest Thou ? "—as if they had said, ' Tell us where we may repair to unburden to Thee our heavy secrets, and, away from the din of these multitudes, sit at Thy feet and behold Thee as the Lamb of God ? '

" Come and see," was the gracious reply.

In obedience to the invitation, the two disciples accompanied Him to the piace where He dwelt, and " abode with Him that day, for it was about the tenth hour."

Where and what was the dwelling of this friendless Messiah, we are not informed.   For the last forty days He had been without home or shelter ; as St Mark in his usual graphic way describes, He was "with the wild beasts."   He may now, like some of the pilgrims who had come to hear the desert preacher, have been under the cover of a canvas tent ; or, like others of them, He may have abode in a little " Succôth "—a sylvan hut made of green boughs from the adjoining forests, having on the top, as we have seen in the Bedawy encampments, oleander and willow, palm and sycamore, with a striped blanket of camel's hair.   Be this as it may, thither, at the tenth hour, which, according to the Jewish computation, would be four o'clock in the

afternoon,[1] they resorted.   How long the interview
lasted that memorable spring evening, we are not informed.   Probably it was far on towards midnight ere
they separated.   The bright stars of that starry land
may have been shining on the white cliffs and foaming
waters of the Jordan when the two disciples came forth
from the most momentous meeting of their lives.   Next
morning still farther reveals what had been the result
of that intercourse on their own souls.   In their dreams,
a ladder, brighter and more glorious than that of their
great ancestor with its troops of clustering angels, had
been present to them, and transformed the banks of
the historic river into a second Bethel—a truer " House
of God " than that of the patriarch.   Andrew, eager to
make others he loved partakers in the joy with which
his own heart overflowed, hurries in breathless haste to
his brother Simon to communicate the tidings : " We
have found the Messias, which is, being interpreted, the
Christ (the Anointed One).   And he brought him to
Jesus."

How much is contained in that brief announcement,
Simon 'brought to Jesus'! the first introduction of Peter
to the heavenly Master, in whose service he was henceforth to be enlisted, and for whom, after a strange
mingling of defeats and victories, he was at last to lay
down his life in willing martyrdom !   The first look of
a great man is always memorable, whether king, or
hero, or statesman.   How profoundly interesting to this
lowly Galilean must have been his first glimpse of One
to whom he was afterwards to stand in so near and

---

1 Ten A.M. would be according to the Roman computation ; but I have
followed what seems the more likely, and which is adopted by Alford,
Neander, Kitto, and others.

endearing a relationship, and compared with whom all rank and greatness and power dwindle into nothing; whose advent had formed the longing aspiration of the holy and the good of the nation for many centuries—the theme of psalmists and prophets—the Seed of the woman—the Shiloh of Jacob—the Star of Bethlehem—the Son and Lord of David—the enthroned Priest of Zechariah—the Desire of all nations of Haggai—" the Wonderful, the Counsellor, the mighty God, the Prince of Peace" of the greatest of their seers !

And if the first *look* be one of deepest interest, much more the first *words* of personal address. How could Simon ever forget that moment when Jesus beheld him, and said, saluting him by name, "Thou art Simon the son of Jona: thou shalt be called Cephas, which is by interpretation, A stone"?[1]   Do not these words seem as if the omniscient eye of Christ had discerned at a glance the strong features in the character of His great follower; his natural weakness, his ultimate greatness, his rock-like boldness, firmness, fearlessness; a nature which, unrestrained and ungoverned by higher principles, might have developed itself into what was violent, headstrong, overbearing; but which, despite of a few exceptions, grace moulded and transformed into what was resolute, stable, inflexible, patient, enduring— the result doubtless of living union and contact with the great living " Rock "?   As in the case of the illustrious father of his nation centuries before at Jabbok,

[1] Cephas—"the rock." The equivocal meaning of the word was, no doubt, evident in the original Aramaic dialect spoken in Galilee. The French alone of modern languages exactly retains it : "Vous êtes Pierre et sur cette Pierre" (Milman's History of Christianity, vol. i. p. 210). Lange renders the words, " Thou art Simon, the son of the shy dove of the rock : hereafter thou shalt be called the protecting rock of the dove."

to whom the new name was given of "the hero of Jehovah," so, "as a prince," he too was "to have power with God and to prevail." The good Shepherd " calleth His own sheep *by name*, and leadeth him out."

From this hour, Peter (for we shall now adopt the new, divinely-given designation) had enrolled himself among the number of Christ's disciples. It was the first and in every sense the most momentous crisis in his life—the time when a hundred hours are crowded into one :—similar to the scene witnessed in a future year on the Damascus highway, when in the twinkling of an eye a proud citadel of unbelief and self-righteousness fell to the ground, and its rare treasures were reclaimed and surrendered for the service of the Lord. In the case of both, " all old things passed away, and all things became new." The suddenness and instantaneousness with which Peter accepted Jesus of Nazareth as his Saviour, was in accordance with the impetuousness of his character. The calm, reasoning, cautious Thomas would have taken days, possibly weeks, to ponder the evidence of the Messiahship claimed by a Galilean workman's son. The other takes his determination at a bound ; and forestals, without hesitation, a future utterance, " Lord, I believe." In the absence of any miracle at this first meeting to authenticate the claims of Jesus, we must infer that there was something in the look and deportment of the Lamb of God, " fairer than the children of men," which attracted and overawed the new disciple with an irresistible sense of the Divine Presence. It was the felt power of intrinsic goodness and holiness, and spoke as convincingly as if the shining hosts of Bethlehem had again hovered over the scene, and repeated their natal song. St Jerome, indeed (although we only accept the great spiritual verity underlying the legend), quotes from a " Gospel to the Hebrews " outside the inspired Canon, fragments of which have come down to us,—that radiations of unearthly brightness came from the face of Jesus at the moment of His baptism, and bore irresistible attestation to His Godhead.

Nor is it unworthy of passing note, that the interesting account of this momentous interview we owe entirely to the fourth Evangelist. An able writer thus comments on Peter's first meeting with his Lord being alone recorded by the friend of his youth at Bethsaida, and the dearest companion of his after-years : " It would almost seem that we might detect the old man's complacency—for John wrote his Gospel in extreme old age —as looking back along the line of half a century of toil and woe, he recalls that scene of his early youth, and with fond and affectionate pride records—what he alone notices—the very marked reception which he saw Jesus give to his friend when they were as yet both strangers to Him. For it is John who tells us that when Andrew introduced his brother to Jesus, the Lord said, ' Thou art Simon the son of Jona,' &c. It is John who tells this, and as we read, we feel glad that of all the Evangelists it is John who tells it." [1]

Shortly after this period (during which more than one interesting occurrence had taken place, on which, however, our limits forbid us to dwell) these earliest disciples of the Messiah seem to have resumed their wonted occupations. We can only picture how the hearts of the " Pilgrim brothers " of Bethsaida burned within them. The summer sun-

[1] Dr Candlish's Scripture Miscellanies, 253, 254.

shine, the song of bird and breath of flower, would be
in accordance with a strange, new inner joy.   When
out on the sea with their boats and nets, girt in their
rough hides, how would they love to rehearse these
memorable hours at Bethabara, when He met them by
the border river, and they pledged their obedience and
love.   They little dreamed, doubtless, then of the higher
vocation and more intimate fellowship in store for
them, which we shall describe in the next chapters, when
summoned from their retirement they were to be made
a spectacle to devils, and to angels, and to men.   Peter's
heart was now given to the Christ of Nazareth, and he
only waited a more definite call to abandon for His sake
his pleasant home and manly toil, and to surrender his
time, his services, and ultimately his life.   Though
sadly failing on several earlier occasions, as we shall
find, to "endure hardness as a good soldier," yet, he
who was reared amid scenes, recalling above all others
in Palestine heroic memories,—Israel's olden age of
chivalry,—was, by a lengthened process of training and
discipline, to be fitted for the stern moral conflicts of
his later career, and finally to be made more than
conqueror through Christ who loved him.

CHAPTER IV.

The Call and Consecration.

PETER'S HOME AT CAPERNAUM.   MIRACULOUS CURE OF HIS
MOTHER-IN-LAW.   THE NIGHT OF FISHING.   THE MIRACULOUS
DRAUGHT AND ACTED PARABLE.   FORSAKING ALL AND FOL-
LOWING CHRIST.

> " Master, speak ! Thy servant heareth,
>   Waiting for Thy gracious word,
>   Longing for Thy voice that cheereth ;
>   Master ! let it now be heard."
> —*Ministry of Song.*

"Under the rough exterior of the young Galilean boatman,
Jesus marked the spirit of hardy zeal, which, purified by contact
with Himself, would fit him for his great initiative mission among
the apostles."—*Pressensé.*

" Admire the dispensation of the Lord, how He draws each by
the art which is most familiar and natural to Him—as the Magians
by a star, so the fishermen by fish."—*Chrysostom.*

"It was desirable that the first impression made on Peter's
mind should continue to act on him in quiet, on which account
Christ first left him to himself.   And when, by repeated operations, everything in his disposition was sufficiently prepared, He
received him into the number of His disciples."—*Neander.*

I must have been now about the end of November the year immediately following, when the sultry heat of summer had disappeared; when the trees were either bared of their leaves, or seared with latest autumnal tints, and the voice of the turtle was silent. A delightful season—in some respects the most delightful on the shores of at other times sultry Gennesaret. Let one who with an artistic eye has tested the charms of atmosphere during that month bear testimony—and the description applies equally to the Apostolic era—" We arrived there on the 17th of November. . . . . There was sometimes a refreshing breeze, especially on the water, and the colouring of the scenery was really beautiful : the mountains, arid and barren masses of rock on the eastern side, were clothed nearly all day in delicate lilacs and purples, sometimes rosy, sometimes golden—the water was always of a light-greyish blue—the nâbk and walnuts that fringe the western shore were in their highest luxuriance, and the blossoms of the oleanders were absolutely glorious. . . . . If any one wants to *feel* the beauty of the Lake of Gennesaret, let him spend a November or December evening on its bosom, watching the varying scene, till all has faded into darkness—till he has done that, he has not understood that lake ; here above all places one realises, in the scenery over which the familiar associations of Scripture have cast their halo, that,—

> " ' The colouring may be of earth,
> The lustre comes of heavenly birth.' " [1]

Our blessed Lord had recently returned into His beloved Galilee.   Several eventful months were now to be spent on the shores of the Lake of Tiberias ere the next Passover in March or April summoned Him again to the capital.   Capernaum was then for the second time, as it continued with little variation afterwards, His Galilean residence, after He had bidden farewell for ever to the sanctities of His old dwelling in sunny Nazareth. It never can cease to be an interesting thought in connection with St Peter, and a special token of honour, distinction, and friendship conferred on the son of Jonas, that it was his home there, as we have already noted, which the divine Messiah made His most permanent earthly resting-place during the years of his public ministry.   Nicephorus tells us that Helen, the mother of Constantine, erected a beautiful church on the supposed site of the apostle's house.   I need hardly say, no

---

[1] Miss Beaufort's Syrian Shrines.

trace of it, amid the modern wilderness of ruin and
desolation, can be found. We cannot tell whether the
blue waves of the lake murmured under its lattice, or
whether it looked out to the vines and olives climbing
the slopes behind. But it is enough to know that
somewhere nigh was that most consecrated of earthly
homes, which stood in the same relation to Galilee
as the dwelling at Bethany did to Judea.[1] On one of
the Sabbaths of Christ's sojourn, after the synagogue
services were over, we read that He repaired, probably
at midday,[2] to the apostle's dwelling, and raised up his
wife's mother from a violent ("great") fever.[3] So that
from that hour Jesus must have been linked, not only
to the apostle, but to his grateful relatives, by ties of
no ordinary gratitude and affection. Here a passing
remark may be interposed, and in doing so I shall use
the words of another : "This part of the history of the
Apostle Peter reminds us that the Evangelists have
left, as it were, their protest in making us specially acquainted with the fact, that the man whom the Church
of Rome exalts to a supremacy above all the apostles
was a husband, and the head of a family. That he
continued to sustain these relations after entering upon

[1] St Mark speaks of it as "the house of Simon and Andrew." St Luke
only as "*Simon's* house," "his stronger personality causing Andrew (though
probably with natural prerogatives as the elder brother, and certainly with
spiritual, as the earlier called and the bringer of his brother to Jesus) here,
as elsewhere, to fall into the background."—*Trench*, p. 234.

[2] "The service in the synagogue, the forms and hours of which appear to
have been studiously conformed to those in the temple worship, would in
all probability have commenced about nine o'clock, and ended sometime
before midday."—*Ellicott*, p. 164.

[3] Dr Thomson remarks, "Fevers of a very malignant type are still prevalent, particularly in summer and autumn. . . . . As there is considerable
marshy land about Tabijah, may not this account for the prevalence of
fevers at Capernaum?" Autumn was the season when this miracle was performed.

his apostolic work is shown by the assertion of St Paul, that he himself had the right, although he did not choose to exercise it, of forming a conjugal connection, and of being accompanied by his wife on his missionary journeyings, as well as his fellow-apostles, naming particularly the subject of our present remarks : ' Have we not power to lead about a sister, a wife, as well as other apostles, and as the brethren of the Lord *and Cephas ?* ' Is it not the finger of God that hath preserved these notices of this apostle's domestic history, immaterial as they might at first have appeared, and yet rendered very important by the subsequent rise, and anti-christian errors, of the great Apostacy ?" [1]

But to return. That Sabbath which witnessed the miraculous recovery in the house of Peter was indeed in every respect a memorable one. As it began with a discourse in the synagogue, followed by more than one miracle, so it ended by multitudes at sunset, after the sacred hours were past, bringing their sick from all quarters—probably to the city gates—to receive the healing touch of the Great Physician. " The gate of an Eastern city is the great place of public resort : it occupies the same position as the Agora of Greek cities. In the burning climate of Syria, the cool hours of evening are chosen by the inhabitants for coming out of their houses ; then begins a singularly noisy stir of life—the women go to the fountain with their pitchers on their heads, the men gather in groups about the gates of the city to talk over the events and interests of the day.

---

[1] Bishop Lee, pp. 28, 29. One cannot note without a smile the easy method by which some Romanists, in their defence of celibacy, get rid of the difficulty of Peter being a married man. The gratuitous assertion is propounded, that he was divorced from his wife after becoming an apostle !

That evening the report of the miracles of Jesus banished every other theme at Capernaum. Every family brought out its sick ; some bedridden, some tossing in the terrible agony of possession. A melancholy spectacle, the epitome in this little corner of the world, of all a world's sufferings."[1] In the same honoured abode where the miracle was performed, Jesus seems to have spent the night as the guest of His disciple and friend, obtaining under his roof needed rest. " The meal would be taken in common ; and the disciples receive, doubtless from the lips of the Master, the explanation of His discourse in the synagogue. We at least know that such was the wont of Jesus in the familiar circle of His friends." From an incidental reference in St Mark's Gospel, we are almost warranted in imagining Peter's surprise, if not disappointment, when he found, at early morning ("a great while before day," ere he himself had embarked in his fisherman's toil), that the Divine Visitor had left His couch of repose, and had retired for prayer and communion with His Heavenly Father, to some "solitary place," up amid these quiet hills. The multitude, whom darkness had dispersed on the preceding night, were already gathered around the dwelling, eager to see the wonder-working Prophet. And the same Evangelist alone mentions, that "Simon and they that were with him followed after Him," somewhat unceremoniously tracking His footsteps and obtruding on His privacy, addressing the urgent plea for His return, "All men seek for Thee" (Mark i. 37).

We have hitherto pictured Simon and his fellow-fishermen simply as disciples of Jesus, who had been

1 Pressensé, p. 351.

warmly associated with their new Master ever since the
memorable interview at the Jordan. "They were
already known as His disciples, and were indeed such
in the affection and respect with which they regarded
Him, but there was as yet nothing definite in the relation which bound them to Him.   On their return with
Him into Galilee, they resume their customary labours ;
but they are ripening for a more positive vocation.
Ignorant as they yet are, they have learnt to know and
love Jesus, and have a vague consciousness of His
exalted dignity. Their hearts are His. There is nothing
to hinder the Master's forming a yet closer tie between
them and Himself." [1]

It is at this period, then, to which we have just referred (perhaps the day following), that we are introduced to one of those gospel incidents in connection
with Capernaum which has a bearing of special interest
on the future apostle. We may suppose it to have
been that morning hour when Nature was waking up
again to life and energy ; the waters of the inland sea
gleaming like silver in the early sun, the innumerable
birds twittering in the thorny brakes greeting his rising.
The wonted traffic had been resumed in the little seaport ; and the fishermen, who had been out the livelong
night, were returning to the nearest landing point with
their spoil. Peter, along with three brother-seafarers
—Andrew, John, and James—had reached the shore.
They had been unsuccessful in their labours. Weary
and jaded, they had pulled up their boat on the strand,
and were in the act of washing their nets before
repairing to their hamlets for refreshment and rest. [2]

---

[1] Pressensé, p. 344.

[2] Luke v. 2 ἀπέπλυναν : "They washed them off—they cleansed them from

But ONE who was no stranger to them had been noting their unrecompensed toil. There was a deep meaning and reason, which they knew not at the time, for the dispiriting results of their midnight industry, but which was, ere long, to be made manifest. Meanwhile, however, Simon's Lord, "as one that serveth," begs from the lowly fisherman the accommodation of his boat— the crowd unduly pressing upon Him—that He might make it a platform from which to address the multitudes who had gathered on the beach.[1]

We may realise the scene. The lake, as we have seen, often fretted with storms, exposed to sudden gusts coming sweeping down the ravines, was now, shall we suppose, either musical with a gentle ripple, or hushed into a dead calm,—tree and rock, fishing hamlet and villa, mirrored in its quiet waters. Hushed, too, was the dense promiscuous throng on the shore; gathered, not on a Sabbath or other holy day, but willingly suspending life's "common task" and toil, that they might listen to the Prophet of Nazareth. The great Object of their eager curiosity sat in meek majesty in the fishing-boat, about to speak the words of eternal life. "I was delighted to find," says Dr Thomson, "small creeks or inlets between Tabiga and Tell Hum, where the ship could ride in safety only a few feet from the shore, and

weeds, &c., and hung them up to dry till they should be wanted again on the following night."—*Wordsworth's Greek Test.* "There is the bag-net and basket-nets of various kinds, which are so constructed and worked as to enclose the fish out in deep water. I have seen them of almost every conceivable size and pattern. It was with some one of this sort, I suppose, that Simon had toiled all night."—*Land and Book,* p. 402.

[1] Dean Stanley, "Sinai and Palestine," p. 373, notes, that on another occasion, when Jesus similarly addressed the multitudes ranged on the level shore, delivering His well-known succession of parables, it was from "*the boat*—the boat of passage that lay close by for the purpose."

where the multitudes, seated on both sides and before
the boat, could listen without distraction or fatigue.
As if on purpose to furnish seats, the shore on both
sides of these narrow inlets is piled up with huge
boulders of basalt." [1]   Although mountain and shore
were not at that particular time of the Gospel narrative
carpeted with the emerald of spring, and decked with
their profusion of flowers, no season of the year could
defraud Gennesaret of its beauty.   The lake itself, and
its varied surroundings ; the balmy air ; the fresh sparkle
of its limpid waters ; its beautiful fringe of rock and
sand ; the rivulets, rare in other parts of Palestine, fur-
rowing the hillsides ; and, above all, glorious Hermon,
like a high altar, or rather, the enduring type of Christ's
own eternal power and Godhead, made it a fit and
glorious temple for inaugurating a ministry of love.
" There was something," it has been eloquently said,
" significant in the place which He chose as the scene
of His earliest ministry.   St John had preached in the
lonely wastes by the Dead Sea waters ; his voice had
been echoed back by the flinty precipices that frown
over the sultry Ghôr.   The city nearest to the scene of
his teaching had been built in defiance of a curse, and
the road to it led through 'the bloody way.'   All
around him breathed the dreadful associations of a
guilty and desolated past ; the very waves were bitu-
minous ; the very fruits crumbled into foul ashes under
the touch ; the very dust beneath his feet lay hot and
white over the relics of an abominable race.   There,
beside those leaden waters, under that copper heaven,
amid those burning wildernesses and scarred ravines,

[1] Land and Book, p. 356.

had he preached the baptism of repentance. But it was, doubtless, a part of Christ's Divine plan that His ministry should begin amid scenes so beautiful, and that the good tidings, which revealed to mankind their loftiest hopes and purest pleasures, should be first proclaimed in a region of unusual loveliness. . . . . If every vestige of human habitation should disappear from beside it, and the jackal and the hyena should howl about the shattered fragments of the synagogue where once Christ taught, yet the fact that He chose it as the scene of His opening ministry will give a sense of sacredness and pathos to its lonely waters till time shall be no more." [1]

His address being concluded, He turns to Peter with the command, " Launch forth into the deep, and let down your nets for a draught." [2] The other replies by telling, despondingly, of their want of success ; that " all night " (the best and most likely time for catching) they had laboured in vain ; but, addressing Jesus as

[1] Dr Farrar's Life of Christ, vol. i. pp. 173,177.

[2] My late lamented friend, Dr Norman Macleod, narrates, in his " Eastward "—a book which combines accurate and reliable information with great charm of vivid description—" There are only two boats on the lake, and we sent a messenger to the town to secure one of them for us after dark, requesting that some fishermen with their nets would accompany it. For other reasons than they could conjecture, we were anxious to 'go a-fishing.' They came, accordingly, when the stars and moon were out in the sky. Few words were spoken ; but each had his own thoughts as these rough men cast out their nets, wholly ignorant of other fishermen who long ago had done the same. It is unnecessary to suggest the memories which arose as the net was dropped in the calm sea, rippling under the moonlight : or as, after encircling a wide space for our prey, we 'caught nothing.' " My own experience, and that of my fellow-travellers, was different. We hired one of these boats. Its two Jewish owners had been out all night ; but, though now wearied and half asleep with their prolonged labours, their toil had not been in vain—as they came for us after landing their "draught of fishes " at Tiberias.

" Master " (evidently showing the relation in which he
already stood to Him), he adds, in simple faith and
submission to a will he had been taught to love,
" Nevertheless, at Thy word I will let down the net."
For, as Dr Trench remarks, " these must not be regarded as the words of one himself despairing of the
issue ; on the contrary, they are spoken more in the
spirit of the Psalmist when he exclaimed, ' Except the
Lord build the house, they labour in vain that build it :
except the Lord keep the city, the watchman waketh
but in vain.' " [1]   The result was, the enclosure of such
a vast shoal of fishes that the overstrained net brake.
It was a momentous act in the history of the Church ;
preliminary to the formal setting apart, on an early
day, of Simon and his fellow-disciples to the office of
the holy apostleship, to feed the flock of God, which
He was about to purchase with His own blood.

In that august sanctuary of Nature, the Lord, alike
of Nature and of Grace, discourses to His disciples and
to the Church of the future by means of an *acted parable.*
He makes the humble calling of the fishermen of Galilee convey—in the first instance to their own minds—
lessons of faith and confidence and hope.   He takes the
nets they were washing as emblems and teachers of
great truths, and prepares to make these simple-minded
boatmen " fishers of men."   We have just seen, that on
the lowering of the nets at the Divine command, the
bootless efforts of the long, midnight hours had been
more than rewarded.   So astonishing, indeed, was the
capture of fishes, that Simon had to beckon to Andrew
and John to come to their assistance from the adjoining

[1] Notes on the Miracles, p. 131.

boat. The net was discharged of its contents, and both
vessels were filled to sinking with the spoil. Peter was
in a moment prostrate at the feet of his Master, with
the exclamation, "Depart from me, for I am a sinful
man, O Lord!"[1] "The man recognises, as he has never
done before, his own vileness and nothingness; rises
out of the dust of self-humiliation, a fitting instrument
to set forward the glory of God, which he never would
have been unless he had first been humbled there."[2]
He had evidently a deepened consciousness, altogether
of an intenser kind than he had at the meeting at
Bethabara, that he was in the presence of no mere prophet or teacher, but of the great Lord of creation, the
Owner of "the fish of the sea, and whatsoever passeth
through the paths of the sea." The words of Jacob may
be taken as the interpreters of his present thoughts and
feelings : "Surely the Lord is in this place, and I knew
it not." It was the lesson that prepared him to make
the more confident avowal at a later time, "We believe
and are sure that Thou art the Christ, the Son of the
living God."

How gently Christ re-assures him, "*Jesus said unto
Simon*, FEAR NOT." And then, having allayed his
doubts, the Master proceeds to unfold the nature and
duties, the responsibilities and discouragements, of the
great work which in due time he was officially to undertake : "*From henceforth thou shalt catch men:*"—words
of deep prophetic meaning. "Sinking, as was so often
His custom, the higher in the lower, and setting forth

[1] The Greek word employed for "man" implies a deep consciousness of
his personal unworthiness and sin. It is ἀνὴρ ἁμαρτωλὸs (not ἄνθρωπος).
[2] Notes on the Miracles, p. 134.

that higher in the forms of the lower," the Divine
Speaker made the mute tenants of the lake—that lay
in dead and dying heaps in the net—a pledge of far
vaster spiritual successes. As, according to the remark of
Origen, Paul the tentmaker was to become " the maker
of everlasting tabernacles," so Peter was to retain his
net, but souls were to be the nobler prey.   He was to
buffet waves still, but they were to be the waves of
human passion, and ignorance, and crime.   He was to
hoist his sail still on a more treacherous sea, but, with a
mightier arm than his own guiding the helm, he would
reach the heavenly shore with the unbroken net, and lay
at his Redeemer's feet joyous multitudes rescued from
the depths of ruin and despair.   Or, as Christ's charge
to Peter has been beautifully paraphrased by a writer to
whose exposition of the miracle we are much indebted,
" Those that were wandering at random through the
Salt Sea waves of the world, among its deep, unquiet
waters full of whirlpools and fears, the smaller of them
falling a prey to the greater, and all with the weary
sense as of a vast prison, thou shalt gather into one,
embracing them all within the same folds and recesses
of the Gospel net." [1]

It is only further added, " And when they had

[1] Archbishop Trench, p. 136. Bishop Wordsworth also notes the force
and meaning of the word " catch" in the original : " This draught of fishes
. . . . foreshadowed the success that would attend the labours of the apos-
tolical fishers of men, in drawing the net of the Gospel through the sea of
the world, and enclosing the wandering shoals of heathen nations within it,
so that they might be 'caught'—not for death, but for life eternal." . . . .
" The expression is stronger than the 'catch men ' of our version. $\dot{\alpha}\nu\theta\rho\dot{\omega}$-
$\pi o v\varsigma$ $\dot{\epsilon}\sigma\eta$ $\zeta\omega\rho\gamma\hat{\omega}\nu$—'Thou shalt be a catcher of men alive. This shall be
thy future occupation—to catch men for life eternal, instead of catching
fish for death.' "—Greek Testament in loc.

brought their ships to land, they forsook all and followed Jesus." Peter was among that honoured band, who have left the Church of God in every age so impressive an example of renunciation and self-denial. It was—it must have been—for him and them a trying hour. At a moment's warning their occupations were to be surrendered. The hallowed scenes of youth were around them. Every rock and ravine, every sheltered nook and bay in that lovely sea, was familiar to them. The Bethsaida hamlet, from which childhood was wont to rush in its sunny morning to welcome their fathers and brothers as their boats rasped the shallows after a night of toil, was in full view. The strange summons addressed to them, and accepted, implied separation from these homes and scenes, probably for ever. They just had, moreover, their boats filled to overflowing. Elated with success, which they might have been perverse enough to attribute to ordinary causes, they never before had so strong inducement to cleave to their nets and prosecute their calling. They were about to exchange their little all, in order to attach themselves to the person and fortunes of the reputed Son of a carpenter, who was often unable to tell of so secure a shelter as had the fox of the mountain, or the bird of the forest! Yet, they "straightway," without deliberating, without conferring with flesh and blood, without reasoning on matters of expediency, willingly surrendered that all, and cast in their lot with the despised and rejected One!

Were they ultimately sufferers by their devotion? "Lo," says Peter on an after occasion, "we have left all and followed Thee." Jesus said, in reply, "Verily,

I say unto you, there is no man that hath left house, or parents, or brethren, or wife, or children, for the kingdom of God's sake, who shall not receive manifold more in this present time, and in the world to come life everlasting." [1]

1 A part of this chapter is abridged from the author's " Memories of Gennesaret."

CHAPTER V.

The Apostleship.

"It is plainly evident that they taught Christianity by a Divine power, when such persons were able with such an uncontrolled success to subdue men to the obedience of His word; for that they had no eloquent tongues, no subtle and discursive head, none of the refined and rhetorical arts of Greece, to conquer the minds of men. . . . I verily believe that the holy Jesus purposely made use of such preachers of His doctrine, that there might be no suspicion that they came instructed, with arts of sophistry, but that it might be clearly manifest to all the world that there was no crafty design in it, and that they had a Divine power going along with them, which was more efficacious than the greatest volubility of expression or ornaments of speech, or the artifices which were used in the Grecian compositions."—*Origen.*

"He whose purpose it was, by the weak things of the world to confound the strong, who meant to draw emperors to Himself by fishermen, and not fishermen by emperors, lest His Church should even seem to stand in the wisdom and power of men rather than of God—He saw in these unlearned fishermen of the Galilean Lake the fittest instruments for His work."—*Trench.*

"No priest of the house of Levi, no warrior of the host of Judah, ever burnt with more fervent zeal than did the fisherman of Galilee as he hung upon the words and looks of that unknown Teacher who appeared on the shores of his native lake."—*Stanley's Sermons on the Apostolic Age.*

"I was no prophet, neither was I a prophet's son; but I was an herdman, and a gatherer of sycamore fruit: and the Lord took me as I followed the flock, and the Lord said unto me, Go, prophesy unto my people Israel."—*Amos* vii. 14, 15.

T was now about the Feast of Pentecost when the wheat harvest and vintage of Gennesaret were being gathered in. Peter, as we have seen, had for a considerable period been warmly attached to the person of Jesus, following His steps alike in Judea and Galilee, the witness of His mighty works, and the hearer of the gracious words which proceeded out of His mouth. It had been a period of important training and discipline in the prospect of the holier relation he was about to hold to the Master. We shall afterwards find, when he came to be an apostle, that he was selected as one of a privileged three who were admitted to be the witnesses of the more sacred transactions of their Lord's life. But even during the present preliminary season when he was no more than a disciple, we find him enjoying

the same distinction.   At the raising of Jairus' daughter
" following out the maxim of law, 'that at the mouth of
two or three witnesses everything is to be established,'
the Lord invested with a peculiar character for that
end Peter and the sons of Zebedee : that such particulars of His ministry as, for good reasons, He wished to
have concealed during His lifetime, might after His death
be attested by a competent number of credible men,
not limited to the very lowest amount of testimony
barely allowed by law, yet not extended beyond what
would be fully acknowledged on all hands to be sufficient."[1]   As yet, though a devoted follower, Peter had
been invested with no official character.   But the time
had arrived when it seemed meet to the great Founder
of our religion to designate a certain number of His
disciples, and Peter among these honoured few, to the
office of the apostolate.

On a hill, somewhere bordering on the lake, our
blessed Lord held a special night season of prayer preparatory to setting up "twelve pillars for the not yet
consolidated yet already endangered Church."[2]   Truly
a night much to be remembered.   Any of these wild
and sequestered nooks immediately behind Bethsaida
might answer the purpose of this midnight oratory or
altar, where the great Intercessor, the Shepherd of
souls, invoked a blessing on His chief under-shepherds.
I remember, as I passed beneath and looked up among
the groups of wild nâbk dotting the sides of these glens,
picturing them as likely spots for this and similar
seasons of sacred retirement.   From the specific mention, however, of " *the* hill " (not " *a* mountain," as in
our version) it has been supposed by some that refer-

[1] Dr Candlish's Scripture Miscellanies, p. 256.   [2] Ellicott.

ence is made on this occasion to the mountain of Hattin, with its bifurcated cone and green summit, which we recognised for the first time to the left of the now desolate plain, when crossing from Nazareth ; but which afterwards mingled conspicuously in several views from the upper portion of the lake itself. From Bethsaida or Capernaum it would be approached by that wild gorge leading from "The land," or "plain of Gennesaret," to which I have previously alluded.[1] And we may readily believe, when Jesus wished to evade the intrusion to which He would be more subject in the familiar hills around "His own city," He would not unfrequently avail Himself of this sequestered dell and the solitude of its guardian mountain for these seasons of holy vigil, holding alike converse with the grandeur of Nature, and fellowship with His Divine Father. "There is something," says Dr Farrar, "affecting beyond measure in the thought of these lonely hours ; the absolute silence and stillness, broken by no sounds of human life, but only by the hooting of the night jar, or the howl of the jackal ; the stars of an Eastern heaven raining their large lustre out of the unfathomable depth ; the figure of the Man of Sorrows kneeling upon the dewy grass, and gaining strength for His labours from the purer air, the more open heaven, of that intense and silent communing with His Father and His God." "What magnificence of the ancient

---

1 We did not visit it, partly owing to the want of time and partly to the great heat. It must, from the accounts of those who have, be eminently entitled to the appellation of picturesque. One traveller speaks of "the romantic glen of the little river," and "the thickets in the bottom of the ravine, where monstrous boulders were lying, and whence the cliffs on either side rose, often quite perpendicularly, to the height of 600 or 700 feet."— *Syrian Shrines*, p. 55.

worship," says another, " could surpass the solemnity
of that sacred season, when Jesus, after passing the
night in prayer on one of the hills which surround
Capernaum, called His twelve apostles ?"—*Pressensé*, p.
357. Whether it were the one mountain ridge or the
other, to which on this memorable evening He resorted,
it was, at all events, the birthnight of the Christian
ministry, that on which the mighty Pleader interceded
not for His own disciples alone, but also for His faithful ambassadors in every age and place of the world :
the " wise" who were hereafter to "shine as the brightness of the firmament," and, turning many to righteousness, " as the stars for ever and ever."

Very early in the morning (at daybreak, before the
crowd from the towns and villages below had time to
gather, and probably in accordance with His own
directions) His disciples come to meet Him. Out of
these unlearned Galileans He selected "twelve, whom
also He named apostles ;" those who were to become
messengers, missionaries, evangelists—persons invested
with a special commission to teach the new Gospel of the
kingdom ; gifted, moreover, with supernatural powers to
attest their Divine appointment. As it is expressed in
the words of consecration, " that they should be with
Him, and that He might send them forth to preach and
to have power to heal sickness, and to cast out devils "
(Mark iii. 14, 15). Among these (shall we say chief
among them) was Simon. We shall come by-and-by
to examine particularly the irrational claims of the
Church of Rome for what is called " the Primacy of St
Peter," in the sense of his being Vicar, or Ruler, in
Christ's stead,—taking the place of his Lord, subsequent
to His ascension, as the Church's divinely-appointed

head. Leaving this question, however, for the present,
it is nevertheless plain, that from his earliest call to the
apostleship, Peter does assume the leading position
among his associates. In every case, in the list of the
apostles, his name stands first. Matthew specially
assigns him this honourable distinction (x. 2), " The
first, Simon, who is called Peter." He is generally addressed by our Lord Himself as their representative and
acknowledged leader ; and as frequently replies as
spokesman in the name of the others. " Thus, when our
Lord had uttered a parable with a solemn call to watchfulness, it is Peter who asks for an application of the
discourse : ' Lord, speakest Thou this parable unto us,
or even to all ?' At a later period, when Christ is
speaking of forgiveness, it is Peter who propounds the
moral problem : ' Lord, how often shall my brother sin
against me, and I forgive him ? until seven times ?' In
reply to the enforcement of self-renunciation, Peter
again speaks for the rest : ' Lord, we have left all and
followed Thee.' Even by the outside world he is tacitly
accepted as the representative of the little company.
In Capernaum it was to Peter that the collectors of the
Temple dedrachma came : ' Doth not your Master pay
the tax ?' "[1] When the apostles are subsequently
mentioned in their collective capacity, the phrase used
is, " Peter and the rest of the apostles ;" " Peter and
the eleven." Paul, when he went up to Jerusalem by
Divine revelation, " took up his abode with Peter."
Add to all this ; Peter's entire life and history, with its
lights and shadows, its ebbs and flows, seemed, more
than any other, to render him a befitting living com-

[1] The Apostle Peter, his Life and Letters, by Dr Green of Rawdon
College, pp. 18, 19. A scholarly volume, whose only fault is its brevity.

mentary on the moral conflict which, in every case, has to be undergone before the natural man is subdued and the spiritual is made triumphant—the weakness of the one, and the strength, through God's grace, of the other. His life, if we may so express it, was "The Pilgrim's Progress" of the apostolic age, with its Sloughs of Despond, and its Doubting Castles, its encounters with Fearful, and Ready-to-Halt, and Despondency, but ending at last with complete victory over Apollyon, reaching the land Beulah, and having "an abundant entrance ministered" (as his own expression is), into the heavenly city. As it has been well said, "The weakness and the strength of our human love for Christ are both mercifully provided for in the character of the greatest of the twelve."[1] In the selection, we may add, not only of Peter, but of his colleagues, Jesus would manifest the sovereignty of His grace, and His independence of human instrumentality. The apostles are chosen, not from the magnates of Jerusalem, not from among phylacteried Pharisees, or learned doctors— the Hillels and Gamaliels of her schools;—but as, in a long preceding age, the God of Israel commissioned no lettered Rabbi of Samaria or Judea, but rather took as His accredited messenger, in the person of Elijah the prophet, a roving Bedouin from the Highlands of Palestine, without the prestige of rank, or birth, or lore, or pedigree ; so now, far away from the corruption of the capital, He selects a fisherman, and gifts him supernaturally to grapple with the powers of evil, and the hostility of the world. Emphatic testimony to the old prophetic utterance, " Not by might, nor by power, but by My Spirit, saith the Lord of Hosts." " About to

[1] Alford.

lay the foundation of the great Edifice, designed to shelter so many generations, He sought, as it were, in the midst of the masses of the people, the block of virgin marble to be fashioned to His will."[1] This Galilean boatman, along with a handful of uneducated men from the darkest of all the Palestine provinces, and, in a later year, a converted Jew from Tarsus, are to hurl Superstition from her throne, to silence her oracles, demolish the temples and shrines of ages, and bring the whole Roman Empire, as by a magic touch, to own a crucified Saviour as its God and King. Truly " God hath chosen the foolish things of the world to confound the wise ; and God hath chosen the weak things of the world to confound the things that are mighty ; and base things of the world, and things that are despised, hath God chosen, yea, and things which are not, to bring to nought things that are : that no flesh should glory in His presence."[2] " The Divine Spirit alone, who filled the Man Christ Jesus," is the reflection of a gifted traveller, as he gazed on the scene of that " calling," " could have transfigured commonplace fishermen and publicans into apostles, and made a commonplace lake a theatre of wonders."[3]

Peter's history from this moment becomes intimately associated with that of his Divine Lord. He is to be a sharer in His earthly humiliation and its manifold accompaniments—fatiguing journeys under the hot sun by day ; often no pillow save the turf of the hillside by night ; no curtains but the silver lining of the olive tree, or canopy of heaven ; no protection from the drenching dews save the long striped Abbâ, crouching

[1] Pressensé, p. 257. [2] 1 Cor. i. 27, 28, 29.
[3] Dr Macleod's Eastward.

F

under which the wandering Arab to this day sleeps amid the flocks outside his tent. The fasting and hunger spoken of by the well of Samaria, and the common bread by which, on that same occasion, hunger was appeased, were doubtless ofttimes the experienced privations in these self-denying journeyings. The comforts of the fisherman's home, and the freedom of the fisherman's life, would be unknown amid the friendless villages, and dusty roads, and overpowering summer heat of the valleys of Galilee and Samaria. "They were to take nothing with them—no scrip for food; no purse for money; no change of raiment; no travelling shoes (ὑποδήματα) in place of their ordinary palm-bark sandals; they were not even to procure a staff for the journey if they did not happen to possess one. . . . On entering a town they were to go to any house in it where they had reason to hope that they would be welcome, and to salute it with the immemorial Shalom lakem, 'Peace be to you,' and if the children of peace were there the blessing would be effective, if not it would return on their own heads." [1]

Peter and the other eleven were sent forth, in the first instance, among the northern towns and villages to testify to Christ's Messiahship, and to say to the cities of Galilee, as well as of Judah, "Behold your God!" The mission-field of labour was not yet, at least, among the way of the Gentiles, "but rather to the lost sheep of the house of Israel." The conversion of the heathen world was to be reserved for a period subsequent to the Lord's ascension, when the separating wall between Jew and Gentile was to be demolished, and in the demolition of which Peter, as we shall find, was

1 Dr Farrar, vol. i. p. 363.

destined to occupy a conspicuous place. The strong
hereditary prejudices these Galileans still entertained
against their Gentile neighbours were, as Neander remarks, "too strong to adapt themselves to their feelings, and to meet the controversies into which they
would be inevitably led along with them. The way in
which the two sons of Zebedee treated the Samaritans
at a later period is a proof of this." He whose standard-
bearers they had become warns them of their trials in
taking up the cross ; assuring them, at the same time,
that "losing their lives for His sake" they would afterwards "find them," and that even the cup of cold
water given to one of the "little ones" would not go
unrecompensed. "Behold," said He, in equipping
Peter and his fellow-apostles, "I send you forth as
sheep in the midst of wolves." A tradition of the second
century, quoted by Lightfoot, represents Peter as saying
in reply to his Master, "But how then if the wolves
should tear the lambs ?" To which his Lord rejoined,
"Let not the lambs fear the wolves when the lambs are
once dead ; and do you fear not those who can kill you,
and do nothing to you ; but fear Him who, after you are
dead, hath power over soul and body to cast into hell-
fire." It was a gracious arrangement on the part of
their Divine Master, and one that has been wisely followed in modern times in the case of several Christian
missions (specially so in India), to send them in their
evangelistic journeys, not singly, in dreary and unsym-
pathetic loneliness, nor yet in a body, but in pairs—
two and two. Andrew would most probably be the
associate of his more impulsive brother ; and it is pleasant to think that the boyish affection of the two, as
they played together in infancy on the pebbly beach of

Bethsaida, was strengthened in the most eventful period of their lives ; that having plied their nets together in early youth on the moonlit sea, they were now associated and united in their nobler calling as " Fishers of men."

To various instructions which their Master gave them in prosecuting their work, " He proceeds with Divine prescience to add warnings of dangers, difficulties, impeachments, imprisonments, and even death itself, to which they should be exposed in after days and in other mission-fields for His sake ; with counsel how to act, and promises to sustain and cheer, under such fiery trials, and in such fearful times. Christ having ' made an end of commanding them,' they went forth on their mission, and ' He departed thence to teach and to preach in their cities,' in the prosecution of His. Thus early did Christianity display itself as a religion not of benevolence merely, but of beneficence ; not of charity only, but of charity organised and in action." [1]

We shall not venture to follow " the footsteps of Peter " during this memorable period of the Saviour's ministry. To do so would only be to rehearse the most familiar incidents in the Gospel narratives. On the occasion of the miraculous feast south of Bethsaida Julias, we find, as an interesting reason given for this retirement from the busier western shores to the solitudes of Naphthali, that the twelve had just returned from their first missionary tour in the towns and villages of Galilee, the first-fruits and earnest of vaster enterprises throughout Judea and the world. Weak and exhausted with their incessant ministrations, their

[1] Anderson's Life of Christ, p. 324.

Lord provides for them this season of needful rest. "Come ye also," says He, "apart into a desert place, and *rest* a little." It was a befitting opportunity too for communicating in private to their Divine Master the result of their preaching. "The apostles," we read, "gathered themselves together unto Jesus, and told Him all things, both what they had done, and what they had *taught*." Another impelling reason may be added for this period of seclusion. The human heart of the great Master had been saddened and crushed as it had never been by any similar cause before, owing to the death, by foulest cruelty and intrigue, of "the friend of the Bridegroom," His noble, self-denying, heroic servant, John the Baptist. This greatest of the prophets had been beheaded, in an act of cold-blooded atrocity, in the castle of Machærus, on the shores of the Dead Sea, where he had for some time been languishing in captivity. No sooner had the axe of the executioner descended, and loving hands had interred the mutilated corpse, than the disciples of the murdered man hastened to communicate this sad intelligence to Jesus. As a partaker of all the most refined feelings and sympathies of our nature, the Divine Saviour gladly sought even a few hours' calm to let the tears of human affection flow over His 'loved and lost.'

We can even picture the scene in the plain of El-balîhah, four miles east of Capernaum, where the toil-worn disciples went to pause for this "little while," and get themselves recruited for fresh labours. We are not to understand by a "desert place" a region of dry, barren sand, such as we are in the habit of associating with the word. On the contrary, it was a spot fertile in itself, but it had not, like the land of Gennesaret, been brought under the cultivation of the husbandman. It remained in a state of nature—cattle browsed on its slopes, or under the shadow of its scattered groups of oak and terebinth. The first flush of spring was again robing both plain and mountain, the vines were showing their tender green, and the olive its brightest silver lining. The rush of the winter torrents was over ; but the brooks and rivulets, not yet dried with summer suns, still sang their way through thickets of nâbk and oleander to the Jordan and the lake. John specially notes the season, "The Passover, a feast of the Jews, was nigh." From every northern outlet, the pilgrims for the feast were streaming down the Jordan valley, and the multitudes from the western cities and plain of Gennesaret (resolved at all risks to track the footsteps of Jesus and His apostles) follow along the northern strand, keeping the sail of their craft in view. Again, as confirmatory of the time, Mark (ever graphic and pictorial, writing with Peter's memory as his guide, and thus always seizing, if I may so say, with a painter's eye, some striking natural feature in the scene he delineates) afterwards represents the multitudes, in his description of the miracle, as seated on the "*green grass.*" [1] Here the little vessel landed its crew. In that peaceful seclusion, the disciples—Peter doubtless the main spokesman—gave their Lord, amid the more sorrowful thoughts then crowding their memories, an

[1] I was unable to visit this interesting spot, but Dr Stanley, in his journey with the Prince of Wales, gives the following account of it :—"Here, through a level plain, almost a morass, entangled with thickets of oleander, which cluster round its tributary brooks, the Jordan passes into the lake under a group of five isolated palms. On the gentle hill which rises immediately at the back of the plain may be traced with sufficient accuracy the situation of the Northern Bethsaida and the scene of the incidents connected with it in the Gospel history. On the first slope of the rising ground

account of their first crusade against the powers of evil. And yet what a picture, too, of the untiring energy of that faithful band; and above all, of Him whom they delighted to serve ! If allowed to enjoy at all their needed season of repose, that season must have been brief indeed. Their boat had been retarded by head winds, and the eager multitude, " with the ordinary contingent of sufferers in various need of healing," had reached the strand before them, while the northern caravan of Passover pilgrims, as we have just noted, had swelled the usual throng. From one of these gentle slopes, or plateaux already indicated, Jesus sees the multitudes, The flocks browsing on the pastoral scenes around Him are carefully tended; but the great and good Shepherd is " moved with compassion " towards the human crowd below, because they were ' shepherdless.' He prepares, therefore, to lead them to green pastures and still waters, and to " give them meat to eat which the world knows not of." The spot on which the multitudes were congregated " was either one of the green table-lands visible from the hills on the western side, or, more probably, part of the rich plain at the mouth of the Jordan. In the parts of this plain not cultivated by the hand of man, would be found the ' much green grass' still fresh in the spring of the year, when this event occurred, before it had faded away in the summer sun ; the tall grass which, broken down by the feet of

are the vestiges of the village (Tell), supposed to mark the site of the old town. On the second stage of the hill immediately above, is a broad green platform where, on the 'much grass,' the multitudes may have been invited to rest. On the third stage, at the summit of the eminence, is a bare ridge, ' the desert place,' the mountain to which our Lord may have retired 'by Himself alone,' overlooking from end to end the whole lake."—*Stanley's Sermons. Prince of Wales*, pp. 195, 196.

the thousands there gathered together, would make, as
it were, 'couches' for them to recline upon. Overhanging the plain was 'the mountain' range of Golan,
on whose heights 'Jesus sat with His disciples' and saw
the multitude coming to them, and to which, when the
feast was over, He again retired." [1] "The apostles
arranged them in companies of fifty and a hundred,
and as they sat in these orderly groups upon the grass,
the gay red, and blue, and yellow colours of the clothing,
which the poorest Orientals wear, called up in the imagination of St Peter a multitude of flower-beds in
some well-cultivated garden. . . . They reclined *in
parterres*, is the picturesque expression of St. Mark." [2]
We need not particularly rehearse the well-known sequel
—how a little lad from one of the adjoining hamlets
had in his possession, probably for the purpose of sale
among these holiday crowds, five barley loaves and two
small fishes. The Divine Master of the feast took the
scanty material that was to suffice for the wants of a
gathering of "five thousand men, besides women and
children." Looking up to heaven for a blessing, He
brake and divided the five loaves and two fishes, giving
the same into the hands of the disciples for distribution.
And yet, after the hunger of the long-fasting multitude
was satisfied, twelve wicker baskets of fragments—more
than the original store—were gathered by the disciples'
hands.

---

[1] Sinai and Palestine, p. 377.
[2] Dr Farrar, vol. i. p. 400. "The πρασιαί," remarks Archbishop Trench,
"are the square garden plots in which herbs are grown. Our English 'in
ranks' does not reproduce the picture to the eye, giving rather the notion
of continuous lines. . . . Perhaps 'in groups' would be as near as we could
get to it in English."

"No fiery wing is seen to glide,
 No cakes ambrosial are supplied,
But one poor fisher's rude and scanty store
 Is all He asks (and more than needs)
 Who men and angels daily feeds,
And stills the wailing seabird on the hungry shore."

"Memorable, indeed, was the scene of the miraculous feeding of this vast multitude ; memorable for the display of the creative power of the Eternal Son that was then made before more than five thousand witnesses ; memorable too for the strange coincidence, that on the eve when the Paschal lambs were being offered up in the Temple courts of Jerusalem, the Eternal Lamb of God was feeding His people in the wilderness with the bread which His own Divine hands had multiplied." [1] The shadows of evening fell, as the multitude, devoutly impressed with the marvellous scene, wended their way homewards by the lake-side. Night doubtless must have overtaken many of them before they reached the plain of Gennesaret. But they were independent of the hour, for the full Passover moon lighted up their pathway. It lighted also the pathway of a solitary Figure ascending once more these familiar, silent hills for purposes of devotion ;—alone, yet not alone, for His Father was with Him.

"The Paschal moon above
 Seems like a saint to rove
Left shining in the world with Christ alone :
 Below, the lake's still face
 Sleeps sweetly in th' embrace
Of mountains terraced high with mossy stone.

[1] Ellicott, p. 196.

" Here we may sit and dream
Over the heavenly theme,
Till to our soul the former days return :
Till on the grassy bed,
Where thousands once He fed,
The world's incarnate Maker we discern."

The incident which followed is too closely bound up
with Peter's history to be dismissed without special
description. It brings out forcibly alike the lights and
the shadows of his composite character, and will form
the subject of the next chapter.

CHAPTER VI.

The Night of Tempest.

> " The feast is o'er, the guests are gone,
> And over all that upland loan
> The breeze of eve sweeps wildly as of old.
> Fain would we grasp the strong right hand
> Reached to Thine own by sea and land,—
> The hand that did Thy saint uphold,
> When love had made him overbold ;
> What time at twilight dawn he stood,
> Half-sinking in the boisterous flood."—*Keble.*

" He brought the apostle to the ship, as a bird brings its young
on its wings to the nest, when it has attempted to fly before its
time, and is about to fall on the ground."—*Chrysostom.*

" This tempest-wrought lake, this tiny, tossing boat, the Master
appearing, to make a great calm within and without, what a sublime parable in action ! It is the very history of the Church in all
ages."—*Pressensé.*

" Lo ! Peter is walking upon the waves. Two hands uphold
him, the hand of Christ's power, the hand of his own faith :
neither of them would do it alone. The hand of Christ's power
laid hold on him, the hand of his faith laid hold on the power of
Christ. While he believed, the sea was brass ; when once he began
to distrust, these waves were water."—*Bishop Hall.*

E may well believe that of the many who could not fail to be impressed by the wondrous miracle described in the close of last chapter, not the least so would be Peter. Perhaps his susceptible and not unfrequently indiscreet nature would be more likely to be perilously wrought upon by the unmistakable feelings and desires of the multitude, who had been spectators of so indubitable a proof of the divinity of the Prophet of Nazareth. Their impulse seemed simultaneous and irresistible to crown Him as their King, even though this would involve the employment of "force." They would put Him at once at the head of their pilgrim caravan; and, joined by other jubilant throngs on their way through Galilee, march in a Messianic triumph to the approaching feast in Jerusalem. The time, however, was premature. The gracious Wonder-worker, knowing all things that were to come to pass, firmly declines the proffered crown. Moreover, He takes immediate means to prevent His disciples becoming partisans in the hollow enthusiasm—abetting these excited Galileans in a design which would only precipitate a collision with the Roman power, and bring His ministry to a premature close. The means He adopts introduces us to one of the most vivid and interesting of Gospel stories, and one which in its sequel brings the son of Jonas conspicuously before us. He gives directions to His apostles to enter their vessel, and recross the lake to the Western Bethsaida. The point is of no importance; but some have supposed that this dispersing of the yet lingering multitude, as well as embarkation of the disciples, must have taken place earlier in the afternoon than we have imagined at the close of the last chapter. For the next day being the Sabbath—and as the Jewish Sabbath began at six o'clock on the preceding evening, it would not have been lawful to undertake the journey by land or the voyage by water, after the sun had set. Very many of the assembled crowd would doubtless be distant from their homes beyond the prescribed 'six furlongs' of the "Sabbath-day's journey." Not to have left, therefore, till the evening had set in, it has been alleged would have involved the alternative of remaining by these lonely reaches of the Jordan without food or shelter till the following sunset. It is probable that His disciples would be the last to linger on the spot.

Either, then, at evening, or anticipating by an hour or two the rapid Eastern twilight (between sunset and darkness), they embarked. Their Lord gives no indication as to how or where He may rejoin them. From the words " *He constrained* them to get into the ship," we may gather that it was with reluctance they consented to this separation. They may have even attempted a remonstrance; preferring the urgent request, either that He would still accompany them, or else permit them again to drop anchor and suspend their voyage over Sabbath. The sky may have already been wearing a threatening aspect; a blood-red sun may have been drooping over the western hills; the hollow moanings familiar to the fishermen's ears may have been premonitory of a storm. Lowering clouds may have been wreathing the brow of the Gadara heights and the headlands of Tiberias.[1] On a former occasion, when the

[1] The day I sailed on the Sea of Galilee, the waters were delightfully calm, or little more than a gentle ripple disturbed their surface. Other travellers, more familiar with its capricious ways, have a different story to record. "My experience," says Dr Thomson, "in this region, enables me to sympathise with the disciples in their long night's contest with the wind. I spent a night in that Wady Shuka-iyf, some three miles up it to the left of us. The sun had scarcely set, when the wind began to rush down toward the lake, and it continued all night long with constantly increasing violence, so that when we reached the shore next morning, the face of the lake was like a huge boiling caldron. The wind howled down every Wady from the north-east and east with such fury that no efforts of rowers could have brought a boat to shore at any point along that coast. In a wind like that, the disciples must have been driven quite across to Gennesaret, as we know they were. We subsequently pitched our tents at the shore, and remained for three days and nights exposed to this tremendous wind. No wonder the disciples toiled and rowed hard all that night. The whole lake, as we had it, was lashed into fury, the waves repeatedly rolled up to our tent door, tumbling on the ropes with such violence as to carry away the tent pins."

"The sea-birds," says another, "sailed with the roaring blast, which rushed on with foam and fury. This torrent of heavy, cold air was pouring over the mountain crests into the deep caldron of the lake below, a headlong flood of wind like a waterfall into the hollow; just as it is said in Luke (viii. 23), 'there came *down* a storm of wind upon the lake.' . . . The peculiar effects of squalls among mountains are known to all who have boated much on lakes, but on the sea of Galilee the wind has a singular force and suddenness, and this is no doubt because the sea is so

disciples encountered another similar storm, they felt that all was safe when their Master had said, " *Let* us *pass over.*" Their adorable Lord, the heavenly Pilot, was with them in the vessel. Now it was different. They had before them *night* and a tempest, and He, whose voice alone could hush its fury, was leaving them apparently to brave it alone. But His word and will were paramount. That great Redeemer whose power and tenderness were so recently manifested to the fainting multitudes, *commands* them to depart. It is enough; they ask no more. Even Peter, so often outspoken, offers no expostulation. Though the storm may have been already beating high, like brave soldiers at the bidding of their captain, they are in a moment launched on the deep, with seven long miles before them, encountering the crested waves and the gathering darkness.

A fair breeze would soon have run them to the western side ; but when midnight came, it found them little more than half-way on their voyage. Owing to a furious head wind, their sail was useless ; and though

deep in the world, that the sun rarifies the air in it enormously, and the wind speeding swift, above a long and level plateau, gathers much force, as it sweeps through flat deserts, until suddenly it meets this huge gap in the way, and it tumbles down here irresistible. We gained at last the windward, and here we could look with safe amazement at the scud of the gale careering across the lake, and twisting the foam in the air as if tied in knots of spray, which sparkled in the sun like ten thousand diamonds, while the sea-birds still flew helplessly downward."—*Rob Roy on the Jordan,* p. 421.

" To understand," says Dr Thomson, again to quote this interesting resident in Palestine, "the cause of these sudden and violent tempests, we must remember that the lake lies low, six hundred feet lower than the ocean ; that the vast and naked plateaus of Jaulan rise to a great height, spreading backward to the wilds of the Hauran and upward to snowy Hermon ; that the water courses have cut out profound ravines and wild gorges converging to the head of this lake, and that these act like gigantic funnels to draw down the winds from the mountains."

for nine hours Simon and his brother boatmen toiled manfully at the oars, three o'clock (the fourth watch of the night) found them still pitching in the midst of that roaring sea with their labouring craft; sheets of white spray dashing over the open deck, a few fitful lights (their only compass) glimmering distant as ever on the longed-for shore. Their seamanship is baffled. The lake was forty-five furlongs in breadth, and they had only accomplished "five-and-twenty or thirty furlongs." The former cry of faithless unbelief may now have been often on their lips, and on none more than on Peter's, as they thought of last evening's mysterious parting, "Master, Master, carest *Thou* not that *we* perish?" 'If He had been with us asleep,' we may picture the impulsive spokesman saying to his fellows, 'If He had been with us asleep, as He was before, on an occasion of similar peril, in the hinder part of our ship, then we could have rushed to His side, invoked His aid, and in a moment the storm would have been changed into a calm. Whither He is now gone, we cannot tell. Our cries are inaudible; our prayers are vain; they are drowned in the rage of that tempest. 'Surely our way is hid from the Lord, and our judgment is passed over from our God!'

But where in reality was their beloved Saviour in the hour they most needed His presence, and most ardently longed for it? He *seemed* to have hid His face from them, but it was in appearance only. "He puts them into danger, as some loving mother-bird thrusts her fledglings from the nest, that they may find their own wings and learn to use them; and by the issue He will awaken in them a confidence in His ever-ready

G

help." [1]   On the heights of one of these lonely mountains that girdled the north-east corner of the lake, in
the silence of midnight, He is alone with His God.   As
He kneels on the dewy grass, that mountain summit is
converted again into an altar of prayer.   His eye is at
one moment on the distant sea, at another uplifted to
heaven ; the breathings of His soul are ascending in
behalf of His disciples ; He is watching every billow
that breaks on their tempest-tossed bark.   The darkness cannot hide them from Him ; their troubled
thoughts " He knoweth afar off."   Though not praying
with them, He is praying *for* them, that "their faith
fail not."

Only one-half, if so much, of their voyage had been
accomplished, when (may we suppose, through a rift in
the driving clouds) the starlight discloses a mysterious,
radiant Object peering out in the gloom, moving on the
crest of the waves.   Jesus approaches, walking silently
but majestically across the billows.   The Lord of the
sea and the storm "made darkness His secret place,
His pavilion round about Him are dark waters and
thick clouds of the sky ; " and as the expression in the
original seems to denote, leading the way for them to
their desired landing place. [2]   He is so near His disciples,
that His *form* might at once have been recognised.   The
joyous utterance might well have passed from tongue to
tongue—" The Master has come ! " the watchword led,
as was wont, by Peter, " It is the Lord ! "

But strange : His appearance seems to trouble and
agitate them more than that vexed and agitated sea.
With those superstitious feelings so proverbially common
among sailors and fishermen, they think they descry in

---

[1] Trench.   [2] See Ellicott, *in loc.*

the hazy darkness, and amid the moaning night winds, no "good angel" of the waters, only some unwelcome messenger from the spirit-world. They imagine, possibly, in their dread, either that one of the demons of darkness, roaming so lately the gorges of Gadara, is now evoked from the depths of the lake, where it had plunged with the mountain-herd; or else that the hour of their own death and destruction had arrived, and a premonitory herald from the regions of Hades—some terrible shape or phantom, such as the Jewish fancy was wont to picture—has come from the world of the dead to give them warning of their approaching end. The Phantom-shape, moreover, appeared as if it were "passing by them." Faith is for a moment eclipsed. The oars hitherto manfully plied are dropped. "They were troubled, saying, It is a spirit; and they cried out for fear."

How great the contrast; the heaving waters, the perturbed disciples, and the calm, majestic tranquillity of the great Lord! Loud above the riot of the storm sound the soothing familiar tones, "Be of good cheer, it is I; be not afraid." Their gracious Master's *form* they had mistaken in the gloom, but the *voice* was well known to them. Peter now becomes the central figure in the night picture. Indeed, had no name been mentioned in this passage, we should at once have been led to fix on Simon as the apostle who went in impetuous haste down from the vessel's side, braved the stormy sea, walked upon it, sank in terror, and rose again in faith. Bold, hasty, forward, ardent, with a soul full of deep emotion, he would, in the fever of the moment, do a brave and hazardous thing from which in a calmer mood he would be deterred. Had he been a soldier by profession, he would have been suited for the brilliant sally, the sudden foray, the impetuous assault (some daring feat of arms) ; not for the slow, wasting, decimating siege and trench work.   His enthusiasm and ardour, honest and sincere at the time, were apt to be damped in the moment of trial and danger.   For emergencies to which he fancied himself equal, the event proved he was not.   A child of Ephraim boldly " carrying his bow," he turned faint in the day of battle ! Judging from his peculiar temperament, perhaps when the mysterious Phantom-form was first seen on the waters, he may have been the most craven-hearted of all.   While the calm John, or Thomas, may have looked their danger sternly in the face, he may have seen in the shadowy Figure nothing but the messenger of death, and fled, cowering in terror, to the hold of the vessel.   But no sooner does he listen to the comforting " It is I," than shame and sorrow overwhelm him that he had been so " slow of heart," and in the very rebound from faithlessness to newly-awakened joy, he resolves by an heroic act to atone for these moments of pusillanimity. " Lord," says he, " if it be Thou, bid me come unto Thee on the water."

Even yet, however, his voice trembles as he speaks. Neither his faith nor his motives will bear rigid scrutiny. The very word with which he begins his presumptuous request implies a secret *doubt*—" *If* it be Thou." His own thought, doubtless, was to make an avowal of his *faith*, but what he did display was *not* faith, but a base, degenerate semblance and figure of the true.   Rightly named, it was forwardness, fool-hardihood, the haughty spirit which is inevitably succeeded by a fall.   His confidence in his Divine Master would have been tempered with a wiser discretion, and a kindlier regard for the feelings of his fellow-apostles, had he simply joined with them in inviting Jesus into their ship. But there was an implied assumption of superiority in the request, "Bid *me*." Farther, he utters on his own authority, and more in the tone of a mandate than a proposal "Bid me come." There is a struggle for pre-eminence, a craving to win the highest encomium from his Master, and to make himself out the boldest and bravest of the apostle-crew. It is the saying and the failure of a future occasion put in another form and other words— "Though all be offended, yet shall not I."[1] Doubtless, had an injunction to leave the vessel emanated from the lips of Christ, it would have been alike his duty and his joy to obey ; there would then have been no sinking, no faltering. If the Lord had " given the word," He would have made Peter's " feet like hinds' feet," and set him upon these " high places." But forgetful of his frailty, he himself takes the initiative ; he makes his own will and wish antecedent to the will of his Lord, and he must pay the penalty of his daring.

How kindly and considerately does Jesus deal with the bold and rash, yet ardent and devoted man ! " Lord, bid me come." He forbids him not. Had He done so, there would have been lost to Peter the most valuable lesson his Master ever taught him. Christ uses the present opportunity to discipline him by his failure to become, as he afterwards did, a spiritual giant and hero. Peter makes his request. A *single word is all he gets in reply.* The same Voice which, a few moments before, gently quieted by a threefold assurance the fears of all the affrighted boatmen, says, in

[1] Arch. Trench, *in loc.*

answer to the outspoken one—"Come!" He does not refuse, but neither does He give any warrant or promise of upholding power. Peter had said, "Bid me;" Christ does not say, "I bid." Peter had said, "on the water;" Jesus speaks of no footway there. Peter had said, "unto Thee;" Jesus gives no such invitation.[1] He utters only the one indefinite word, "Come!" "Come," He seems to say, "bold one, make trial of thy strength; come if thou canst; but it is on thine own responsibility; I give no pledge or warrant of success to thy carnal presumption."

He *does* come! He descends the side of the lurching vessel. The next moment his feet are on the unstable waves. His faith is for the moment strong, and fixing his countenance on his great Redeemer, though drenched and dripping with the spray, he travels in safety along that strangest of pathways :—"Christ thus," says Chrysostom, "adding to a great miracle one even greater." But a wandering eye is the first symptom of a mournful reverse. He turns his face from his Master; he transfers his glance to the rolling waves, with their black chasms at his feet, and the storm sighing overhead. "When he saw the wind boisterous, he was afraid." It was no new tempest that had sprung up; the sea was not opening its mouth wider than before; the sky was no gloomier; the hurricane no louder; the waves were beating as high when he first sallied forth. But with his eye and his heart on the Lord of the storm, he had no room *then* for a thought of danger. Now it was different : gazing on the tempestuous elements, he trembled at his own courage. He took his eye off the Secret of his support, and down he sank like lead in that raging sea.

[1] See Stier and Trench, *in loc.*

But pass we now to a more favourable turn in Peter's case. He had presumed, faltered, was fast sinking. Is all to end in ignominious failure? or by some strong effort will he yet retrieve his honour, and convert that midnight sea into a moral battlefield where a great fall is turned into a great victory? Yes; as *unbelief* sank, so *faith* is to raise him again. How is he raised? He honours Christ throughout in this memorable crisis. He might have dreamt at that moment of other ways of extricating himself from his peril. Was there no rope in the hold of the boat? Could he not have asked one of the apostle-rowers to stretch him one of those oars with which, a few minutes before, they had been toiling in vain to make head against the storm? Or where was his natural or acquired skill in swimming, of which we read afterwards, when, near the beach of the same lake on a later occasion, he plunged headlong into the water and swam manfully ashore.[1] But he resorts to none of these expedients. Having dishonoured Jesus by distrusting Him, he will honour Him once more by fresh confidence in His power and love. He cries, " Lord, save me, else I perish!" No artificial props can raise up the battered, down-trodden flower so well as the genial sunshine. So this drooping flower turns his leaves to the Great Sun of Righteousness. The apostle is sinking, but even "as he sinks, he sinks 'looking unto Jesus!'"

And as the servant honoured his Master; as the disciple honoured his Lord; so does the Lord and Master honour and deal tenderly with him in return.

He might righteously have left him for a while in his anguish and trepidation to feel the consequences of his rashness. With the horrors of death taking hold on

[1] John xxi. 7.

him, He might have addressed him in words of cutting rebuke and upbraiding. But He will first restore his confidence. "Immediately Jesus stretched forth His hand and caught him." The Lord's hand was not shortened that it could not save. Peter's experience was that of the Psalmist—"When my foot slipped, Thy mercy, O Lord, held me up!"

And now comes the gentle rebuke. It would not have been well for Peter—it would not have been well for the Church of the future, which was to read and ponder this scene—had the salutary, needed reproof been allowed to pass. Gentle, however, it was! He does not address him as the presumptuous *unbeliever;* neither does He reprimand him for making the attempt to come. This might have had the effect of damping his energies for bolder deeds yet in reserve for him. Thus is he addressed by Him who "breaketh not the bruised reed, nor quencheth the smoking flax"—"O thou of little faith, wherefore didst thou doubt?" That sensitive heart required no harsh or severe word to enforce the appeal. A look—a glance, in impressive silence, yet of deep significancy—we shall find afterwards covered his face with bitter tears. So now, that one brief question would bring before him the memory of many other acts of love and power, all of which would aggravate the unkindness of distrusting that gracious Saviour. It was equivalent to saying, "Peter, after what I *have* done for thee in the past, why hast thou now dishonoured Me? Why refuse reliance now on My all-powerful arm? I still acknowledge thou hast faith, but in this critical emergency it has shown itself to be small. Wherefore hast thou wounded Me so by this unworthy doubting?"

The accused is silent. He attempts no reply. Perhaps his tears forbid it. Doubtless he returned to the vessel a humbled man. It was a night which to his dying hour would be much remembered. Yet, could it fail to rivet his affections more strongly than ever around that Saviour? If we put a "song of the night" into his lips, may it not be appropriately that of the great prophet—"Behold, God is my salvation. I will trust and not be afraid, for the Lord Jehovah is my strength and my song. He also is become my salvation."

Then was Peter received into the vessel along with his Divine Lord. The gusty squall is over. The disciples no longer cower in terror. No miracle of their Master seems to have exercised a greater power over them than this. The contrast has been noted between the effect produced on their minds by the miraculous multiplication of the loaves and fishes, and the stilling of the tempest. Even though they were the spectators and ministers of the former, Peter himself, in his relation of the scene by Mark, notices and acknowledges their dull perception of the Lord's power in the feeding of the five thousand (Mark vi. 52). But "here was something that appealed to those hardy boatmen as nought else could have appealed, and made them, both with their lips and by their outward and unforbidden posture of worship, avow for the first time collectively that their Master was, what one of them had long since separately declared himself to be, not only 'the King of Israel,' but 'the Son of God.'"[1] The waves of the lake resume their wonted quiet play. The sun is breaking with his first faint ray over the Gadara hills, and probably at Ain et-Tin they reach the shore. Often as in future they called to remembrance the Voice which chained the tempest on Tiberias and laid to sleep its waters, would

[1] Ellicott, p. 210.

they employ the words of the Psalmist in a nobler than their primary meaning—" O Lord God of hosts, who is a strong Lord like unto Thee ? Thou rulest the raging of the sea ; when the waves thereof arise, Thou stillest them."[1]

Who knows but this scene and incident may have been specially memorable—specially comforting—to them on its first anniversary ; that next Passover season when they were to be tossed and driven by a more awful tempest—the Master apparently gone, and the frail bark He had " constrained " them to enter, the sport of the wild waves ;—that Passover moon shining down on the agonies of Gethsemane ; and Peter, belying his boasted bravery, sinking in deeper waters of faithlessness and despair ? In that darkest of all nights, moreover, might not the sequel to this parable of the lake possibly occur to some of them—the Master returning in the hour of hopeless despondency ? And when He did return, would they not recognise His " Peace be unto you," as but a repetition, in another phrase, of the " It is I, be not afraid ? " Would not the special message which we shall find was sent on that great Easter day to our Apostle, be the echo of the present rebuke on the moonlit sea—" O thou of little faith, wherefore didst thou doubt ? "

[1] The greater portion of the preceding is also abridged from " Memories of Gennesaret." It may not be out of place here to note that " Christ walking on the sea " formed, from the pictorial elements in it, a favourite subject with the painters of the Middle Ages. " The most ancient and most celebrated representation is Giotto's Mosaic (A.D. 1298), now placed in the portico of St Peter's, over the arch opposite to the principal door. The sentiment in the composition of this subject is generally ' Lord, help me, or I perish.' St Peter is sinking, and Christ is stretching out His hand to save him. It is considered a type of the Church in danger, assailed by enemies, and saved by the miraculous interposition of the Redeemer ; and in this sense must the frequent representations in churches be understood." —*Mrs Jamieson's Sacred and Legendary Art*, p. 196.

CHAPTER VII.

The First Confession, and what led to it.

CRISIS IN THE SAVIOUR'S MINISTRY. SERVICE AND DISCOURSE IN THE SYNAGOGUE OF CAPERNAUM. THE BREAD OF HEAVEN. SYMPTOMS OF DISSATISFACTION. DEFECTION AMONG HIS OWN DISCIPLES. HIS APPEAL TO THE APOSTLES, AND PETER'S RESPONSE.

> " The waning winds have died away,
> And clouds, beneath the glancing ray
> Melt off, and leave the land and sea
> Sleeping in bright tranquillity."

"O Almighty God, who hast built Thy Church upon the foundation of the apostles and prophets, Jesus Christ Himself being the head corner-stone : grant us so to be joined together in unity of spirit by their doctrine, that we may be made an holy temple, acceptable unto Thee through Jesus Christ our Lord. Amen."

E shall now proceed to describe the morrow's sequel to this most dramatic incident in Peter's life—a sequel in which his name is specially associated with the first of two memorable confessions.

In order to understand the value of that earlier confession, brief as it was in words, and falling far short of subsequent fuller and nobler avowals, it may be pardonable to advert a little more particularly than would otherwise have been needful, to the crisis which had now been reached in the ministry of his Great Master.

We may picture in thought, which is often the case with that fitful, capricious lake, with which we are now so familiar, that the night of storm had been followed by a morn of sunshine. These waves, so easily roused

by the great winds which revel in the wadŷs all around,
are as easily rocked to rest; so that, in a brief hour,
the ridges of wild foam are lying placid and calm as a
mirror, with the snowy crest of Hermon reflected
serenely in their depths.   It is then, shall we suppose,
in the quiet of the following morning, that the town of
Capernaum is in a state of unusual bustle.   Boats,
large and small, had the previous afternoon come in
from different quarters—several of these driven for
refuge by the last night's tempest from Bethsaida-
Julias, Gergasa, Magdala, Tiberias, and other border
cities.   The occupants of these varied vessels, leaving their craft moored on the beach, are seen hastening in one direction—across through the wharves and
along the narrow streets towards the White Synagogue,
which, with its Greek columns and their capitals of
acanthus-leaf, crowns a gentle swell about a quarter of
a mile from the shore.   A dense, excited crowd are
already there, discussing in animated tones, under the
marble portico, the strange events of yesterday.   Among
them are numbers from Northern Galilee, who have
for days been streaming down to the approaching
feast in Jerusalem, and have pitched their tents outside
the walls of the lake-town.   Some, from the cities we
have just mentioned, had doubtless been present on the
previous afternoon at Bethsaida-Julias.   They had been
among the privileged multitude who had sat on the
green turf and ate the loaves and fishes—personal eye-
witnesses of the miracle.   Others had only heard of
these things; tidings had reached them about this
second Moses, who, on the shores of their own inland
sea, had given a repetition of the wilderness banquet
of quails and manna.   Attracted not only by the

report of the astounding exhibition of supernatural power, but also by the poor, carnal motive of having their wants supplied without toil or labour, they had hastened to the well-known home of the Wonder-worker, expecting to see Him personally, and themselves to share in some similar material benefit. Perhaps a still farther purpose may have animated not a few of the motley crowd, viz., to carry into execution the design, which yesterday had failed, of crowning Him as King, and following Him with acclamations to regal Jerusalem.

There is every likelihood, too, that their cravings will so far be satisfied ; for Jesus, the Object of all this transient burst of enthusiasm and curiosity, has already, as His wont was, taken His accustomed seat in the upper end of the synagogue, nigh to the ark ; and ere the ritual is concluded, some present will avail themselves of the usual privilege of putting to Him a series of questions relative to His claims and pretensions as a messenger from heaven.

The ordinary service begins. The Shĕlîach, with the attendant Batlanim, their heads muffled in the white keffiêh, have taken their appropriated places on the upper platform, close to where Jesus of Nazareth is seated along with His apostles ; the women have screened themselves behind the lattice. The responsive Amen follows the liturgy of petition, confession, and blessing, and more especially during the reading of those beautiful psalms which have been used in common for three thousand years, alike in Jewish synagogue and Christian temple. The *Chazzân*, the same officer we have alluded to in connection with Peter's early education, proceeds to the ark, and opening the *Côphereth*, or lid

of the holy chest, takes out the scroll containing
"Moses and the Prophets." This, unrolled, is handed
to the presiding Shĕlîach, who in plaintive monotone
reads the portion for the day. The scroll, re-adjusted,
is deposited in its sacred receptacle, and on the *Chazzân*
returning to his seat, the *Derash*—or, in other words,
the exposition or sermon—completes the service.

And now that the formal ritual has ended, all eyes
are directed to the Great Teacher of Nazareth, and one
voice (the spokesman and interpreter of the rest) breaks
silence thus :—

"Rabbi ! how camest Thou hither ?"

In His reply, He says nothing about the miraculous
walk on the waters, the pathway of tempest and wave
by which He had reached Capernaum. He proceeds at
once to dissipate their base, carnal expectations and
delusions ; rebukes and reproaches them for that mean,
unworthy motive of self-interest which had induced them
to follow His footsteps to the present place of assemblage, hankering after miraculous provision only to
satisfy the wants of their lower natures. He declares
Himself, not in a carnal, but in a lofty, spiritual sense,
to be the true "Bread of God," and delivers an earnest
exhortation couched in words of withering reproof :
"Labour not for the meat which perisheth, but for
that meat which endureth unto everlasting life, which
the Son of man shall give unto you : for Him hath God
the Father sealed."

Then come the first symptoms of dissatisfaction which
were to end in bold and defiant unbelief. *Shĕlîach* and
Batlanim and *Chazzân*, and some of the leading Jews of
the town, backed by malignant emissaries from Jerusalem who were secretly conspiring His ruin, exchange

with one another significant glances. These glances shape themselves in undisguised words, "What! this Son of a Galilean carpenter, whose mother and brothers we know well, to arrogate to Himself the title 'Bread of heaven,' and 'Giver of Everlasting Life!' averring, too, that he that eateth this bread (meaning Himself) would live for ever—that no one had seen the Father but Him—and that the highest 'work of God' was to believe on Him!" The resentment is intensified with every new question and answer. This apparently reached its climax when He asserted His power and prerogative to "raise up at the last day."

Nor was it the haughty Pharisee and sceptic Sadducee alone that had the curl on their lip and the flash of indignation in their eye.

Jesus too well knew what the result of this plain speaking would be on many who were hitherto favourably disposed to His claims,—who had loved His lofty morality and tender ways, as well as wondered at His mighty deeds. They, too, began to suspect and distrust Him, and to look coldly on His claims. However varied, indeed, the shades of opinion might be—whether passively friendly or inveterately hostile—all that crowded auditory would be at one in pronouncing His present mystical avowals unsatisfactory, and very unlike those expected from their ideal "Anointed One." Sacred books, which they had put on a par with the Old Testament Scriptures, had superadded brilliant though unauthorised visions of Messiah's person and reign to the pictures of the true Hebrew seers. The land flowing with milk and honey was to be a land full of wine and royal banquetings — golden platters with

H

birds of Paradise—jars of luscious manna, in comparison with which the manna and quails of the desert were common food. What, to them, were all these high-flown spiritualistic doctrines which He had just uttered? It was neither heavenly bread nor even everlasting life they wanted. Their immediate demand was the advent of the Messiah-Redeemer, to break the cursed Roman and Edomite yoke from their necks, and give them back their inviolate right to vineyard and olive-yard, untaxed by Cæsar, and rid of his odious tribute. Many of those present and absent could understand the boon of a free, unbought banquet on the green grass at Bethsaida, and the shout of a king to follow, leading to nobler festivals in His own hill of Zion, and within His temple of Moriah; but they could not comprehend or tolerate this mystic partaking of His own flesh and blood, without which life was declared to be an impossibility. They wished Him to sit on a throne, judging the twelve tribes of Israel. He had mocked them with some transcendental visions, worthy only of the Essenes of Engedi, or the fanatic dreamers of Egypt or Chaldea. On other occasions, too, so far had He forgot the national *prestige*, as to speak of the Pagan nations east and west enjoying with the patriarchs the Sabbatic rest of heaven. They could not brook apostate latitudinarianism like this! Too well did He Himself know and realise that He had reached a great crisis-hour in His life and ministry. To use a modern expression, His popularity was on the wane. "From that hour many (many He had trusted and confided in) went back, and walked no more with Him" (John vi. 66). "The desertion," in the words of Dr Kitto, "was so general, that He, who that day might

have mounted a throne amid the acclamations of assembled thousands, was, before its close, left almost, if
not quite, alone with His chosen few of the apostles."

It was in this hour of sadness and distress, when,
after the toils and labours of the preceding day, and
the weariness of a sleepless night, His bodily exhaustion—the infirmities of innocent humanity—weighed
down His sensitive spirit; when, too, as we have seen,
in the bitterness of His soul, He was mourning the loss
of His best and noblest human friend,—it was amid
these hard words, and scornful looks, and diminished
numbers, and the memory of buried love, He turns
with a deep sigh and yearning for sympathy, to the
fishermen friends at His side—" *Will ye also turn
recreant?* Will ye also fail, and forsake, and 'go
away?'"[1]

Peter, who, from his elevated seat in the synagogue,
had watched the surging tide of human faces, has his
answer ready. Yes; he whose ideas and apprehensions
were often material enough—clinging with fond avidity
to dreams of temporal glory—showed, at all events, the
strength and ardour of his personal devotion to the
great Being who had recently spread the feast and
stilled the storm, and by these two things had read to
himself and his fellow-apostles a lesson in diviner
verities. With all the intensity of his loving nature
burning to give vent to his own strong convictions, he
repels the unworthy creed and imputation of other
fickle disciples, and exclaims, " *Lord! to whom shall we*

---

[1] John vi. 67. In the original, the "ye" is emphatic, while the form of
the question implies that a negative was sought: "Ye do not, do you?"—
See Dr Green, p. 21 ; also, Dean Stanley's "Sermons on the Apostolic Age,"
in loc.

*go ? Thou hast the words of eternal life.   We believe
and are sure that Thou art the Holy One of God."* [1]

[1] Nearly all exegetical scholars are now at one in rejecting the commonly-received words of our Authorised Version—"Thou art the Christ, *the Son of the living God."* This latter confession we shall speak of in next chapter; but in the present case, it would seem to have gone no farther than the avowal and recognition of his Master as "The Holy One of God."—*See* Tischendorf, Meyer, Alford, and others.

CHAPTER VIII.

The Second Confession and the Primacy.

CÆSAREA PHILIPPI.   ITS SITE AND SURROUNDINGS.   PETER'S
AVOWAL OF HIS LORD'S DIVINITY.   THE ROCK ON WHICH THE
CHURCH IS BUILT.   PETER'S ALLEGED PRIMACY.   "THE
POWER OF THE KEYS."

> "On Christ, the solid Rock, I stand,
> All other grounds are sinking sand."

"He did not say, Upon Peter; for He did not found the Church upon a man, but upon faith. What, therefore, means, 'On this rock'? upon the confession contained in his words."
>   —*Chrysostom.*

"Upon this rock which thou hast professed, I will build My Church, because the rock was Christ; upon which foundation even Peter himself was built."   —*Augustine.*

"The twelve apostles are the twelve patriarchs of the spiritual Israel, and the relation of St Peter to the other apostles appears to be similar to that of Reuben to his brethren: a relation of primacy, not of supremacy. He was 'primus inter pares: non summus supra inferiores.'"   —*Bishop Wordsworth.*

"Utterly groundless is the notion that Peter had, or pretended to, any claim to dictate to the other apostles, to decide finally on all questions of faith or practice, and to bear rule over the universal Church. . . . We find him when censured, either vindicating himself where he was right, or where he was *not* right, modestly submitting to reproof and correcting his fault.—*Arch. Whately.*

ITHIN a few years, the writer was
privileged to visit two very dissimilar
places, both having a close and interesting connection with the history of
Peter, or rather with a specially memorable event in his
life.

The one was a spot rendered alike beautiful by
Nature and by Gospel association, in the extreme
northern limits of the Holy Land. The other was
standing under the vast dome of St Peter's in Rome,
and reading the well-known Latin inscription which, on
a blue setting, surrounds the base of that wonderful
canopy :—" Tu es Petrus, et Super hanc Petram
Ædificabo Ecclesiam Meam; et tibi dabo Claves
Regni Cœlorum."

As my readers are aware, that inscription, in what
certainly architecturally is the cathedral church of

Christendom, was first spoken at the former of these two places—the ancient Cæsarea Philippi, romantically situated at the roots of Mount Hermon.   It was called by its Roman name, after Philip the Tetrarch of Trachonitis, in conjunction with that of his imperial master, Cæsar Augustus.   But previous to this, the limestone rock on which the city was built was crowned by the Greeks with a temple to the God Pan, in which were recesses filled with sculptured effigies of his fabled wood-nymphs.   Hence it was designated Paneas ; which again, in modern times, has been easily changed by the substitution of a letter, into *Banias*.   It was doubtless much resorted to as a " summer city " by the Roman population on the town and shores of Tiberias. When the intense tropical heat, specially to strangers, rendered residence in lower Galilee well-nigh intoler- able, the wealthier classes of Greeks, Jews, and Italians would retreat thither to enjoy the breezes as well as the picturesque scenery of the Lebanon.   Our Lord and His disciples, rejected by the Galileans, and experi- encing increasing animosity at the hands of those from whom He merited only gratitude and love, journeyed up by the eastern banks of the Jordan, past the waters of Merom, to that comparatively quiet retreat.   Being in relation to Palestine a border city, it was farther removed at all events from the hatred and intrigues of the Jewish sects.   Of no place in that hallowed land have I more charming recollections.   Though doubtless altered in many minor features, the magnificent sur- roundings continue the same and unchangeable.   Art must at the apostolic age have added to the material beauty.   From the middle or near the base of the high cliff of which I have spoken, issuing forth from a

" cavern sanctuary " or grotto, is the most conspicuous and impressive of the sources of the Jordan. The lime-stone is now festooned with lichen and fern, half conceal-ing from view Greek inscriptions. A temple of pure white marble, erected by Herod in honour of Augustus, had superseded the ancient pagan one, although only fragments of this now remain. We can picture palaces and gardens occupying the undulating ground, where amid olive groves and the rush of the river the modern traveller pitches his tent. While towering as a glorious back-ground, Hermon, " that goodly mountain, and Lebanon," with his coronal of snow and nearer bold ridges, must have given then, as now, character to the whole scene. It recalled the Val-D'Aosta and Cor-mayeur with the gigantic spurs of Mont Blanc. No hills that surround the lake of Gennesaret can lay claim to picturesqueness in outline : but here you are at the base of an Alp with all its bold and ragged appurten-ances, while " its exuberance of water, its olive groves, and its view over the distant plain," have given to it the still more appropriate designation of " a Syrian Tivoli." [1]

I may venture to add one out of many graphic descriptions of the same scene, given by a modern traveller, whose accuracy all who have been eyewit-nesses will endorse : " The path led through an ancient square tower of bevelled stones, over a picturesque bridge, under which a cataract of foaming water, the Za'areh, dashed down to the Jordan ; the rocks over which it tumbled, and the old stones of the bridge,

[1] Sinai and Palestine, *in loc.* See woodcut at the head of the chapter, engraved by permission from one of the photographs of the Palestine Exploration.

were thickly hung with long streamers of vines and
blackberries, bending down to catch the light spray from
the water, and with lovely fronds of harts-tongue and
giant maiden-hair fern of deliciously fresh green ; then
the stream tumbled on under an arched avenue of large
plane and willow trees, which met and interlaced at the
top. . . It is no wonder that travellers coming up from
the arid, stony ugliness of Judea should think Banias a
perfect paradise of loveliness, and as Josephus calls it,
'a place of great pleasure, famous and delightful;' its
freshness and luxuriant verdure are remarkable even to
eyes lately come from the thick foliage and flowers of
Damascus. . . . We scrambled down the hill, and
followed the stream into its delicious and lofty thickets
of ash, bay, laurustinus, myrtle, vine, clematis, night-
shade, ever so many different roses, and a thousand
other plants, shading the little cascades of water, and
hiding many remains of ancient buildings." [1]

It was here, then—with all that wealth of Nature in
view, although we cannot fix on any particular spot,
(shall we picture it in one of the quiet wadŷs at the
base of Hermon ?)—that a most momentous interview
took place between Christ and His disciples. Perhaps it would be more correct to say that Jesus had a
twofold object during that week of memorable seclusion
in the northern borders of Palestine. It was "from

[1] Syrian Shrines, Vol. II., 29, 30.

Dr Robinson of America, who is not much given to enthusiastic description, has the following remarks on Banias :—"The situation is unique,
combining in an unusual degree the elements of grandeur and beauty. It
nestles in its recess at the southern base of the mighty Hermon, which
towers in majesty to an elevation of 7000 or 8000 feet above. The abundant
waters of the glorious fountain spread over the terrace luxuriant fertility
and the graceful interchange of copse, lawn, and waving fields " (Vol. III.
404).

that time" He began to speak of His sufferings. Hitherto He had unfolded the ethical laws of His kingdom. Alike by teaching and example He had laid the broad basis of His Church. But from the outer courts of the temple He was now to take His disciples into the inner shrine, and instruct them on the great work He came to accomplish,—in comparison with which all else was subordinate, viz., *offering up His life as a ransom for the world.* He had another purpose in view. As the chosen band were quietly surrounding their Master, now that His ministry was approaching a close, He was desirous of testing, not their personal attachment, for of that He was assured, but of ascertaining their matured views about His Messiahship and Divinity. He prepares the way for this, by putting first the general question as to the public and prevailing impression regarding His claims : " Whom do men say that I, the Son of man, am ? " Their rejoinder was, that few imagined Him to be the Messiah. Some thought that John the Baptist had risen again in His person from the grave ; others, that the great Elijah, according to the prophetic announcement of Malachi, had descended from heaven invested with the old miraculous power which had so conspicuously distinguished the Prophet of Cherith ; others, perhaps from the plaintive yet tender tones which had greeted their ears, that Jeremiah, the mourning prophet of the captivity, whose advent the Jews had long expected, had come back to take up his parable in the second temple, and, as was supposed, to restore the ark and altar of incense, which he was said to have concealed in a cavern at the destruction of the temple by Nebuchadnezzar.[1] Or failing him, that

[1] Macc. xv. 13, 14.

in accordance with the doctrine of Pythagoras (then current alike in the Jewish and Pagan world, of the transmigration of souls) that the spirit of one of the old Hebrew prophets—one of the illustrious roll of Hebrew worthies—had retenanted a mortal body.

Perhaps in one sense these were to Jesus saddening announcements. But He was too well aware, and specially (as we have noted in the preceding chapter) from indications of public sentiment since the miracle of the loaves, that His influence was greatly on the decline. There was a marked defection among His followers. Indeed we have seen that it was on that occasion, that sorrowful crisis in His history, when He had to learn the lesson of human instability,—when to His fore-seeing gaze the dark clouds of the not distant future were gathering ominously,—" when the human agents of the kingdom of darkness were arraying themselves against the Lord of the kingdom of light " (Ellicott), that He turned with the tear in His eye from the fickle throng to His own apostles, and made the appeal which the true-hearted Peter so nobly answered. When, therefore, after the lapse of some days, Jesus put a still more urgent question to His disciples, He could have expected no more favourable reply as to the estimate of the undiscerning and self-seeking multitudes. " He came unto His own, and His own received Him not." But when they had answered the preliminary inquiry, He ventured on that which lay next His heart, as to their own individual and conjoint estimate of Him. If, misinterpreting the ancient prophecies of His coming, the rest of His countrymen had rejected His claims and refused to credit Him with any loftier official dignity than that of an inspired teacher or prophet, He turns with deep anxiety to the favoured few who had for nearly three years been closely associated with Him—who had seen His mighty works and heard His gracious and mighty words. If He were misunderstood by His own apostles at this time, and specially when He was about to unfold the still more humiliating story of His approaching decease, His cause, humanly speaking, was lost. While, on the other hand, if His constant associates had learnt to recognise His true dignity as the Divine Son of God, the estimate of the rest of His kinsmen according to the flesh would sit lightly on Him. Armed by the sympathy and allegiance of His personal followers, He would " set His face steadfastly to go up to Jerusalem."

We may imagine, therefore, with what deep interest (if with reverence we may say so) the great Redeemer waited for an answer to the question—" But whom do YE say that I, the Son of man, am ? " " Am I regarded by you as human alone, or human and Divine ? am I a mere prophet, or am I the Immanuel predicted by the greatest of your prophets ? "

Peter, as usual, was ready with the reply. It seems to have been a momentary one—without hesitation—without deeming it necessary to consult in the first instance with his brother-apostles. But from previous confidential intercourse apart from their Master, he knew he was warranted to give it as the deliberate and concurrent testimony of their deepened experience—" THOU ART THE CHRIST, THE SON OF THE LIVING GOD " (literally " the Son of the God—the living God "). Brief, but most weighty words—full and glorious confession of faith, although one sentence embraces it all.

" The excellence," says Dean Alford, " of this confession is, that it brings out both the human and the Divine nature of the Lord : the Messiah, the son of David, the Anointed King ; and the Eternal Son, begotten of the Eternal Father, as the last word most emphatically implies ; not Son of God in any inferior, figurative sense ; not *One* of the sons of God, of angelic nature ; but ' THE SON OF THE LIVING GOD,' having in Him the lordship and the Divine nature *in a sense in which they could be in none else.*   This was a view of the Person of Christ quite distinct from the Jewish Messianic idea."[1] " The heavenly truth flashed on him," it has been similarly remarked, " did indeed contain the meeting-place between the two dispensations ; the Anointed Messiah whom prophets and kings had desired to see ; the Son of Him who once again, as at the burning bush, had come with ever-living power to visit and redeem His people. . . . In that confession were wrapt up the truths which were to be the light of the future ages of Christendom."[2]

The confession was uttered by him " in one of those ecstasies of faith which raise him for the moment above himself, and reveal that ardent courage which characterises all mighty workers on the great heart of mankind." Is it not allowed us to picture the joy which that announcement must have imparted to the human soul of Him, whose joys were so few and whose sorrows were so many ?   The expression of His satisfaction may be found in the ready acknowledgment and answer He gives to the testimony borne by His open-hearted friend, when for a second time He bestows upon him his

1 Greek Testament, *in loc.*
2 Stanley's " Sermons on the Apostolic Age," pp. 86, 87.

descriptive name. It was as if He had said—Simon, you have bestowed upon Me My true title, and owned My Divine prerogatives; I shall now bestow upon you your new name in token of My approval, and in recognition of the rock-like strength of your belief. Hitherto you have been called *Simon*—but "blessed art thou, Simon Bar-jona: for flesh and blood hath not revealed it unto thee, but My Father which is in heaven. And I say also unto thee, That thou art Peter, and upon this rock I will build My Church; and the gates of hell shall not prevail against it. And I will give unto thee the keys of the kingdom of heaven: and whatsoever thou shalt bind on earth, shall be bound in heaven; and whatsoever thou shalt loose on earth, shall be loosed in heaven" (Matt. xvi. 17–19).

"This acknowledgment itself," says Neander, "might have been made by Peter at an earlier period; but the way in which he made it at that critical moment, and the feeling which inspired it, showed that he had obtained a new intuition of Christ as the Son of God. It was for this that Christ called him 'blessed,' because the drawing of the Father had led him to the Son, and the Father had revealed Himself to him in the Son." [1]

---

[1] It may not be out of place to note, that Cephas, not Peter, was the name by which, though now almost extinct, Peter was known and addressed by the Lord and his brother-apostles, as well as subsequently by Jewish Christians. I quote in full the following *addenda* to an able article on the apostle in Smith's Bib. Dic. p. 810 :—" Cephas (κηφᾶς) occurs in the following passages : - John i. 42; 1 Cor. i. 12, iii. 22, ix. 5, xv. 5; Gal. ii. 9, i. 18, ii. 10, 14 (the last three according to the text of Lachmann and Tischendorf). Cephas is the Chaldee word *Cepha*, itself a corruption of, or derivation from, the Hebrew *Ceph*, 'a rock,' a rare word, found only in Job xxx. 6, and Jer. iv. 29. It must have been the word actually pronounced by our Lord in Matt. xvi. 18, and on subsequent occasions when the apostle was addressed by Him or other Hebrews by his new name. By it he was

It is worthy of remark in passing, that in this reply to Peter we have one of the only two occasions in which the word (now so familiar to us) "Church" is found in the Gospels, although often recurring in the Acts and Epistles.

The metaphor employed by Christ is a strong, and remarkable one, "The gates of hell (or Hades—the place of departed spirits) shall not prevail against it." The gates of Oriental cities formed the place of judgment and counsel—often in the evil sense of intrigue and conspiracy. The figure employed evidently means, that all the machinations and stratagems of Satan and his emissaries will fail in shaking the foundations of his rock-built, spiritual citadel; and though assailed for eighteen centuries, He has been "faithful that promised."

My readers are aware that these few words from the lips of the Divine Redeemer, which took only a moment to repeat, have influenced the outer history and creed of the Church in a way which no other single utterance of His ever did. They are boldly assumed to have specially conferred at the time upon Peter what is called "the power of the keys," and to have invested him with an

known to the Corinthian Christians. In the ancient Syriac version of the New Testament (Peshito) it is uniformly found where the Greek has Petros. When we consider that our Lord and the apostles spoke Chaldee, and that therefore (as already remarked) the apostle must have been always addressed as Cephas, it is certainly remarkable that throughout the gospels, no less than 97 times, with one exception only, the name should be given in the Greek form, which was of later introduction, and unintelligible to Hebrews, though intelligible to the far wider Gentile world among which the gospel was about to begin its course. Even in St Mark, where more Chaldee words and phrases are retained than in all the other gospels put together, this is the case. It is as if, in our English Bibles, the name were uniformly given, not Peter, but Rock; and it suggests that the meaning contained in the appellation is of more vital importance, and intended to be more carefully seized at each recurrence, than we are apt to recollect."

unlimited ecclesiastical supremacy not shared by his brother-apostles—authority to remit or to retain sin at his discretion. But for this declaration, indeed, the Church of Rome with its haughty usurpations would never have existed; millions would never have recognised in the Pope the successor of Peter—the reigning vicar or representative of Christ—infallibly guarded from all possibility of error in doctrine. Perverted from the meaning the Divine Speaker intended them to convey, they have been thus made the occasion and authority for building up a compact system of spiritual delusion and despotism, supreme among the many which, in the sacred name of religion, have in different ages been palmed on human credulity.

In order to avoid any ambiguity or misstatement regarding the Roman assumptions, the words of her own canon law are these—"The Pope by the Lord's appointment is the successor of the blessed apostle Peter, and holds the place of the Redeemer Himself upon the earth." "The Roman Pontiff bears the authority, not of a mere man, but of the true God upon the earth." "Christ, the King of kings and Lord of lords, gave to the Roman Pontiff, in the person of Peter, the plenitude of power." "In the creed of Pius IV. we read, ' I acknowledge the Holy Catholic and Apostolic Church of Rome to be the mother and mistress of all Churches ; and I promise and swear true obedience to the Roman Pontiff, successor of the prince of the apostles, St Peter, and the vicegerent of Christ.' The catechism drawn up by command of the Council of Trent, declares ' the visible head of the Church to be he who, as the legitimate successor of Peter, the prince of the apostles, holds the Roman chair.' In defining the authority

I

and power which they allege were given to Peter, the Romanists affirm that the grant included *temporal* as well as spiritual power; and that the Pope, who is Peter's successor, is 'Bishop of bishops, Ordinary of ordinaries, Universal bishop of the Church, Bishop or diocesan of the whole world, Divine monarch, Supreme emperor, and King of kings. Hence the Pope is crowned with a triple crown as king of heaven, of earth, and of hell.' "[1]

"To give," says the same writer to whom I am indebted for these statements, "but one example of those astounding claims as preferred by a Pope, we give an extract from the Bull of Pius V. against Queen Elizabeth. The Bull is entitled, 'The Damnation and Excommunication of Elizabeth, Queen of England, and her Adherents, with an Addition of other Punishments,' and declares, 'He that reigneth on high, to whom is given all power in heaven and in earth, committed one Holy Catholic and Apostolic Church (out of which there is no salvation) to one alone upon earth, namely, to Peter, the prince of the apostles, and to Peter's successor, the bishop of Rome, to be governed in fulness of power. Him alone He made prince over all people and all kingdoms, to pluck up, destroy, scatter, consume, plant, and build.' "[2]

One thinks how Peter himself would have shrunk back appalled at the blasphemous assumptions which have been cruelly thrust on him, causing him to be identified with that "man of sin who opposeth and exalteth himself above all that is called God or that is worshipped; so that he as God, sitteth in the temple

---

[1] West, "Scenes in the Life of St Peter," pp. 112, 113.
[2] Ib. 113, 114.

of God, showing himself that he is God" (2 Thess. ii. 3, 4).

I shall not attempt to enter exhaustively into a question upon which volumes have been written, alike defending and combating this strange dogma. But neither can a topic that has so close and intimate a bearing on Peter's life be summarily disposed of or entirely slurred over. In pondering it, to any candid or dispassionate mind melancholy proof is afforded on what a slender and worthless foundation men can build up crude assertions into religious beliefs, revolting alike to reason and common-sense, and in this case derogatory to the Great Being whose distorted words have been made responsible for a system of gigantic error.

It is not unworthy of preliminary note, that there are two words employed in the Saviour's address to His apostle—Thou art Peter, a stone (*Petros*), and upon this rock (*Petra*) I will build My Church; Petros being simply a stone : Petra a bold, immoveable rock. So that the Romish writers are wide of the truth who would represent Christ as asserting that Peter was the rock on which the Church was to be built, seeing if our Lord had intended to convey any such meaning, He would not have employed a mixed metaphor, but would at once have said in direct words—"Thou art *Petros;* and upon thee will I build," &c. An excellent practical expositor puts this same observation in a different form : " When our Lord says, ' Thou art Peter,' or thou art a stone, He makes use of a masculine substantive, and one usually applied by the classical writers to a fragment of a rock, or such a stone as a man can lift. When He continues the sentence, ' and upon this rock,' He changes the word into a feminine noun, which is always employed by the classical writers to express the solid rock itself, and He continues to refer to this feminine noun throughout the sentence. A change of expression, which, to say the least, would be extremely improbable, if our Lord were speaking of the same person or the same thing throughout." [1]

I shall endeavour, with as much brevity as the theme will allow, to make a few remarks upon the much-controverted passage.

I. The first which occurs is : If Peter were thus invested by his Lord with such tremendous prerogatives ; if he were selected specially from among his brother-apostles, not as the chief or representative (for that, as we have already noted, owing to his natural character, and possibly from his age, he in one sense was), but to be accredited with powers superior to theirs—their prince and the prince of all succeeding ecclesiastics ;—not only so, but that the power bestowed upon him was to be transmitted from age to age to a successor, seated as " vicar of God " in the city of Rome :—surely we must at all events look for the record of so remarkable an appointment in all the four gospel narratives. If Peter was to be the future " rock " on which the Church was to be built, that rock would surely, so to speak, appear conspicuous in the foreground of all the four inspired pictures. His alleged Primacy would be considered far too important to be left to the description of only one evangelist. [2]

1 Blunt's " Lectures on St Peter," p. 50.

2 " Had they suffered Peter to be content with a primacy of order (which his age and gravity seemed to challenge for him), no wise or peaceable man would have denied it, as being a thing ordinarily practised among equals, and necessary to the well-governing of a society ; but when nothing but a primacy of power will serve the turn, as if the rest of the apostles had been inferior to him, this may by no means be granted " (Dr Cave, p. 17).

How stands the case? *Matthew alone records the saying of Christ, and none of the others do so.* Possibly it might not have been deemed of sufficient importance to be chronicled even by the former, had not his Gospel been written mainly, in the first instance, for behoof of Christians claiming Jewish descent, and among whom Peter had alike a special mission and a special influence. All about the personal history of the apostle of the circumcision would be of peculiar interest to his converted countrymen. " 'Tell us,' they may well have said when they came to this point of the Gospel teaching, 'tell us something of our great apostle; tell us not only what he said of his Master, but what his Master said of him ; tell us what prophetic anticipations were uttered in this, the crisis of his life, concerning those mighty works which he has done and is doing amongst us, concerning those awful responsibilities which have been entrusted to him alone in his dealings with his Jewish and Gentile brethren?' And to this question the blessing on St Peter in St Matthew's Gospel was the answer."[1] Bishop Wordsworth, in referring to the passage in Matthew xvi., and vindicating the reference of the Rock there spoken of to Christ, remarks—"The evangelists St Mark and St Luke would not have omitted the words in St Matthew, if the declaration of St Peter's privileges and not of our Lord's Person and office had been the main scope of the conversation."[2]

II. If Peter had been thus accredited with special and distinctive powers apart from his brother-apostles, we should naturally look for these being referred to

[1] Stanley's "Sermons on the Apostolic Church," p. 11.
[2] Greek Testament.

frequently in subsequent inspired writings—not only in the later Gospels, but in the epistles, and in the Acts of the Apostles. His " beloved brother Paul," who occupies so prominent a place in later years in the Church of the first century, was too magnanimous to refuse honour to whom honour was due, if such had been Peter's pre-eminent place, as the divinely-appointed, first universal bishop. What do we find in all the letters of the great apostle ? *Not even one reference to Peter's alleged official dignity* as *the " Rock-man of the Church."* On the contrary, as is well known, he is the only prominent leader of apostolic days whose fallibility and instability drew forth a reluctant rebuke from the apostle of the Gentiles. For owing to his brother's inconsistent con-duct at Antioch (A.D. 51), which we shall come after-wards to note, Paul tells frankly that he withstood him to the face, because he was to be blamed. " If thou, being a Jew, livest after the manner of the Gentiles, and not as do the Jews, why compellest thou the Gen-tiles to live as do the Jews " (Gal. ii. 14). " What language," as has been well observed, " is this to the prince of the apostles, the vicar of Christ, the man who had the keys of heaven, and earth, and hell ! " This circumstance is so fatal indeed to the pretensions which have been urged in favour of his supremacy over the other apostles, that from a very early age attempts have been made to set aside its force by the hypothesis, that it is not of Peter the apostle, but of another person of the same name, that Paul speaks in the passage referred to (Euseb., Hist. Eccles. 1–13). " This hypo-thesis, however, is so plainly contradicted by the words of Paul, who explicitly ascribes apostleship to the Peter of whom he writes, that it is astonishing how it could

have been admitted even by the most blinded zealot." [1]
In the Acts of the Apostles, while Peter undoubtedly
occupies not only an honourable, but unquestionably
the leading place in the Pentecostal days and in the first
gatherings of the Church, and, though in a very special
sense, may " the keys of the kingdom " be said to have
been put into his hands, first in the revivals of Pentecost, and afterwards as the honoured instrument employed in opening the door for the reception of the
Gentiles in their representative Cornelius (Acts xv. 7),
yet so far as official rank is concerned, James the Just,
as we shall by and by find, is the acknowledged President or Chief of the Council in Jerusalem. He never
on that occasion accorded any deference to Peter as the
vicar of Christ. Nor did Peter urge or assert his
delegated supremacy. He simply rose up after the
expression of diverse opinions, and stated his own on a
parity with Paul and Barnabas ; and then the aged
president, " after they had held their peace," answered,
saying, " Men and brethren, hearken unto *me*." It is
not Peter, but James who delivers the finding or verdict
—" Wherefore my sentence is," &c.

III. What light do the inspired writings of the New
Testament throw upon the equality of the other apostles
with St Peter ? To begin with the words and utterances of Peter's Lord and Master :—

Had He committed to Peter alone " the power of the
keys," the right of binding and loosing ; how comes it,
that in the immediately succeeding context in St Matthew, when He is speaking, not to Peter, but to all the
disciples collectively, we should have the virtual repetition of the very words on which the zealots of the

1 Kitto's " Biblical Literature."

Church of Rome have arrogated for him exclusive claims and jurisdiction : (Matt. xviii. 18) "Verily, I say unto you, Whatsoever *ye* shall bind on earth, shall be bound in heaven ; and whatsoever *ye* shall loose on earth, shall be loosed in heaven."

Subsequent to this same rock-charge, we find the disciples—evidently all-unconscious of any such distinction or acknowledged superiority as Romanists claim, but rather in one of those mournful exhibitions of frail human nature—disputing on the way to Jerusalem "which of them should be the greatest" (Mark ix. 33). What an opportunity this would have been for their Divine Head putting them right on the subject of Peter's priority ! Rather, might we not have expected His answer or rebuke to them to have been somewhat as follows : "Why this disputation, when I so lately solved and settled that very question at Cæsarea Philippi by awarding the chief dignity to the son of Jonas ?" How different His reply : "And He sat down, and called the twelve, and saith unto them, If any man desire to be first, the same shall be last of all, and servant of all. And He took a child, and set him in the midst of them : and when He had taken him in His arms, He said unto them, Whosoever shall receive one of such children in My name, receiveth Me ; and whosoever shall receive Me, receiveth not Me, but Him that sent Me" (Mark ix. 35–37).[1] When Jesus felt that the hour waited for by all time was drawing on, when He would surrender His own life for the life of the world, He thought it meet to prepare the minds of His confidential followers for the scenes of humiliation which were close at hand.

[1] See all this question very clearly and admirably handled by the author of "Essays on the Church."

He would impress upon them, that though (according to their joint confession) He was indeed the Son of the living God, yet they must moderate their expectations, for He was to be made the victim of cruel suffering and death. Though He had on previous occasions given more than one obscure intimation of coming sorrows, it is now for the first time He announces so plainly this mystery of woe, and scatters all their false dreams and expectations of a mere temporal kingdom : " And He began to teach them, that the Son of man must suffer many things, and be rejected of the elders, and of the chief priests, and scribes, and be killed, and after three days rise again " (Mark viii. 31).

How was the startling announcement received ? " We may imagine," says Stier, " the different effects produced on the other disciples, according to the individual peculiarity of each—the still, astonished feelings of a John or a Nathanael—the prostrate sadness of a Thomas, Is this the end to which He is to come ?—the crafty listening of a Judas—and the *naïve* questioning of an Andrew or Philip, ' What is this that He saith ? We cannot tell what He says.' " We know, however, with certainty the expressed feelings of their ever-impulsive spokesman. Peter has evidently been falsely elated with the words of encomium lately pronounced on him ; so much so, as to lead him in the present instance to unwarrantable presumption. In the quaint words of Dr Cave, " His spirits were now afloat, and his passions ready to overrun the banks ; not able to endure the thought that so much evil should befall his Master, he broke out into an over-confident and unseasonable interruption of Him." Taking Him, as the expression would seem to indicate, familiarly aside by the hand or garment, apart from the others, he ventured on a private remonstrance. "He took Him, and began to rebuke Him, saying, Forbid it, Lord; this shall not happen to Thee." The feeling, doubtless, mainly in the heart of the apostle was, that such a revolting end would be unbefitting and unbecoming the dignity of Him who had so lately appropriated the designation, "The Christ, the Son of the living God." But, over and above this, there may have mingled a feeling of personal disappointment. He had clung with fond avidity to the carnal dream of a temporal kingdom : his mind recoiled from the thought of so sudden an eclipse of his cherished expectations of a share in the grandeur and glory of that kingdom, by these humiliating revelations of approaching suffering and death.

His Divine Master, however, as Bengel expresses it, "reduces him to his proper level. He meets the unwarranted expostulation with a stinging rebuke, uttered in the presence of all the others, ' Get thee behind me, Satan (or adversary), thou art an offence (or stumblingblock).'" It has been supposed by some that Jesus here had still in His mind the emblem of the rock. ' Thou Petros, who wert lately by thy confession a living stone of the temple of which I am the foundation, art become as a stone of stumbling—an offence in My way, with which, if thou couldst, thou wouldst make Me fall.' And it is the more evident, perhaps, that our Lord had such a reference in His rebuke, from the way in which Peter, many years afterwards, speaks of those who became an offence to the great Headstone: "A stone of *stumbling* and a *rock of offence*." [1] Nor is it without

[1] "These words (of stern admonition) open up to us the fact, that this period of the ministry was a time of special trial and temptation to the sin-

significance, that in none of the Gospels is this sharp and stinging rebuke more faithfully recorded than in what we have already called Peter's "own gospel." The honest, genuine, outspoken man is the first to proclaim, as with a trumpet, his Lord's merited censure, the severest that ever came from lips of love and tenderness ; as if he would have all future ages to know that instead of occupying the chief seat, he was truly "a man of like passions," who had greater reason than his brother-apostle of Tarsus to call himself "less than the least of all saints." "The very point and occasion of that rebuke," as has been well observed, "is his inexcusable want of discernment in spiritual things, his betrayal of so earthly a judgment and so carnal a heart. . . . It is at once a most overwhelming disproof of the baseless and arrogant pretensions of the Papacy, and also an affecting comment on the weakness, blindness, and fallibility of man, even when most honoured and privileged. On the very same day, we find this apostle commended most honourably for his faith and attachment to his Lord, and reproved in terms of the utmost severity for his blindness and unbelief. One moment he is the most favoured of the apostles, a chosen foundation-stone of the Church, presented with the keys of the kingdom of heaven ; and the next, he is visited with his Lord's stern displeasure, and addressed

less Son of God. 'Escape from sufferings and death. Do not drink the cup prepared of Thy Father ; it is too bitter ; it is not deserved.' Such was the whisper of the Prince of this world at that time to our Lord ; and Peter has been unwittingly taking it into his mouth. The doctrine of a suffering Messiah, so plainly exhibited in the prophets, had receded from sight in the current religion of that time. The announcement of it to the disciples was at once new and shocking. By repelling it, even when offered by the Lord Himself, they fell into a deeper sin than they could have conceived. The chief of them was called 'Satan,' because he was unconsciously pleading on Satan's side."—Bib. Dic. Art. "Jesus Christ," p. 1059.

as if he were Satan himself, the great enemy of God and man. Surely such an incident in the life of such an apostle should teach us to cease from man, whose breath is in his nostrils, for wherein is he to be accounted of ? " [1] " The two things he wanted were just those two qualities which the Romish expositors insist on finding in him. He was very fallible, often making mistakes ; and he was unstable, the very opposite to that characteristic of a *rock* which they always ascribe to him." [2]

We may add yet one other reference to the Saviour's declarations. When imparting His last injunctions to His Church before His ascension, these were His emphatic words, addressed not to one, but to all the apostles without distinction : " As My Father hath sent Me, even so send I you. And when He had said this, He breathed on them, and saith unto them, Receive ye the Holy Ghost. Whose soever sins ye remit, they are remitted unto them ; and whose soever sins ye retain, they are retained " (John xx. 21-23).

To pass from the testimony of the Master to that of His other apostles and disciples, St Luke tells us that he had carefully collected in his Gospel " all those things that are most surely believed among us." Strange it were, had there been authority for it, to have omitted such a foundation-truth as this ; while in the Acts of the Apostles, where the same Evangelist records the later biography of Peter, his priority is not once referred to. Here unquestionably, had there been any similar authority, we should have found the " Prince of

<hr />

1 Bishop Lee on St Peter, pp. 64, 65.
2 Author of " Essays on the Church."

the apostles and Vicar of God" claiming his Divine right, and exercising his Divinely-conferred supremacy. But there is not the trace of it, either by word or deed. Surely, to take one important official act, if such had been his special prerogative, as the infallible representative of Christ on earth, to him would have appertained the filling up of the vacancy in the apostleship caused by the treachery and death of Judas Iscariot. But, as we shall ere long find, and as we are expressly told, *this was done by the whole company of the apostles.* " *They* appointed two—Joseph and Matthias," and the solemn appeal was made to lot. " There could not have been a fitter opportunity for the exercise of Peter's supremacy than this. It was clearly the part of the vicar of Christ to appoint to the vacant bishopric a new suffragan ; but he did not do so, or attempt to do it ; he was only the spokesman. All united in the nomination of two, and then in prayer to God that He would choose between them." [1]

It is equally strange to find St John, Peter's most intimate associate, utterly silent about his friend's alleged official distinction. Both he and St Luke could not fail to have known this appointed primacy ; how then can we explain that they have not so much as a passing reference to it ? We have already shewn that St Mark's Gospel was in some way written under Peter's own dictation, and we should naturally look in it for the full explanation of these exceptional powers. Not one word is there mentioned, either about " the power of the keys," or the pretentious " rock." We may surely confidently rely upon it, that if Peter had been invested with any such vicarage, the most intimate sharer of his

[1] West, p. 120.

thoughts, and recorder of his sayings, who stood to him
in much the same relation that Timothy did to Paul,
would have been the very first to put it in writing. He
would never have done Peter the injustice to leave
unnoticed the great fact of his history, and the chief
honour of his life ; but, on the other hand, would have
felt the pride of a disciple in placing him on the conspicuous pedestal.

The sacred writers, however, are *n t* silent regarding
the Rock on which the Church was to be built, although they refuse any such assumption to the son of
Jonas. To begin with a passage in the Old Testament,
we may use the comment of an eminent expositor :—
" In the book of Daniel the kingdom of the Son of man
is compared to a *Stone*, which becomes a great *Rock*
(Dan. ii. 35) and lasts for ever, and is called ' the kingdom of the God of heaven' (ii. 44). It is a prophetic
representation of our Lord's words to St Peter—'On
this Rock (*i.e.*, on Myself, the Son of man, confessed
also to be the Son of God) I will build My Church, My
kingdom, which is the kingdom of *the living God*, and
it shall last for ever, and I will give to thee the keys of
that kingdom.'"[1] St Paul describes the Church as being
" built upon the foundation of the apostles and prophets,
Jesus Christ Himself being the chief corner-stone "
(Eph. ii. 20). Twenty years after Christ had spoken
the memorable words to Peter, and by which time surely
their truth and application must have been fully
ascertained, the apostle of the Gentiles says, " Other
foundation can no man lay than that is laid, which is
Jesus Christ." St John, in the allegorical description
of the New Jerusalem in the Apocalypse, speaks

[1] Bishop Wordsworth's Greek Testament.

of it as having "twelve foundations," in which were
the names of the twelve apostles of the Lamb
(Rev. xxi. 14). No foundation, let it be observed,
is ascribed to Peter different from the others; no
indication that one stone was to be regarded as
more precious or distinguished than the others.
"There are *twelve stars* on the crown of the Church
militant sojourning on earth, and *twelve foundation
stones* in the wall of the Church glorified in heaven;
and if Peter, who is one of these twelve stones, is taken
from the other eleven and made to be their *foundation*,
the whole structure is disturbed, and the whole fabric
falls."[1]

And what, perhaps, is more to the point than all,
what says St Peter himself? It would only be natural
to expect from him an explicit statement as to the distinctive powers his Lord had conferred on him. The
Christian modesty and humility which so specially
characterised his old age, might have deterred him
from speaking of what savoured of egotism or vain-
glory. But not, certainly, if, as the Papal writers
allege, the interests of the Church were, by Divine
authority, surrendered to his keeping. It would have
been a false delicacy and reticence surely, unworthy of
his brave, outspoken manliness, to have preserved these
prerogatives as a secret. What, however, *does* he say
of "the Rock" on which the Church is to be built?
Is that Rock himself, or another? "Unto you, therefore, which believe, HE is precious;" "Unto whom
coming, as unto a living stone, disallowed indeed of men,
but chosen of God, and precious, ye also, as lively stones,
are built up a spiritual house, an holy priesthood, to offer

1 Wordsworth.

up spiritual sacrifices, acceptable to God" (1 Peter ii. 5). The inscription at the opening of his first epistle is not "Peter *the* apostle, the vicegerent of God," but "Peter, *an* apostle of Jesus Christ." There is no instance on record of his ever having exercised any such supposed power. On the contrary, there are instances, if we may here for a moment anticipate, when he went forth a delegate, in obedience to the injunction of his brethren, as when he was sent, at their command, along with John, to minister to the infant Church of the Samaritans.

Some have ventured to affirm that Peter received on the shores of Tiberias the special commission we shall come afterwards to consider—"Feed My sheep." "But it was not certainly as one endued with exclusive or paramount authority, or as distinguished from his fellow-disciples, but rather as one who had forfeited his place, and could not resume it without such an authorisation." [1] On the other hand, surely if Christ had purposed to invest him with any alleged primacy in the Church, that final interview would have been the most befitting occasion. But there is no such purpose : while at a previous period of his history, to one of his own bold assertions, he received from the lips of his Lord an answer which implies, as distinctly as language can assert, a parity or equality among the apostolic band, to which he was no exception ;—" Then answered Peter, and said unto Him, Behold, we have forsaken all, and followed Thee ; what shall we have therefore ? And Jesus said unto them, Verily I say unto you, That ye which have followed Me, in the regeneration, when the Son of man shall sit in the throne of His glory, ye also shall sit upon twelve thrones,

[1] Bib. Dic. *in loc.*

judging the twelve tribes of Israel" (Matt. xix. 27, 28).
How singularly, to revert once more to his epistles, does
he seem to protest against any such primacy or priority
of claim, when he speaks thus regarding pastors, "Neither
as being lords over God's heritage, but being ensamples
to the flock ;" and turning, as it were, the eye of false
teachers away from himself to the brotherhood of the
faithful—" the Church throughout the whole world," he
exclaims, " Ye are a chosen generation, a royal priesthood." He tells us in his last epistle of some things
he would wish his converts and the early believers to
have always in remembrance after his decease ; but any
claim of authority over his colleagues was not among
these, nor in other parts of his writings does he trans-
mit any such. When he came at last to lay down his
life for the sake of the Master he loved so well, how
would the remembrance of rashness, impulse, fear,
cowardice, mingling with deeds of heroic devotion and
allegiance, make him shrink from the assumption of
any lordship over God's heritage ![1] Stier succinctly remarks: "In the Gospels, the Acts of the Apostles, and the
entire New Testament, there is no trace to be found of
such a supremacy, but the contrary, indeed, everywhere.
In Acts vi. the twelve call together the multitude of
the disciples. Acts x. 47, Peter asks permission
from the inferior attendants who were present,
as at chap. xi. he vindicates himself before God
and man by a ' What was I ?' " " Thus is wholly

[1] "Even in the time of Cyprian when communion with the Bishop of Rome
as St Peter's successor for the first time was held to be indispensable, no
powers of jurisdiction or supremacy were supposed to be attached to the
admitted precedency of rank. . . . Peter held no distinct office, and certainly never claimed any powers which did not belong equally to all his
fellow-apostles."—*Bib. Dic. in loc.*

K

set aside anything like the institution of an official
primacy, which would make a man the sovereign dispenser of God's pardons.   To Peter belongs, nevertheless, the honour of having been the first to give utterance to the creative word of the Church, and of having
displayed in action that great quality of conquering energy, which procured for him a moral supremacy
at Jerusalem.   If the Church had no more stable basis
than the impulsive heart of a man, it is evident how
frail would be her foundation."[1]   " Sure I am," says
old Dr Cave, with whose words we may appropriately
sum up the argument, " that, as Origen tells us, every
true Christian that makes this confession with the same
spirit and integrity which St Peter did, shall have the
same blessing and commendation from Christ conferred
upon him."[2]

Yes, thanks be to God, the Church is not built *upon
the shifting sand*, but upon " Jesus Christ, the same
yesterday, to-day, and for ever."   Her foundation is
upon the holy mountains.   She looks to no prince of
the apostles, but to the " Prince of the kings of the
earth :" as it had been predicted ages before by the great
evangelical prophet,—" Therefore thus saith the Lord
God, Behold, I lay in Zion for a foundation a stone, a
tried stone, a precious corner-stone, a sure foundation :
he that believeth shall not make haste" (Isa. xxviii. 16).
To One alone, and to no other, has been given the keys
of the kingdom of heaven.   " I am He that liveth, and

---

1 Pressensé, p. 393.

2 " If we shall say, like Peter, 'Thou art the Christ, the Son of the living
God,' not by the revelation of flesh and blood, but by the light of our Father
which is in heaven shining into our heart, we become Peter, and to us
might be said by the Word (*Logos*), 'Thou art Peter.'   For every disciple of
Peter is a rock."—*Ib.*

was dead ; and, behold, I am alive for evermore, Amen :
and have the keys of hell and of death " (Rev. i. 18).[1]

Thus, then, do all these " wise master-builders," and
none more than St Peter himself, point away from
every human foundations to their great Lord, saying,
" He *only* is my ROCK and my salvation."[2]

[1] As to the latter prerogative, indeed, alleged to have been bestowed on
the apostle, the possession of the keys of the kingdom of heaven, a writer,
already quoted, observes, "It is said that when the Jews made a man a
Doctor of the Law, they put into his hand the key of the closet in the Temple
where the sacred books were kept, and also tablets to write upon ; signifying
by this that they gave him authority to teach and to explain the Scriptures
to the people. Peter had the honour of opening the Christian dispensation.
He was the first to preach after the effusion of the Holy Ghost on the day
of Pentecost, when the evangelical dispensation was fully and formally
opened. The promise was fulfilled to him, he receives the keys of the
kingdom of heaven, and opened the door to both Jews and Gentiles."—
West, 107, 108.

[2] Archbishop Leighton, referring to Peter's failings, says, "These, by the
providence of God being recorded in Scripture, give a check to the excess
of Rome's conceit concerning this apostle. . . . Whatsoever he was, they
would be much in pain to prove Rome's right to primacy by succession.
And if ever it had any such right, we may confidently say it has forfeited it
long ago, by departing from St Peter's footsteps and from his faith."—*Commentary on 1st Peter*.

CHAPTER IX.

Peter on the Mount.

GRANDEUR OF THE TRANSFIGURATION. ITS LOCALITY AND DESIGN.
PETER ONE OF THE FAVOURED EYE-WITNESSES. HIS EXCLAMA-
TION. RETURN FROM THE MOUNT TO CAPERNAUM.

" The light o'erflowed Him as a sea, and raised His shining brow ;
And the voice went forth that bade all worlds to God's Belovèd
bow."   *—Aird.*

" Hermon, as connecting Palestine geographically with the
Gentile world beyond, was a fitting place for such a revelation of
Jesus, in whom alone Jew and Gentile were to become one."
     —Eastward, 279.

" We may, not without reason, regard the whole as in mysterious connection both with St Peter's profession of faith and
with that saddening prediction which followed it."
     —Bishop Ellicott.

" The apostle Peter, towards the close of his life, in running his
mind over the proofs of Christ's majesty, found none so conclusive
and irrefragable as the scenes where he and others were with Him
in the Holy Mount, as eyewitnesses that He received from God
the Father honour and glory."   *—Kitto's Cyclopedia.*

IX days later from the date of the incidents narrated at the beginning of last chapter, Peter occupies a prominent and distinguished place in that most marvellous and glorious of the occurrences in the life of our Lord—the Transfiguration on the Mount. This great transaction, which concluded the week's seclusion at Banias, formed a befitting climax to the Saviour's ordinary teachings and ministry, preparatory to the last all-momentous act in the Divine drama. It was like the robing of the Jewish High Priest before entering the most Holy place on the great Day of Atonement. Peter seemed afterwards to have a lively remembrance of the surpassing grandeur and privilege of the scene—"We were with Him in the Holy Mount."

The traditional locality of the Transfiguration which,

as early as the fourth century, was assigned to Tabor, is now abandoned by all modern writers. That it was ever selected seems to have arisen from the one fact, or rather misconception, that this beautiful mountain, with its "woody coronal," answered apparently better than any other single eminence in Palestine to the description of the evangelist Mark, "an high mountain apart." Before the close of the sixth century three churches and a monastery were built on the summit of the mountain in commemoration of the great event. Arculf, A.D. 700, says, "At the top is a pleasant and extensive meadow surrounded by a thick wood, and in the middle of the meadow a great monastery with numerous cells of monks. There are also three handsome churches, according to the number of tabernacles described by Peter." Dr Porter mentions that "the Crusaders crowned the fable by establishing on Tabor a Benedictine monastery, whose abbot claimed the jurisdiction of a bishop."[1] When, however, the passage in the Gospel comes to be examined, the word "apart" is found really to refer, not to the position of the *mountain*, but to that of the *disciples*. Besides, the objections to Tabor are, in other respects, insuperable. It is shown by the most learned of Biblical travellers[2] that a fortified town —Itaburion—must, during this very period of our Lord's life and ministry, have occupied the summit of the hill, the ruins of which are still remaining. More than this, the Redeemer, as we have seen, had just been sojourning with His disciples in the region round Cæsarea Philippi, the extreme north of Palestine. It is far from probable that during the intervening six days,

---

1 Quoted by Andrews, "Life of our Lord," p. 282.
2 Dr Robinson, vol. ii. p. 359.

He would take the long journey of fifty miles to the foot of Mount Tabor, on the confines of Zebulon and Naphtali. It is much more likely that He would select one of the spurs or ridges of snow-covered Hermon as a meet high-altar for this scene of "excellent glory." The expression in the original of St Luke is, " He went up into *the* mountain." As He was at that time under the shadow of this great giant—the solitary Alp of Northern Palestine—no eminence could so well answer the distinctive epithet applied by the evangelist. " It is impossible," says Dr Stanley, whose words I read on the spot, and could then fully subscribe alike to their beauty and accuracy, " to look up from the plain to the towering peaks of Hermon, almost the only mountain which deserves the name in Palestine, and one of whose ancient titles was derived from this circumstance, and not be struck with its appropriateness to the scene. That magnificent height, mingling with all the views of the north, from Shechem upwards, though often alluded to as the northern barrier of the Holy Land, is connected with no historical event in the Old or New Testament. Yet this fact of its rising high above all the other hills of Palestine, and of its setting the last limit to the wanderings of Him who was sent only to the lost sheep of the house of Israel, falls in with the supposition which the words inevitably force upon us. High up on its sunny slopes there must be many a point where the disciples could be taken 'apart by themselves.' Even the transient comparison of the celestial splendour with the snow, where alone it could be seen in Palestine, should not perhaps be wholly overlooked."[1]

---

[1] Sinai and Palestine *in loc.*

" What other hill could it be than the southward slope of that goodly mountain, Hermon, which is, indeed, the centre of all the Promised Land, from the entering in of Hamath unto the river of Egypt—the mount of fruitfulness, from which the springs of Jordan descended to the valleys of Israel ? Along its mighty forest avenues, until the grass grew fair with the mountain lilies, His feet dashed in the dew of Hermon, He must have gone to pray His first recorded prayer about death : and from the steep of it, before He knelt, could see to the south all the dwelling-place of the people that had sat in darkness, and seen the great Light—the land of Zebulun and of Naphtali, Galilee of the nations ; could see even with His human sight the gleam of that lake by Capernaum and Chorazin, and many a place loved by Him and vainly ministered to, whose house was now left unto them desolate. And chief of all, far in the utmost blue, the hills above Nazareth sloping down to His old home : hills on which the stones yet lay loose that had been taken up to cast at Him when He left them for ever." [1]

It was then, after the season of unremitting labour described in previous chapters, that the Redeemer thus ascended one of these lofty eminences for rest and prayer. We know that the evening was the time He usually selected for these " Sabbaths of His soul," when the burning heat of the day was over, and the thronging multitudes following His steps had retired to their several homes. Moreover, as the same evangelist informs us that the three disciples who accompanied Him were " heavy with sleep," and finishes his account of the transaction by stating that " on the

[1] Ruskin on Mountain Beauty : " Modern Painters," vol. iv. p. 392.

next day they came down from the hill,"—are we not warranted in entertaining the supposition that the Transfiguration took place during *night?* If this conclusion be correct, what an additional pictorial interest does it impart to the scene ! The sun had already set, far to the west, over the Great Sea; all Nature was hushed to repose ; nothing heard but the rippling of the mountain streams ; nothing seen before them but the pale, silvery moonlight, falling on the everlasting snows of the mountain ; or above them, myriad stars, like temple-lamps lit in the outer court of some august sanctuary; behind them the hill-tops of their own covenant land—the land of the patriarchs and prophets —but the land too, alas ! that was now manifesting daily and increasing symptoms of enmity towards Him whose presence and footsteps had given its "holy fields" their highest consecration. It evidently was a season of rare peacefulness and elevation to the soul of the Redeemer. Away from the bustle of cities, which He always seemed to shun, He was permitted, amid these cool, dewy uplands, to hold a season of sweet communion with His Father, to forget the shamefulness of the world's present rejection, and the deeper shame of that world's approaching crime, in putting the innocent One to a death of agony.

The three disciples selected from the apostolic company to be the representatives of the Church on earth, at their Lord's Transfiguration,—to be " eyewitnesses," as St Peter afterwards expresses it, " of His majesty," (or, as that word means, " of His excellent glory,") were the apostle himself and the two sons of thunder. Peter, " the Rock ;" James, the first of the twelve who was to suffer death for his Master's sake ; John, the favoured

disciple, whose head afterwards leaned on his Master's
bosom—the three who have been called, not inaptly,
"the flower and crown of the apostolic band." [1]
Wearied with the fatigues of the day, these privileged
watchers wrapped themselves in their *abbas,* and fell
asleep. They continue locked in slumber till a strange,
unearthly light is felt playing on their eyelids. Is it a
dream? a trance? They wake up; and lo! a spectacle
of overpowering glory bursts upon them. The Lord,
they left praying, is now seen before them arrayed in
garments woven as with sunbeams—His raiment emit-
ting light, vying in whiteness with the virgin snow
which crested the higher ridges, or lay lapped in the
gigantic corries around them, gleaming in the moonlight
—green sward and thorny nâbk and mountain flower
luminous with the strange brilliance. St Mark, in his
own graphic way of delineation, adds, " So as no fuller
on earth can white them." [2] A bright, fleecy cloud sur-

[1] Trench.

[2] The graphic detail in St Mark's narrative of the Transfiguration, is an
additional confirmation of the surmise that one of the apostle-spectators of
the scene had dictated the account from vivid personal reminiscence. A
recent writer, in an interesting article on the characteristics of Mark's Gospel,
specially vindicating it from the theory of being a late made cento from the
other two Synoptists, notes (and the accuracy of the observation will be confirmed by all who have seen the great original in the Vatican)—"Look at
Raphael's picture of the Transfiguration, and see for how much the painter
is indebted to St Mark alone (ix. 2-29). All the Synoptists have recorded
this event, as well as the healing of the lunatic child which followed it, and
which forms the subject of the lower half of the picture. But St Mark's
narrative may be recognised in it at once by its features of characteristic
description—the shining garments of the Lord, exceeding white as snow,
&c., &c. . . . In the scene at the foot of the mount, St Mark's peculiar
style is abundantly apparent. . . . We feel sure, as we read his words, so
abounding with minuteness of description, that we have before us the narrative of one who was on the spot. . . . It is no mere adaptation of St
Matthew we are perusing: it is the work of one who was of a different
character from the publican-apostle, and abounds with strokes of word-
painting with which there is nothing comparable to be found in the writings
of St Matthew."—*See the entire article,* " *The Graphic and Dramatic Character of the Gospel of St Mark,*" *in* " *The Expositor,*" *October* 1875.

rounds Him with a halo of glory, and on either side of the transfigured Saviour there is a glorified form. The apostles gaze in mute wonder. As their adorable Master is engaged in converse with these mysterious visitants from another world, the question must have passed from lip to lip, in all probability Peter taking the initiative, "Who are these arrayed in white robes, and whence came they?" He and his two favoured brothers do not require, however, to wait a reply. Either by revelation, or, more probably, from hearing their Lord addressing the glorified delegates by name, they know that they are in the presence of none other than Moses and Elias. With what profound interest would they gaze on the two fathers of the nation, whose names must have been embalmed in their holiest memories since the dawn of earliest childhood! The two, may we not venture to add, who were in character most like-minded with our apostle, having natural constitutional frailties most nearly allied to his own :—Moses, who once " spake unadvisedly with his lips ;" Elijah, whose great heroic heart, in a moment of weakness, had cowered before the impotent threats of a woman, and fled ignominiously from work and duty ; but both of whom, through that same Divine grace which was yet to prove omnipotent with Peter, had gotten them the victory. The eyes of the earthly and the heavenly representatives are alike fixed on the great central Figure of the group—the toilworn, sorrow-stricken MAN, who, a few hours before, had climbed the steep ascent with weary limb and burdened soul, but who is now radiant with superhuman glory, the true Apocalyptic Angel " standing in the sun." If silent up to this time, Peter, as we have found in other memorable seasons, cannot longer

repress his emotions.   If mistaken before, now, at all
events, he imagined to himself that the long expectation of Messiah's kingdom was at last realised.   He would
render his impressions at once permanent, and make the
grassy meads of Hermon better than the pagan dream
of Elysium.   In an ecstasy of ravishment, he exclaims,
" Lord, it is good for us to be here."   He even proposed
the erection of three tabernacles, where their Master and
His glorified attendants might take up a lasting abode,
and, enthroned on these majestic peaks of Hermon,
reign over regenerated Israel, away from the intrigues
and plottings of Pharisees, and the wily expedients of
Pilate and Herod.   His Lord, too, would avoid the
humiliation and shame of the " decease at Jerusalem."
There is a beautifully natural touch given in St Mark
in describing the agitation which had accompanied
Peter's enthusiastic proposal—" *Not knowing what he
said* " (Mark ix. 6) ; indicating also, as it does, the
humility of the venerable apostle, when he came to
speak of the past in his old age, taking the least favourable view of his conduct on the occasion.

A new phase occurs in this diorama of heavenly
splendour.   A cloud of yet more transcendant brightness descends on the head of the Saviour and His two
celestial companions.   " Here is something more than
the radiance of a heavenly Soul occasionally seen on a
human countenance, more than one of those glances
which, like lightning-flashes, reveal its moral beauty." [1]
It is nothing less than the Shekinah, or Divine glory,
the symbol and emblem of a present Deity ; the same
cloud which of old preceded in a pillar-form the march
through the wilderness ; which hovered over the ark in

[1] Pressensé

the tabernacle ; and over the Holy of holies in the
Jerusalem temple ; the same " cloud " which, not long
afterwards, when His work was finished and the victory
won, received the ascending Redeemer out of the sight
of the apostolic band on the heights of Olivet : "And a
cloud received Him out of their sight" (Acts i. 9).
Peter and his fellow-disciples seem, at this juncture, to
have been shut out and excluded by the new canopy.
They became greatly afraid ; the appearance of the
cloud struck them with awe. They fell prone on the
ground, touching the dewy herbage with their faces
(Matt. xvii. 6). This feeling, moreover, increased as
they felt themselves thus dissociated and severed from
their Lord, whose presence a moment before, radiant
though it was with almost intolerable brightness, had
yet been to them the blessed pledge of security and
safety. A Voice issues from the cloud. A message
comes to them from the midst of the excellent glory—
"This is My beloved Son, in whom I am well pleased :
hear ye Him." It is the sublime attestation of God the
Father installing the Son as Sovereign of the kingdom,
consecrating Him as Prophet, Priest, and King for
evermore.

" That Transfiguration united the old dispensation
and the new. For Moses, the representative of the law,
and the representative of the prophets, witnessed to
Him who had fulfilled both the law and the prophets.
Their work was finished. The stars which had illumined
the old night were lost in the blaze of this risen Sun." [1]
" It was intended also to illuminate with a ray of
glory the dark days that were about to begin ; it was
designed to strengthen Jesus for His conflict. It was

[1] Eastward, 279.

His first watch before the battle; the next would be in Gethsemane." [1] But the hour of triumph is at an end; the dazzling lustre has faded from the Redeemer's raiment; the celestial voices are hushed; the vision has passed away. Emerging from the cloud, and returning to Peter and his two companions, Jesus touches them, and with gentle voice, says—"Arise, be not afraid." For them, too, as for Him, that Transfiguration had a special purpose, and for none more than the son of Jonas. In the words of Chrysostom, "It was to comfort Peter and those who regarded with fear the suffering (of Christ), and to raise up their thoughts." They, too, had their own fierce fight before them, and one of them, at all events, was often cheered in his after battles by the memory already quoted, "We were with Him on the Holy Mount." They lifted up their eyes; the cloud, the glory, the heavenly visitants, the Voice, were gone. They glanced round in every direction, as the word in the original means,[2] but "they saw no man, save Jesus only." The morning light was again tipping the brows of the kingly mount, and they must hasten down its slopes once more to encounter stern duty, temptation, and trial. Who can doubt but that this rare privilege of being "eyewitness of His majesty" as it was designed, so it *did* prepare Peter and his associates for those scenes of ignominy and humiliation which were so close at hand?[3]

The great annual celebration of the feast of tabernacles was now drawing nigh: "the olives were being shaken

---

[1] Pressensé, p. 400. [2] Περιβλεψάμενοι, Mark ix. 8.

[3] The reader is referred to a fuller account of the Transfiguration in the author's "Prophet of Fire," from which this chapter is abridged.

from the trees, and the grapes were being trodden in the winepress." Both Master and disciples purpose going up to the feast on their return to Capernaum. In the meantime they would seem to have there enjoyed a few weeks' comparative calm. For the reason stated in a previous chapter, the intense heat was still detaining multitudes of the usual inhabitants in their summer retreats in North Galilee, and thereby left the little company free from the intrusions to which they were subjected in former visits. Peter and his Bethsaida brothers may possibly have resumed, as we know they did at a later period, their old occupations ; while in the middle of the day, when work was impossible, they would not improbably in 'Simon's house' gather around the Divine Teacher, and receive important directions regarding their future work. "These rough, uncultured natures," says a writer, "were like precious marble not yet polished, but from which the great Master would bring forth a monument to His praise." When the time came that it was necessary to leave for the Jerusalem festival, it would appear from the narrative that they pursued together the longer route by Samaria, Shechem, and Bethel, while some other of the disciples in Capernaum joined the caravans of pilgrims by the shorter one along the Jordan valley.[1]

---

[1] I have passed over, without comment, the only other incident which occurs at this time in connection with Peter, on his return, along with his Lord and the rest of the apostles, to Capernaum. It is recorded alone by the evangelist Matthew : "And when they were come to Capernaum, they that received tribute-money came to Peter, and said, Doth not your Master pay tribute ? He saith, Yes. And when he was come into the house, Jesus prevented him, saying, What thinkest thou, Simon ? of whom do the kings of the earth take custom or tribute ? of their own children, or of strangers ? Peter saith unto him, Of strangers. Jesus saith unto him, Then are the children free. Notwithstanding, lest we should offend them, go thou to

the sea, and cast an hook, and take up the fish that first cometh up ; and when thou hast opened his mouth, thou shalt find a piece of money : that take, and give unto them for Me and thee" (Matt. xvii. 24-27). The "tribute" here spoken of, or the Græco-Roman " *didrachmon,*" is given outside this Volume, both as an illustration of this occurrence in the life of Peter, and as a specimen of the most current of the coins of the time in Judea.   It was equivalent in value to the Jewish half-shekel, and was devoted to the expense connected with the temple-offerings and sacrifices.   Though in one sense a voluntary offering, it was expected of every Jew, rich and poor, in whatever country he resided.   " It should be observed, however," says Dr Kitto, "that although the people usually paid the collectors in this coin, the coin itself could not be paid into the temple on account of the symbols and effigies, deemed idolatrous, with which it was charged, and had to be changed for Jewish money at Jerusalem.   Hence the vocation of the money-changers' whom our Lord expelled from the temple."—*Daily Readings,* vol. i. p. 333.

CHAPTER X.

During the Last Days of the Passion.

> "The Saviour looked on Peter. Aye, no word,
> No gesture of reproach ; the heavens serene,
> Though heavy with armed justice, did not lean
> Their thunders that way : the forsaken Lord
> *Looked* only on the traitor. None record
> What look that was, none guess :   *   *   *
> He went out speechless from the face of all
> And filled the silence, weeping bitterly."
> —E. Barrett Browning.

"Peter may have thought that his untruth could not injure any person, while it might profit him and insure his safety ; and hence that it was lawful, or at least a matter of small moment But he soon experienced what consequences the commencement of sin entailed."—*Luther.*

"He must have now felt fully the truth of his Lord's declaration of the preceding day, 'Without Me ye can do nothing.' He now learnt, no doubt, to distrust his own unaided strength."—*Archbishop Whately's Lectures on the Apostles.*

"If Christ had not *looked* upon Peter, Peter had not wept. Peter's tears flowed first from the eyes of Christ. . . . 'I came, I saw, I conquered'—may be inscribed by the Saviour on every monument of His grace. I *came* to the sinner. I *looked* upon him, and with a look of omnipotent *love* I overcame him."—*Toplady.*

HE crowning miracle of the raising of
Lazarus shortly afterwards occurred.
As Peter, however, though doubtless
present, occupies in connection with
it no more prominent place than the other Apostles, we
shall not dwell on the many touching incidents of that
loveliest " Idyll " in our Lord's life.   The miracle itself
had the effect of greatly exasperating the hostility alike of
Pharisee and Sadducee against the great Conqueror of
death, and of hastening on the awful end.   Meanwhile,
however, in anticipation of the Passover, Jesus and His
Apostles retired to the seclusion of a little village on
the borders of the wilderness, called Ephraim ; supposed
to be situated in one of the undulating valleys which
cluster around the ancient Bethel.   Work seems to
have been here suspended.   Ere the final scene and

conflict, Master and disciple once more have turned
aside there together "to rest awhile." Nearly twenty
miles of road would lie between them and Jerusalem.
Their spirits would be refreshed on these breezy uplands, hallowed with the old memories of Abraham's
first altar and Jacob's mystic ladder; commanding in
unusual impressiveness, from my own recollection, a
prospect of the Mountains of Moab, which, next to
Hermon, form the grandest hill scenery visible in Palestine. Doubtless these weeks of calm would be employed by the Divine Pilot in strengthening the vessel
for the coming storm. Those quiet hills would be
turned into oratories. Many a warning and encouragement too would drop from the lips of the Master into
the ears of His soon to be scattered followers ; chiefly,
we may suppose, would He seek to reconcile their minds
to that mysterious revelation which He had recently
made as to His approaching death.

From one of these watch-towers of lonely Nature He
could descry, in the distant Valley, the troops of worshippers on their way to the city of solemnities, carrying branches of palm, citron and myrtle, and singing
their Shemas and other appointed festal songs. It was
again Earth's loveliest season, when the corn was
ripening, and the hill sides were flushed with red
anemones ; when the birds were twittering among the
branches, and making the groves vocal with their earliest
melodies. It must have been a solemn and sustaining
thought to Him, that in these caravans were many
devoted followers from Galilee, who would be present in
Jerusalem during His coming hours of suffering; perhaps His own Mother among the number, and the other
holy women who were to be the last at His cross and

the first at His tomb. Ere long, He and His disciples joined the group of Pilgrims at the Ford of Jordan; crossing that burning plain,—at present the dreariest of wastes, baked with furnace heat; a heat which was then doubtless, however, tempered by the abundant vegetation. There, surrounded with gardens, palm forests, and olive groves, rose on a gentle swell where now there is nothing but a cluster of the meanest hovels, the City of Palms. " Its towers, its gates, and theatres might have won the prize from Cæsarea, and Ptolemais ; gardens of oranges, dates, and pomegranates extended from its ramparts on every side; a circus stood beyond the wall ; a college flourished within ; a town adding the charms of a Nilotic climate to the artistic beauties only to be derived from Greece. This shining city was no fit home, not even for a night, of poor Galilean boatmen, carpenters, and potters ; men who drove their own asses, baked their own bread, drew their own water, and either carried their own tents, or slept on the bare ground. So the caravan of pilgrims marched through the city, in by one gate, out by another ; the women seated on asses, the men and lads trudging beside them, bearing sprigs of myrtle and fronds of palm, the whole company singing hosanna as they wound their way past the portico of Herod and the temple of Zeus. In the western suburb of this royal city they encamped. Jesus passed through the streets with this caravan." [1]

Next day (Thursday) the procession was renewed. Passing near the fountain of Elisha, and entering the Wady Kelt, the grandest gorge in Southern Palestine, they pursued their way up the steep road, with valleys

[1] Dixon, p. 353.

of limestone on either side, leading from Jericho to Jerusalem.   The pass of the Kelt, by some (though we venture to think erroneously) identified with the Cherith of the Prophet Elijah, "is 'the going up of Adummim,' that is 'the red pass' which was on the western border of Judah ; the word is the plural of the same Hebrew root as Adam, Edom, &c., all meaning *red*. St Jerome says that the name refers to the blood so often shed by robbers on this road ; but in the Septuagint it is given as the 'pass of the red ones.'"   "It is," continues the same writer, giving a faithful description of its present features, unchanged in all material respects since Peter trode it that day with his Master—"It is a very steep and rugged ascent, with sharp angles, turning on the edge of the cliff, with the 400 or 500 feet of chasm below : but the road is everywhere protected by rough walls.   It bears traces of the old Roman work at intervals all the way to Jerusalem. From the summit we looked back once more over the plain, now beautiful in the morning light—the orange and green foliage by the winding river, like a green serpent on the sands—the blue sea, and the stern and lofty cliffs with the cleft of Wady Hesban, through which probably the Israelites arrived at the Promised Land—the Eastern and Western Mountains gradually closing in at the far north." [1]   They would pause for the night in all likelihood at the good Samaritan's Inn, the only place of shelter probably then as now in that dreary road,—the modern Khan Hoadjar, where alone among these rainless wastes a well of water is to be found : then on the morrow making an early start to complete the fatiguing journey.   The last pause

[1] Miss Beaufort's "Syrian Shrines," p. 140.

would probably be made when within sight of Bethany, to quench their thirst at the fountain then known as En Shemish, with its screen of rock and trickling water, now so familiar to all travellers as " the Fountain of the Apostles." " There are few pictures," it has been well said, " in the Gospel, more striking than this of Jesus going forth to His death, and walking alone along the path into the deep valley, while in awful reverence and mingled anticipations of dread and hope—their eyes fixed on Him, as with bowed head, He preceded them in all the majesty of sorrow—the disciples walked behind and dared not disturb His meditations. But at last, He paused, and beckoned them to Him, and then once more, for the third time, with fuller, clearer, more startling, more terrible particulars than ever before, He told them that He should be betrayed to the Priests and Scribes, by them condemned, then handed over to Gentiles ; by the Gentiles mocked, scourged, and He now for the first time revealed to them without any ambiguity the crowning horror—*crucified*, and that on the third day He should rise again." [1]

This last and most sacred pilgrimage was probably that afternoon terminated at Bethany. There the Prophet of Nazareth and His chosen followers parted company with the rest of the multitude that kept holiday. These latter would pour by thousands across the shoulder of Olivet, their enthusiasm breaking into most joyous strains at that well-known turn in the road when Herod's magnificent Temple burst in a moment on their sight on the other side of the Kedron—the same spot that was watered by the Redeemer's tears, and which, when we saw it, was sprinkled with " blood-drops "

[1] Dr Farrar, vol. i. p. 179.

(as the red anemone has after Him been touchingly called by Christian pilgrims).

From the name given it by the Latin and Greek Christians (Viri Galilæi), it has been conjectured that the most northerly summit of Olivet was the spot where the disciples and the other worshippers from Galilee were in the habit of pitching their tents on the recurrence of the great festivals.[1] On the present occasion, however, it is more than probable that night quarters would be provided for the immediate followers of Jesus in the home of Lazarus, which we have reason to believe from various incidental touches in the story of Bethany was not the dwelling of poverty, as it is often represented to be, and therefore not so limited as others in its accommodation. To be lodged however in a house, or even within walls, was, at the time of the Passover, the exception, not the rule.   " The thousands on thousands were content with the little green booths called *Succoth*, a wattle of twigs and leaves, such as Jacob had made for himself in Canaan, and such as the Sharon peasant still builds for his family at the Jerusalem gate.   Mizpeh, Olivet, Gibeon, Rephaim, sparkled with these booths and tents.   The slopes of the Kedron being alive with men and women with sheep and goats, with camels and asses, while the great fountains of En-rogel and Siloam were thronged with girls drawing water for man and beast." [2]

Such is a picture of that eventful evening when Peter, and Peter's great Lord, saw the sun sinking over the brow of Olivet, and lighting up with varied hues of purple and amethyst the line of the Moab hills.

[1] Reland *in loco*.   [2] " The Holy Land," p. 145.

During that ever-memorable week, Jesus crossed and recrossed Olivet by the familiar road to the same congenial home ; forgetting, amid the scenes matchless in Palestine for their varied interest, the strife of tongues in Jerusalem ; and in the sweet friendship of those He loved, banishing deeper sorrows, which like gathering thunder-clouds were closing around Him.

It was on one of these journeys (the second morning of the Passion week), that He pronounced the doom on the barren fig-tree. This must have occurred some time in the early part of the day. On returning to Bethany, the disciples might possibly fail in the dusk of evening to recognise the completeness of the withering ; but following the same path next morning, Peter, ever vigilant, turned his Master's attention to the solitary, shrivelled, blighted cumberer, "Master, behold the fig-tree which Thou cursedst is withered away." Upon which the Divine Teacher inculcated a lesson, needful for them all in the future of their Apostleship, and specially when in a few days they would see Him scorfed and buffeted and crucified. They might take this exercise of His power and sovereignty in the world of nature as a pledge of similar potency in the domain of Providence and grace, " Have faith in God " (Mark xi. 22).

Either the same, or possibly the next day, was one which seems to have impressed itself deeply on the mind of Peter ; for in St Mark's Gospel, he specially puts his own name first, in describing a memorable scene and interview on the summit of the Mount of Olives.

Jesus had quitted the Temple for the last time. One of His many adherents had directed His attention to the grandeur of the pile of buildings He was now leaving ; to stair and cloister, gate and pillar, stones of cyclopean size, plates of gold and silver gleaming on wall and roof in the sunset.

His own Apostles listened for the moment in silence to His strange reply, that the hour was on the wing when all that mass of gorgeous magnificence would become a pile of desolation ! They retain their silence till they have crossed the Kedron gorge and climbed the caravan road to Bethany,—the same which He had traversed on the occasion of His triumphal entrance, and from which the city appears, despite of the intervening valley, so peculiarly near. " The stones could be seen from the opposite hill, so that a man might have counted the tiers, and told off the mason work ; here the grand art of Solomon, marked with the Tyrian bevel ; there the more hasty labour of Nehemiah, showing columns of porphyry and serpentine flung into the mass ; the whole riveted and topped with the less solid, but more regular masonry of Herod the Great."[1] The hum of busy tents and encampments is all around ; but they select some secluded grassy knoll where they may seat themselves in the cool of the evening and unburden their thoughts. Peter, joined by James, John, and Andrew, interrogate confidentially the Master about the strange mysterious prediction they had just heard Him utter. No wonder that both the scene and the prophetic utterances imprinted themselves indelibly on the mind of our Apostle. The discourse was the most solemn and impressive of all Jesus had delivered : and the outer framework surely was a fit setting to it. As they gazed right and left on the mountains round about Jerusalem,—and

" The Holy Land," p. 366.

in front, across the deep *crevasse* of the Kedron, on the glittering masses of white marble reddened with the last fires of day, there was truly no hyperbole—no poetical licence or exaggeration—in the words of the Minstrel King as applied to the " perfection of beauty " beheld at that sunset hour—" Beautiful for situation, the joy of the whole earth, is Mount Zion ; on the sides of the north, the city of the Great King ! " Who need wonder that one of those, whose eyes then gazed upon this earthly " apocalyptic vision," should afterwards, when the visions of Heavenly glory were stealing over him, have made the transcendent human scene suggestive of a grander and more enduring verity—" the holy city, the New Jerusalem," with its gates of pearl, and its streets of gold, " coming down from God out of Heaven prepared as a bride adorned for her husband " (Rev. xxi. 2). Let the minstrel of the " Fall of Jerusalem " complete the picture of that vision of loveliness on which the eye of Peter, and we may add the eye of Incarnate glory, fell.

" How boldly doth it front us ! how majestically!
  Like a luxurious vineyard, the hillside
  Is hung with marble fabrics, line o'er line,
  Terrace o'er terrace, nearer still, and nearer,
  To the blue heavens. Here bright and sumptuous palaces,
  With cool and verdant gardens interspersed ;
  Here towers of war that frown in massy strength,
  While over all hangs the rich purple eve.
          .   .   .   .   Behold the Temple
  In undisturbed and lone serenity,
  Finding itself a solemn sanctuary
  In the profound of Heaven. It stands before us
  A mount of snow, fretted with golden pinnacles !
  The very sun, as though he worshipped there,

> Lingers upon the gilded cedar roofs :
> And down the long and branching porticoes,
> On every flowery, sculptured capital,
> Glitters the homage of his parting beams." [1]

" Master, seest Thou what manner of stones and what buildings are here ? "

" There shall not one stone be left upon another that shall not be thrown down."

Peter might afterwards contrast this with another saying regarding a more enduring Rock and Temple. " Upon this Rock I will build my Church, and the gates of hell shall not prevail against it ! "

On the Thursday morning of that great week, the favoured Apostle was selected along with John to go into Jerusalem to make preparation for the keeping of the Passover. Jesus gave these two messengers specific directions as to how, in the densely-crowded state of the city at that time, a chamber could be secured for the sacred celebration. Dr Hanna observes with regard to this joint errand of Peter and John, that " though often singularly and closely associated afterwards, this, I believe, was the only time that Christ separated them from all the rest, and gave them a conjunct task to perform. In sending them before the others, He could easily and at once have indicated where the room was in which they were to meet in the evening; instead of this He gives them a sign, the following of which was to conduct them to it. This way of ordering it, whatever was its real purpose, served effectually to conceal from the others the locality of the guest-chamber, and may have been meant to keep the traitor in the meantime in

---

[1] Milman's " Fall of Jerusalem."

ignorance of a fact, his earlier knowledge of which communicated to the Chief Priests might have precipitated the catastrophe, and cut off Gethsemane from our Saviour's passion."[1]

Their omniscient Lord told them, that on entering the Eastern gate of the city they would meet a hired servant bearing a pitcher of water from one of the fountains of the Kedron. They were to follow the footsteps of this water-carrier till they reached a house the master of which would bid them welcome, and shew them an upper room already furnished and plenished for the feast. "At noon all work was laid aside, and all leaven destroyed, unleavened bread alone being lawful food for the next eight days. In the Temple the evening sacrifice was offered an hour earlier than on other days, for the number of Passover-lambs to be slain before night-fall was immense. During this week the whole company of priests was on duty; and the courts of the Temple were crowded with the multitudes of Jews who had come up to the city to keep the Passover and brought their lambs to slay for the Paschal supper, which had to be eaten that night; the first day of the Passover beginning as soon as the stars became visible in the sky. Peter and John . . . had to choose and buy a suitable lamb, carry it up to the Temple, and see that it was roasted for supper. . . . .

"On this day the evening sacrifice was offered about half-past two, immediately after which the slaying of the Passover began. Probably the disciples were in the first division of those who brought their lambs; for at the fall of evening, as soon as the stars shone in the sky, the feast was ready. Christ had been lingering on

[1] Dr Hanna's "Passion Week," p 280.

Olivet, where the hymns and hallelujahs from the
Temple might reach His ear, with the blast of the silver trumpets which told that the Paschal lamb was
slain.   But as the evening drew on, He descended the
Mount with His disciples, and entered the city unob-
served in the twilight. . . . .

" The pre-occupation of the people freed the little
group of men from observation, as well as the twilight,
which was darkening the streets.   Every Jew must eat
the Passover that night, in his best and festive garments.
Many of those who had been latest in the Temple, were
hurrying homewards with the lamb that had yet to be
roasted for the supper.   All of them were too much
engrossed in the celebration of the feast to give more
than a passing thought to the band of Galileans, but
dimly seen, who were following the Prophet of Nazareth through the streets. . . . .

" It was still early in the evening when they reached
the large upper chamber where the feast was prepared
for them." [1]

Peter, as he had been sent beforehand to prepare, so
was he conspicuous as one of the privileged guests in
the *Cœnaculum*.   After partaking of the Paschal Supper, the sacramental memorial of Redeeming love was
instituted.   All that is hallowed and sacred in thought
must ever gather round that quiet sanctuary.   It is a
beautiful family meeting where He who on other occasions
is either brought before us as the Homeless One, or else
as the guest of others, is now Himself the Master of the
feast.   The disciples are " seated under their Beloved's
shadow with great delight."   It was a second Mount of

[1] "The Wonderful Life," pp. 177-8, a recent history of our Lord, written with the charm of simplicity and reverence.

Transfiguration. But besides the " decease that He was so soon to accomplish at Jerusalem," there were super-added themes of ineffable comfort for the Church on earth, with sublime vista-views of the " many mansions," and the Eternal glory ;—the crown rising above the Cross. Well might Peter on that hallowed ground have renewed his exclamation, " Lord, it is good for us to be here."

Before partaking of the sacred symbols, there occurs the touching incident of the washing of the disciples' feet by the Great Master Himself. " When the Holy Jesus," says Jeremy Taylor, " had finished His last Mosaic rite, He descends to give example of the first fruits of Evangelical grace." The act itself was in harmony with the other parts of our Lord's teaching. We have indeed at times that teaching enforced and illus. trated in the continuous, systematic discourse ; but we have, more frequently still, great and eternal truths which He wished to impress on the heart not only of His hearers but of humanity, set forth in significant rite and emblem. Now it is outer nature—the scenes around Him,—now it is the bread which feeds the hungering multitudes, or the water drawn at the way-side well—(the conjoint staff of daily life) which are made the exponents and interpreters of spiritual verities. And so it was in the present case. A lesson is to be read to the disciples and the Church by means of an acted parable.

The simple Gospel narrative has thus been graphi-cally expounded by a recent writer. " On arriving in the upper room, after the hot and dusty afternoon walk from Bethany, the first refreshment needed by the weary disciples was the loosening of their sandals, and the bathing of their feet. To perform this kindly office was usually the duty of the host, but on occasion of the Passover when rooms were lent gratuitously to parties of visitors to Jerusalem, it was expected that the guests would provide for their own comfort in this, as in other respects. Nor could the household servants be spared at so busy a time to wait upon the visitors. Only the laver was ready, with the cool water, and the linen towels. Yet no one of the disciples would stoop to perform the service to the rest. The condescension seemed too great, the old strife broke out, as to " which of them should be the greatest." In the end it seemed as if they would have to take their places at the table weary and unrefreshed, and with mutual rancour in their hearts, when Jesus Himself solves the difficulty, inculcating at the same time great lessons of purity and humility upon them all; " He riseth from supper," *i.e.* from the supper-table, before the meal had begun, " and laid aside His (upper) garments, and took a towel and girded Himself. After that He poureth water into the laver, and began to wash the disciples' feet, and to wipe them with the towel wherewith He was girded." [1] How impressive an example for engaging in those lowly works and services of charity which He had so often inculcated; denying themselves, and stooping to the infirmities and necessities of the poor and suffering! He administers a significant rebuke to human pride. " Ye call me Master and Lord, and ye say well; for so I am. If I then, your Lord and Master, have washed your feet, ye also ought to wash one another's feet. For I have given you an example, that ye should do as I have done to you" (John xiii. 13–15). It was a pattern

[1] Dr Green, pp. 42, 43.

exhibited by the Master to be followed, not in the letter, but in the spirit; not by the ostentatious ablutions practised in Easter week by the Papal hierarch, who in affected humility washes in a golden ewer the feet of twelve extemporised pilgrims; but the exercise of those silent offices of love, by which the greatest as well as the humblest member of the household of faith can help and comfort those who are in anywise afflicted and distressed in mind, body, or estate. " Inasmuch as ye did it to one of the least of these my brethren, ye did it unto me." [1]

When Peter's turn came in the touching ceremonial, with mingled humility and pride he resents the thought of his Master stooping to so mean an office, and curtly refuses the offered service. He asks, with astonishment and displeasure, and under a deep consciousness of his unworthiness, " Lord, dost Thou wash my feet ?"—' Thou whose brows I so lately saw encircled with unutterable glory on the Mount, receiving homage from the greatest of Hebrew sires, and pronounced by the Divine voice as the Father's Beloved Son ! ' It recalls the spirit and emotions of the trembling fisherman of a former year, kneeling on the shores of Gennesaret, and exclaiming, " Depart from me, for I am a sinful man, O Lord ;" as well as the bold and arrogant reprover of his Divine Master, on the way from Hermon, " This be far from Thee, Lord." " Then cometh He to Simon

[1] Regarding the question we have already discussed of Peter's primacy or precedence over his brother Apostles, a discerning writer, previously quoted, here well remarks : " Peter is again, as in many other places, prominent— an eager speaker. But this prominence is not assigned to him by his Lord. We are not told that Jesus began with Peter. On the contrary, He began with some other of the Apostles, and ' *then* cometh He to Simon Peter ;' who does not appear to have been either the last or the first."—*Author of Essays on the Church*, p. 6.

M

Peter; and Peter saith unto Him, Lord, dost Thou wash my feet? Jesus answered and said unto him, What I do thou knowest not now; but thou shalt know hereafter. Peter saith unto Him, Thou shalt never wash my feet. Jesus answered him, If I wash thee not, thou hast no part with me. Simon Peter saith unto Him, Lord, not my feet only, but also my hands and my head" (John xiii. 6-9).[1] They then return to the table, reclining, as was the Jewish wont, on couches and cushions around it. Their Lord begins to discourse more fully than He had done before, on the mysterious cross and passion now so close at hand. The joy moreover of an otherwise joyous feast was darkened by a new, portentous shadow of evil. The startling announcement was made by those lips of tenderness, that one of their number was to turn false-hearted—"Verily I say unto you, that one of you shall betray me." The question was asked by one after another of the sorrowful guests—blank astonishment on every face—none suspecting a brother, each suspecting himself, "Lord, is it I?" Peter, under the agonizing memories of former instability and faithlessness, seems to dread more than all the rest the possibility that he may be the dastard apostate. As if anxious to be relieved of the horrible suspicion of any complicity in so foul a deed, he can, unseen by Jesus in the place he occupied on the *triclinia*, make a silent but

---

[1] The subject of Christ washing Peter's feet was often selected by the religious painters, Giotto and others. But by far the most beautiful and reverential treatment, in harmony with all the works of the great artist who was said never to have used his brush without previous prayer, is a picture by Fra Angelico. (See a careful reproduction in outline in Mrs Jameson's vol., p. 16.) She also refers to the oldest art treatment of the same Gospel incident on a sarcophagus found in the Roman catacombs.

sufficiently understood sign to the Beloved Disciple. He beckons to the latter, as he was leaning on his Master's bosom, to ascertain the whole sad truth—so that the hypocrite and traitor may be at once exposed—" Ask Him who is it."

Supper being ended, and Judas having gone out to consummate his villanous purpose, renewed reference was made by the Divine Lord to the hour of trial. " Little children, yet a little while I am with you. Ye shall seek me : and as I said unto the Jews, Whither I go ye cannot come, so now I say to you." Peter was again the first to speak. The words jarred and grated on his spirit. The others maintained awe-struck silence —they sit like Mary of Bethany at the Master's feet; but this Martha of his sex must probe the mysterious secret about these valedictory utterances. " Lord, whither goest Thou ? " Jesus intimated to him that the awful journey to the mount of suffering was to be made alone —" Whither I go thou canst not follow Me now." But, giving His disciple the first hint of future and remote fellowship in His sufferings, He adds " thou shalt follow Me afterwards." The latter is not content with the reply ; he is doubtless honest and sincere in his expression and feeling of reverence and devotion, nor can we even question his courage. Perhaps at that moment he carried on his person the sword which he afterwards unsheathed in defence of a life dearer than his own. Little knowing the weakness and treachery of his own heart, and the fitfulness of his best frames, he presumptuously refuses to acknowledge any reason why he may not accompany his Lord, even if that should involve martyrdom ; — " Why cannot I follow Thee now ? " adding the still more confident assertion, " I will lay

down my life for Thy sake." Jesus addresses to him
the severest of rebukes, couched in the announcement which Peter could not fail to reject with in-
credulity, viz., that before cock-crowing, or the early
morning watch, he would be guilty of a shameful
threefold denial of Him he now boasted that he would so
faithfully serve.[1] It is worthy of note also, that on this
one occasion alone, as given by St Luke, Jesus calls him
by his Rock-name, "Peter;" perhaps to remind him of
his own weakness and recal the source whence alone his
rock-like strength was derived.   Moreover He made no
secret to him, as they still sat at the Feast, that he
would become the victim of Satanic assault; Satan
would try to "sift him as wheat:" revealing too sadly
that all these loud vain-glorious protestations were but
as the chaff of the summer's threshing-floor; accompanying, however, the warning with the gracious assurance
that "though he fall, yet would he not be cast down
utterly," for He, his faithful Lord, would "uphold him
with His right hand."   "*But* I have prayed for thee,
that thy faith fail not."   "The vision set before him,"
says Dean Stanley,[2] "is not of the future, but of the
present and the past; not clothed in the imagery of the
national prophecies, but of that Book which above all
others in the Old Testament speaks of the struggles and
temptations of the individual man in the presence of his
Maker.   It is the opening of the Book of Job that fur-
nishes the medium through which the inward and
spiritual contest is represented to the outward sense.

---

[1] St Mark, as usual, records two points which enhance the force of the
warning and the guilt of Peter, viz., that the cock would crow twice, and
that after such warning he repeated his protestation with greater vehemence.
—*Bib. Dict.*, ii. 800.

[2] Stanley's Sermons and Essays on the Apostolic Age, pp. 152, 153.

As in a previous occasion peculiar to this same Gospel, it had been said on the return of the Seventy, ' I beheld Satan fall from heaven like lightning,' as if the court of heaven had been opened before him, and at the triumph of good the Accuser had visibly fallen from his wonted place amongst the sons of God ; so here the same scene is again displayed, but with its brightness overcast by the coming on of the 'hour and the power of darkness,' brought before us also in this especial Gospel with a vividness and emphasis peculiar to itself (Luke xxii. 53). ' It is,' if we may so far bring out the latent image implied in the sacred words, ' It is no light trial which is now impending over you ; it was no slight demand which has, as it were even now, been made and obtained by the Great Adversary as he stood before the throne of heaven, and received permission from the Most High to sift as on a threshing-floor the good from the bad who are mixed up in your company. But, great as the trial will be to all, and, above all, to thee, the first and chief Apostle, fear not. One there was, who at that moment sent up His prayer to the Father that *thou* at least mightest come through victorious, that *thy* faith might not sink under the terrors of the coming distress ; and it will be for *thee* therefore, whensoever the time may come, that thy spirit shall revive, and that thou shalt turn again from thy flight . . . to support those whose faith has even more than given way under the danger ; when thou hast known what it is to be tried thyself, thou wilt be the better able to strengthen others.' " [1]

[1] It has been noted that in this address of Jesus, the word "you" (plural in the first part) includes all the Apostles, who were to be subject to this assault of the Evil One, and to succumb to it. But "thou," in the second part, is addressed to Peter, as the one against whom the onset would be mainly directed, and moreover who was specially to enjoy the benefit of

The great Hallel was now sung—that cluster of time-honoured Psalms which had been for long centuries used on the same occasion by thousands and tens of thousands, and which that very evening were being intoned by thousands more, closing with the strangely appropriate words—words that became for all future ages the Hymn of Redeemed Humanity in looking back on that night of nights and on the day which followed :—

> "God is the Lord, which hath shewed us light :
> Bind the sacrifice with cords,
> Even unto the horns of the altar.
> Thou art my God, and I will praise Thee :
> Thou art my God, I will exalt Thee.
> O give thanks unto the Lord ; for He is good :
> For His mercy endureth for ever."—*Ps.* cxviii. 27-29.

Then followed the valedictory address contained in the 14th, 15th, and 16th chapters of St John's Gospel ; and though Peter's name is not specially mentioned as one of the auditors, we know that he was so. At the close of the 14th chapter the Divine Speaker suddenly interrupts His farewell words of comfort, as if some sudden impulse had seized Him, or some inner voice had whispered that "His hour was come." He pauses, and gives the summons, " Arise, let us go hence !" Hence ! Where ? From the hour of sweet communion to the place and the season of conflict.

They descended from the large upper room to the streets jubilant with the festive music and the hurrying crowds. Then issuing forth by the southern gate, the

---

his Master's prayers. "I have prayed for *thee,* that thy faith fail not," and yet farther, that there was a promise that through him his brethren would be strengthened. "When *thou* art converted, strengthen thy brethren."— *See Arch. Whately's Lectures,* p. 19.

distant olive-grove would come in sight. He dare not keep His disciples longer in ignorance of the impending trial. Proceeding, as we may suppose for a while in profound silence, wrapt in meditative thought, with a strange undefined presentiment of what was at hand, He makes the revelation, "All ye shall be offended because of Me this night: for it is written, 'I will smite the Shepherd, and the sheep of the flock shall be scattered abroad'" (Matt. xxvi. 31). Peter is the first as usual to speak. His words are a renewed protestation of his fidelity and allegiance. Perhaps from former reproofs, he had good reason to believe that his great Master had little confidence in his steadfastness, less so than in all the others. His natural pride was wounded at such implied exception ; and in half resentful language he makes anew the asseveration, " Though all shall be offended because of Thee, yet will I never be offended." His Lord briefly repeats the warning of the cock-crowing, which would ere long convict him, not of one, but of a three-fold denial. We might have expected that he would have received the renewed reproof in silence and in tears. But nothing will daunt his boastful fortitude. " Though I should die with Thee," is his avowal, "yet will I not deny Thee." His Lord does not condescend on a second answer. He meets the assertion with an ominous silence. A few hours would reveal the sad fickleness and frailty of a wavering heart. " The hour is *now* come," says Christ again, as they have reached the depths of the valley (to Him truly in a figurative sense " the Valley of the Shadow of Death ") " that ye shall be scattered every man to his own, and shall leave me alone." The disciples were very familiar with that road, especially so during the preceding days. Each evening of that eventful week, as we have seen, had been spent in the Village of Bethany. Doubtless therefore, in rising from the supper table, and taking the wonted path conducting to the Mount, most (or all) of them would imagine that their Divine Master was about to resort as heretofore to the same hallowed retreat, and renew congenial seclusion and fellowship among the friends He loved. But on reaching the gate of the olive garden, there is a different resolve announced, and He thus alike prepares them and Him-self for His hour of trial, " Sit ye here while I go and pray yonder."

Let us endeavour farther to picture that walk in which Peter occupies so prominent a place. They would descend from Mount Zion either by the King's Gardens, or else traverse the pathway, which in all likelihood would lead then, as it does now, under the Eastern wall of the city. In either case, they would cross the Valley of Jehoshaphat where the Kedron, swollen it may be by the last of the latter rains, mur-mured along its rocky gorges, " flowing through ranges of graveyards into the desert on its way into the Dead Sea : the ledges of hill dropping down to this brook being terraced for vineyards and olive woods ; . . . the bare rock on its sides shaped into the monuments of forgotten priests and kings." [1]   It was not my privilege to be at Jerusalem during Passion Week, but under a clear full moon with its attendant stars a month pre-vious, I was able by looking in the direction of Geth-semane from the opposite side of the Valley, to carry away undying impressions of that supreme moment of

[1] "The Holy Land," p. 336.

the Incarnation ;—the descent to the Kedron—the smooth grassy plateaux of " The Mount " studded here and there with groups of olive, all under the impressive silence and stillness of an oriental night. Imagination was perhaps left the more free to reject the traditional site of the Garden, with its present obtrusive modern wall, and to follow that company of woe-worn, sorrow-stricken pilgrims of old to some quieter nook, not far off, bathed in that same silvery moonlight, and before Olivet's wealth of trees had fallen under the axes of the Roman conqueror. The disciples with their adorable Master ascended slowly that opposite sward or pathway, probably between our eleven and twelve o'clock. Doubtless, other lights lingered in the city or among the white tents that covered the slopes of Olivet. The shadow from the opposite side of the ravine may have been projected upon Gethsemane, veiling it in partial darkness. Jesus was no stranger to that olive-grove. Some indeed suppose it to have been an orchard or farm, belonging to a disciple who had joyfully granted it to his Divine Master. St Luke, introducing the history, says, " He went *as He was wont* to the Mount of Olives." That same spot had doubtless oft before listened to His prayers ; as if He had been desirous by previous fellowship with His Father in heaven on the same hallowed ground, to consecrate *it*, and to nerve *Himself* for that struggle on which He was now to enter ! The betrayer, too, seemed to have been familiar with the favoured resort. He may have often tarried at the gate of that garden, and heard the same direc tion which was now to be given under more awful circumstances. " Sit ye here, while I go and pray yonder." Nor need we limit it to a place of devotion.

It may have shared the honour with Bethany, of being the Judean Home or lodging-place of the Divine Pilgrim. That houseless Wanderer, who slept on the plank of a fishing-boat on the Sea of Galilee, may have pillowed His weary head oft and again, on the sod underneath these sheltering olive boughs. As a stranger in the land, and a wayfaring man, He may have turned oft aside here to tarry for a night.

Peter has again a conspicuous post allotted to him in this momentous hour. While the rest of the eleven are left at the outer precincts reclining on the sward, he, along with other two out of the sacred band are permitted more nearly to approach and to be within a stone's cast of their Master. These spectators of His humiliation are the same three, the favoured "triumvirate," who we recently found had been the witnesses of His glory on the Mount of Transfiguration. "James and John had but a short time before boldly asserted that they were able to be baptized with His baptism of suffering and to drink of His cup of sorrow. Peter had just declared that he was ready to go with Him even to prison and to death. Of all His disciples, none had so confidently demanded a scrutiny; none therefore had less reason to complain that they were now placed in the front row of the battle." [1] While they follow Him amid the deeper shades of the plantation, the august Sufferer Himself seems to have plunged further still into the solitude. He must be alone. No inviolate mountain-oratory indeed has He now, as on the silent hills around Bethsaida and Magdala; but the present, as it had been with every other momentous crisis of His life, must be entered on by prayer, even though the din

[1] Blunt, p. 144.

of the festal encampments all around may, late as the hour was, have invaded and disturbed the moments of supreme devotion. A horror of great darkness comes upon Him. Mark says "He became sore amazed and very heavy." Matthew says "His soul became sorrowful"—"exceeding sorrowful" (encompassed and environed, as the word means, round and round with grief), "sorrowful even unto death." [1]

Too soon was Peter's weakness revealed and His Lord's warnings fulfilled. The divine Sufferer, coming no less than three times in these moments of intense and vehement emotion from the depths of the Olive grove to the gate of the Garden, finds His boastful disciple and his two associates asleep under the trees. He utters the withering rebuke which might well have gone as an arrow to their hearts. "What, could ye not watch with me one hour?" The slumberer in whom we are chiefly interested is specially selected for a personal reprimand. "*Simon, sleepest* THOU?" 'Thou didst promise to *die* with me, canst thou not *watch* with me? O faithless one! for whole nights hast thou toiled at thy nets at Gennesaret and surrendered hours of needed repose—on this *one* night of temptation and anguish canst thou not spare thy Lord one hour?' Coupled indeed with his previous bold and energetic protestation of unalterable devotion, Peter's faithless conduct is most strange and his guilt most aggravated. It was the season of all others when his sympathy was most needed; —when strong crying and tears and great drops of blood were the exponent of divine-human anguish. Could

---

[1] On this as specially recorded by Mark in Peter's own Gospel—Bishop Wordsworth observes:—"St Mark takes care to show that Peter had all necessary training from Christ before the denial."

he ever possibly forget these burning words of tender rebuke, I had almost said irony, with which the awful transaction closes, as perchance the red glancing torch-lights of the approaching murderers were seen, and the noise of their footsteps was heard,—"Sleep on now, and take your rest." As if He had said, 'The hour when you could have aided and comforted me is now past. You have by your unwatchfulness forfeited the one opportunity of sustaining me in the crisis of the battle.' Faithless ones, your wakefulness can be of no use to me now, "sleep on and take your rest." [1]

It would seem however, too, as if Peter had treasured up in special memory for after years the prayer of that hour of agony. It would seem as if he could not have been so oppressed with sleep as to be unconscious of some of its utterances. For it has been discriminately noticed that in his special Gospel alone, the expression "Abba, Father" is found; as if that precious name had mingled with the recollection of his disturbed slumbers.

As Peter's Lord uttered the last words I have quoted, the tramp of hostile feet seems to have been borne yet nearer to His listening ears. The first, sorest, most mysterious part of the spiritual struggle was over. He had made in vain the appeal, "Have pity upon Me, Have pity upon Me, O ye My friends, for the hand of *God* hath touched Me." Now He was about to enter on the second part of the awful drama, and to be seized by the hand of *man*.

But we need not more minutely detail the well-known narrative. Immediately after this came the armed troop with their lighted torches and rough staves,

[1] This latter portion is mainly abridged from the author's "Memories of Olivet."

THE LAST DAYS OF THE PASSION.

Roman soldiers and some emissaries from the High
Priest. Those who have beheld what I have just been
describing, a full Passover moon in Palestine, making
the night clear as day, will only see in these needless
lanterns the firm determination to prevent the possibility of escape, and of tracking, if need be, the footsteps of the Divine Victim in case He might seek
concealment amid the deeper shades of the olive-
groves. Unsanctioned by their Master, a collision
takes place between the handful of disciples and the
assassin band. As we might expect, the ungovernable
spirit of Peter takes the initiative ; and yet, may we not
extenuate his rashness by making it share the better interpretation of an act of heroic devotion in a desperate
hour,—as if he would redeem, if he could, his recent
unfaithful vigils ? Unsheathing one of the two swords
we have already noted as having been taken by the disciples to the garden, he assaulted Malchus, the High
Priest's servant. But missing a more deadly aim and
purpose he cut off his ear. Jesus at once interferes.
Mingling mercy and forgiveness in that hour of unmerited vengeance, He heals the wound, making the
last miracle before His death a deed of kindness to an
enemy,[1] and then addresses His impetuous disciple in
words of rebuke for this fresh act of indiscretion and
temerity :—"Then said Jesus unto him, Put up again

[1] The same writer on sacred art already quoted, referring to this incident, says :—"There was perhaps a tradition in the fifteenth century of the
servant having carried a lantern ; for from about that time it is always introduced (in pictures) and seen fallen with him to the ground. In a manu-
script in the Brussels Library . . . the prostrate servant catches hold of
the robe of Judas to save him : a touch of bitter satire on the painter's part,
on the blindness which could thus appeal to the sinking sinner with the Ark
of Refuge standing by."

thy sword into his place: for all they that take the sword shall perish with the sword. Thinkest thou that I cannot now pray to My Father, and He shall presently give Me more than twelve legions of angels?" (Matt. xxvi. 52, 53).

"Peter's precipitate sword," says a recent writer, "strikes a random blow; all in keeping, it might be thought, with the flashing of lanterns and the glitter of weapons, and the clamour of voices which now broke upon the still night; but all violently out of keeping with the deep resignation of the soul of Christ, and that final act of self-consecration which the band of men and officers were bringing to its accomplishment. If the sword were to be used at all, Malchus was not the person to strike at. The only chance was to slay the leader of the band, and escape, if possible, in the confusion. But, indeed, it was a mistake altogether. The sword was utterly out of place. Whole armies of men, or twelve legions of angels, were as powerless here as that one futile blow. Those awful world-moments held the everlasting ages in their grasp. Stand all aside. It was the Son's supreme agony of self-sacrifice and of obedience to the Father's will. 'Put up thy sword into the sheath.'" [1]

The Divine Sufferer having meekly resigned Himself into the hands of His captors, was led at dead of night, not in the first instance to the "*Lish-cath ha-gazith*" the meeting-place of the Sanhedrin on the Temple-hill, (that court could not be convened until the morning had advanced) but to the dwelling of Annas or Hanan, the High Priest; situated near the great bridge over

---

1 See a thoughtful and suggestive volume, "Waiting for the Light, and Other Sermons," by Rev. Mr Wright, Vicar of Stoke-Bishop.

the Xystus, " between Millo and the Armoury on the North-Eastern slope of Mount Zion."[1] All the disciples in abject terror had forsaken Him and fled, ere He had recrossed the Kedron. They may have expected some divine intervention;—the advent of some strong angel to effect His liberation. But when they beheld His hands bound with cords and no effort made on His part to wrench them away, some plunged ignominiously into the thickets or grottoes around ; others betook themselves within the walls of the city, and left their Divine Master to His fate—

> " All My disciples fly ! Fear put a bar
> Betwixt my friends and Me ; they leave the star
> Which brought the wise men from the East from far.
>   Was ever grief like Mine ! "—*George Herbert.*

Peter, however, timidly followed the crowd, but it is specially noted he " followed afar off." Had his nobler and braver nature risen to the ascendant ;—facing the jeers and buffetings of the rabble had he walked by his Master's side, and listened to the same majestic words which had calmed his fears on Gennesaret, he might have saved himself the bitterest and most mournful hours of his history. Nerved with such Divine utterances, and receiving the fresh promise of supporting grace, he might have renewed his strength and mounted up as on eagles' wings. But he cowardly skulked away in the distance. He was once more on the midnight waves and " beginning to sink."

> "Forsake the Christ thou sawest transfigured, Him
> Who trod the sea, and brought the dead to life ?
> What should wring this from thee ? Ye laugh and ask
> What wrung it ? Even a torchlight and a noise,

---

[1] Dr Barclay's " City of the Great King."

The sudden Roman faces, violent hands,
And fear of what the Jews might do !   Just that,
And it is written, ' I forsook and fled.'
There was my trial, and it ended thus."—*Browning*.

It has often been remarked in connection with this melancholy defection, how the most distinguished saints of Holy Writ are found to have made shipwreck of faith and of a good conscience in the very circumstances where we might least have expected failure or disaster: —that the graces which shone most conspicuous in their characters were those which were most mournfully blighted in the hour of strong temptation.   It was the Father of the faithful who swerved from his fidelity by stooping to unworthy equivocation.   It was the meek Moses who spake unadvisedly with his lips.   It was the patient Job who gave way to murmuring and fret-fulness.   It was the lion-hearted Elijah who fled panic-stricken at the threats of an impotent woman.   It was the loving and tender-hearted John who in a moment of strange passion would call down fire from heaven. It was the courageous Peter who could defy winds and waves, or do battle in later times with a whole San-hedrin, who became renegade and coward in the hour when heroic heart and deed were most needed : aye, whose cowardice was about to shape itself into crimes of yet deeper dye.   Truly over his failure and that of all the others, the utterance of the Great Apostle may well be written " By the grace of God I am what I am."[1]

" Thus," says a writer whose description brings suc-cinctly together the salient parts of the narrative, " the sad procession passed on to the High Priest's house,

---

[1] See Blunt on St Peter.

which, though it was night, was lighted up for the trial; a kind of irregular assembly, preparatory to an early meeting of the Sanhedrim, being convened at that unusual hour, perhaps to make sure of their fatal work, perhaps from fear of popular tumult, perhaps to save appearances, and to procure the condemnation and death of Jesus before the Passover festivities.   John, who was known to Caiaphas, went boldly into the place of assembly; Peter remaining at the doorway until John used his interest with the portress, and brought Peter into the court—the great quadrangular hall, shut off from the street by a high wall, in which were folding gates, with a wicket at their side for passing in and out on foot.   Here, no doubt, stood "the damsel who kept the door" after the mass of people had been admitted through the large gates, now closed.   The rooms of the Palace were entered from the three sides of the square: in one of these the council was assembled, with Jesus before them: the soldiers remained in the quadrangle, the entrance from which to the council hall remained open.   It is necessary to bear all this in mind, fully to understand the melancholy scene that followed."[1]   "Besides the *mandarah*, some houses have an apartment called *mak'ad*, open in front to the court, with two or three more arches, and a railing and a pillar to support the wall above (*Lane*, i. 38).   It was in a chamber of this kind, probably one of the largest size to be found in a palace, that our Lord was being arraigned."[2]

The night being cold, coming from the frosty air and

[1] Dr Green, 49, 50.   "Tradition asserts that John had become acquainted with the family of the High Priest while still engaged in his original calling."—*Lange*.

[2] Bib. Dict. vol. i. 838.

chill dews of the Jehoshaphat Valley, Peter joined the
soldiers and servants as they gathered around a brazier
or charcoal fire in that open quadrangle, warming his
hands.[1] He had foolishly imagined that he would
have been unrecognised in the strange place. It is
even evident that he had injudiciously and discredit-
ably entered into promiscuous conversation with those
sharing in the popular frenzy, traducing his Master
and thirsting for his Master's blood. The foretold
hour of unworthy denial came. The young portress,
probably a female slave, who had first admitted him,
appears to have been relieved at her post by another,
and meanwhile joined the circle round the brazier.
Holding up her lighted lamp to Peter's face, as he sat
in ill-suppressed terror and excitement, she charged
him with being a friend and accomplice of Jesus :
" Thou also wast with Jesus of Nazareth." But
he seeks by an unworthy equivocation to evade an
answer, pretending not to comprehend the precise drift
of the question ; he thought that perhaps thus he
might escape a further scrutiny and be saved the baseness of a more direct falsehood—" I know not what
thou sayest." The first fatal step being taken, another
quickly follows. According to Peter's own recollection
(for the picture seems to have been minutely engraven
in his inmost heart, Mark xiv. 66–72), he seems to
have stealthily crept away from the glow of the

---

1 It was now past midnight. Those who have travelled in Palestine at
the same season of the year will endorse the naturalness and accuracy of this
incidental touch in the narrative, as to the grateful heat from the brazier.
Often have I felt in tent-life there, that when the early part of the night
was balmy, pleasant, and "summer-like," the early morning hours were intensely cold, so much so as to render additional clothing not only acceptable but necessary.

firelight to the outer porch of the hall, possibly to secure a retreat from his perilous position. As daybreak was approaching, he heard, and yet he seems to have heard as if he heard not, a strange reprover there in the crowing of a cock. The glance of another suspicious eye is upon him. The second portress, to whom we have just alluded, repeats the accusation. She communicates her shrewd suspicions to "them that stood by:"—these bystanders, we may well believe, being animated with the deadliest hatred to the cause of Jesus. The miserable man plunges deeper into the morass. It is indeed with him the hour and power of darkness. A second denial follows. He now disclaims all knowledge of his kind and affectionate Master. Who can imagine the conflict of cowardice and shame and mental reproach which he then must have undergone?

But lower still has he to sink ere he emerges from the depths of his degradation. He felt retreat from where he was now to be impossible; and yet with that foolhardihood in its most terrible phase which we have seen to be his natural characteristic and failing—as if he would brave his baseness to its direful end rather than surrender, he returns again to join the group of servants and idlers at the fireplace. His doom and disgrace are now inevitable. They confront him anew with the charge. They are fortified and confirmed in their accuracy by hearing his Galilean accent, the peculiarity of which, says De Wette, was "that the gutturals were not properly pronounced;"—to which Lange adds the curious statement, that "the pronunciation of the people of Galilee was so uncouth and indistinct, that they were not allowed to read aloud in the Jewish Synagogue. The Talmudists relate a number of anecdotes about the curious misunderstandings occasioned by the indistinctness of pronunciation in Galilee." "Thy speech bewrayeth thee,"—was therefore a new, and to Peter an unexpected testimony confirmatory of his guilt. A relative of the servant he had wounded at Gethsemane, and who had seen him there, adds his damning testimony; one after another of the excited group hurls a missile on the unhappy apostle. But it only makes him turn to bay, and with the coarse aggravation of oaths and curses once more to deny any knowledge of the Lord who bought him. "It is to be observed," says Greswell, "that the moral lesson furnished by this most impressive and instructive incident is wonderfully enhanced, if it appears, as it must do now, that the number of times for which it was predicted that Peter should deny his Master, and the number of times for which he protested, in the confidence of a genuine sincerity, that he would rather die than deny Him, and the number of times for which, on being put to the test, he *did* deny Him, were precisely the same."[1] Thus tersely too does Lange note the gradations of his guilt. "Ambiguous evasion, distinct denial, awful abjuration." He has reached the sad climax—a position, excepting that of Judas, unparalleled almost in the annals of human ingratitude.

But He who came to His sinking disciple in the deepest darkness of stormy Gennesaret, comes to him now. He sends, probably at this moment, for the second time, the same humble instrument already employed to enkindle feelings of shame and remorse. While the stars are still shining in the early morning sky, the shrill voice

1 Greswell's Dissertations.

of the cock again greets the ear of the self-blinded one. And far more than this—more than gleam of lightning or voice of thunder, or sword of avenging angel—a LOOK penetrates to the inmost recesses of his soul. Peter had imagined he was beyond the cognisance of Jesus. He never dreamt that his words of denial and perjured curses would reach his Master's ear. It has been surmised that the eyes of the Master and the disciple may have met as the former was being led away bound to Caiaphas across the court where the Apostle was then standing.[1] At all events, at that moment, with a glance not to be mistaken, never to be forgotten,—"a glance of more than human power, and more than human tenderness,"—"the Lord turned, and looked upon Peter. And Peter remembered the word of the Lord, how He had said unto him, Before the cock crow, thou shalt deny Me thrice. And Peter went out, and wept bitterly" (Luke xxii. 61, 62). Or, as St Mark expresses it, "And when he thought thereon, he wept." The simple wording of Peter's repentance in "Peter's own Gospel" is surely

1 I have followed the "harmony" which seems the most satisfactory one and most generally accepted, detailed in the following note:—"The difficult question of the harmony of the various accounts cannot here be fully entered into. If we allow ourselves to conceive that in the narrative of St John the first and second denials are transposed, and that the first took place at going *out*, rather than coming *in*, there would seem to result this very natural account,—that the *first* denial took place at the fire (Matt. xxvi 69, Mark xiv. 66, Luke xxii. 55, John xviii. 25), and was caused by the fixed recognition (Luke xxii 56) of the maid who admitted St Peter ; that the *second* took place at or near the door leading out of the court, to which fear might have driven the Apostle (Matt. xxvi. 71, Mark xiv. 63, Luke xxii. 58, John xviii. 17), and that the *third* took place in the court about an hour afterwards (Luke xxii. 59), before several witnesses who urged the peculiar nature of the Apostle's harsh Galilean pronunciation, and near enough to our Lord for Him to turn and gaze upon His now heart-touched and repentant follower."—*Ellicott's Life of Our Lord*, p. 333, *with authorities.*

worthy of passing note, as an additional testimony to what has often been observed, how when in his declining years he came to dictate the story of his life, he ever seeks to keep his goodness in the shade, and brings always into emphatic prominence his faults and failings. He authorises, or rather instructs, St Mark graphically to describe the sad story of the threefold denial; but in the present instance, lest he should seem to exaggerate his feelings of penitential sorrow, he records of himself simply that "he wept," while the other faithful chroniclers specially mention that "he wept *bitterly*." We can picture, and no more, what that soul-penetrating "look" would be! How, like scathing fire of heaven, it would flash conviction and rebuke on his seared conscience. All the more so, that it would not be a look of wrath and vengeance, but rather such as would instantaneously photograph all the three past years of unvarying kindness and amazing privilege. The Apostle's heart was broken.

> " The rock is smitten, and to future years,
> Springs ever fresh the tide of holy tears."
>
> .   .   .   .   .
>
> " That gracious chiding look, Thy call
> To win him to himself and Thee,
> Sweetening the sorrow of his fall,
> Which else was rued too bitterly."

We cannot truly wonder at the bitterness of these tears, when, at the risk of recapitulating, we attempt to gather up in a sentence all the peculiar aggravation of Peter's sin. None of the Apostles had been more loved, more trusted, more honoured than he; enjoying constant and endearing intercourse with his Lord; ad-

mitted into the inner circle of fellowship; the auditor
of these matchless discourses spoken on Mount Hattin;
the witness of these miracles of power alike in Capernaum and Jerusalem. He had beheld the glory of the
Transfiguration—an eye-witness there of his Lord's
majesty; he had sat a guest at the supper-table, listening
to those valedictory words of kindness which must have
reminded him more of a Parent speaking to his children,
than a Master to disciples; he had partaken of the
consecrated bread, and drank the sacramental cup, the
emblems and memorials of Redeeming love, and the
ratification of previous vows of allegiance. With reiterated protestations he had said, "Whatsoever others
do, as for me, I will serve the Lord." We might well
have expected that if any grew apostate and renegade,
it would not be he who walked fearlessly at his Master's
bidding on the midnight wave, who nobly confessed His
Divinity at Cesarea Philippi, and avowed, almost in
the words spoken by the young Moabitess of olden time,
"Where Thou goest, I will go; . . . death itself shall
not separate between Thee and me." Yet at this critical
moment, when his Redeemer stood companionless and
alone among His foes, "a lamb dumb before His
shearers," uncheered by one sympathising look in the
palace-hall of Caiaphas—nay, rather, surrounded by
an infuriated throng of blasphemers, who are soon to
wreak upon Him their vengeance—His tender heart is
wounded most of all by the faithlessness of His own
familiar friend. Peter might even have made some
partial amends and compensation now for the slumber
of Gethsemane. He might by his presence and looks
have given the meek Sufferer the assurance that

amid that surging crowd, with their rough jostling, cruel taunts, and ribald jests, there was one heart at least that beat true to Him in its unvarying and unswerving attachment. But memory and heart seemed to be strangely dormant and extinct; the lips that should have been employed in intercession and sympathy are debased by a cruel falsehood; and the profane swearing, which we could only expect in the mouth of Roman soldier, or debased publican, or sceptic Sadducee, is emitted from the tongue of him who a few hours before had exulted in being a disciple of "the Holy One of God."

> " Did I yesterday
> Wash thy feet, My beloved, that they should run
> Quick to deny Me, 'neath the morning sun?"
> —*Browning.*

As he rushed out amid the chill of early morn to the grassy ridges of Jehoshaphat, "dewy with Nature's tear-drops," how the recalled words of better days must have rung like a knell in his ears:—"Whosoever shall be ashamed of Me and of My words, of him shall the Son of Man be ashamed, when He cometh in the glory of His Father, with the holy angels." "O Lucifer, how art thou fallen! The Elijah of New Testament story turns coward the very moment we look for stout heart and brave deed. Other inspired words might be added to those which emblazon Peter's reputed tomb in Rome, '*When thou thinkest thou standest take heed lest thou fall.*'"

Such was our Apostle's deepest and saddest humiliation. But that look of penetrating love melted the faithless one. Tradition asserts, that every time afterwards Peter listened to the crowing of a cock, he fell on his knees and mourned; and that it was his wont to rise at midnight and spend the hour between cock-crowing and morning in acts of penitence and devotion. We may well reject the tradition while we accept the truth it embodies. From that day he was alike an humbled and an altered man. "Peter," says Lange, "went out into the black night, but not, as Judas, into the blackness of despair. Weeping bitterly, he awaited the dawn of another and a better morning. The Angel of Mercy accompanied him on that heavy road to spiritual self-condemnation, which issued in the death of his old man, more especially of his former pride and self-confidence. And thus it came that he really accompanied Christ unto death, though in a very different and much better sense than he intended."[1] With one solitary exception his path, in future years, is no longer chequered with shadow and darkness, but rather begins that brightness which deepened and increased to the perfect day, till at last the promise was made good, "At evening time it shall be light." The sun which had waded among threatening clouds sets in vermilion and gold; and the words thus confidently spoken were shown not to have been spoken in vain, "Lord, to whom shall we go? Thou hast the words of eternal life!" The invocation and prayer of the poet of the "Christian Year" was in his case most faithfully answered—

---

[1] Lange's Life of Christ *in loc.* The great German commentator naively adds, "Will the so-called Romish Peter ever go forth from the Palace of the High Priest, when he has denied Jesus, to weep bitterly?"

" When brooding o'er remembered sin
The heart lies down—O mightiest then,
Come ever true, come ever near,
And wake the slumbering love again,
Spirit of God's most holy fear."[1]

---

[1] "The denial of Peter occurs frequently on the ancient sarcophagi as the symbol of Repentance; and is treated with classical and sculptural simplicity, the cock being always introduced." The same writer however adds, "It has not been often painted; it seems to have been avoided in general by the early Italian painters, as derogatory to the character and dignity of the Apostle." . . . "The maiden, whose name in the old traditions is Balilla, is always introduced with a look and gesture of reproach, and the cock is often perched in the background."—*Sacred and Legendary Art*, p. 197.

CHAPTER XI.

The Dread Interval.

PETER'S FEELINGS DURING THE CRUCIFIXION. HIS ABODE WITH
JOHN. THE LORD'S RESURRECTION. THE SPECIAL MESSAGE
TO PETER. THE SPECIAL INTERVIEW. PEACE BE UNTO YOU.

> " And can I be the very same,
> Who lately durst blaspheme Thy name,
> And on Thy Gospel tread !
> Surely each one who hears my case,
> Will praise Thee, and confess Thy grace,
> Invincible indeed."—*John Newton.*

" Except Judas the traitor, none fell so low as Peter. . . . .
Lord, what is man ! What is our boasted strength but weakness !
and if we are left unto ourselves, how do our most solemn resolutions melt like snow before the sun ! Be Thou surety for Thy
servants for good ! "—*Doddridge.*

" A piece of timber on the water may easily be drawn with the
hand of a man ; but on the land it cannot be stirred without much
greater strength. So is it with sin upon the conscience. In the
time of committing it, nothing is more easy ; but in the time of
judging it, nothing is more insupportable."—*Bishop Hopkins.*

" A bruised reed shall He not break, and smoking flax shall He
not quench, till He send forth judgment unto victory."—MATT.
xii. 20.

THE Crucifixion with its story of love and suffering is now over.

To all the disciples unspeakably bitter must have been that season of their Master's unknown anguish. How heavily must the hours have passed between the time the procession moved along the Dolorous Way and the Resurrection morning! What a different Sabbath from the pleasant ones of Galilee, when, as on their way to sick and desolate homes and weary hearts on errands of mercy, they had plucked the ears of corn, or hung on their Master's lips as He addressed the assembled crowds in Synagogue or on hillside or by pebbly beach:—Sabbaths, in which active work and deeds of divine philanthropy were beautifully blended with hours of teaching and devotion. How many hallowed unrecorded conversations on these Jewish high days must have come back to their memory, like gleams of light in the thick darkness, making them stand aghast at the thought of the present awful contrast. But specially to the one smitten heart with which we are now so familiar, almost intolerable must have been the gloom and misery and consternation. The others doubtless had their own sad reflections at the timidity which led to unworthy abandonment of their gracious Shepherd in His trial-hour :—they would mourn over the severance of a hallowed friendship :—and if they still hoped on, it was hope cherished amid almost despairing anxieties. But Peter had sorrows and remembrances too deep for tears. If he were lurking, as he may possibly have been, within hearing of the taunts and jeers and hootings of a ruffian soldiery and debased populace as they hurried his Lord to Golgotha, how must these infuriated shouts have made every wound of his spirit to bleed afresh. The usual type of Jewish mourning was the rent garment, the sprinkling with dust and ashes, and sitting in sackcloth. But these outer symbols were all too feeble to express, in his case, the intensity of his grief. As the air was rent with the exclamation, " Crucify Him, Crucify Him ;" or as the Eloi-cry ascended apparently unsuccoured to heaven—how terrible to think that to all that bitter anguish of the forsaken Jesus he had basely contributed ;—that one of the sharpest and most poignant thorns in the Crown which wreathed these bleeding brows was inserted by his ungrateful hands ; and that as memory did its work during these long and silent hours of torture, the Divine Sufferer could say with equal truth of another as of Judas—" He that ate bread with Me hath lifted up his heel against Me !" Add to all these bitter reflections, his injured Lord was now beyond reach of any renewed expression of the sincerity of His disciple's repentance. The eye which cast upon him its look of reproachful love in the courtyard of Caiaphas was now sealed in death! Well has it been observed, "There can scarce be a more poignant remorse than that which results from the conviction of unkindness to the departed,—to those who are now beyond our reach, inaccessible to the expressions of our regret, or to the offers of reparation. Such must have been the nature of Peter's grief in this mournful interval. If he could but come again to his Master, clasp His feet, confess his offence, and assure Him of his unfeigned contrition, what a relief to his burdened soul! But that Master is no more. He hath died with those grievous words ringing in His ear, with that odious ingratitude pressing heavily upon His heart. And often at the thought the Apostle's grief is renewed, and his tears flow with increased bitterness." [1]

Had he been permitted indeed to know all, it might have been different. For may we not confidently surmise that in these hours of agony and shame, when Jesus was transfixed to the cruel cross, His thoughts towards the erring one were thoughts not of severity but of love? He who pled for the expiring felon, and opened for him the Gates of Paradise—He who with His dying breath sought forgiveness for His own very murderers, would not be likely to forget the Prodigal Apostle, who had already, through passionate tears, breathed the Prodigal's prayer—"I will arise and go to my Father." "Father, forgive *them :*"—"Father, forgive

---

[1] Bishop Lee's Life of St Peter, pp. 134-133.

HIM." "I will not blot out his name out of the book of life, but I will confess his name before My Father."

Peter would seem to have taken up his abode during these never-to-be-forgotten days with John :—so we are led to infer from the fact of Mary Magdalene, as we shall presently note, finding them together (John xx. 2). Whether after the burial they had lingered nigh the grave, or, stupified with grief, had shut themselves up in John's wonted place of sojourn in Jerusalem, we cannot tell. There is something remarkable and significant, however, in their fellowship at such a time. We can only conjecture the reason. Could it be that Peter, penitent as he was, still cowered away in shame from his old associates? Or, on the other hand, might it not be that, truants as they all were from the fold, this unhappiest of wanderers was discredited and disowned by the rest? They would remember perhaps his vain boasting and bravado—the precedence he so often assumed, and which now would rekindle jealousies so recently manifested. They would have little confidence in the genuineness of his tears. While this, however, might be the case with the others, the one disciple most like his Lord in tenderness to the erring still clung to his rejected companion. Perhaps John had stolen out after him into the night, and had witnessed his bitter weeping. Perhaps he knew the solitary chamber whither his erring brother had repaired to brood gloomily on the horrible past, and had there found him out. They had mingled perchance their prayers and tears together. "As we find John at the foot of the cross, receiving the charge which, in the midst of all His own agony, the Son of Mary committed to him, 'Mother, behold thy Son; Son, behold thy Mother,' shall we say that after leading that Mother to his own house, and soothing her poignant grief as best he might, he bethought himself of his fallen friend, and went in search of Peter, whom he had seen, under the piercing, yet melting glance of their common Master's eye. . . . What might be their converse, who can guess? 'We did trust,' they might be sadly saying to one another, 'that it was He that should have redeemed Israel.' But He is gone, it may be for ever; and all seems to be lost: Hope is withered, and for our consolation, memory is all that now remains; memory, in John, of that last endearment at the Supper; in Peter, of that last offence at the trial. And yet, friendship can blend the two. The bosom on which John leaned—the eye that looked upon Peter—are now common in the sad retrospect to both. They mourn, in their sad bereavement and bitter penitence, together." [1] Peter, treated, as we have surmised, with not unmerited scorn by all the others, thus discovered in the Disciple of love a friend that sticketh closer than a brother, and saw in his generous kindness the type and pledge of a forgiveness still more coveted. Hence, we may conjecture, was the reason that Mary Magdalene revealed the astounding tidings in the first instance to these two *alone*.[2]

While the Apostles were thus indulging in conflicting feelings of amazement, and shame, and terror, others had been busy with their ministry of love and affection to the Beloved dead. Joseph of Arimathea had, on the afternoon of the Crucifixion, begged the body of Jesus, and wrapping it in a linen shroud, "laid it in a new tomb." Nicodemus too had provided a mixture of

---

[1] Dr Candlish's Scripture Miscellanies, pp. 267-269.
[2] See this well stated by Dr Green, p. 54.

myrrh and aloes, an hundred pounds weight, and embalmed the corpse. The first funeral ceremonies were necessarily hurried and incomplete. The last offices of affection to the departed were required by Jewish law to be completed before sunset, at which time the Hebrew Sabbath began, and during whose sacred hours the rites of sepulture were rigidly forbidden. Mary Magdalene, Mary the mother of James, and Salome, had after a time of sacred watching in the Garden, hurried to their homes to prepare additional costly spices for the final interment on the first day of the week,—what Lange calls "the Great Burial;"—adding, as an additional reason for a renewal of sepulchral rites, that "by the first anointing, they sought simply to preserve the body; by the second, they wished to fulfil the ceremonial requirements, for which no time remained upon Friday evening." Jesus indeed had told them, as we have found He had done His Apostles, of His death, burial, and resurrection (Luke xxiv. 6, 7). But the preparations we find them making for a more complete embalmment too truly reveals the conviction which had seized their minds, that His flesh was to share the doom of mortality and be laid in "the long home."

The spices and perfumes accordingly were duly purchased on the Friday evening; and after the hours of the Paschal Sabbath had elapsed, Mary Magdalene is seen, in the early dawn, ere the first golden beam was tipping the summit of the Mount of Olives—doubtless, too, after a day of agony and a night of sleeplessness— hastening to the spot where all she most loved lay silent in the domain of death. As she and the other Galilean women, guided by the moonlight, enter the

garden gate, their first thought is as to how they shall
be able to remove the gravestone. They are nearing
the spot. Lo! the stone is already rolled aside from
the mouth of the sepulchre. Mary, in a moment of
panic, leaves her companions, and rushes into the city,
to carry the tidings to the disciples. The thought of
rude hands pillaging the tomb and taking the loved
inmate away, alone seems to have occupied her. She
has never entertained the possibility of her Lord having
risen. She had expected to have seen His cherished
form again; to have bathed His pale countenance
with her tears, and relaid the embalmed corpse in its
rocky bed. Blinded to grander realities by her grief,
in an agony of sorrow she pours out her painful tale to
the disciples: "They have taken away the Lord out of
the sepulchre, and we know not where they have laid
Him."

Meanwhile the other women, who have lingered behind, see a young man seated in the vacant tomb, clad
in long white raiment—the emblem of gladness. He
announces the startling tidings that the Lord they loved
had risen; that He was to go before them into Galilee;
that the Sea of Tiberias and its shores were again to hear
the familar music of His voice. "He goeth before you"
(the word would seem to indicate "as a Shepherd")
"into Galilee; there shall ye see Him as He said unto
you."

Peter and John heard the strange account from the
lips of Mary. Her words to these two disconsolate
brothers seemed "foolishness." They run toward the
sepulchre; and surely the very fact of Peter thus
hastening, shows that though overwhelmed with anguish
at his aggravated sin, he was not absolutely "crushed

by his fall." The beloved Disciple, younger and fleeter in foot, outstrips his friend ; but, with feelings of sacred awe, he can do no more, on reaching the spot, than "look in." Peter, on the other hand, "with characteristic ardour"—disregarding, as other Jews would have done, ceremonial pollution—rushes inside the rocky grave, followed by his more timorous companion. They beheld with their own eyes the folded napkin and 'sindon' —the fine linen given by Joseph of Arimathea, lying by themselves (the undoubted trophies of victory), indicating no hasty or furtive abstraction of the body. With mingled doubt and perplexity, yet consolation and hope, they "went away again unto their own home !"

Does the narrative, however, furnish us with no other and more interesting clue to Peter's present conduct ? After all the sad and recent story of his apostasy and ingratitude, would even such startling tidings as he had heard tempt or warrant him without hesitation to leave the hiding-place of his cowering shame and remorse ? Had no new ray of light pierced that horror of great darkness ? Had no word of encouragement and hope, better and stronger than man could give him, been conveyed to his ears ? Yes ; undoubtedly there was. A special and most wondrous message had been brought to him by Mary Cleophas—a message direct from the celestial Warder at the tomb—which might well have brought burning tears to the eyes of one of sterner mould. "*Go*," said that Angel-guardian ; "*go your way, tell His disciples*, AND PETER." Often has imagination sought to picture the interview between this messenger of reconciliation and the trembling Apostle on that memorable morning. When Mary rehearsed to him the Angel's words, would he not be disposed at first to listen

to them as idle tales,—as a message too good, too kind
to be true? "'What!' may he not have said to her,
'have you not mistaken the name? John or Andrew,
James or Matthew, it may have been; or some peculiar
message of love and affection to His sorrowing but devoted mother; but I am the last, surely, who would
have been singled out with this special remembrance of
a love I so basely requited.'"[1] Yet it was all true; a
new testimony that "God's thoughts are not as man's
thoughts, and God's ways are not as man's ways." He
who guaged all the anguish of that smitten heart, knew
that better than all the balm of Gilead would be a
single expression of affectionate recollection and kindness from the lips of Him he had denied. "AND
PETER!" How these two little words would linger like
a strain of music in his soul. How they would follow
him every step in his way back to his native Galilee,
haunt his sleeping and waking hours, and prove like a
bright gleam in his lonely watches on the midnight sea.
Well does Bishop Wordsworth observe, on the fact of
these same words being recorded by *St Mark alone*:—
"The recital of them, treasured up by the thankful
Apostle, and recorded by his son in the faith, seems
like the thankful acknowledgment of a contrite heart,
overflowing with love for the Divine tenderness to him
after his denial. And they beautifully illustrate our
Lord's saying, that 'there is joy among the *angels* of
God over one sinner that repenteth.'"

His anxiety would seem to have led him a second
time to the vacant tomb. But now the angels were
no longer keeping vigil. After gazing on the place of
mysterious silence, "he departed, wondering in himself

[1] Water from the Well Spring, p. 65.

at that which was come to pass." Moreover, during the day, at some time and in some way not revealed to us, he evidently had a special appearance of his Divine Lord vouchsafed to him, similar to that given to Mary. We are curious to know the particulars of what doubtless must have been a most touching interview ;—where it was—how it came to pass—what words were spoken. But regarding all this, Scripture is silent. "The details may have been too personal to be revealed to us." Beautiful, however, and deeply touching is this earliest evidence of Christ's forgiving love.[1] The Risen Saviour, with His old unchanging kindness, makes it His first business to seek out the deeply erring but now deeply humbled and penitent man. The Good Shepherd's first errand is to go to rescue the one of the fold most entangled in the thorny brake—bleeding, and footsore, and weary ! All we know for certainty is that such a meeting did take place. For in the evening of that ever hallowed day, when the two disciples from Emmaus hastened to the chamber in Jerusalem to convey the wondrous tidings that Jesus had been " made known to them in the breaking of bread," they were welcomed with the joyous announcement : " The Lord is risen indeed, *and hath appeared unto Simon.*" The same special interview is expressly mentioned by St Paul in the beginning of his Great Resurrection-chapter. There, in specifying the evidences of the Saviour's rising from the dead, he commences with the distinct announcement, as if the appearance were one pre-eminently

---

1 "It is observable that on this occasion the Apostle is called by his original name Simon (not Peter) ; the higher designation was not restored until he had been publicly reinstated, so to speak, by his Master."—*Bible Dic., art. "Peter."*

noteworthy and remarkable : " He was seen of CEPHAS, then of the twelve."

It has been well remarked, "The absence of all description, and even of any direct mention of this interview, is strikingly characteristic of that which is a peculiar feature of the Gospel history, whether told by Matthew, or Mark, or Luke, or John—we mean, the studied avoidance of that which we now describe as 'sensational.' There probably never was, during the whole world's history, such another interview between two persons in human shape as this between Peter and his injured Master. But, with one consent, all the Evangelists avoid the subject. Every one of the four must have been cognisant of the fact ; yet they are all not only reserved, but absolutely silent. This could not be because they deemed the fact an uninteresting one. No ; a contrary feeling prevailed. The meeting was felt to be one which, as no human eye beheld, so no human pen should attempt to describe. Peter's own attached friend, whom he calls 'Marcus, my son,' was one of these Evangelists. But he is as silent as the other three. The Apostle had kept silence even to him, or he had forbidden all allusion to the subject." [1] And yet, is it vain curiosity which tempts us in thought to lift the curtain and try to get a glimpse into the sacredness of that interview? We can picture Peter covered with confusion, dumb with emotion. How strange, how thrilling, to meet for the first time all alone—unseen by any third person —the glance of that eye which when last confronted had pierced him to the heart's core, and sent him away weeping in the darkness ! If silence and tears on

[1] Author of Essays on the Church, p. 89.

the present occasion had found vent in words, we can
suppose that they were either a repetition of his Transfiguration experience, "Not knowing what he said,"
or else that, in spirit at least, he adopted the plaintive
wail and confession in that "Psalm of a broken
heart"—"Against Thee, Thee only, have I sinned, and
done this evil in Thy sight, that Thou mightest be
justified when Thou speakest, and be clear when Thou
judgest."   But whether the interview was thus one
of "mute expressive silence"—where exchanged looks
were sufficient between the Forgiving and the Forgiven,
—or, as is more likely, there were the penitential
sighings and avowals of a contrite soul on the one
hand, and the assurance of generous oblivion extended on the other, we cannot fail to recognise, at
all events, the extreme tenderness in the dealings of
Him of whom it was truly predicted that "He would
not break the bruised reed nor quench the smoking
flax."   By this considerate means the Lord spared
Peter the pain and shame of encountering *for the
first time*, in the presence of his brethren, One whom
he had so deeply injured.   Unless this private preliminary meeting had first taken place, in vain, at
least to one heart present, would the benediction
have been uttered, "*Peace* be unto you."   He could
have seen only the spirit-form he once beheld on
the stormy waters, the vision which led him to "cry
out for fear!"   Jesus, however, by this gracious anticipation seemed, in divinest sympathy, to exemplify
His own law in dealing with the erring: "If thy
brother shall trespass against thee, go and tell him
his fault between thee and him *alone*."

That "upper chamber" within which, on that Easter

evening, Peter and the rest of the eleven were gathered, was most probably the same which had been so recently and sacredly associated to them with the institution of the Holy Supper, the washing of the disciples' feet, and the last sacerdotal discourse and prayer. All at once, in mysterious silence, with no footfall heard, and no opening of door, the Great Lord Himself appears with the familiar words we have just quoted, gently upbraiding them for their unbelief, and graciously exhibiting the spear and nail marks on hands and side, to attest the identity of His resurrection-body. Then breathing upon them, He said, "Receive ye the Holy Ghost." And so also, eight days later, must our Apostle have been present with the waiting ten, who had again gathered on the second Easter Sunday to commemorate their Lord's rising, and when the slow, doubting Thomas had his misgivings removed by reaching forth his finger and touching the crucifixion wounds;—exclaiming in reverential faith, "My Lord and my God." It was on the same occasion Jesus repeated the gracious word for His Church in all ages : " Blessed are they that have not seen and yet have believed." " An echo of which saying," as has been observed, " we have, years after, in the first letter of Peter to the Churches ; "—" Whom having not seen, ye love ; in whom, though now ye see Him not, yet *believing*, ye rejoice with joy unspeakable and full of glory " (1 Peter i. 8).

CHAPTER XII.

The Lake Shore.

> "The storm is o'er—and hark! a still small voice
> Steals on the ear, to say, Jehovah's choice
> Is ever with the soft, meek, tender soul:
> By soft, meek, tender ways He loves to draw
> The sinner, startled by His ways of awe:
> Here is our Lord, and not where thunders roll."
> —*Keble.*

"He loved St John exceedingly, but it was by Peter that he was exceedingly beloved."—*Chrysostom.*

"In the interview that follows, the Lord addresses Himself to Peter alone. All the past is buried in oblivion: forgiveness begets love: much forgiveness, much love. The fallen Apostle is restored: the Shepherd's crook is again put into his hands—the Martyr's crown is suspended over his head."—*Dr Candlish's Scripture Miscellanies.*

"There was no Apostle who appeared from this hour so remarkably by the power of Divine grace to have overcome the natural frailties of his temper and disposition as St Peter."—*Blunt.*

"Peter was now 'converted:' converted from self-confidence to humble distrust of his own strength. He must have been now qualified, at least by a general firm reliance on his Master, for his destined office of administering consolation and support to the other Apostles—'strengthening his brethren.' He was prepared to live the life and to die the death of a Martyr in his Master's cause."—*Archbishop Whately.*

E owe to the Fourth Evangelist a new
and most touching chapter in the life
of Peter, and one which, as we shall
come to note, forms an important key
to the position he afterwards assumed
in the Infant Church. The 21st chapter
of St John's Gospel has been regarded
by scholars as an appendix or postscript.[1] The surmise
has even been ventured, that in his last abode in
Ephesus, when laid on his death-bed, the season when
memory is often peculiarly vivid, and when scenes and
visions of the past stand out with photographic detail,
he either transcribed himself, or dictated to another, an
episode we should not willingly have missed from the
sacred canon. It has been further surmised, that the

---

[1] " If we call John i. 1-14 the Prologue, this we might style the Epilogue
of his Gospel."—*Trench.*

main and immediate object the aged Apostle had in
view was to contradict the rumour of his own immor-
tality—the saying that had gone abroad, and gained
wide acceptance among the Brethren, " that he should
not die " (v. 23). This he does at the close of the
chapter.[1] But as he recalls the spot where Jesus had
spoken words which had thus been misinterpreted—" If
I will that he tarry till I come, what is that to thee ? "
(v. 22)—all the memorable accessories of the scene so
rose like one of his own apocalyptic visions before his
dimming eye, and especially those in connection with
his earliest and dearest human friend and fellow-Apostle,
that he bequeathes this precious codicil to the Church
of the future.   It has been noted also, that the saddest
event that had darkened in past years the prospects of
the early Christians had been Peter's violent death.
But his aged surviving brother was able in this, the
closing chapter alike of his life and of his writings, so
far to calm the agitated minds of those mourning so
irreparable a loss, by testifying that the addition of
Peter to the noble army of martyrs—nay, even the
manner of his death—was no matter of capricious
chance or hapless misfortune—but the event had been
foreseen, or rather appointed, by Him whose very
words came to his own dying remembrance fresh as when
they were spoken (v. 18).   And better than all, what
seemed to be the Church's loss would in other respects
be her gain ; for assurance was given that by that appalling death he would " glorify God " (v. 19).

---

[1] Dr Macleod well remarks that there is " a lesson here taught to the
Church of the untrustworthiness of even apostolic traditions, seeing that
in the very lifetime of the Apostles a false tradition had gone abroad regarding the death of St John."—*Eastward*, 265.

But not to anticipate. We are once more summoned in thought to the Sea of Tiberias. Since we last followed the footsteps of Peter there, the mighty debt of ransomed millions had been paid; glory had been secured to God in the highest, peace on earth, and good-will to men! We do not wonder to find that the disciples have retraced their steps to their native sea, when we recall the announcement referred to in the preceding chapter, made first by the angels and repeated by the Lord Himself, that He was "to go before them into Galilee," and that there they were to see Him.

It would be, then, shortly after the termination of the Passover festival they would thus return to their northern home; probably immediately after this second Easter day. We naturally love those localities which have been specially consecrated to us by early and hallowed associations. By that Lake shore they had listened to their Lord's earliest utterances of matchless wisdom—there they had been summoned by Him to undertake their great Embassy. Wherever Peter and his brothers of Bethsaida and Capernaum turned their eyes, its undulating beach must have been fragrant with His name and presence. Capernaum rose before them with its crowded memories of power and mercy. Yonder were the bifurcated peaks of Hattin, where the most wondrous of discourses was uttered;—yonder was the plain, flushed now with the full loveliness of Spring, where the Sower had sowed;—yonder in the far north was the green tableland where the barley loaves were dealt out as emblems of mightier spiritual blessings;—yonder, hiding itself amid sterner nature, was the scene of demoniacal conquest; there, yet again, was the bleak mountain-oratory, where the Lord

of all this wondrous panorama poured out His soul
into the ear of His Father. And when night fell, and
the stars looked down at one moment from their silent
thrones, and the next were swept from the heavens
by the sudden blast, the Apostle-fishermen would remember the august form of Him who trode these very
waters, and the voice that mingled with the moanings
of the tempest, saying " Fear not, it is I ; be not
afraid."

Can we doubt that these solemn and manifold remembrances would now oft tune their lips on their
lonely night-watch ;—that day after day they would be
thus interrogating one another as to the one absorbing
expectation, " Where shall we see Him ? " " When
shall we again hear His longed-for voice ? " He is
faithful who promised that He would meet us here
again.   " Even so ; come Lord Jesus, come quickly ! "
Other six of them—James and John, Thomas, Nathanael, and probably Andrew and Philip—have followed
the example of Peter, who said " I go a fishing." It
has been remarked that we are not warranted to infer
from these words the abandonment of hope in Christ
as Messiah and the permanent resumption of the old
secular calling, but simply the resort to former occupations in order to furnish them with what was needful
to supply their daily necessities. Circumstances had
now altered. They had no longer a common purse to
provide for these necessities, and it was incumbent on
them therefore to resume their boats and nets, leaving
their future destination in the hands of their loving
Saviour. Accordingly the old sail is unfurled, and they
have been out on the Lake the livelong night. But
their toil, as on a former occasion, is unrecompensed.

Morning begins to streak the mountains of Naphtali—
distant Hermon is unveiling his diadem of snow. The
lark was singing his early song and the flowers inhaling
their earliest perfume. In the appropriate words of
the Christian poet, who had the picture of the Galilean
Sea before him as he wrote them—

> "Slowly the gleaming stars retire,
> The eastern heaven is all on fire;
> The waves have felt the unrisen sun,
> Their matin service is begun."

As they approach within a few cubits of the shore, in
the grey dawn of that morning light, a Figure attracts
their eyes. We are not informed as to what particular
part of the Lake the interesting scene and meeting
which follows occurred. We could not help, in sailing
past, associating it, as suggested in "Sinai and Palestine," with the rim of broad and pearly sand at the
shore of El-Tabijah—a spot which would be silent and
secluded enough at that early hour. "The early dawn
had broken, revealing as it does every cleft and broken
cliff in distinct proportions all down the rocky sides of
its enclosing hills. On the beach stood the solitary
Figure, and through the stillness of the morning air, not
yet disturbed by the waking hum of the surrounding
villages, came the gentle voice calling in the manner of
the East, ' Children.' " [1] " They knew not that it was
Jesus!" That first friendly word He uttered might
have told them all! Yet still they recognise Him
not! They regard Him as a chance " early traveller."
It seems a strange thing, as it has been well remarked,
that they did not almost immediately " discover the

[1] "Eastward," 374.

presence of Christ, inasmuch as the whole was so manifestly a repetition of that former event, by which the commencement of their ministry had been signalised when He called them to become 'fishers of men.'"[1] Their eyes, however, are holden : He appears but as a passing wayfarer whom curiosity has drawn to watch the mooring of the boat on the shingle. He inquires if they have any fish captured that might serve for a morning meal? " Have ye any meat?" Strange that the recognition still fails. The question might have recalled to them many a hallowed hour among the hills and valleys of Galilee, when, after a hot day of toilsome journeying and teaching, they gathered at sundown in the cool of the evening for their frugal repast, ere retiring to rest : and when He who was dependent for His own human necessities on what His disciples were able to procure in the shape of victuals, oft doubtless put the same question, as they reclined on the grassy turf which served alike for couch and table— " Children, have ye any meat?" They answer despondingly that they had none! The mysterious stranger bids them " cast out on the right side of the ship." The result was so vast an enclosure of fishes—no less than 153—that they were unable to draw it to land. The quick-sightedness of love discerns the Divine Presence ;—the similarity of the present with a former occasion has led the beloved John—" him of the eagle eye" —to scrutinise more closely the person of the Speaker. Catching up the music of that well-known voice, he is the first to reveal the joyous secret, whispering it first with half-trembling lips into the ear of his chief associate, " It is the Lord!" Peter, with his old impetu-

[1] MacLaren's Sermons, p. 183.

osity and fervour, girts around him with his "zummar"
(girdle) his loose fisherman's tunic of which he had
divested himself for work,[1] springs into the sea and
swims a hundred yards to shore, in order that he may
cast himself soonest at the feet of his Great and Good
Master. What a rush of thought must have come upon
him with that place, that hour, that voice! How
vividly it must have recalled a similar season, when at
the first miraculous draught he flung himself at the
Divine Teacher's feet confessing his sinfulness. How it
must have brought to his mind his vows of heart and
life consecration on these same shores : and not only
how poorly they had been kept—but how miserably
they had been broken ! Far more than on that first
occasion had he reason to say, " Depart from me, for I
am a sinful man, O Lord ! "

The other disciples follow at leisure in a small boat,
—the larger vessel being unable to reach the shore
from the shallowness of the water—dragging with them
the net with its encumbering load. " When they recognise the Lord," says Chrysostom, " again do the
disciples display the peculiarities of their individual
characters. The one, for instance, was more ardent,
but the other more elevated—the one more eager, but
the other endued with finer perception—on which
account John was the first to recognise the Lord, but
Peter to come to Him."[2]

Who can describe the profound emotion of that
meeting ? It is simply and artlessly told in the gospel

[1] It was that same kind of upper garment which the soldiers at the Crucifixion cast lots for after they had divided among themselves the rest of our
Lord's apparel. In Peter's assuming of the tunic, Ambrose sees an act of
becoming reverence to his Master.

[2] Chrysostom Hom. quoted by Ellicott.

P

story. No strong or exaggerated effects are inserted
by the Apostle to mutilate the simple grandeur of the
picture. "If ever a narrative," well remarks Dr Macleod in the description of the scene in his travels,
"shone in its own light of divine truth, it is this one.
Its simplicity and pathos, and its exquisite harmony
with all we know and believe of Jesus, invest it with
an interest which must ever increase with its study."[1]
Not a tear, not a word, not a question is recorded.
Nay, in significant silence they confront The Holy One :
—"None of the disciples durst ask Him, Who art
Thou ? knowing that it was the Lord."

How different was the latest similar meeting! How
great the contrast with the recent Paschal Feast in the
upper chamber, where all was unrestrained fellowship ;
—where the disciples unburdened their inmost thoughts
in freest intercourse. But even the Master now, for a
while, seems to say nothing. There was a reason indeed
for the silence of one of the guests who had been ready
at other times to initiate the conversation, but all the
others seem for the moment awe-struck in that august
Presence. If there be an interchange of words—these
must originate with Him. They recognised the mystic
glory of His resurrection-body ; and though unchanged
in all the sympathies and realities of His humanity,
they were conscious that they stood to Him in a new
relation, and therefore maintained towards Him the
profound reverence of silence. Even when that silence
as we find after the meal, is broken, there is an arrest
put on all vain questionings and idle speculations—
"What is that to thee"—"If I will."

But there was a strange—it may be a miraculous

—provision ready for them at that landing-place. A fire, the fuel of which was probably the drift-wood brought down by the upper Jordan, and which may still be seen strewing the beach, was

" Kindled by no mortal hands,"

"some fish from the lake were laid thereon, and bread." The feast had been prepared by their adorable Lord. Ere inviting to partake of it, however, He bade them pull their nets to land. Peter in a moment complied with the request, "dragging it up the shelving bank, and spreading it upon the white margin of the sandy beach;"[1] and it is specially noted that full as the net was, and that too of "great fishes," it was brought on shore, unlike the former one, unbroken.

"Come and breakfast" was the brief invitation tendered and accepted. The Master and His seven disciples surround that lowly board; "Jesus came, and took bread, and gave them, and fish likewise."[2]

"We sat down," says the same interesting traveller from whom we have previously quoted, "under the shade of the rocks, and one of our boatmen walked knee deep into the lake with a little net; in a few minutes he had a dozen fish, each about the size of a mackerel; the other man collected two or three sticks and built up a little pile over a morsel of charcoal, on which he

---

[1] Stanley's Sermons, who notes that "the scene is marked by the word αἰγιαλος ; one of those spots where the shore of the lake descends to the water-side, not in a steep grassy slope but a white sanded beach."

[2] The same writer just quoted, in his sermon preached by the Sea of Tiberias before the Prince of Wales during his tour in the East, thus remarks on the similarity between that "Feast on the Shore," and the ordinance of the Lord's Supper :—"Some of the oldest pictures in the Roman Catacombs represent the Holy Communion under this very figure ;—not the twelve disciples but these seven, with the thin round loaves as of Arab bread, and the fishes lying beside them, as from this Sacred Lake," p. 56.

placed the fish ; . . . . it was interesting for us to have them thus cooked, remembering the 'fire of coals' (charcoal) and the 'fish laid thereon,' and the blessed invitation of the Risen Lord to His Apostles, 'Come and dine,' while we could look round at the very mountains and lake that had met His own human eyes and feel that we were indeed seeing the same objects, breathing the same air, and treading the same shell-covered shore that our blessed Saviour Himself had done." [1]

This is not the place to dwell on the deeper inner and spiritual meaning of the symbolic feast, in which Peter was immediately to have so deep an interest. I cannot forbear to quote the beautiful words of the ablest expositor of that miracle : 'As that large capture of fish was to them the pledge and promise of a labour that should not be in vain ; so the meal, when the labour was done, a meal of the Lord's own preparing, and "*upon the shore*," was the symbol of the great festival in heaven, with which, after their earthly toil was over, He would refresh His servants, when He should cause them to sit down with Abraham, and Isaac, and Jacob in the kingdom. And as they were bidden to bring of their fish to that meal, so should the souls which they had taken for life be their crown and rejoicing in that day,—should help and contribute to their gladness then.' [2]

The feast is followed by a solemn and touching interview between the Lord and the Apostle-guest in whom we are most interested. Peter's downfall had, indeed, been humiliating. We could not have wondered, if, covered with confusion at the thought of his recent treachery, and

<hr>

1 Egyptian Sepulchres and Syrian Shrines, p. 52.
2 Trench on the Miracles, p. 462.

refusing ever again to meet the glance of his injured Master's eye, he had fled back in terror to Galilee, and hid himself for very shame, in one of its most secluded hamlets. But what will not the consciousness of devoted love brave and overcome? Never more convinced than now of attachment to that Lord he had deeply wounded, he is the first of all the seven to throw himself at His feet and implore His forgiveness. It were strange too, had it been otherwise; or rather, when He who sent the special message—" Go and tell *Peter* "—is standing before him in peerless majesty in the morning light, can we wonder that, unable to repress the outburst of his grateful feelings, he is seen plunging into the water, cleaving the waves with his brawny arms that he might be the first to reach the land!

The feast was partaken of in silence;—but when concluded, the risen Lord is the first to speak; and Peter's name is the first on His lips. The latter had, on the evening of the Resurrection-day, in common with his brother Apostles, received the world-wide commission to " disciple " all nations. But having more grievously apostatised than the others, it was needful that his reinvestiture with the Apostolic authority and office should have greater publicity. He had been forgiven in *private*—that secret interview to which we previously adverted, had probably put the seal of gracious pardon on an erring past; but it was needful also, that in presence of his brethren as the representatives of the Church, he should be formally reponed in the position from which like Judas he had by transgression fallen.

The fishermen Apostles, we may remember, were previously addressed figuratively through the occupation with which from youth they had been familiar—their

nets being taken as typical of the Gospel Church, and
the fish enclosed, of the living souls they were to capture.   Our Lord, however, now changes the metaphor.
He passes to one with which these villagers of Bethsaida, amid the abounding green slopes and pasture-
lands which bordered their lake, must have been equally
familiar.   Perhaps where they now were, a flock of
sheep might have been seen browsing on one of the
adjoining mountains : these may at the moment have
attracted the eye of the true " Shepherd of Israel " as
they emerged at that early hour from their fold.   Be
this as it may, the old figure which David loved so well,
when he sang of the Shepherd-love of God, is now taken
by the GOOD SHEPHERD to instruct His own Disciple.
The figure of *the net* spoke emphatically of the magnitude of the ministerial work.   Now He proceeds to unfold the principle or motive by which that work could
alone be successfully prosecuted, and the method of at-
taining the great final recompense.

How does our Lord address the erring but penitent
Apostle ?—" SIMON, SON OF JONAS."

Simon ! He had surnamed him after his noble confession at the coasts of Cæsarea Philippi, " *Peter*, the
Rock." But the Rock that should have manfully braved
the storm had become the brittle reed, shattered by the
first blast of temptation.   His conduct had belied his
loud protestations, and forfeited the nobler title.   His
Lord, therefore, goes back to the simple name of his
old fisherman life—the one which He employed on
another occasion already noted, when a fall seemed imminent—" Simon, Simon ! Satan hath desired to have
thee that he might sift thee as wheat." Or again, as may
be remembered, when he was found slumbering at his

post, instead of being, as he ought, the wakeful attendant and guardian of the Great Sufferer, "*Simon, sleepest thou?*" (Mark xiv. 37.)

'We read of one of the Caliphs,' says Dr Trench, happily illustrating from Eastern manners the significance of this change of name, 'that he used to give his principal officers an honourable surname suited to their qualities; when he wished to show his dissatisfaction, he used to drop it, calling them by their own names; this caused them great alarm. When he resumed the employment of the surname, it was a sign of their return to favour. This passage helps us, I think, to enter into the significance of the " Simon, son of Jonas" here.' [1]

And while there is a thrice-repeated *name*, there is also a thrice-repeated *question*, "LOVEST THOU ME?" A knowledge of the original brings out tender touches of meaning in this remarkable passage which are not discerned in our English translation.[2] There are two entirely different words in the original Greek which are rendered in our Bibles by the word " lovest " (*agapas* and *phileis*). The first time the question is asked by our Lord it is the word *agapas* which He uses;—a word which denotes more a feeling of general reverence, honour, respect, than any intense personal attachment. Peter in his reply employs a different term (*philo*). His sensitive heart would doubtless be wounded to think that his Lord saw needful to use what implied a less ardent affection. He therefore in his reply adopts not the word his Master had done—(for that would inade-

[1] Trench on the Miracles, p. 464.
[2] See Notes in Alford and Trench *in loco*.

quately have expressed his feelings)—but he takes the one indicative of deep personal love.

" Honourest thou Me more than these ? "

" Yea, Lord, Thou knowest that *Thou art dear to me.*"

Jesus puts the question a second time; but still continues to use the less fervent word. He would still perhaps remind the penitent of past boasting and profession and failure.

" Honourest thou Me ? "

Peter, however, will not abate the avowal of a deeper affection; conscious of the reality of his love, he still clings to his former expression (*philo*).

" Yea, Lord, Thou knowest that *Thou art dear to me.*"

And now the Great Master, despite of the remembrance of former expressions of allegiance which had grievously failed, can resist no longer the ardent profession of His attached disciple after this double avowal of them. In putting the question for the third time, He changes His former word for the one of deep personal love—

" Am I dear to thee ? "

" Lord, Thou knowest all things, *Thou knowest that Thou art dear to me.*" [1]

There can be no doubt as to Christ's intention in the thrice-repeated question. He wished by reminding of the *threefold denial*, to convey to His servant a gentle *threefold rebuke*. He could not have done so more impressively ; while in the addition He makes to the first query, " Honourest thou Me *more than these?* " there is

[1] The stronger of the two words is that used by the Jews at the grave of Lazarus, " Behold how He *loved* him " (ἐφίλει).

an equally manifest reference to that occasion when, in a self-sufficient boastful comparison of his own moral heroism with that of his fellow-disciples, Peter had said, " Though all should be offended because of Thee this night, yet will not I " (Mark xiv. 29).

Simon heard the first two questions unmoved ; but when for the third time it was uttered, the questioned Apostle " was *grieved*." He began to suspect there must be some good reason for these implied doubts. He knew that the loving heart which so interrogated would not unnecessarily wound him ; that his gracious Lord would not utter a needlessly unkind word or question. Could it be that He who knew all things, might see foreshadowed some future denial, which led Him to receive these ardent protestations with such caution ? Could it be that his heart, which had so deceived him in the past, was to prove a traitor-heart again, and that he would have to renew his bitter weeping over the humiliations of a still sadder fall ?

It was, however, the very grief his Lord desired. He wished to humble him, to annihilate his self-confidence and self-sufficiency.

That our Lord's reiterated appeal had the intended effect we cannot doubt. It read a lesson the Apostle never forgot to his dying hour. We may regard this interview, indeed, as a crisis in Peter's history—the date of a new development in his inner life. The proud self-sufficient disciple becomes, from this day onward, a little child. He comes forth from the furnace into which his Lord had cast him, purified as gold—humbled but really exalted. We see in his very reply to the threefold question the germ of this new grace of future poverty of spirit. His answer in former times would probably have been "I know that I love thee." But Jesus has taught him a different estimate of himself. He appeals from his own untrustworthy heart, to that of the great Heart-searcher, " Lord, Thou knowest all things, *Thou knowest* that thou art dear to me." His Lord had asked him as to the relative intensity of his love, whether it was now according to his former boasting estimate of it—" more than these." The humbled Apostle takes no note of the comparison. His silence is its own interpreter. There was once a time when he would have been arrogant enough to say, " Yea, Lord ; none can honour Thee or love Thee as I do." But the remembrances of the past and the rebukes of the present, have seated him in the dust. He can only make the confident appeal to Him who knew the heart, as to the sincerity of present resolutions, and the depth of present attachment.[1] 'It was once my feeling and my boast,' we may imagine him saying, 'that I was bold enough for anything. But I am covered with humiliation, and my sins of pusillanimity and apostasy are blackened with aggravations I shudder to recall. I dare boast no more. I can say nothing as to the dependence to be placed on my devotedness. Fitful in the past, it may be fitful still ; but at present, Lord, it is with no sembled lips that I declare, with Thy scrutinising glance upon me, THOU *knowest that I* LOVE *Thee.'*

> " He loves and weeps—but more than tears
>   Have sealed Thy welcome and his love ;
> One ' look ' lives in Him, and endears
>   Crosses and wrongs where'er he rove."

Jesus forthwith proceeds to reinstate him in the

---

[1] See Maurice on St John.

Apostolic office. Anew He affixes the seal on his previous high commission, "Feed My lambs," "Feed My sheep." And here too there are three, or rather five, different words, though they are translated by two only in our version : "Feed My little lambs," "Shepherd My sheep," "Feed the choicest of the flock."[1] Jesus had listened to his protestations of love. He accepts them ; and in token of acceptance He tells His disciple to go and act a shepherd's part to the Church purchased with His blood. His words are equivalent to saying : 'Simon, if you indeed love me, make proof of the reality of your love, not by your words but by your acts. Prove by newly baptized zeal and unremitting labour that I have not unworthily confided in your resolute assertions.' "The peculiarly Hebrew imagery," it has been observed, "is dropped ; the particular features of the Rock and the Keys, and the binding and loosing, which were to be exemplified in his rule of the Palestine Church, disappear ; and we have instead the more universal metaphor with which the readers of this Gospel must have been already familiar from the parable of the Good Shepherd. . . . It is at least a striking coincidence and illustration of this passage that there is no part of the New Testament (with the exception of John x.) where the image of the Shepherd is so prominently brought forward as in the 1st Epistle of Peter, where almost the very words of this passage are repeated— (1 Peter v. 2-4)—'Feed the flock of God which is among you, taking the oversight thereof, not by constraint, but willingly ; not for filthy lucre, but of a ready mind ; neither as being lords over God's heritage, but being ensamples to the flock. And when the Chief

[1] See Alford and Tregelles.

Shepherd shall appear, ye shall receive a crown of glory that fadeth not away.' " [1]

Jesus not only receives the once erring Apostle, but even in rebuking him, what tenderness, what unutterable gentleness, is mingled with that rebuke! We quite expect, after so black a catalogue of guilt, a reprimand of corresponding severity. When the words are first uttered—" Simon, son of Jonas"—we expect to hear the enumeration of his bygone sins :—his arrogance, his presumption, the oaths and curses and cowardly desertion. But we see "the end of the Lord, that the Lord is very

---

[1] Stanley's Sermons on the Apostolic Age, pp. 139, 140.

The following observations of the same thoughtful art-critic, from whom we have previously quoted, are curious and noteworthy : "There is something singularly unadapted to the reading of the eye in this incident. 'Art requires action.' Here there is none, except by one figure addressing another. . . . It therefore might be predicted that this subject remained unthought of in Art before the dogma of the Supremacy of the Roman Church arose, and also during those times when that dogma was not questioned. We therefore look backward for the appearance in Art of 'the charge to Peter,' to a particular period in the history of Christianity, as men look forward to the appearance of a comet at a particular junction in the heavenly bodies. And we find it accordingly emerging above the horizon at the close of the fifteenth century, and completely above it in the reign of Leo X. : also first seen in works of importance in the locality most suited to its presence—viz., in the Sistine Chapel of the Vatican. Perugino's fresco of the charge to St Peter still exists on the right hand wall, and Raphael's cartoon of the subject is one of the series originally intended to adorn the lower part of the same walls. In both these, and generally in all representations, the giving of the keys is added to the subject of the charge ; or rather, in point of art, it may be said to supersede it ; for this assertion of a dogma, under the form of the giving and taking of a conventional implement, shuts out all remembrance of the Scripture narrative. This is especially the case with Raphael's cartoon, which suffers by comparison with its fellow works ; for after standing before the Death of Ananias, the Preaching of St Paul, and others, which bespeak the closest adhesion to the spirit of the Sacred text, the eye turns away with more than indifference from these actual sheep and these gigantic keys which have no possible point of congruity except that of an equal departure from the laws of Art and the simplicity of the Gospel." The same writer farther notes, what no observant eye can fail to recognise, that the remaining ten Apostles' figures in the cartoon, which are without any distinguishing action, are masterpieces of composition.—See Mrs Jameson's Sacred and Legendary Art.

pitiful and of tender mercy." He knew well that that wounded spirit did not require to be needlessly lacerated. There is no direct reference therefore to the past, no catalogue of former errors dragged afresh to the light of day. Like the Shepherd in the parable of The Lost Wanderer, in silent love " He lays him on His shoulders rejoicing, saying : Rejoice with Me, for I have found My sheep which was lost."

When Peter writes these verses in his old age, who but himself must have filled the foreground of the picture—" Love shall cover the multitude of sins " (1 Peter iv. 8) ; " Ye were as sheep going astray, but are now returned unto the Shepherd and Bishop of your souls " (1 Peter ii. 25).

Nor is it unworthy of note, that not only does the Great Master from this hour preserve a significant silence regarding Peter's fall ; but it is a beautiful illustration of the generous love and affection which animated the breasts of his fellow Apostles, that never once afterwards, in all the record of their dealings, did one of them ever ungraciously recall the past, ever once taunt or upbraid their brother for his former failings and inconsistencies. In a true spirit of Christian courtesy and delicacy, the sad story of the denial and the curses seems buried in everlasting oblivion.

Jesus having calmed the spirit of His ardent disciple by the assurance of forgiveness and reponement in the Apostolic office, proceeds to predict his future martyrdom :—that after serving Him in the vigour of manhood, he would in old age have his hands nailed to the cross ; —" girded " too, or bound to it with cords, as was the manner in that cruel death—and thus give the costly and unmistakable proof of his avowed love, by shewing what great things he was willing to endure for his dear Lord's sake. As the words have been well paraphrased in a sermon preached on the very shores : " *Verily I say unto thee, when thou wast young*, when thou wast a fisherman's boy on the shores of the Galilean Lake, *thou girdedst thyself* in thy fisher's coat, *and walkedst* over these hills and valleys, *whither thou wouldest : but when thou shalt be old*, as years and duties and infirmities increase, thou shalt stretch forth thy hands, even on the cross of martyrdom, *and another*—the Roman executioner—*shall gird thee* with the bonds of imprisonment, *and carry thee whither thou wouldest not*, even to the place where thou must glorify God by thy death." [1] It must have been unspeakably comforting to Peter to listen to these declarations, even although they predicted a baptism of suffering. They would assure him, at all events, that he was not again to prove a renegade and coward in the hour of trial. Jesus had warned him of his approaching fall, and His intimation had come too sadly true. Now, however, the same lips declare that he was to "glorify God" by being faithful unto death. Moreover, that it was "when he was old" all this was to happen ; so that he had before him many years of active service and devotion in his Lord's work. When the sickle came, he would be cut down as a shock of corn fully ripe—he would fall a veteran in the field.

"Follow thou Me." The privileged son of Jonas seems to have obeyed literally this last injunction. As the Divine Master walks along the sandy beach, the footsteps of His devoted Apostle are behind him. At that same moment Peter hears or sees the Beloved

[1] Stanley's Sermons in Palestine, p. 59.

Disciple following, and with his thoughts full of his
own destiny as just declared by the lips of Omniscience,
he puts the question regarding one who, as we have
seen, had been knit to him as the soul of David was to
Jonathan (v. 21), "What shall this man do?" or as
it has been rendered, "What shall his lot be?"
He has never been like me a traitor and renegade.
There has been no failure, as in my case, in his love
and allegiance. Will he on that account be exempted
from my baptism of suffering, and go to heaven, not, as
in my case, in a chariot of fire, but on the wings of
loving angels? We would fondly believe that the
question was thus prompted; not, as some have
thought, by mere idle curiosity, but from the ardent
love he bore his best human friend in the past, and who
was destined to be his fastest friend in the future.

Jesus, with a gentle rebuke, reminds him of his
personal duty, "What is that to thee, follow thou Me."
As if He had said ' He may have a different niche to
fill in My Temple—a different lot in the shepherding of
My sheep. He may be called to lead the flock in the
quiet valley beside the green pastures and the still
waters—whilst thou mayest be summoned to the moun-
tain-heights to battle with the storm and encounter
the wolves. He may have to undergo years of lonely
banishment and silence, serving me by recording
heavenly visions, or by days and nights of rapt devotion—whilst thou art in the thick of the open fight,
storming the citadels of Jewish prejudice and Gentile
unbelief. He may have his eyes closed by loving
hands in his own home—whilst a ruffian throng may
hound thee to the most tragic of ends. But what
signifies to thee or to him the nature of these diverse

appointments—whether for life or for death. Ye can both serve Me ; the one it may be by active work, the other by passive obedience and suffering ; the one in the seclusion and exile of a lonely isle, the other by meeting in street and market place the frowns of bigot Jew and Pagan Roman ; the one in a death that is like ' taking of rest in sleep ; ' the other by a repetition of the scene at Golgotha. To every man there is his assigned work, what the unbelieving world has mis-named as " destiny." Do thine bravely, whatever it be :—leave to Myself My own dealing and appointment with My own Beloved Disciple—" Follow *thou* Me." '

These are the last recorded words spoken by Jesus to Peter. How he treasured them in his heart of hearts we shall ere long see evidenced by noble deeds. He was, a few weeks before, braced up for a new life of devotion and service by Christ's look of rebuke, pity, forgiveness, love. This was a second strengthener of his reviving fortitude. " Out of weakness " he was now made still more strongly prepared to " wax valiant in fight, and to turn to flight the armies of the aliens." He gladly and heroically resumes the cross, and

" With brightening heart he bears it on,
His passport through th' eternal gates,
To his sweet home."

With this scene on the shores of the Northern Lake may be said to close the period of the Apostle's train-ing for the great work of the future. His composite character, in which naturally there were so many mingled elements of good and evil, is now finally, so far as a fallible nature could be, purged of the latter. By his various humiliations and rebukes, he comes forth from the furnace as gold doubly refined. All presumption, loud protestation, and arrogant bravado are henceforth at an end. His armour has been proved. Now that he is soon to dispense with his Lord's presence,—with his whole character elevated, he is to enter the battle alone, and by unceasing labour and godly patience and endurance to upbuild the walls of the Gospel Zion.

" Meanwhile, however," to use the words of another, " let us look for a moment at the simple fulness, and the exact suitability of this closing chapter of St John's Gospel to the plain necessities of the case. Something was obviously needed. Peter had fallen most deplorably—most perilously fallen—but yet not quite irretrievably. Still, had this closing chapter of St John not been written, we could hardly have borne to read the first three chapters of the book of the Acts. . . . We should have been startled, and almost shocked, at Peter's forwardness in Acts i. 15, and ii. 14. We should have said, ' Surely we might have expected, for a time, a little more reserve, a kind of shamefacedness, in him who had so recently declared, before many witnesses, ' I know not the man.' But this 21st chapter of St John places everything in its destined position. . . . Christ had met him as the prodigal had been met. The ring is put upon Peter's finger, and the shoes on his feet. Most distinct and emphatic, most full and complete, is the restoration of the penitent to his former place. Thrice had he sinned, and thrice shall he be pardoned, recognised and anew commissioned. The entireness of the restoration is seen in this, that no one has ever dared to breathe a syllable of surprise when, at the opening of the Church's history in the

Q

Acts, we find Peter at once assuming his accustomed place, as an Apostle, and a warm-hearted, prominent, and earnest servant of Christ.'"[1]

In the one sublime closing act, Peter's name is not specially mentioned. But that he formed one of the most eager and earnest of the spectators, we cannot for a moment doubt. On one of those silent heights of the Mount of Olives to the north of Bethany so familiar to him, and which are at this day clothed with fig, almond, and carob, or possibly on one of those secluded eminences overlooking the Hosannah road, the scene of the only earthly triumph of the divine King, a nobler, though unseen triumphal procession was about to ascend to the gates of the Heavenly Jerusalem. What a solemn and momentous gathering! The Master confided to His chosen followers His last words, that the Gospel of the Kingdom was by them to be carried to "*the utter-most parts of the earth.*" As His final personal word to Peter was " Follow thou Me," so here He gives him, along with the others, the limits of that "following." Their footsteps were to tread, not the sacred ground of Palestine only, which had hitherto formed the horizon of their thought,—but they were to go on their God-like errand, from nation to nation, from kingdom to kingdom, from shore to shore, until Christendom be another name for the world. " With His disciples around Him, standing on a mountain top, heaven above and earth below, He thus proclaimed His kingdom 'All power is given to Me in heaven and in earth:" here was the King. ' Go :' here were the ministers and army,—an embassy of peace. ' Teach :' here the weapon,—the Word of God. ' All nations :' here the

1 " Life and Writings of St Peter," pp. 94, 95.

extent. 'Baptizing them in the name of the Father, and of the Son, and of the Holy Ghost:' here the badge of citizenship. 'Teaching them to observe all things whatsoever I have commanded you:' here the statute law. 'And lo, I am with you:' here the royal presence and glory of the kingdom. 'Always unto the end of the world:' here its duration." [1]

And so in the Ascension-cloud, what Chrysostom calls "the royal chariot," He was parted from them in the act of breathing a divine benediction; and with hands extended in blessing, He was borne higher and higher from their sight. [2] In no bosom of the trans-fixed assemblage during these thrilling moments would there be a greater rush of conflicting emotions, than in that of the Son of Jonas. His gracious Master's voice, never more to be heard in this world, would seem to ring louder than ever in "the ear of the soul" the imperishable words "Lovest thou Me," "Follow thou Me." In that moment of uncontrollable emotion, he saw through his tear-dimmed eye, in common with his bereft brethren, a vision of angels. Delegates from the upper sanctuary had sped down with the message of consolation to the orphaned band, "Ye men of Galilee,

[1] Arthur's "Tongue of Fire," p. 9.

[2] The recorded meeting with "the 500 brethren at once," in Galilee, does not specially fall to be noticed in connection with Peter's life. The meeting we know took place on some mountain. It may have been the Mount of Beatitudes or Mount Tabor—or the same spur of Hermon which formed the scene of the Transfiguration. Whether the last named may have been the hallowed spot of this farewell convocation or no, Lange notes the following points of similarity and contrast between the two memorable scenes:—"The two agree in kind. There Peter confessed 'Thou art the Christ the Son of the living God:' here, a disciple-band of more than five hundred believing souls, fall in adoration at the feet of the risen Lord. There Christ confirmed Peter's confession as a revelation from the Father: here, He declares all power is given unto *Me* in heaven and upon earth."—*Lange's Life of Christ.*

why stand ye gazing up into heaven? This same Jesus, which is taken up from you into heaven shall so come in like manner as ye have seen Him go into heaven" (Acts i. 11). It is evident that these balm-words of comfort had the effect of soothing their hearts and drying their tears. The thought of present duty, and the prophetic announcement just listened to, which so vividly recalled His own words, "If I go and prepare a place for you, I will come again and receive you unto Myself," reconciled them to the " little while in which they should not see Him." Accordingly we read, "And they worshipped Him, and returned (it has been thought probably on a Thursday evening) to Jerusalem with great joy, and were continually in the Temple praising and blessing God" (Luke xxiv. 52, 53).

Can we doubt that the hero heart and retuned lips of Peter would lead the strain? That while others of the timid band might well be downcast under so unutterable a bereavement as that of the withdrawal of their Lord's earthly presence, this Luther of the infant Church would wake the Temple-court with the song, " God is in the midst of her, she shall not be moved,— The Lord shall help her, and that right early?" Often had they entered that Temple before, cheered with the presence of their Master; and in one sense their plaint might have been " Ichabod—the glory has departed;" —but " Again a little while and ye shall see Me" was the promise with which He had cheered their drooping hearts; and " though now they saw Him not, yet believing, they rejoiced with joy unspeakable and full of glory."

CHAPTER XIII.

———

After the Ascension.

> " The Spirit
> Poured first on His Apostles (whom He sends
> To evangelise the nations), then on all
> Baptized, shall them with wondrous gifts endue
> To speak all tongues, and do all miracles,
> As did their Lord before them. Thus they win
> Great numbers of each nation to receive
> With joy the tidings brought to them from heaven."
> —*Paradise Lost*, Book XII.

" Peter came forward, with the rest of the Eleven ; and as the
Apostles spoke in the name of the whole Church, so Peter spoke
in the name of the Apostles."—*Neander*.

" Immediately after the Ascension, Peter, the first of the
Twelve, . . . the holder of the Keys of the Kingdom, becomes
the great Actor under God in the founding of the Church. He
is the centre of the first group of sayings and doings."—*Alford*.

" That this Society or Church was 'that Kingdom of Heaven'
of which the keys were committed to them, and which they had
before proclaimed as 'at hand,' they could not doubt. They
could not have been in any danger of cherishing any such presumptuous dream as that they or any one else, except their
Divine Master, could have power to give or refuse admittance to
the mansions of immortal bliss."
　　　　　　—*Arch. Whateley's " Kingdom of Christ."*

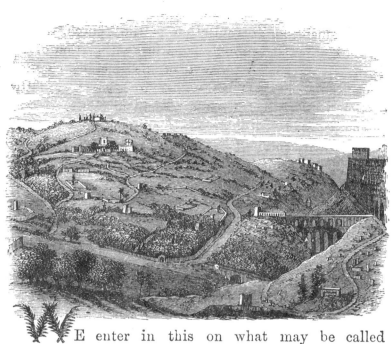

E enter in this on what may be called
the second great chapter in the Apostle's
history. Hitherto we have contemplated him as
the personal follower and associate of his Divine
Lord, following his Master's footsteps, witnessing His
miracles, listening to His gracious teachings :—the
spectator of His agony in the garden, the witness
of His resurrection, a participant in that never-to-be-
forgotten last blessing, which like a golden shower
came from the ascending cloud on Mount Olivet.
Peter up to this time had been like a wayward child,
led, controlled, disciplined by the tenderest of parents.
Now the parent's guiding hand and voice have been
withdrawn, and he and his fellow-disciples are left
friendless in the world. For the future story of his
life we are mainly indebted to the " Acts " or doings of

the Apostles—a permanent record of the rise, growth, establishment, and organisation of the Church, written by Luke, the beloved physician, in continuation of his Gospel. The main interest of its opening chapters centres in our Apostle; while, in the larger latter portion, St Paul becomes the prominent figure.

The period which intervened between Ascension and Pentecost, resembling, as it must often have done, the sad sequel of a family bereavement, was spent by the disciples in a chamber in Jerusalem — what is significantly called, not, as in our translation, " an upper-room," but " *the* upper-room." It might have gratified curiosity to have known what and where this meeting-place was, where assembled the first congregation of the infant Church of Christ. Some have deemed it probable that it was one of the many chambers above the temple cloisters, which were open for the use of religious assemblies. Olshausen favours this view. He says, " The accounts given by Josephus of the construction of the temple guide us here to the right conclusion. According to his description the main building was surrounded by thirty rooms, which he names οἴκους; and it is probable the apostles, along with their little company, assembled in one of these spacious apartments. And thus," he adds, " the solemn inauguration of the Church of Christ presents itself as an imposing spectacle in the sanctuary of the Old Covenant."[1] But when we remember the hatred with which the Nazarenes were regarded, it is improbable that the Temple guardians would have permitted this daily assemblage of the sect most odious to them. It

[1] Olshausen, vol. iv., p. 362. See also Note, with references, in "Fleetwood's Lives of the Apostles."

is much more likely that the meeting took place in one of the oratories common in most of the private houses of the Jews. These were situated on the top of their dwellings. Thither they were in the habit of retiring for personal devotion, or convening their families to read the law. Such was the "upper-chamber" (for it is the same word that is used) where the body of Dorcas was laid (Acts ix. 37). Similar also, to take an older illustration, was the chamber which Daniel frequented, "as he was wont," in the land of his captivity, and which a writer of the Middle Ages, speaking of the Jews in Babylon, mentions as having been pointed out long after his death by those who lingered in the Chaldean capital.[1] It is more than probable then, that in one such well-known private house, probably the same where the Holy Supper a few weeks previously was instituted, the first converts and disciples were now convened.[2] It has been suggested that it may have been the usual residence of the mother of John, "whose surname was Mark"—a home, we know, which was familiar to Peter on a future occasion.

In this chamber at all events, be where it might, the entire Judean Church met together for fellowship —"breaking of bread and prayers;"—a meeting truly which will continue ever memorable as the fountainhead of that river, the streams whereof have since, in every quarter of the earth, made glad the city of God. We have the names specially given of a few of those forming the Assembly, "Peter, and James, and John,

---

[1] See Cave, *in loco.*

[2] Epiphanius places it on Mount Zion, and further asserts that it became one of the holy places, and the site of a Christian church.

and Andrew, Philip and Thomas, Bartholomew and
Matthew, James the son of Alphæus, and Simon Zelotes,
and Judas the brother of James." Besides these, were
some of " the holy women " who in former years had
ministered to Jesus of their substance, who had followed Him on His journeyings among the cities and
villages of Galilee, and who more recently had tracked
His footsteps along the Dolorous way, stood weeping
at His cross, and brought costly spices to His tomb.
Specially interesting is the last reference made in sacred
story to one of these, the Blessed Mother of our Lord.
She had doubtless repaired thither under the guardian-
ship and tender care of " the son of her old age," who
we know, at the hour of deepest agony and humiliation,
had " taken her to his own home." As we have already
noted that Peter and John at this momentous time seem
to have lived together, it adds a solemn association to
the present history of the former, that the one whose
soul was pierced by a more painful than material sword,
had shared his companionship also, probably had been
witness of the Apostle's profound emotion, his bitter
penitence and tears. To one other ear in addition to
that of John he may have confided the burdening secret
of his heart, and possibly the private and confidential
sayings of her loving, dutiful Son and his forgiving
Master. In addition to the other Galilean women
assembled in that " Jerusalem Chamber," may we not
be warranted from Paul's reference (1 Cor. ix. 5) in
including the wife of Peter ; also the sisters of the
raised Lazarus, Martha and Mary,—full as they must
have been with the recent recollections of the Bethany
tears, and Bethany sayings, and Bethany departure ?
Nor is it unworthy of observation, that the only other

individuals specifically mentioned in addition to those already named, are " our Lord's brethren "—evidently his brethren " according to the flesh," the sons of Joseph by a former marriage ; those who during His public ministry had persistently rejected His claims to the Messiahship, but who it is supposed had been so impressed with the crowning miracle of His resurrection, as to unite with the confession of the Roman soldier, " Truly Thou art the son of God " — and were now found waiting, along with the others, for the promised Pentecostal blessing.

The statement that " the number of the names together was an hundred and twenty," does not in any way conflict with the fact mentioned by St Paul, that our blessed Lord had been seen by 500 brethren in Galilee. It may well be believed that the number of His adherents was much greater in that favoured scene of His northern labours. Moreover that some of these had been unable to give their personal presence at distant Jerusalem during the celebration of the Feast of Pentecost; others had not yet reached the city of solemnities.

These days we may describe as a memorable series and succession of prayer-meetings. St Luke tells us, " they all continued with one accord in prayer and supplication," preparatory to the Apostles going forth on the Great Mission to which their Lord had destined them. There was to be no literal restoration, as some of them had dreamed, of the Kingdom to Israel. A nobler enterprise, as we have seen, was in prospect for Peter and his associates, viz., to preach repentance and remission of sins to all nations ; to tell, not to the little world of Palestine only, but to every kingdom under heaven, the story of redeeming love. They were to "begin at Jerusalem." A mysterious, super-human energy was to be communicated in order to qualify them for the world-wide embassage; and mean-while, until that was vouchsafed, they were to tarry in the Holy City. "Behold, I send the promise of My Father upon you, but tarry ye," said their Lord, "in the city of Jerusalem, till ye be endued with power from on high." "And being assembled together with them, He commanded them that they should not depart from Jerusalem, but wait for the promise of the Father, which, saith He, ye have heard of Me." "Ye shall receive power," He added, "after that the Holy Ghost is come upon you."

Such were the thoughts and words which filled their minds and prayers, during these solemn days of patient waiting; a picture of union and devotion which has had no parallel since in the Church of Christ.

Meanwhile at their first gathering, an important transaction takes place. Peter, who as we have already said, forms undoubtedly the conspicuous personage, the recognised leader in these opening chapters of the Acts, takes the initiative in addressing the little Assembly.[1] In brief but expressive words he rehearses the mournful story of Judas' apostacy and fall. He narrates circum-stantially the tale of his base treachery and miserable end. Bold and fearless as the speaker was by nature, we can well imagine with what profound emotion he

---

[1] "Peter's situation among the Apostles was, manifestly not that of Supreme Ruler, but apparently that kind of Presidentship which, in every kind of Assembly among ourselves, is conferred on some one who, under the title of 'Chairman' or 'Speaker,' *presides* in the Assembly, though without any thought of dictating to, and bearing rule over, the other members."—*Whateley's Lectures on the Apostles*, p. 16.

narrated the successive incidents in that awful tragedy. How nearly he too had been involved in similar guilt and shame! Rather how vividly the thought must have come home to him, that while the one wretched Apostle had sought no place of repentance, but in a fit of wild remorse threw down the wretched lure of blood-money, and perished in his sins, he had been made a monument and miracle of mercy and pardoning love. How keenly and gratefully he must have felt, as he contemplated this awful "bankruptcy of hope" in another, "by the grace of God I am what I am." It would seem, too, to indicate the depth and genuineness of his repentance. "Only let the heart be at bottom sincere and true to God," is Olshausen's remark, "and the soul may soon rise again from a very deep fall."

The object of his address is to invite his fellow-disciples to take immediate steps to fill up the vacant place caused by the defection of their erring brother. Though Judaism was now to be for ever superseded by Christianity, the type by the Antitype, it would seem, nevertheless, to be in accordance with the Divine Mind, that the number of the Apostolic band should still continue its correspondence with the number of the twelve Hebrew tribes. They were to be the representatives of God's spiritual Israel. Peter's friend, who in a later year saw in vision "the Holy City, New Jerusalem," describes its "twelve foundations" as bearing "the names of the twelve Apostles of the Lamb." It is more than probable that one among the sacred private injunctions of the Master, given to the Apostles during the forty days, was to fill up without delay the place rendered vacant. A special qualification in the candidates for the sacred office was that of having been a personal witness of the Lord's resurrection. Even St Paul at a future, time in vindicating his own claims to the Apostleship, alludes to the fact that he had " seen the Lord ; " adding, as he enumerates the other names of those similarly privileged, " Last of all of me also." "Wherefore," says Peter in summing up his statement, " it is necessary that of these men who have accompanied us all the time that the Lord Jesus went in and out among us, beginning from the baptism of John unto the day when He was taken up from us, one should become a witness with us of His resurrection " (Acts i. 21, 22).   Let me give, however, in full the recorded address of the speaker.   And in doing so, it may be worthy of note, that here, as in all his speeches and preaching, Peter enforces his arguments and appeals by quotations from Old Testament Scripture.   " And in those days, Peter rising up in the midst of the brethren, said (the number of the names together was about an hundred and twenty), Men and brethren, it was necessary that this scripture should be fulfilled which the Holy Ghost foretold by the mouth of David concerning Judas, who was guide to those who took Jesus.   For he was numbered among us, and received the office of this ministry.   Now this man purchased a field with the wages of iniquity ; and falling headlong, he burst asunder in the midst, and all his bowels gushed out. And it was known to all the inhabitants of Jerusalem, so that that field was called in their own dialect, Aceldama, that is, The field of blood.   For it is written in the book of Psalms, ' Let his habitation be desolate, and let there be no dweller therein,' and ' his office let another take.'   Therefore it is necessary that of these men that have accompanied us all the time that the

Lord Jesus went in and out among us, beginning from the baptism of John unto the day when He was taken up from us, one should become a witness with us of His resurrection." [1]—*Tischendorf's Translation.*

After what has previously been said, it will be unnecessary here to revert to the question of Peter's primacy, save to note in passing, that had his claims been of that exclusive character which the Roman Church advances, unquestionably he would, *ex cathedra,* and on the ground of his own paramount authority, have proposed the successor to Judas. He would not have deemed it needful, but, on the contrary, derogatory to his official rank and prerogatives, even to solicit the assent and ratification of the assembled brethren. So far, however, from any lording it over God's heritage, he arrogates no higher power than that of being simply the mouthpiece of the assembly, leaving the final result to the great Searcher of hearts. Indeed, even the suggesting of the names rested not with him, but with them. "THEY appointed two," &c. The candidates were selected for suffrage, evidently from the number of the seventy disciples. Joseph, called Barsabas, first named, was supposed by some to have been one of the brothers or relatives of the Lord, surnamed " Justus " probably on account of his high character for probity. A legend has found its way among the early writers regarding him, that he drank poison, but, by faith in the Divine power, the potion failed to have a fatal effect. A more reliable testimony is, that he continued Christ's faithful soldier and servant unto the end ; and at last, from the hands of Jewish bigots, received the crown of martyrdom. [2] The other was

---

[1] Acts i. 15–22. [2] Calmet.

Matthias, who, on the authority of Nicephorus, was said to have preached the gospel, and suffered martyrdom in Ethiopia. From both names signifying "the gift of God," he has been supposed by some to be none other than Nathanael. This, however, is purely conjectural. Thus far, then, in the election of an apostle to fill the vacant place, were all the preliminary steps taken by the "hundred and twenty :"—but farther they cannot, on their own responsibility, proceed. "The subsequent selection between the two," says a writer, "was referred in prayer to Him who, knowing the hearts of men, knew which of them was the fitter to be His witness and apostle. The brethren, under the heavenly guidance which they had invoked, proceeded to give forth their lots, probably by each writing the name of one of the candidates on a tablet, and casting it into the urn. The urn was then shaken, and the name that first came out decided the election. Lightfoot describes another way of casting lots which was used in assigning to the priests their several parts in the service of the temple. The Apostles, it will be remembered, had not yet received the gift of the Holy Ghost, and this solemn mode of casting the lots, in accordance with a practice enjoined in the Levitical law (Lev. xvi. 8) is to be regarded as a way of referring the decision to God. (Comp. Prov. xvi. 33.")[1] Chrysostom remarks that it was never again resorted to in the Christian Church after the descent at Pentecost. The Moravians alone, among the

[1] Bib. Dic., ii. 279. See, too, the explicit Divine command to Moses, in the original division of the land among the tribes of Israel (Num. xxvi. 52). The soldiers selected to make the attack on Gibeah were chosen by lot, which seems to point to its sanction even in Hebrew warfare (Judges xx. 9).

existing Churches of Christendom, still follow what they regard as the Apostolic practice and obligation.

It has been maintained indeed by a few modern writers, those too of some name—and their theory is not without plausibility—that this election of Matthias was a precipitate and unauthorised proceeding on the part of Peter—another example, added to the many of his previous history, of rash and inconsiderate impulse. Sanction, it has been alleged, he had none, for taking the responsible and momentous step of filling up the vacancy in the apostolic number; that such an appointment rested not with himself and his brethren, but with their glorified Master, who had Himself chosen each of them, and delegated to them authority to choose for Him; that the appointment of Matthias was practically annulled and set aside by the subsequent "call to be an Apostle" of the great Apostle of the Gentiles, who claims and appropriates the name :—"Am I not an Apostle?" "I was the least of all the Apostles, not worthy to be called an Apostle." "Are they Apostles? So am I :"—who, moreover, gives as the special qualification he possessed to fill the vacant office, that he had "seen Christ;" and witnessed, though in a peculiar way, His resurrection, when on his way to Damascus he saw his Lord's living form, and heard his Lord's living voice. We cannot, however, believe, if Peter had on this occasion committed the infant Church to an unlawful "human act" (an interference with the Divine prerogative), that it would have been apparently homologated, and that no reference, by way of rebuke or condemnation, would have been made in the sacred narrative. It surely is not in itself a likely thing that the very first public deed of the Christian Church would be permitted

R

by its Lord and Head to be a serious error ; that the
first of the "Acts of the Apostles" was an act of unauthorised presumption, in contrariety with the Divine
will ; that the first trumpet-blast in preparing for the
battle had proved an uncertain, or rather a false sound.
Matthias, however little known to us, does not stand
alone in that respect among the others of the apostolic
band.   We have reason to conclude, as has been already
observed, that he formed one of the seventy mission
disciples ; and if so, he fulfilled, even more than St
Paul, the special qualification in those selected to fill
the office, as having companied with the Lord Jesus
during His public ministry, as well as being eyewitnesses of His resurrection.   Nor can we accord with
the harsh verdict which, in the present instance, has
been by some pronounced on Peter.   The words with
which the responsible choice was entered upon, do not
indicate presumption and self-confident assertion.   Devoutly realising a present though unseen Saviour, he
thus leads the devotions of the hour with the solemn
appeal, "Thou, Lord, who knowest the hearts of all,
show whether of these two Thou hast chosen."   Moreover, St Paul seems to occupy a niche peculiarly his
own in the gospel temple—the Apostle of the uncircumcision, as distinguished from the twelve apostles of the
circumcision—an Apostle truly in the best sense of the
word, but "one born out of due time," and unable, from
personal observation, to attest the great facts of gospel
history, and the crowning evidence of all, "The Lord is
risen."   Although, therefore, the former view is supported with great ingenuity and ability by Stier, as well
as writers of note in our own country, the deliverance

thus tersely summed up by Lange seems the more reliable one, and that too accepted by the great majority—
"We find not the least trace in Scripture, or in the ancient Church, that this step taken by Peter had been disapproved of. As regards Paul, he himself better understood his position in the kingdom of God. He is contrasted with the apostles of the Jews as the apostle of the Gentiles, or more exactly, the apostle of progress as contrasted with the apostles of the foundation."[1] A recent writer uses language of still stronger commendation—"Surely it was an act of no common courage to take upon themselves to elect and consecrate a new apostle. How many of us would have thought it safer to leave all exactly as Christ had left it! Not so these hundred and twenty; they see the wisdom of St Peter's counsel that they should at once complete their organisation; and they act upon it, certain their unseen Lord and Master will stay them if they are wrong. And clearly they were right! Dead things only are fixed and stationary. Living things ever are growing and acting. Life, and life means growth, is the essential condition of Christ's Church."[2]

In closing this chapter, we can only think of the increase in Peter's devotedness to his Redeemer's cause and service. When a beloved earthly friend is withdrawn from sight, how the affections of the bereaved are deepened and intensified! Death is often the test of the strength and reality of our love. Peter, and the sympathetic hearts around, were only more feelingly alive, alike to the greatness of their loss, and the

[1] Lange's "Apostol." vol. ii. p. 12.
[2] Canon Norris' "Key to the Acts of the Apostles," p. 5.

warmth of their attachment. May we not also suppose that they were so absorbed in the thought of His mediatorial glory and joy that they repressed every tearful emotion? In the mysterious, undefined future, there mingled, with all its dimness and darkness, the assurance of a "blessed hope," an unseen Presence, a coming reunion of "loved and lost."

CHAPTER XIV.

Peter at Pentecost.

> " O golden rain from heaven!
> Thy precious dews be given
> To bless the Church's barren field!
> And let thy waters flow
> Where'er the sowers sow
> The seed of truth, that it may yield
> A hundredfold its living fruit,
> O'er all the land may take deep root,
> And mighty branches heavenward shoot."
> —*Lyra Germanica.*

"Peter (in the storm on the lake) was the image of weak faith, staggered by the storms of this world; but after he had received the gift of the Holy Ghost, he who was like a fluent wave became a steadfast rock, unmoved by the tempest of persecution and the fear of death."—*Augustine.*

"One colossal figure emerges from the gloom, now more than ever the representative of his brethren. Can we doubt that when they saw him stand forth in the front of the whole body of the believers, in their first days of bereavement, for the election of a new apostle; in their first hour of exultation on the day of Pentecost; that when they witnessed the thousands upon thousands of his converts, they felt that it was the rolling back of the everlasting doors by him who had the keys of the kingdom of heaven?"—*Stanley's Sermons on the Apostolic Age,* pp. 89, 90.

"In him is found that bold spirit of the pioneer which, when purified in the crucible of trial and repentance, will make him the man of action and preponderating influence in the first period of the apostolic age."—*Pressensé.*

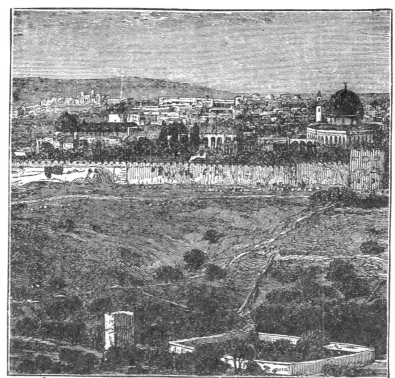

HE vacancy in the Apostolic number being now filled up, they must continue to wait patiently for the fulfilment of the great promise of the Holy Spirit, whose advent their Divine Lord had said would more than indemnify them for the loss entailed by His departure. "It is expedient for you that I go away; for if I go not away, the Comforter will not come unto you; but if I depart, I will send Him unto you" (John xvi. 7). The present position and attitude of the infant Church remind us of Zechariah's symbolic vision of the candlestick "all of gold," with its seven lamps—the Jewish number of completion — and their connecting seven pipes. All was in readiness for the distilling of the oil from the "two olive-trees;" above all, for the Divine *fire* which was to complete the object for

which the candlestick was erected—the illumination of
a dark world.   When is the Church's Lord to "answer
by fire"?

Peter's feelings at this crisis were doubtless those of
a brave soldier eager to begin the assault which would
lead to the deliverance of beleaguered captives, but
who must continue in a state of inaction till the per-
missive word be given.

That word would not be delayed.   A faithful Saviour
had expressly said that it would be "not after many
days."   What the precise boon was which was to be
conferred they appear to have had an indistinct idea.
It is evident that with some, possibly Peter among
the number, there had lingered up to the last interview
with their Master previous to the ascension, the fond
dream of the setting up of a temporal Messianic Kingdom.
"Lord!" was the question which very possibly emanated
from the lips of our apostle as spokesman, "restorest
Thou at this time the kingdom to Israel?" (Acts i. 6).
It has been noted that Jesus, in His reply, does not
give a precise and definite answer to their query: as
if He would leave the clearer light, which this new
Divine agent would impart, to dispel their darkness, and
unfold the full grandeur of a sovereignty very different
from what was associated in their minds with the
limits of Palestine and the sceptre of Judah.

The hours, the days pass, and yet it is with them
"hope deferred."   When the Sunday came round, the
first Easter day after the great Assumption, we may
imagine with what sanguine hearts they would look
for the bestowment of the promised Gift, which was,
as it were, to clothe them with invisible armour, and
turn them into spiritual giants.   As they sat together

at the fellowship feast, and called to memory the events which from their recency required no outward visible memorial, how must guest have whispered to guest, "Surely it must be to-day!" How will "the promise of the Father" be communicated? Will the white-robed angels of the sepulchre be delegated to bring down this Divine Comforter from the heavenly sanctuary? Will a burst of angel-song welcome in the Paraclete, as it did the Saviour thirty-three years before on Bethlehem's plains? Or might Peter have heard and garnered in his mind an old saying he had listened to on the banks of the Jordan, " He shall baptize you with the Holy Ghost and with *fire?*" Will it be the seraphim of Isaiah who will be employed to fetch some live coals from off the holy Altar before the Throne, and to touch therewith each lip of the waiting throng?

The hours of that Lord's day pass in silence; the lengthened shadows are projected athwart the Valley of Jehoshaphat; but no sign appears in the serene heaven above Mount Olivet, where last they strained their eyes in watching the receding cloud which bore their best Friend away. Ere evening closes, surely, at all events, they will see once more the " gates ajar," and these longing prayers of theirs will be answered! But the sun has set over the mountains of Bether; the stars resume their silent watch, and all is still. We may imagine them stealing hour after hour during the day to the flat roof of the dwelling, and gazing up into the ethereal blue of an eastern sky, longing for some harbinger of the great Gift. We may think of them at night on the outlook for some bright meteor such as that which led the sages of Persia to the manger cradle. But, like the answer of the prophet's child, each delegate returns with the reply, "There is nothing!" No "still, small voice" steals on these saddened hearts. And so day by day, and eve by eve, all that next long week, prayer ascends—an "ecstasy of worship"—and still no answer; the earth is as brass, and the heavens as iron. Will not the outside Jewish world be confirmed in its scorn of these lofty pretensions of a crucified Galilean, and pity the reckless and persistent fanaticism of the poor dreamers who are still clinging with the desperation of drowning men to a baseless delusion? In vain the psalm is sung, and the invocation and pleading prolonged. The God they invoke seems to be like Baal, "asleep or on a journey." One of these whom we now know well, more impatient naturally than the others, may at times be ready to abandon hope. Fancying perhaps that something in himself might be the hindrance, he might be tempted to utter the old upbraiding cry of the misgiving prophet, "Surely my way is hid from the Lord, and my judgment is passed over from my God." Mysterious and unaccountable delay! The reapers standing with their whetted sickles in hand, and the fields "already white unto the harvest" inviting an abundant ingathering; and yet the command, amounting to a present prohibition, is "*Tarry* ye in the city of Jerusalem, until ye be endued with power from on high."

It was the solemn preparation season;—"the hour of expectancy," which has ever been found to prelude a time of true revival—the season when the furrows are being prepared to receive the precious seed and the falling shower; the tolling of the bell preceding the time and the act of worship. All God's greatest works are characterised by deliberation—slowness of development. Specially is this the case in the growth of His Church, and in the hearts of His people. " He that believeth shall not make haste." What a discipline for persevering prayer! What an occasion for continued importunate pleading! Some of these earnest, longing suppliants would perhaps remember a parable which now-glorified lips once spake to them, " How that men ought always to pray and not faint."

But " the Lord is good to them that wait for Him, unto the soul that seeketh Him." After a few additional days, in which faith was disciplined and prayer loaded the cloud of mercy, that cloud burst in showers of blessing on the disciples' heads. The heavens are opened, and the true baptism of fire takes place!

It was early, probably very early in the morning (as we gather from Acts ii. 15),[1] long before the smoke of the sacrifice was seen rising from the temple courts— Nature's sweet hour of calm and refreshment, when the dews were lying thick on Olivet, and the rising sun was bathing the tops of the Moab mountains. It was, too, on the Feast of Pentecost, the great feast of Wheat-harvest, or Fiftieth Day, as it was familiarly called among the Hellenistic Jews, a feast which differed from the two other great national anniversaries of Passover and Tabernacles by occupying only a single day in its celebration. And there was a beautiful and befitting reason why our blessed Lord, in the plenitude of His wisdom, should have selected the old typical festival to form in future the commemoration of a mightier event. Pentecost occurred the fiftieth day after the killing of the Paschal Lamb in Egypt, and the sprink-

[1] The third hour of the day would be 9 A.M.

ling of its blood on the lintels and doorposts of the
dwellings of Israel. Accordingly its first celebration
took place among the valleys around Sinai, amid the
thunderings and lightnings of the Mount of God. It
was surely alike appropriate and remarkable that the
very same day in the year on which the law was given
to Israel, that law " which gave them national life and
unity," the Holy Spirit should come down to give life and
unity to the Church. " As the possession of the law
had completed the deliverance of the Hebrew race,
wrought by the hand of Moses; so the gift of the
Spirit perfected the work of Christ in the establishment of His kingdom upon earth." [1] That mount of
Jehovah in the great and terrible wilderness, was a
permanent monument and memorial of the *power*
of God; and although there was in the antitypical
" Whitsunday" no element of terror or awe, though
the new voice was not to be emitted amid cloud,
and tempest and quaking precipices, yet they had
reason, too, to expect some manifestation of Divine
majesty or omnipotence; for it had been expressly intimated that that favoured handful of spiritual Israelites,
under a new dispensation, were to be " endued with
POWER from on high :" " Ye shall receive *power* after
that the Holy Ghost is come upon you." Nor was
this the only reason for the appropriateness of Pentecost as the season selected for the bestowment of this
promised outpouring of the Spirit. There were others
also. It was a harvest-festival, the great day of thanksgiving for the wheat ingathering. On the morning of
the most memorable day of Peter's life, when his Divine
Master rose triumphant from His grave on Golgotha,

[1] Bib. Dic., Art. Pentecost.

the first sheaf of barley harvest had been waved before the Lord in the temple; and now when the main harvest-treasure, the great cereal of Palestine, had fully ripened, a second offering takes place: and prominent in the rite is a similar presentation before Jehovah of the two first wheaten loaves. While the former was eminently typical of Him who, in His glorious resurrection, was the first-fruits of a multitude which no man can number, redeemed by His precious blood; equally beautifully and significantly surely did the latter point to those who were to form "the first-fruits of the Spirit," gathered in and consecrated to God. The rite, moreover, next to the Feast of Tabernacles, was celebrated with greatest joy. It partook much more of a jubilant festival than the Passover. It was an occasion of liberality to the poor; and though its duration does not seem to have exceeded one day, brief as the ceremony was, it was attended, and more especially in later times, by Jews from all parts of the world. So Josephus specially notes (Ant. xiv. 13), and his statement is amply corroborated in the inspired narrative before us. Many Jews who, from distant homes, came up to the Passover, were in the habit of remaining till the Feast of Pentecost; and when we bear in mind the statement of the same historian, that at the siege of Titus during the former season, three millions were crowded within the walls of the city of solemnities, we may have some approximate idea of the vast throng which must have been brought together at this time. We may even believe that on the present occasion an unusual number would be assembled in consequence of that universal expectation, to which we have more than once referred, over the length and breadth of the Roman empire, as to the coming of the Messiah of ancient prophecy. Besides what we have indicated, we have no very reliable knowledge as to what were the other special symbols of joy and thanksgiving which distinguished the celebration of Pentecost. They may possibly have been similar in character to those at the Feast of Tabernacles—the waving of myrtle, and olive, and palm branches; certainly the singing of the Hallel. We know that in the modern keeping of the feast, the Jews have their houses festooned with flowers, wearing chaplets of the same on their heads, to testify their joy in the possession of the law. The same writer who mentions these facts adds, as a remarkable peculiarity which is of interest to us in the life we are now tracing, that "they eat such food as is prepared with milk, because the purity of the Divine law is likened to milk; hence the significance of the expression used by St Peter in his second epistle, "The sincere *milk* of the word." [1]

On that memorable day of joy, then, the disciples were gathered in the place where prayer was wont to be made; and although the assertion cannot be made absolutely, there is another probable coincidence which adds to the interest of the occasion. Those best conversant with Jewish chronology suppose, that the present Pentecostal season must have occurred on "the Lord's-day"—not the Jewish Sabbath, but the commemorative Resurrection-day—the new Sunday of the Christian Church. "The Jewish Pentecost," to quote Olshausen, "in the year of our Lord's death, fell upon Saturday; but it began at six o'clock in the evening,

1 Bib. Dic., Art. Pentecost.

when the Sabbath was at a close, and it lasted until six o'clock on Sunday evening." "If the Paschal Supper was eaten on the 13th, and Christ was crucified on the 14th, the Sunday of the Resurrection must have been the day of the omer, and Pentecost must have occurred on the first day of the week." [1] Full of earnest hope the gathered disciples would in all likelihood be engaged in united supplication, " preventing the dawning of the morning." We know not whose voice at the moment may have been ascending to the Great High Priest ; who it was that was pleading the recently guaranteed promise, " Whatsoever ye shall ask the Father in My name, He will give it you." Would it be Peter, the " Rock-man," wrestling as the Patriarch " Prince" did of old at Peniel, and prevailing ? We are not told. Be that as it may, without note of warning, a noise " like to " ($\omega\sigma\pi\epsilon\varrho$) the sound of a rushing mighty wind, which has been compared to that with which Ezekiel was familiar in his Chebar visions, is heard. " Tempests blow commonly horizontally. This appeared to come *from above,* and this is all that is meant by the expression ' from heaven.' " [2] It was neither earthquake, nor tempest, nor whirlwind, as some would explain away the supernatural element in it. The walls, and doors, and rafters of the dwelling are unmoved. The 120 startled disciples remain uninjured. " The Lord is in His holy place, as in Mount Sinai." It was an unmistakable announcement, by an outer audible sign, of the advent of the promised Divine Invisible Spirit, and the direction of the sound indicated His descent from heaven. " It may be remarked," observes the same commentator, " that this

[1] Art. Pentecost, Smith's Bib. Dic.   [2] Barnes.

miracle was *really* far more striking than the common
supposition makes it to have been. A *tempest* might
have been terrific ; a mighty *wind* might have alarmed
them ; but there would have been nothing unusual or
remarkable in it. Such things often occurred, and the
thoughts would have been directed, of course, to the
storm as an ordinary, though perhaps alarming occurrence. But when all was still, when there was no
storm, no wind, no rain, no thunder, such a rushing
sound must have arrested their attention, and directed
all minds to so unusual and unaccountable an occurrence."[1]

Cloven or divided tongues, like as of fire, came down
separately on the heads of each of them, and remained
settled there.[2]

> " The days of hope and prayer are past,
> The day of comfort dawns at last.
> The everlasting gates again
> Roll back, and lo ! a royal train,
> From the far depth of light once more
> The floods of glory earthward pour.
> They part like shower-drops in mid air,
> But ne'er so soft fell noontide shower,
> Nor ev'ning rainbow gleam'd so fair
> To weary swains in parched bower.
> Swiftly and straight each tongue of flame,
> Through cloud and breeze unwavering came."
> —*Christian Year.*

[1] Barnes on Acts, p. 29.

[2] Renan and his school, with the usual rejection of the miraculous, suggest, to account for these appearances, a flash, or successive flashes of
lightning. Others a *semblance* of these fiery tongues, arising from the
spectators being in a trance or ecstasy, superinduced by their prolonged
devotions—the vision of distempered and excited imaginations. But all
these are gratuitous, inadmissible, and totally at variance with the plain
meaning of the passage. " The writer," says Olshausen, "manifestly in-
tends that we should form to ourselves the idea of a fiery stream which
divided itself, and whose radiations spread over all, and rested upon them."

If it had been intended that Peter was to become, according to the Roman theory and claim, his Lord's vicar and successor, doubtless on him alone would the fiery " mitre " have been placed. But while he wears this strange coronal of flame, he looks around him, and beholds his brethren and sisters bearing the same, from John and James, Andrew and Philip, to the latest chosen Matthias, and the female watchers by the Cross and the Sepulchre. Even the Virgin Mother, doubtless, was there, crowned in a nobler sense than by the idolatries of an apostate Church of later ages. Recognising in her own case, as in that of those gathered around, the blessed token that her Son, ' being by the right hand of God exalted, and having received of the Father the promise of the Holy Ghost, had shed forth this,'—might she not have resumed on that festival of double joy the strains of her old song of praise—" My soul doth magnify the Lord, and my spirit hath rejoiced in God my Saviour." We may feel sure the substance, at all events, of that hymn would be on every heart and lip of that rapt assembly.

But as we linger on the scene, and behold Peter with the flaming Symbol on his head, let us pause, and more particularly inquire as to its meaning.

The Fire was no strange or novel emblem. It was the invariable token and sign of present Deity. Jehovah in ancient days preceded the Host of Israel in the wilderness by a Pillar of *fire :*—out of a Canopy of flame (a *fire*) He delivered the law :—out of a bush of flaming fire in that same wilderness He had first spoken to Israel's leader. The vision Ezekiel had of his great Lord was that of " a cloud and a fire unfolding itself " (Ezek. i. 4). The Fire which now descended, therefore,

S

was the undoubted indication and symbol of the Divine nearness and presence. It was as if the Shekinah of the first Temple had reappeared in the inauguration of the Great spiritual Temple of the future. That Temple, in a new sense, was " filled with the glory of the Lord."

But while the fire doubtless indicated " Surely the Lord is in this place," and converted that upper chamber into a Bethel; there was a latent significancy in the novelty of the form in which the flames appeared—" tongues," and " cloven tongues."

Tongues! These were symbolic of the instrumentality which was to be employed, and to become effectual in extending the kingdom of Christ. " Go ye into all the world," were among the last words which fell from the Master's lips, " and *preach* the Gospel to every creature." " It hath pleased God," was the comment of the greatest of ministers, on his Lord's injunction, " by the foolishness of *preaching* to save them that believe." Human *speech* was to form, in the future, God's noblest means in making known the Great Salvation. In a sense the wise seer of Israel never dreamt of, " Death and life were to be in the power of the *tongue*." By that mighty power, proud Pharisees, sceptic Sadducees, effeminate Greeks, haughty Romans, slaves and beggars, publicans and harlots, soldiers and merchant princes and members of Cæsar's household, were all alike to accept with gratitude and joy the tidings of Redeeming Love.

And it is specially worthy of note in the conversions to which we shall presently allude, that it was not the *miracle* which directly led to these. The manifestations of supernatural agency produced only amazement in some, and mockery and scorn among the many. But it was when the *tongue* of the unschooled speaker was unloosed,—in other words, when the Gospel was preached—that eyes were dimmed with tears, hearts humbled and broken, quickened and saved.

They were, moreover, Tongues of *fire*, the tongue of man but inflamed and inspired by God. The rushing mighty wind and the phenomenon of flame, together significantly proclaimed the Divine power, and the superhuman ability with which that power would endow.

Nor was the " cloven " tongue, the divided, forked flame, without significance. The tongues in which that Gospel was to be proclaimed were to be many :— one element of fire, but diverse in shape to suit the varied languages, and it may be characteristic of earth's diverse peoples. For in connection with the external symbol was another marvel, and the greatest of all, that each came to speak previously unknown languages, ejaculating words probably unintelligible to themselves, but understood by those in whose dialect they spake. It was the fulfilment of one of the " wonders " predicted by Christ Himself in His memorable Sermon on the Mount of Olives: " These signs shall follow them that believe . . . they shall speak with new tongues " (Mark xvi. 17).[1] Babel's old confusion of language is no barrier to the Spirit's divine energy. " We are at once led to ascribe to the historian the

[1] Chrysostom's view, which was followed by several of the early Fathers, is untenable on several grounds, viz., that the gift was bestowed for the ultimate dissemination of Christianity :—that each Apostle was miraculously gifted at the moment with the power of speaking *one* language other than his own native Aramaic, and that whatever the new tongue was, it was designed thus preternaturally to indicate to him the country he was

idea that an effect was here exhibited, exactly the reverse of the separation that once took place among the
nations by the confusion of tongues. The outpouring
of the Spirit of God through the instrumentality of the
gift of tongues, melted together again the broken fragments into a new unity.[1] " Is not My word like fire ?"
—Though a different emblem, it recalls the flight of the
Apocalyptic Angel of Patmos with " the little book" in
his hand, speeding " to every nation, and kindred, and
tongue, and people."

" Then they were all filled with the Holy Ghost."
Every soul was made a Temple of indwelling Deity.

Soon the strange fact obtained publicity. Soon it
was noised about street and Temple-court, and crowded
tent on Olivet and Jehoshaphat, that the unlearned
and ignorant men of Galilee were speaking no longer
in their native Aramaic, but in diverse languages, previously unknown and unacquired. Probably the small
upper room is too limited to contain the crowd that is
hastening to see and hear this new marvel, and so the
fire-crowned company descend themselves to the streets
to proclaim the Name that is above every name. " Like
the school of the prophets of old who went forth to
greet King Saul, this new school of prophets go forth
into the streets of Jerusalem, and meet the crowds who
would be already assembling for the Temple service."[2]
Their ecstatic theme was " The mighty things of God"

commissioned to evangelise" (Homil. on Acts, *in loco*). " I believe," says
Dean Alford (Greek Test. vol. ii. p. 12), " the event related to have been a
sudden and powerful inspiration of the Holy Spirit, by which the disciples
uttered, not of their own minds, but as mouthpieces of the Spirit, the
praises of God in various languages, hitherto, and possibly at the time itself,
unknown to them."

[1] Olshausen, *in loco*.
[2] Canon Norris, " Key to the Acts," p. 8.

(Τὰ μεγαλεῖα ῥοῦ Θεοῦ), a noble birth-song for this second Genesis of the Church—a prelude at least of that Gentile Hosannah which was yet to unite with the Hebrew Hallelujah, in hailing the ascended Christ of Nazareth as Son of God and Saviour of the world; and that too in every tongue and language under heaven. "They spake," we read, "as the Spirit gave them utterance"—an unequivocal testimony that they were inspired men—uttering not their own thoughts or words—but speaking under the direct control and impulse of the Holy Ghost.

We may follow in thought the footsteps of Peter in this his first embassage of power. Shall we suppose him hastening to the cloisters of the Temple where Jews and proselytes from all countries, representatives from Europe, Asia, and Africa, were fast gathering at that early hour, to secure places at the opening Pentecostal services? It has been surmised from the word employed, that several of these foreign Jews had taken up their abode in the ancient capital; that, in the same way as those who have visited the modern Jerusalem never fail to be struck with the many Israelites gathered from all nationalities, who have been attracted in their latter days to the city of their fathers, in order that they may lay their dust in the Valley of Jehoshaphat;—so it may have been then. It is manifest, however, that these permanent residents were exceptional — that the vast majority were composed of caravans of pilgrims who had come from a distance to attend the feast, who were naturally most familiar with the language of the varied countries of their adoption; many of whom indeed were unable to converse in the current Syro-Chaldaic speech of Palestine. There is an

Egyptian here, a Roman there, a Persian there, an Ethiopian there. Peter has a word in their own native vernacular for each and all of them. The Jewish onlookers may mock and jeer, and with a contemptuous smile of disdain say 'these men are inebriated'—"full of new wine"—apprehending danger and riot from the violent outward excitement. But the imputation is not credited by any means universally. Even those who can only gaze with dumb amazement have the inward conviction that something strange and unwonted has happened. The awe-struck foreigners, with the eager enthusiasm peculiar to Eastern crowds, carry the tidings from group to group, and from cloister to cloister. A congregation is speedily formed: " Yonder," may be the cry as they see a bold figure making his way through the crowd, and taking his place on an extemporised pulpit in one of the Temple-courts, " Yonder is Simon of Galilee. Let us follow and listen to his own account of these strange things."

So, like the Athenians of a later age, as they gathered around a more accomplished Orator on Mars Hill, to hear the new doctrine of "Jesus and the Resurrection," the Pentecostal worshippers assemble around this bold Bethsaida fisherman. We long to obtain a momentary glimpse of the living man, and note how he comports himself in this the first great emergency after the ascension of his Master. How changed in many respects he must have been, since the day when we spoke of him in opening manhood, pursuing his worldly calling on the shores of his native lake, without having so much as a thought of his conspicuous future! The last few months—rather we should say the last few

weeks—of the three past eventful years, must especially
have left on his countenance the traces of that struggle
which had so nearly ended in the doom of a traitor,
but which had left him more than all his fellow-apostles
a debtor to grace — that grace bringing him anew
out of darkness into "marvellous light." The last
few hours had done more than all. We may imagine
him coming forth like Moses from the presence of God
on the mount, with his face still lustrous with the recent
glory—resolute, undaunted, self-possessed. No sign
of the timidity or vacillation of former years ; no skulk-
ing now away in the dark from duty and peril. His
subsequent words attest his fearlessness, when with
unhesitating tongue, in language not to be evaded or
misunderstood, he serves on his audience the awful indictment of having with wicked hands plotted and consummated the murder of the Lord of Glory ! There
is an end to all captious difficulties and objections,—
" Thou shalt never wash my feet :" of all mistimed and
unwarranted questionings as to the necessity of his
Master's sufferings,—" This be far from Thee, Lord."
The baptism of fire has shed a new and lurid light on
much that was before incomprehensible regarding that
cross and passion. Impressed with the dominating
thought that the death of Jesus was the life of the
world, his whole resolve and desire now and subsequently seems to be, like his brother-Apostle, to glory
in the cross of Christ, and to lead others to espouse
the creed that " there is none other name under heaven
given among men whereby we must be saved."

As we follow him, then, from the fiery baptism of the
" upper room," his whole soul seems kindled with the
symbolic flame which, a few moments ago, played on his

head.   The oft-before "Ready to halt," is now a "Son of Thunder;" a mouth and wisdom has been given unto him, which all his adversaries will be unable to gainsay or resist.   He knows well the complex character of his hearers, their scornful prejudices, and vengeful religious hates.   There were indeed doubtless among these, not a few who were "religious according to the light they had previously enjoyed;" for we are expressly told in the narrative, that among the multitude there were "*devout* men out of every nation under heaven," earnest seekers after the truth; of the same stamp as those names afterwards familiar in the Acts,—like the Ethiopian Eunuch, or the noble-born Roman Cornelius,—proselytes who had come to worship the God of Israel at His appointed festival, and who, though unattached to the person and cause of Jesus, recognised Him as a Holy teacher and prophet, worthy of all reverence.   But doubtless the great majority was composed of a totally different class; and among these again, would be comprehended wide diversities of feeling. There would be haters and bigots of every hue and type, jealous of the traditions of their fathers; from the phylacteried Pharisee and sceptic Sadducee down to the base traffickers in the Temple merchandise, who would see their godless gains imperilled in a new sect that made so little of letter and ceremonial, and so much of spirit and spiritual worship.   Many of all these varied characters had been spectators of the scene on Calvary; many more, it is evident, had been active participators in the gigantic crime,—had joined in the cry, "He is a deceiver of the people, and worthy of death," "Not this man but Barabbas," "Crucify Him, crucify Him," "His blood be on us, and on our children." This is manifest from the language used by Peter in his sermon ; for, as we have just noted, he directly impeaches them with the death of the Lord of Glory. "Him, being delivered by the determinate counsel and foreknowledge of God, *ye* have taken and by wicked hands have crucified and slain : "—" God hath made that same Jesus, whom *ye* have crucified, both Lord and Christ." And when the arrow of conviction "pricked their heart," they cried out in the agony of conscious guilt and self-condemnation—" Men and brethren, what shall we do? [1] "

The sermon or address delivered by the Apostle is not in itself distinguished by what we would now call great qualities. It is simple in the extreme ; without metaphor, or subtlety, or eloquence, or declamation. He seeks calmly yet fearlessly to convince them of the erroneous impressions of some and the slanders of others, and leads them to the acceptance of the "blessed hope" which was the anchor of his own soul. It formed, indeed, an illustrative comment on words he wrote in his later life : " Be ready always to give an answer to every man that asketh you a reason of the hope that is in you with meekness and fear" (1 Peter iii. 15). He begins with repudiating the false surmise of the mockers, who had mistaken the visible effects of a divine manifestation for a fit of inebriety. The very hour and season were conjointly sufficient to refute such an imputation, seeing it was " but the third hour of the day;" and until the sixth hour, till after the sacrifices were offered and the oblations made, the Jews observed on

[1] See Prof. James Buchanan on the "Office and Work of the Holy Spirit," p. 370-1.

festive seasons a rigid abstinence from wine and meat.[1]
He claims for that strange scene of apparently unnatural
excitement, the fulfilment of a prophecy of Joel, when
that seer predicted that in the waning of the Jewish
dispensation God was to pour out of His Spirit upon
all flesh.   " Meantime, and in the midst of these signs,
the covenant of the spiritual dispensation is (ver. 21),
' *Whosoever* shall call on the name of the Lord shall
be saved.'   The gates of God's mercy are thrown open
in Christ to all people ; no barrier is placed, *no union
with any external association or succession required :*
the promise is to *individuals* AS *individuals*." [2]   Then
at once he takes up the key-note of all future Apostolic discourses, and proclaims in the hearing of " the
men of Israel," heirs of promise, the Divine Person of
Jesus of Nazareth.   He feels that in thus holding up
before their view the Prince of Life, he is not speaking
to them of a stranger.   For three years they had been
conversant with His " signs and wonders," His labours
of love, His works and words of mercy and kindness,
His holy life, His death of agony and humiliation
suffered at their hands.   Fortified farther by one of
David's Messianic Psalms, he proceeds to refer to the
resurrection and exaltation of Jesus at the Father's
right hand.   In that Psalm, the inspired minstrel of

---

[1] Lightfoot, Hor. Heb. iv. 29, with references to Josephus and the Talmudists.   " What is in the A. V. rendered ' new wine,' ought rather to be
translated ' sweet wine,' newly-fermented wine being an impossibility at
the season of Pentecost.   This sweet wine, preserved in cool places to preserve its luscious flavour, was greatly esteemed by the ancients, though
very intoxicating, and as quoted in one of the satires of Horace (Lib. ii.
Sat. 1), seems to have been a favourite *morning* draught ; hence the appropriateness of the false assumption made regarding the Apostles."—See Dr
Kitto's Pictorial Bible.

[2] Alford's Greek Test., vol. i. p. 19.

Israel in speaking of God "not suffering His Holy One to see corruption," but "making known to Him the way of life," could have no primary or even secondary reference to himself, for they could point to the monarch's sepulchre nigh at hand, on the brow of Zion, where his royal dust had been laid for centuries, and had been subjected to the common doom of mortality. He must, therefore, with prophetic insight, have been speaking of another and a Greater, even of Him who had proved Himself by many unquestionable miracles to be the "Sent of God," who had both died and rose again, and of whose resurrection they were witnesses; and that that very outpouring of the Spirit which had caused mingled wonder and mockery, was nothing else than an attestation by the Divine Redeemer Himself of His completed work,—the promised evidence and pledge of His own exaltation and glorification. The speaker sums up all with the words, "Therefore let all the house of Israel know assuredly, that God made Him both Lord and Christ, even this Jesus whom ye have crucified" (ver. 36).

Olshausen observes, "We discover already in this first sermon, all the peculiarities of Apostolic preaching. It contains no reflections nor deductions concerning the doctrine of Christ—no proposition of new and unknown doctrines, but simply and entirely consists of the proclamation of *historical facts*." Although Peter refers to "the powers, and wonders, and signs" which had been done in the midst of them by "Jesus the Nazarene," also to the great central truth of Christianity and of their teaching — the resurrection of Christ from the dead, it is noteworthy that he grounds his main appeal not on these miraculous deeds of which he had been himself a distinguished witness, but rather on the fulfilment of *prophecy*. The reason of this was obvious. He was addressing those who were living in vivid expectation of the Messiah's advent; who were moreover thoroughly conversant with the utterances of their own prophets on this great theme, and he knew well that no argument would prove more potent and convincing than to show how these predictions had their signal fulfilment in the mysterious events that had been, and were being, transacted before their eyes.[1] Still more noteworthy is that which is remarked upon by Archbishop Whateley in his " Lectures on the Apostles " (p. 93): " Peter dwells especially on the very circumstance which had been to himself the chief stumblingblock—the *sufferings* and *death* of the Messiah; so completely at variance with all the expectations cherished by the Jewish nation. The Apostle who had, a very short time before, incurred rebuke for saying, ' Be it far from Thee, Lord; there shall no such thing happen unto Thee,' we now find declaring (Acts ii. 36), ' Let all the house of Israel know assuredly, that God hath made that same Jesus, whom *ye have crucified*, both Lord and Christ.' "

Like the prophet Elijah confronting the King and Queen of Samaria and the scoffing priests of Baal,—with the best eloquence of earnestness he thus speaks, in the Aramaic language: " Ye men of Judea, and all ye dwellers in Jerusalem, be this known unto you, and hearken to my words. For these men are not drunken, as ye suppose, for it is the third hour of the day. But this is that which was spoken by the prophet, ' It shall be in the last days, saith God, that I will pour out of My

---

[1] See this well stated in Dr Gloag's Commentary on the Acts, p. 104.

Spirit upon all flesh; and your sons and your daughters shall prophesy, and your young men shall see visions, and your old men shall dream dreams. And on My servants and on My handmaids I will pour out in those days of My Spirit, and they shall prophesy. And I will give wonders in heaven above, and signs in the earth beneath : blood, and fire, and vapour of smoke. The sun shall be turned into darkness, and the moon into blood, before the great and illustrious day of the Lord come. And it shall be, that whosoever shall call on the name of the Lord shall be saved.' Ye men of Israel, hear these words : Jesus the Nazarene, a man approved of God among you by powers and wonders and signs, which God did by Him in the midst of you, as ye yourselves know : Him, being delivered up according to the determinate counsel and foreknowledge of God, having crucified by the hand of lawless men, ye have slain : whom God raised up, having loosed the pains of death, because it was not possible that He should be holden by it. For David says with reference to Him, 'I saw the Lord always before Me, for He is on My right hand, that I be not moved. Therefore did My heart rejoice, and My tongue was glad ; moreover also My flesh shall rest in hope, because Thou wilt not leave My soul in Hades, nor give Thy Holy One to see corruption. Thou hast made known to Me the ways of life ; Thou wilt make Me full of joy with Thy countenance.' Men and brethren, I may speak to you with freedom of the patriarch David, because he is both dead and buried, and his sepulchre is among us unto this day. Therefore, being a prophet, and knowing that God had sworn with an oath to him, that of the fruit of his loins one should sit on his throne, he, fore-seeing this, spoke concerning the resurrection of Christ, that He was not left in Hades, neither did His flesh see corruption. This Jesus did God raise up, of which we all are witnesses. Therefore being by the right hand of God exalted, and having received of the Father the promise of the Holy Spirit, He shed forth this which ye see and hear. For David is not yet ascended into the heavens, but he says, The Lord said unto my Lord, ' Sit Thou on My right hand, until I make Thy foes Thy footstool.' Therefore let all the house of Israel know assuredly, that God made Him both Lord and Christ, even this Jesus whom ye have crucified."—*Tischendorf's Translation.*

I cannot forbear to add, though in a somewhat lengthened extract, partly too rehearsing what has been already said, an able writer's graphic description of this unparalleled gathering : " Never was such an audience assembled as that before which this poor fisherman appeared. Jews, with all the prejudices of their race, inhabitants of Jerusalem, with the recollection of the part they had recently taken in the crucifixion of Jesus of Nazareth, met in the city of their solemnities, jealous for the honour of their Temple and law ; men of different nations, rapidly and earnestly speaking in their different tongues ; one in Hebrew, mocking; another inquiring in Latin, another disputing in Greek, another wondering in Arabic ; and an endless Babel beside, expressing every variety of surprise, doubt, and curiosity. Amid such a scene the fisherman stands up ; his voice strikes across the hum which prevails all down the street. He has no tongue of silver, for they say, ' He is an unlearned and ignorant man.' The rudeness of his Galilean speech still remains with him ; yet, though 'unlearned and ignorant' in their sense, as to polite learning, in a higher sense he was a scribe well instructed. As respects the Word of God, he had been for three years under the constant tuition of the Prophet of Nazareth, hearing from His lips instruction in the law, in the prophets, and in all 'the deep things of God.' . . . The tongue of fire by degrees burns its way to the feelings of the multitude. The murmur gradually subsides; the mob becomes a congregation; the voice sweeps from end to end of that multitude, unbroken by a single sound; and, as the words rush on, they act like a stream of fire. Now one coating which covered the feelings is burned, and starts aside; now another, and another; now the fire touches the inmost covering of prejudice, which lay close upon the heart, and it, too, starts aside. Now it touches the quick, and burns the very soul of the man! Presently, you might think that in that throng there was but one mind—that of the preacher—which had multiplied itself, had possessed itself of thousands of hearts, and thousands of frames, and was pouring its own thoughts through them all. At length shame, and tears, and sobs overspread that whole assembly. Here, a head bows; there, starts a groan; yonder, rises a deep sigh; here, tears are falling; and some stern old Jew, who will neither bow nor weep, trembles with the effort to keep himself still. At length, from the depth of the crowd, the voice of the preacher is crossed by a cry, as if one was 'mourning for his only son,' and it is answered by a cry, as if one was in 'bitterness for his firstborn.' . . .

"No part of the proceedings of the day strikes us with a deeper or more lasting impression than the amazing change in Peter which is here manifest. . . . Here was a man who, in all probability, had passed the period of life when eloquence is most forcible without having distinguished himself by any such power. He comes forward with a most unwelcome message, to address an unfavourable audience, himself unskilled in the arts of oratory ; and yet such is the power of utterance given to him, that he produces an effect the like of which had never been known before in the history of mankind. Never has it been recorded in any other instance that three thousand men were in an hour persuaded by one of their own nation, of obscure origin and uninfluential position, to forego the prejudices of their youth, the favour of their people, and the religion of their fathers. ' I will be with thy mouth' is more strikingly fulfilled here, in those extraordinary effects of the speaking of an ordinary man, than in any other form in which the power of God could be displayed through the instrumentality of a human tongue." [1]

I need not dwell on the exhortation which followed Peter's sermon ;—as with rent garments and loud wailing, such as may be heard and seen to this day at the wailing wall of the old Temple, the terror-struck thousands cried, " What, oh, what shall we do ? "

" Luke," says Calvin, " doth now declare the fruit of the sermon, to the end we may know that the power of the Holy Ghost was not only showed forth in the diversity of tongues, but also in the hearts of those who heard." That sermon was addressed, as we have seen, to those who had been guilty of earth's greatest sin. If any individuals could be for ever excluded from hope of pardon and mercy, surely it would be those who had joined in the savage cry against that innocent Redeemer ; who

[1] Arthur's " Tongue of Fire," pp. 89–92.

had uttered the blasphemous taunt and jeer ; who had helped to put on the robe of mockery, or to weave the crown of thorns. But yet, in the most unqualified manner, the apostle preacher proclaims in the ears of the stricken multitude the fulness and freeness of the great salvation—that all are warranted, all are welcome, to come to the fountain opened for sin and for uncleanness, and have their crimson sins washed away,—the promise of the new covenant, thus ratified and sealed by the death of Jesus, being the property alike of themselves and their children :—" Repent, and be baptized every one of you in the name of Jesus Christ, in order to the remission of sins, and ye shall receive the gift of the Holy Ghost. For the promise is to you, and to your children, and to all that are afar off, as many as the Lord our God shall call " (Acts ii. 38, 39).

In many, in most, of the other religions of the world, their doctrines were ' esoteric.' They were never publicly enunciated. A knowledge of them was restricted to the privileged, exclusive few, who must be content to receive dubious oracular responses.

But THE WORLD was now to be the auditory. The faithful saying was to be made " worthy of all acceptation." As it had been in the case of their Divine Master, " the common people " were to hear His servants " gladly ;" and, as we shall presently see illustrated, the injunction was given and obeyed, " Go, speak to the people all the words of this life."

It is added at the close of the address, " And with many other words did he testify and exhort, saying, Save yourselves from this untoward generation." Here, as in all cases where the truth of God is faithfully preached, if it be not the savour of life unto life, it will prove the

T

savour of death unto death; while some are convicted
and converted, some remain obdurate and impenitent;
what melts and subdues the one, inflames and exaspe-
rates the other. As it was subsequently with the martyr
Stephen, whose address was rudely interrupted by
hostile bigots, so now, it has been suggested, amid that
stricken and agitated audience, signs of hostility may
have been manifested. Some adverse voices were
raised, if possible to counteract the effects of the
speaker's stirring appeal. In brief, sententious language, if he cannot still the murmur of the gainsayers
and disarm their opposition, he will exhort at least to
steadfastness and boldness those who had, before many
witnesses, avouched the Lord to be their God. He
uplifts the warning voice, reminding them of their perils
and temptations, that a man's worst foes are often those
of his own household—" Save yourselves from this untoward generation"—save yourselves from the certain ruin
and destruction impending over the heads of those now
present, who, along with their infatuated countrymen,
are precipitating the ruin of their city and nation.

Thus ends the narrative of the first, and in every
sense the greatest, revival in the Christian Church; one
in which Peter holds, as an honoured instrument in
the hands of the Spirit, the most distinguished place.
" The Lord gave the word," and if not "great" in the
sense of intellect, or wisdom, or numbers, yet great in
faith, and holy energy, and zeal " was the company of
them that published it." Wondrous, too, must have
been the indirect as well as direct results, when we
remember that the precious seed sown at the feast in
Jerusalem must have been so widely disseminated.
Among those congregated in the city of solemnities were

" Parthians, and Medes, and Elamites, and the dwellers in Mesopotamia, and in Judæa, and Cappadocia, in Pontus, and Asia, Phrygia, and Pamphylia, in Egypt, and in the parts of Libya about Cyrene, and strangers of Rome, Jews and proselytes, Cretes, and Arabians" (Acts ii. 9–11). Little, perhaps, did our Apostle calculate the ultimate consequences of that first-fruit gathering. Little did he dream that thirty years after the preaching of this his first sermon, the Gospel of his heavenly Lord would be carried to every part of the civilised world, and even among some of its savage tribes. Vast, truly, was his privilege to be the chief speaker in this birthday of Christendom. It imparted to Pentecost in all time to come a twofold commemoration, at once of the sublimest incident of the Old Testament, and in one sense the greatest and most momentous of the New. To Peter it would ever afterwards be a special anniversary. Nor need we be surprised at the anxiety of his " beloved brother Paul," in a future year, to go up to Jerusalem and keep this now doubly-hallowed feast—the last of Israel's festivals probably observed by him (Acts xx. 16). He would not spend the time in Asia, for " he hasted if it were possible for him to be at Jerusalem *the day of Pentecost.*" We are told, on the authority of Tertullian and Jerome, that in subsequent years these fifty days between the Passion and Pentecost were specially set aside for the baptism of converts. Hence the new name transferred to the festival of the Christian Church, " *Whitsunday,*" or White Sunday, because those presenting themselves to receive the sacred rite were generally habited in white garments.[1]

[1] See Dr Kitto's " Cyclopædia of Bib. Lit."

In speaking of the baptism of converts, it will not be out of place to close this chapter by referring to the sequel of the wondrous scene we have just been contemplating. These three thousand who had "gladly received the word" at the mouth of Peter, were also, at his exhortation, baptized. "Repent, and be baptized every one of you." It is the first recorded dispensation of this Christian sacrament. Those who had repented of their sins, and avowed their faith in Jesus, receive the outward visible sign of admission into the Church of the Faithful. That dispensation would, owing to the numbers, be shared by the other Apostles. "Almost without doubt this first baptism must have been administered, as that of the first Gentile converts was (see chap. x. 47), by *affusion or sprinkling, not by immersion.* The immersion of three thousand persons, in a city so sparingly supplied with water as Jerusalem, is equally inconceivable with a procession beyond the walls to the Kedron or to Siloam, for that purpose." [1]

This administration of the initiatory ordinance of the Church is mentioned in the most cursory way in the narrative ; and yet we can well realise that the act must have involved, on the part of those baptized, no small amount of heroism and moral courage. It was, first of all, a public acknowledgment of their own guilt in having rejected Jesus, and given Him up to death : perhaps, in the case of not a few, of having taken active part in the cruelties inflicted on the innocent Sufferer. Doubtless, this open acceptance and avowal of a hated faith, would subject them to no small obloquy and persecution. It was pledging themselves to be the servants and faithful followers of Jesus in the very city

[1] Alford, II. 25.

where they had themselves slain Him as a malefactor. In the "breaking of bread," here spoken of, we have the additional fact that the other sacrament of Divine appointment was not forgotten by them; that often (possibly daily) they sat round the holy table of communion, probably at the conclusion of their *agapæ* (evening meals), and that in the most solemn sense of the words, as Peter distributed the sacred elements, he obeyed his Lord's farewell injunction, " Feed My sheep." [1] It demonstrates the thoroughness and completeness of the change wrought upon them through

[1] Tertullian gives the following account of these *agapæ* :—"Our feast," he says, " shows its character by its name; it bears the Greek name of love; and however great may be the cost of it, still it is gain to be at cost in the name of piety, for by this refreshment we make all the poor happy. No one sits down at the table till prayer has first been offered to God ; we eat as much as hunger requires; we drink no more than consists with sobriety ; while we satisfy our appetites, we bear in mind that the night is to be consecrated to the worship of God. The supper being ended, and all having washed their hands, lights are brought in, and every one is invited to sing, either from Holy Scripture, or from the promptings of his own spirit, some song of praise to God, for the common edification."

In employing the word *agape*, however, in connection with this "breaking of bread" in the early apostolic days (see interesting article by Dr Plumptre in "Dic. of Christian Antiquities "), we anticipate the language of a somewhat later date. This special name seems not to have been attached to the meal before the close of the apostolic age, and by that time the original simplicity, which at Pentecost characterised this " witness and bond of the brotherhood of Christians," seems to have been departed from, and various causes led to the discontinuance altogether at the close of the third century.

"When Christians came to have special buildings set apart for worship, and to look on with the same local reverence that the Jews had had for the Temple, they shrank from sitting down in them to a common meal as an act of profanation. The *agapæ*, therefore, were gradually forbidden to be held in churches, as by the Council of Laodicea (c. 27). This, of course, together with the rule of the third Council of Carthage (c. 29), that the Eucharist should be received fasting, and the probable transfer, in consequence of that rule, of the time of its 'celebration' from the evening to the morning, left the 'feast of love' without the higher companionship with which it had been at first associated, and left it to take more and more the character of a pauper meal."—*Dic. Christian Antiquities*, p. 41.

the Divine instrumentality.   It was no mere ephemeral
and transient outburst of emotional feeling.   With a
few, such may have been the case, as in all periods of
intense religious excitement.   But with the vast majority it was evidently a season of the oft-misquoted
and misapplied word " conversion"—a turning from sin,
and from the great sin of hostility to the Lord of Life
and Truth, and in broken-hearted penitence looking
alone for salvation to the cross of Him whom they or
their countrymen had basely crucified.   That " day of
the Lord " was a great turning-point in their lives.
The saying was exemplified in their experience, " If
any man be in Christ, he is a new creature, old things
are passed away, behold all things are become new."
For neither were they content with the mere outward
badge and seal of the Christian profession in partaking
of the rite of baptism and communion; they persevered
in the diligent use of the appointed means of grace.
Many of these converts, coming from distant regions
and cities to attend the yearly solemnity, must have
had a very partial and imperfect acquaintance with the
life and doctrines of the Great Founder of the new
faith, and willingly submitted to the teaching of His
followers.   No longer would the one small upper room
now suffice for these oral instructions and communion
fellowships, but each Apostle would probably gather his
separate group—a church in various private dwellings
—and unfold to wondering ears their own hallowed
reminiscences of Him who spake as never man spake.
They came, too, to understand and value the precious-
ness of prayer,[1] and to live under the influential power

1 It has been noted that the word is in the plural, not in the singular
("prayers "), apparently indicating that they had stated times for devotion

of new principles and affections. Being forgiven much, they loved all the more. By a voluntary act they sold their worldly possessions, and consecrated these in a common fund for the relief of their poorer brethren; remembering, doubtless, as they did so, the words of the Lord Jesus, how He said, "Inasmuch as ye did it to one of the least of these My brethren, ye did it unto Me."[1] "They continued steadfastly in the Apostles' doctrine and fellowship, and in breaking of bread and in prayers." "And they, continuing daily with one accord in the Temple, and breaking bread from house to house, did eat their meat with gladness and single-ness of heart" (Acts ii. 46). An attractive picture, surely, as to how the new inner life, with which they were imbued, hallowed and consecrated their whole natures, diffusing an atmosphere of holy love even in the par-taking of their ordinary meals, and in their hours of social intercourse—their common "daily bread" trans-muted into the bread of heaven. "The joy of the Lord was their strength." Nor could they resist giving outward expression to their feelings, "praising God."

We need not wonder at the last entry in this beau-tiful description, "having favour with all the people." Their blameless, charitable, self-denying lives disarmed opposition,—raised them from the position of a despised and hated sect, and gained them, for the time being, tolerance and goodwill. The spectacle was as winning as it was novel and strange. "See how these Christians love one another."

over and above the appointed hours of Temple worship. Perhaps we may add, unpremeditated or extempore prayers, in addition to those of the Jewish Psalter, which have been the common liturgy and inheritance of the Church in all ages.

[1] See some excellent observations and practical thoughts on this subject in Dr Buchanan's Work on the Holy Spirit.

CHAPTER XV.

The Beautiful Gate.

THE LAME BEGGAR. THE HOUR OF PRAYER. CURE EFFECTED BY
PETER. HIS ADDRESS TO THE MULTITUDE. SEIZURE OF THE
APOSTLES. ARRAIGNED BEFORE THE SANHEDRIM.

> " On! champions blest, in Jesus' name,
> Short be your strife, your triumph full,
> Till every heart have caught your flame,
> And, lighten'd of the world's misrule,
> Ye soar, those elder saints to meet
> Gathered long since at Jesus' feet ;
> No world of passions to destroy,
> Your prayers and struggles o'er, your task
> All praise and joy."

" Everywhere we find these two Apostles, Peter and John, in
great harmony together."—*Chrysostom, Hom. viii.*

" Methinks Erasmus's reflection is here not unseasonable ; that
no honour or sovereignty, no power or dignity, was comparable
to this glory of the Apostle ; that the things of Christ, though
in another way, were more noble and excellent than anything
that this world could afford. And therefore he tells us that
when he beheld the state and magnificence wherewith Pope Julius
II. appeared—first at Bononia, and then at Rome—equalling the
triumphs of a Pompey or a Cæsar, he could not but think how
much all this was below the greatness and majesty of St Peter,
who converted the world, not by power or armies, not by engines
or artifices of pomp and grandeur, but by faith in the power of
Christ, and drew it to the admiration of himself."—*Cave's Lives
of the Apostles, p. 119.*

W E are, in the present and succeeding chapter, to have another and more signal instance brought before us of the new life which, since the Great Pentecostal effusion, animated St Peter. Intrepidity, sagacity, prudence, dignity, take the place of cowardice, vacillation, wayward impulse, loud bravado. That righteous man has become bold as a lion. From among the "many wonders and signs" which we are told were wrought by the Apostles immediately following the gift of tongues, the beloved physician selects one in which our Apostle occupies a prominent part. At the close of his own Gospel (Mark), he specially records the authority for the "boldness" with which we shall immediately find him acting. He remembered the words of his Divine Lord and Master, "And these signs shall follow them that believe. In My name shall they cast out devils ; they shall speak with new tongues. . . . *They shall lay hands on the sick, and they shall recover*" (Mark xvi. 17, 18). Similarly, at a much earlier period of the Divine ministry, it is recorded in the Gospel of St Matthew, that while the same gracious commission was given to them to heal the sick (Matt. x. 8.), there were two specific injunctions coupled with it. The one of these was to "provide neither gold nor silver in their purses ;" the other was that they were to "go to the lost sheep of the House of Israel." These three conditions seem remarkably to meet in the case of the lame mendicant we are now to consider, whose cure Peter was employed as the instrument in effecting. He was one that needed healing ; he was a Jew, one of the lost sheep of the House of Israel ; and, as we shall find, true to their Master's charge as He equipped them for service, the Apostles, who were honoured in performing the miracle, had neither gold nor silver in their purses. The same Divine Lord who had spoken to His followers words of encouragement in the prosecution of their spiritual calling, had forewarned them also of great and imminent tribulation ; and the inspired historian seems purposely, or, as an additional reason, to have selected the incident now to engage our thoughts, because it was the occasion of the first of those many fearful persecutions to which the Church, from that hour onwards, became too painfully familiarised.

The Beautiful Gate of the Temple, although it is impossible with absolute precision to indicate its position, seems with greatest likelihood to have been situated opposite the Gate Shushan, or eastern entrance.

If correct in this supposition, it would lead from the Great Court of the Gentiles into the Court of the Women, which, however, notwithstanding the name, was open to both sexes. It would face eastwards the marvellous porticoes or cloisters which, with their rich elaborations, formed the most costly contribution of Herod to the great building which crowned the summit of Moriah. These cloisters would recall to the modern traveller the Piazza of the great Roman Basilica, only on a more imposing scale, with tesselated pavements and double rows of Corinthian columns—monoliths of dazzling marble—whose capitals were exquisitely carved with acanthus and lily, supporting a roof of cedar. A covered way was thus made round the vast quadrangle, the open porticoes affording agreeable retreats from rain and sultry sun ; while to the spectator standing at the Beautiful Gate on its elevated platform, the triple Mount of Olives would be seen rising behind, and apparently so near as if no Kedron Valley intervened. Out of nine other similar entrances, adorned with plates of silver and gold, this appears to have been a triumph of artistic skill, the most magnificent of them all, and forming the main entrance to the Temple. So ponderous was the Gate, forty cubits high, that Josephus tells us " it could be with difficulty shut by twenty men." The material composing it was of world-wide celebrity, being bas-relief lily-work of Corinthian brass, more precious than gold.[1] It was approached by a flight of fifteen steps. Nearly two centuries before, the renowned city of Corinth had fallen before the armies of the Roman general Mummius. After being sacked it was burned to the ground,

[1] See Josephus, Bel. v. 53.

because of the insolence of the citizens towards ambassadors that had been sent to treat with them. It
was set on fire in diverse places on the outskirts ; and
the flames, rolling towards the centre of the city, met
with prodigious fury. There had been collected a
vast number of images and statues in gold, silver, and
copper. These, melted by the intense heat of the
burning city, were fused, and ran down the streets
in a gleaming molten stream. When the flames were
extinguished, this novel combination received the name
of Corinthian brass. It was prized in value beyond
all other precious metals, being, it was said, beyond
the imitation of art. Herod had secured a portion of
the rare compound for the main entrance to the Jewish
Temple. The Gate was of Greek design, and by some
it was said to have been brought from Alexandria by
Nicanor, and to have been called by his name.[1]

Such was the scene of the coming miracle. If we
are correct in the position we have assumed, it was in
the most public and conspicuous position of the outer
court of that vast pile which, a few weeks before, on
one of those green eminences rising behind, had elicited

[1] "There is probably, from imperfect information respecting these gates,
a general impression that the *outer* gate was meant, founded perhaps on
the notion that beggars were not likely to be admitted *into* the Temple
court, and that it is expressly said that this beggar was placed there to
ask alms of those 'that entered into the Temple ;' but we have shown that
no particular sanctity was attached to the other court, and that the second
gate was properly the entrance into the Temple. There was nothing to
prevent a beggar from being stationed there ; and if he could be placed
there, he was more likely to go there than to remain at the outer gate.
These grounds of doubt cannot therefore stand, and we are at liberty to
suppose that the gate really most beautiful was the one distinguished as
the Beautiful Gate."—*Kitto's Daily Bible Illustrations.*

Lightfoot differs from most others in supposing it to be the Gate Hulda—
"the Gate of Time"—situated at the west or opposite entrance to the
court of the Gentiles.

the exclamation even from the untutored and unsophisticated peasants and fishermen of Galilee, "Master, see what manner of stones and buildings are here." No traveller who has crossed by the Bethany road to Jerusalem and seen that unparalleled view, traditionally (we may rather say undoubtedly) associated with Christ's weeping over the city, but must have recalled the familiar description of Josephus. If the scene be so impressive even now amid ruin and desolation, what must it have been in the time of our narrative, when the gigantic pile stood forth in its fully completed magnificence after the toil of "forty-and-six years ?" " The outward face of the Temple in its front wanted nothing that was likely to surprise either men's minds or their eyes ; for it was covered over with plates of gold, which at the first rising of the sun reflected back such a splendour as made those who forced themselves to look upon it to turn away their eyes, just as they would have done at the sun's rays. This Temple appeared to strangers, when they were at a distance, like a mountain covered with snow, for those parts of it that were not gilt were exceeding white." [1] It is interesting at the outset to note the lingering fondness the Apostles still had for the holy building and its services. They knew, from lips incapable of deceiving, that that mass of wondrous magnificence was too surely doomed to destruction. But with some feeling akin to the tender love which we bestow on an aged and beloved relative on whom disease and death have unknown set their irrevocable seal, they seem to have clung to the old venerated haunts that were within a few years to be razed to the ground. In common with the disciples

[1] Bel. v. 5, 6.

of the infant Church, they had doubtless their own lowlier places of assemblage for praise and prayer and the celebration of the last memorial rite; but these did not diminish their love for the gates of Zion. With the memory of all their pleasant Passover festivals, when they had "gone to the house of God with the voice of joy and praise, with the multitude that kept holiday;"—with the more sacred remembrances also of Him who so often trod these Temple-courts and made them for ever fragrant with memorable words, they were still as ready as ever to say, "If I forget thee, O Jerusalem, let my right hand forget her cunning. If I do not remember thee, let my tongue cleave to the roof of my mouth; if I prefer not Jerusalem above my chief joy" (Ps. cxxxvii. 5, 6). It is a remarkable statement (ver. 46) "They continued *daily* with *one accord* in the *Temple*." It is worthy of note, too, in connection with the miracle now to be considered, that it was at "the *hour of prayer*" the Apostles entered its gates. From this it would almost seem that they did more than merely visit the sacred locality as a place full of hallowed associations, or one also where they might have ampler opportunities of proclaiming the Name and cause that was dear to them. May we not be warranted in entertaining the thought, that they most probably were present joining in the Temple worship? In the truest sense of the word, indeed, these services, that ritual, had been abrogated, ever since the cry was heard on Calvary, "It is finished!" The object of their institution being fulfilled, the shadows were superseded by the substance; old things had passed away, and all things had become new. If, therefore, we think of the Apostles and followers of the Great Antitype standing by the huge altar of unhewn stone with its blazing fires, spectators of the bleating lamb, or by the brazen altar gazing on the ascending incense-cloud,—both of these had to them a new and more wondrous significance. They were no longer typical, but memorial, reminding them of the *One* Offering which had " perfected for ever them that are sanctified," and the fragrance of those spotless merits ascending for them from no human altar but within the heavenly veil, whither the Great High Priest had entered, carrying with Him the virtues of His own precious Sacrifice.

There were three distinct hours of prayer among the Jews, each appointed (so ran an unauthorised tradition) by one of the patriarchs. The morning prayer, at nine o'clock, was said to have been instituted by Abraham ; mid-day prayer, at twelve, by Isaac ; and evening prayer, at three, by Jacob.[1] It was at the latter of these stated hours of devotion, at the offering of the evening sacrifice, corresponding with our three o'clock, that Peter and John went up with the stream of worshippers.[2] And here we have again to note the brotherly association of these two Apostles. Recent hours of sympathetic sorrow had brought and bound them closer together ; and as, doubtless, in the secrecy of their common home they took sweet counsel together, so now " they walked to the house of God in company." They would go, shall we suppose, by the Gate of Ophel,

[1] Cave.

[2] " Being the ninth hour." " The division of the day into twelve hours— a mere conventional division—was unknown among the Jews until the Babylonish captivity. The first mention of it is in the Book of Daniel. Before that, the periods of the day were distinguished by natural appearances, as morning, noonday, and evening. Herodotus informs us that the Babylonians were the first to divide the day into twelve parts."—*Dr Gloag on the Acts*, vol. i. p. 93.

and through the Stoa Basilica, to the court of the Gentiles. It was that same court which we find from sacred story was, on the great festal seasons, specially the Passover, with its crowds of pilgrims, ignominiously transformed into a scene of barter and exchange,—its tesselated pavement polluted with the erection of pens for cattle, and cages of doves for sacrifice, also tables and booths for the exchange of money, traffickers in live-stock and coins driving their usurious gains, and "making the Father's house a place of merchandise." It was not, doubtless, so thronged now ; yet as there were few Jews who did not inherit the pride of their ancestral religion, and who failed to frequent their Temple at one at least of the hours of prayer, the Beautiful Gate was seldom without its complement of worshippers. Of all places, indeed, within or without Jerusalem, it was the likeliest rendezvous for the diseased and crippled,—those wrecks and outcasts of humanity, to be found in all cities and countries, who haunt the most public resorts in order to elicit the sympathy and the alms of the benevolent. "We know," says Dr Kitto, "that the Pharisees and others in those days bestowed much alms in the most public places, that their ostentatious charity might be 'seen of men ;' and the perception of this weakness, in a class of people so wealthy, had doubtless considerable influence in causing the beggars of Jerusalem to resort in large numbers to places so public, and through which the Pharisees were so continually passing, as the gates of the Temple—these people being more constant than others in their attendance at the sacred courts." It seems to have been a privilege accorded in ancient times to such sufferers, even in pagan cities, to seat themselves at the doors or gates of the temples [1]—a custom which has lingered on to this day, as those can testify who are familiar alike with the Brahminical temple or the Mohammedan mosque,—in accordance, too, with the practice recommended by Chrysostom for Christian churches. Who, that is conversant with these cities, can fail to recall groups of importunate beggars or limping cripples outside the great basilicas of Florence, Venice, and Rome? In sad agreement with the scene here described by St Luke, there is no memory of Jerusalem more vivid to the writer of these pages than the rows of wretched men and women, mainly lepers, outside the Jaffa and Damascus gates, who to this day repeat this early story of the Acts. We read, in connection with the Jewish towns, of no hospitals, or infirmaries, or homes for such hapless outcasts. Indeed, the Jew was apt ungenerously and superstitiously to regard bodily infirmity and disease as the result of sin, or rather as a Divine judgment,—that those so circumstanced (and including among them the greatest Sufferer of all) were " stricken, smitten of God, and afflicted."

Outside this " Beautiful Gate of the Temple " there sat one such hapless mendicant, who had been " lame from his mother's womb." For forty long years had he suffered from his grievous infirmity; for many of these, we may suppose, he had been daily carried by his relatives and laid at the same portal. During that dull, monotonous period, we cannot doubt that, as in the case of some privileged blind and lame in our own cities, he had become well known to the frequenters of the Temple; his features and tones of voice familiar as the gate itself; that morning, noon, and evening wor-

---

[1] Martial, quoted by Barnes.

U

shippers had often and again dropped their alms into the folds of his tattered garment as they passed through the gorgeous portal. They could entertain no doubt as to the reality of his infirmity. It was not a case of disease from sudden accident, involving a temporary dislocation of knee or ankle bone, which it was in the power of human skill to rectify.[1] He was a born cripple. So long had he presented his dull, monotonous petitions, with these powerless limbs and outstretched hands, that not one of the thousands who walked daily past him,—proud Sadducee, or ostentatious Pharisee, or robed Levite, thus familiarised with his appearance, —but must have felt satisfied that restoration to health and deliverance from his ailment, would only be effected by a notable miracle, and by special Divine intervention. All ordinary means, we may suppose, had been employed in vain to effect his cure. It was now one of those " all things" possible only with God. The unhappy object himself had doubtless long ago given himself up to the abandonment of despair, only thankful that he was permitted to escape the additional miseries of abject penury by sheltering himself from a burning Palestine sun under the shady portico, and to claim the beneficence of the passengers at a spot where not the Pharisee only, actuated by the base motive of display, but where hearts, stimulated and quickened by the services of devotion at the holy altar, would be the more ready to relieve the necessities of the poor and suffering.[2]

---

[1] Dean Alford remarks that "Luke the physician had made himself acquainted with the peculiar kind of weakness, and described it accordingly."

[2] It has been well observed, with reference to the manner in which this whole narrative is recorded, that " when a story is told in general terms,

It was about three o'clock in the afternoon, when the sun was westering, and the shadows from the Beautiful Gate were projected along the variegated pavement of Solomon's porch, that two men, whose faces were perhaps not unfamiliar, attired in the humble garb of Galilee peasants, stood before him, and from whom, uttering the wonted tale of distress, he asked an alms. Some had passed with averted head; others, as aforetime, had tossed some small pittance into the sufferer's lap to get rid of his importunity. But these two worshippers have paused under the portico; and one of them, in the emphatic words of the original, "fastened his eyes upon him;" a word significant of intensity of gaze, as if all at once the Apostle were seized with a Divine impulse, not his own, to use the authority which had been delegated to him, and make this familiar cripple a monument of Divine power and mercy. Could Peter at that moment have recalled a most remarkable, a strangely memorable, saying of his Master, when they were sitting in confidential fellowship around the Last Supper table—could that saying have prompted the

without date, or place, or any circumstance which an inquirer might lay hold of to ascertain its reality, there is reason to suspect it to be a fiction, or at least, that the writer knows nothing about it but by vague and uncertain tradition. . . . In the present case Luke does not content himself with saying that on a certain occasion the Apostles, somewhere in Judæa, cured a lame man; but he points out the individual by such marks as are equivalent to giving his name. He is represented as a sort of public person, having been often seen by those who frequented the Temple; the gate at which he was wont to lie is specified; and thus an opportunity was given to every reader at that time to bring the narrative to the test. No reason can be conceived why Luke has inserted, in a history so concise, a circumstance apparently of so little importance as his being laid at the gate of the Temple called Beautiful, but his knowledge that what he was writing was true, and his willingness to subject it to the most scrupulous examination. Impostors do not write in this manner. They dread inquiry, and use every precaution to elude it."—*Dick on the Acts,* pp. 48, 49.

strong impulse to translate it into fact? " Believe Me
that I am in the Father, and the Father in Me ; or else
believe Me for the very works' sake. Verily, verily, I
say unto you, He that believeth on Me, the works that
I do shall he do also ; and greater works than these
shall he do ; because I go unto My Father. And whatsoever ye shall ask in My name, that will I do, that the
Father may be glorified in the Son" (John xiv. 11-13.)
Be that as it may. " Look on us," was the sudden
command of Peter. Instantaneously were the eyes of
the cripple uplifted to the speaker. But he had no
thought other than receiving, from the limited means
of those accosting him, a denarius or " penny." Doubtless, it was with disappointed look he listened to the
response to his earnest appeal, " Silver and gold have
I none."[1] But the speaker added in brief, sententious words, yet in tones indicating unhesitating confidence and faith, "In the name of Jesus Christ
of Nazareth"—the very name which had been written in letters of scorn and derision on His cross—
" rise up, and walk." How different, we may remark in passing, from the formula used invariably by
Peter's Master, whether to winds and waves, or helpless
paralytic, or raging demons, or death itself. " Verily,
verily, I say unto thee : " " Peace, be still : " " *I will*, be

[1] A severely practical comment on the words of Peter, made by Thomas
Aquinas to one of the alleged successors of the Prince of the Apostles and
"Vicar of Christ," is worth recording :—"Thomas Aquinas, surnamed 'the
Angelical Doctor,' who was highly esteemed by Pope Innocent IV., going
one day into the Pope's chamber, where they were reckoning large sums of
money, the Pope, addressing himself to Aquinas, said, 'You see that the
Church is no longer in an age in which she can say, '*Silver and gold have
I none* ' 'It is true, holy Father,' replied the Angelical Doctor, 'nor
can she now say to the lame man, 'Rise up and walk.'"—*Quoted by West*,
pp. 208-9.

thou whole : " " *I say* unto thee, 'Young man, arise : ' "
" Lazarus, come forth." He spoke in no name but His
own. Forth went the omnipotent fiat ; storms were
hushed, and demons chained, and sickness cured, and
death uncrowned. But Peter, in this his first miracle,
as in all subsequent ones, announces himself as merely
the delegate and servant of a Greater. If that helpless,
lame petitioner is restored, the cure is effected in the
name of "Jesus the Nazarene." We may imagine the
man's astonishment at the strange words which fell on
his ears. Would he not likely have been in the same
spot a few weeks before, when crowds were hurrying
from every direction to Calvary to see the Prophet of
Galilee die a malefactor's death—the reputed Saviour
and Restorer of others, unable to save or rescue Himself ? 'What,' we may picture him exclaiming to
himself, ' are these Galileans adding insult and injury
to this life-long curse of God ? How can the name of
Him who perished by a felon's death have any charm
or potency to give strength to these shrivelled limbs?
No, it is only mocking a miserable being with wild
delusions. If silver and gold you have none to bestow,
then go your way, and leave me to my fate.' Or possibly these momentary thoughts may have been of an
entirely different kind. The magic name, Jesus of
Nazareth, may have awoke within him gleams of ardent
hope. That Name could not have been strange to him as
the wondrous Healer and Restorer of sick and diseased,
blind and impotent and dead. May he not often have
longed to hear spoken to himself the gracious word
which had proved so efficacious in the case of others ? He
had, however, no time or leisure given him for such
reflections, even if they had been tempted to arise ;

for in a moment, Peter, without any parade of caba.
listic words or mystic incantation, "caught him by the
right hand, and lifted him up." The cure is complete.
"Immediately his feet and ancle-bones received strength,"
and owned the might of the all-powerful word and Name.
In the further artless description of the narrator, " he,
leaping up, stood, and walked, and entered with them
into the Temple, walking and leaping, and praising
God." With all the ecstatic feelings of a man who,
after a night of hideous dreams, has suddenly awoke
amid the glare of sunshine and singing of birds—the
cripple cannot conceal or repress his jubilant emotions in the use of his new-born physical energies.
With tears of gratitude and joy in his eyes, he leaps
exultant to his feet ;—recalling doubtless to the wondering spectators the words of the old prophet, never
before more literally fulfilled, " Then shall the lame
man leap as an hart." It is surely, moreover, worthy of
note, that it was not Peter, the instrument in his deliverance, whom the restored one praised, but Peter's
God. In what words or songs he vented these praises,
we are not told. But the Eucharistic hymn of the
sweet singer of Israel might appropriately embody his
marvellous experience, " I waited patiently for the
Lord ; and He inclined unto me, and heard my cry.
He brought me up also out of an horrible pit, out of
the miry clay, and set my feet upon a rock, and established my goings. And He hath put a new song in my
mouth, even praise unto our God : many shall see it, and
fear, and shall trust in the Lord " (Ps. xl. 1–3). How
Peter, in his heart of hearts, must at that critical hour
have re-echoed the subsequent utterance of his brother
Paul, when he " thanked God and took courage !"

It was in the truest sense of the word a crucial moment for the cause he had at heart. If, in that place of public resort, with no partial spectators gathered around, the attempt to perform this miracle had proved a failure—if the cripple, in attempting to rise, had only reeled back again to his old helpless seat on the steps of the gate—that cause, dear to both Apostles, could not fail to receive a damaging, or rather an irrecoverable blow. They would be denounced loudly as bold impostors. It would have confirmed most of the bystanders in the foregone conclusion, that the Name which had been solemnly pronounced over the cripple— the Name which by their rulers had been branded with scorn—was as powerless as they supposed it, or perhaps wished it to be. Peter, however, at once saw that a rare opportunity was now given him, as herald of the good tidings, of unfurling his banner, and advancing the cause and kingdom of his Divine Master. For as the grateful mendicant accompanied his benefactors to the Temple—the mouth speaking ' out of the abundance of the heart '—the assembling worshippers heard the joyous outburst, and knew at a glance that it was he who sat for alms at the Beautiful Gate; and " they were filled with wonder and amazement at that which had happened unto him." They could not long be in doubt as to who his benefactors were. Most naturally is the scene depicted. The man "*held* Peter and John;" partly, perhaps, as with faltering gait, half distrustful of his new power, he clung to their support; partly as keeping hold of his deliverers, that he might not be severed from them, and the better exhibit to the wondering crowd unto whom it was that he owed his cure. The throng of spectators rapidly increases. That a

notable exercise of superhuman power had taken place,
none could deny.   They dared not resist the testimony
of their senses.   There was no room in such a case for
artifice or collusion.   The most persistent opposition, the
most malignant prejudice, could not impugn the reality
of the miracle transacted before their eyes.   How great
indeed (we cannot resist remarking parenthetically in
passing) the contrast of the present with those pseudo-
miracles pretended to have been wrought in the earlier
centuries and in the Middle Ages—or those which have
their credulous supporters still in the lying wonders of
an apostate Church—winking images, bleeding pictures,
supernatural cures wrought at so-called " holy wells," or
by coming in contact with the bones and relics of departed saints !   The cure of this mendicant was not
done in a corner.   It was effected in open light of day
on the person of one too notorious to admit of his identity being questioned, or the alternative supposition
that for forty years he had been a successful deceiver.
However tempted, therefore, to have their judgment
swayed and perverted by prejudice, they dare not, in the
presence of such an infallible proof, withhold the admission extorted from the magicians of Egypt, " This
is the finger of God."

There is a rush made from divers quarters to Solomon's Porch.   It was that singular spot in connection
with the sacred building, which has its counterpart and
resemblance still in the " precincts " of a few of our
own and in many more foreign cathedrals, where shops
and booths may be seen clinging as unsightly appur-
tenances to Gothic shafts and porticoes, for the sale
of articles in connection with the religious services.   In
the case of Roman Catholic places of worship, such as

at Rouen, Bruges, and Ghent, we have mean, wooden stalls for poor venders, driving their trade in rosaries, beads, crucifixes, wax tapers, and such like. In the Temple of Jerusalem, these were on a more extensive scale in front of Solomon's cloisters. There were pens of cattle, and coops of doves, for offerings and sacrifice. There were money-changers with greedy eyes standing behind their "hhanoth" clutching the Roman drachm and stater, and giving in usurious exchange the only coin current in the holy place, the Jewish shekel. During the great festivals in the time of our Lord, that sacred platform had been degraded into a base, mercenary rendezvous for unseemly wrangling between buyer and seller,—scenes which those who have been in the bazaars and market-places of Alexandria and Cairo, Beyrout and Damascus can well understand,—and which drew down the withering rebuke from the Divine denouncer of such sacrilegious traffic, " Get you hence ; make not My Father's house a house of merchandise."

The place, then, where the multitudes were now crowding, was one pre-eminently associated to the disciples with the teaching of their divine Master, for there He had proclaimed Himself to be the Son of God and Saviour of the world. It was that broad level platform or terrace, partly artificial, overhanging 200 feet the steep gorge of the Jehoshaphat valley, the work of the great King of Israel who gave it its designation. It was entered by the gate Shushan and buttressed by the Cyclopean stones still surviving in the Temple wall. The memory, we repeat, of the Master's presence and words, who there spake as never man spake, as well as His deeds of irresistible power, was well calculated to inspire His servant and give him " strength equal to his day." The crowd had gathered, and had now evidently become a dense multitude. Every eye was fastened with amazement on these wonder working Galileans, who had effected what the hierarchy of their own Temple, with all their religious and spiritual prestige, had been utterly unable to perform. Indeed it was a moment of peril and temptation to the Apostles themselves. If Peter had not been recently re-baptized with the Holy Ghost and with fire, and made strong in the grace which is in Christ Jesus, we might almost have trembled as to the effect on his naturally bold, fervid, ambitious spirit. The unholy strife manifested only a few weeks previous as to who should be the greatest, might have now reasserted itself. The son of Jonas, borne on the plaudits of the multitude, might have arrogated to himself the glory of the miracle, claimed an apparently justifiable precedence, and ante-dated the arrogant pretensions thrust on him in after ages, as the Vicegerent of God and Prince of the Apostles. How different! With a holy jealousy for his Master's honour, Peter repudiates every such claim for distinction, and ascribes the glory to whom alone it was due:—" Ye men of Israel, why marvel ye at this? or why look ye so earnestly on us, as though by our own power or holiness we had made this man to walk?" And then, having made this disclaimer, he proceeds to speak of the God who had given Jesus as not a strange God, but their own God—the God of their own patri-archs—disarming at the outset any opposition which might have arisen from the impression that they were striving to introduce a religion antagonistic to their an-cestral faith, by assuring them that the author of the Mosaic was the author also of the Gospel dispensation:

that the God of Abraham and Isaac and Jacob had in this miracle glorified His Son,[1] and it was specially to attest and verify the reality of His resurrection, that power had been delegated to himself and his fellow Apostles. In the performance of the present supernatural cure, they had invoked, not the name of God Almighty, but the name of Him whom their rulers had treated as a blasphemer and impostor, and had wickedly crucified, but who was truly the " Prince " or rather " Author of Life." " Was it not an obvious inference from this view of the case, that Jesus of Nazareth was the very person whom He had announced Himself to be, the expected Saviour of Israel ? Had He been still in the state of the dead, He could have imparted no extraordinary powers to His disciples, nor would there have been more virtue in His name than in that of any other deceased malefactor. It being manifest then, that He had triumphed over death and was invested with sovereign authority, the house of Israel were bound to acknowledge Him as the Messiah, and to embrace His religion. Thus the Apostles acted the part of faithful servants, concerned only for the glory of their Master, and willing to retire from view that He alone might be contemplated and admired. 'Look not earnestly on us ; but consider Jesus, whom the God of your fathers hath glorified.' "[2]

---

[1] Rather " His Servant." The word is $\pi\alpha\hat{\imath}s$, not $\upsilon\iota\acute{o}s$—the same word that is used in St Matthew in the quotation, " Behold My Servant ($\pi\alpha\hat{\imath}s$) whom I have chosen "—the reference being not to His divine Person and nature, but to His official and mediatorial office as the Father's Servant—specially and frequently designated as such by the Evangelical prophet in his closing chapters. See Dr Gloag *in loc.*, who adds, " In the Acts of the Apostles it occurs four times in reference to Christ. . . . The title is once applied to Israel and twice to David. None of the Apostles however is ever called $\pi\alpha\hat{\imath}s$ $\Theta\epsilon o\hat{\upsilon}$ but only $\delta o\hat{\upsilon}\lambda os$ $\Theta\epsilon o\hat{\upsilon}$."

[2] Dick on the Acts, p. 55.

Let the Apostle however speak in his own words. These vividly reproduce alike the style and theme of his great Pentecostal sermon—Jesus and the Resurrection. Moreover, as it has been observed, " while strikingly characteristic of Peter, it is also a proof of the fundamental harmony between his teaching and the more developed and systematic doctrines of St Paul." [1] " The God of Abraham, and of Isaac, and of Jacob, the God of our fathers, hath glorified His Son Jesus; whom ye delivered up, and denied Him in the presence of Pilate, when he was determined to let Him go. But ye denied the Holy One and the Just, and desired a murderer to be granted unto you : and killed the Prince of Life, whom God hath raised from the dead ; whereof we are witnesses. And His name, through faith in His name, hath made this man strong, whom ye see and know : yea, the faith which is by Him hath given him this perfect soundness in the presence of you all. And now, brethren, I wot that through ignorance ye did it, as did also your rulers. But those things, which God before had shewed by the mouth of all His prophets, that Christ should suffer, He hath so fulfilled. Repent ye therefore, and be converted, that your sins may be blotted out, when the times of refreshing shall come from the presence of the Lord ; And He shall send Jesus Christ, which before was preached unto you : whom the heaven must receive until the times of restitution of all things, which God hath spoken by the mouth of all His holy prophets since the world began. For Moses truly said unto the fathers, A prophet shall the Lord your God raise up unto you of your brethren, like unto me; Him shall ye hear in all things whatsoever

[1] Smith's Bib. Dict. *in loco.*

He shall say unto you. And it shall come to pass, that every soul, which will not hear that prophet, shall be destroyed from among the people. Yea, and all the prophets from Samuel and those that follow after, as many as have spoken, have likewise foretold of these days. Ye are the children of the prophets, and of the covenant which God made with our fathers, saying unto Abraham, And in thy seed shall all the kindreds of the earth be blessed. Unto you first, God, having raised up His Son Jesus, sent Him to bless you, in turning away every one of you from his iniquities."

This is a bold appeal, not surely in accordance with the dictates of human policy or worldly wisdom. Peter had too recently and vividly in his memory the scenes in the house of Caiaphas, the hall Gazith, and the place of public execution, not to know at what peril to himself and to his associate he uttered this strong indictment. Had he been the disciple once familiar to us, he would have been less outspoken and courageous. But true to his new name, the Man of the Rock, he had in him the fear of God, and no other fear. At that moment too, he rose with the occasion, and takes advantage of an opportunity that may possibly never again recur. With a notable miracle appealing to their outer senses, he brings home to their consciences in the strongest language he can employ, the various aggravations of their guilt, by crucifying an innocent man,—that too in defiance of the remonstrance of their own timid, irresolute judge,—and giving a preference to a base murderer (lit. "a man, a murderer"), when they raised the infatuated cry, "Not this man, but Barabbas." They had preferred (for there is this antithesis implied in his charge) the man that took away life, to the Divine

Author and Restorer of life.   In such burning words he executed the prophet's commission, "Cry aloud, spare not, lift up your voice like a trumpet."

At the same time, as on the previous occasion at Pentecost, he opens the door of mercy.   There was this extenuation of their enormous crime, that in the case of many, possibly the majority, they "did it in ignorance." They had blindly refused to weigh and estimate the claims of Jesus to the Messiahship.   Their ideal Messiah was so different to that lowly Man of Sorrows.   They would never have stooped to the committal of such a deed had they known that He whom they crucified was in truth the Lord of glory.   Peter recals his Lord's prayer on the cross, which had doubtless been repeated to him—"Father, forgive them ; *for they know not what they do.*"   In the spirit of that prayer he makes a free unlimited offer of pardon and salvation ;—that even with sins of crimson and scarlet recorded against them in the Book of God, there was forgiveness in the cross of Christ, if they would repent and believe.   The cripple had been cured in "the name of Jesus," and that name, so potent in the cure of a physical malady, was still more potent to cancel the foulest guilt that had ever defiled a fallen earth.   He used no flattering words, but yet he would doubtless gain their attention and conciliate their good will, by addressing them as "Brethren."   He points them onwards to those times of refreshing, of which their own prophets had spoken, and which alone would come through Him who had been "exalted at the right hand of God a Prince and a Saviour." Standing as they were at that moment on the Temple area, with the proud traditions of the past vividly recalled, while he speaks in the first instance to each individually, he addresses them in their national and corporate capacity. As the children of the prophets and of the covenant which God made with their fathers, he implores them to accept forthwith the Crucified One as their Messiah King, that so they might participate in the countless spiritual blessings of His reign—the regeneration of the world, "the restitution of all things."

Among the last questions, it will be remembered, put by the Apostles to their Lord previous to His ascension, and to which we have alluded in a previous chapter, was this, "Lord, wilt Thou at this time restore again the kingdom to Israel?" Peter indirectly alludes to this in his present discourse with special reference to his brethren according to the flesh. And it was surely meet that the Apostle of the circumcision, Hebrew to the last in all his sympathies and yearnings, should, amid longings for the spread of Messiah's cause, look forward with eager hope and expectation to the era of which his brother Apostle of the Gentiles afterwards spoke when "all Israel would be saved," and when, the veil removed from their hearts, the Jewish nation would welcome in the Christ of Nazareth, as the promised Shiloe—the Son of David—the Lord of Glory —the Prince of Peace.

The effect of the miracle and the discourse following was most powerful. We believe we may with reverence say, no miracle of Peter's Great Master, not even His crowning one, the raising of Lazarus, produced such startling and astounding effects as did the present. The Pentecostal gift of the Spirit had been shared by many more than the Apostles and their followers. This divine influence, deepest in the centre, was sending its concentric waves all around. The Lord had given the word, and great was the company of them that received as well as of them that published. " Many of them," we read, " that heard the word believed, and the number of the men was about five thousand " (iv. 4). " When, at what time or in what place, were any other such sermons as these ever preached? So far as we can see, Paul, a man of far greater genius and learning, never wielded a multitude after such a fashion. When he addressed an assembly of Greeks, ' some mocked, and others said, We will hear thee again of this matter.' When he spoke to the Jews at Jerusalem, ' they cried out, Away with such a fellow from the earth, for it is not fit that he should live.' " [1]

But while Peter is still speaking, his address is interrupted ; the measured tread of soldiers is heard, coming from the direction of the adjoining barrack. The cause of this sudden change on the scene is not difficult to explain. The Jewish leaders, ever on the watch, had already noted the excited crowd which had gathered in one of their sacred cloisters. They begin to apprehend that the Nazarene sect, which they had hoped had been effectually crushed and silenced, might re-assert the influence of recent months or years, and their doctrines again come into dangerous conflict with the ancestral beliefs. A new impulse had evidently been given to the former by the reported miracle. The " pestilent heresy " must be crushed at once, and its two abettors consigned to imprisonment for this fresh outrage ; all the more daring, because perpetrated within the sacred ground of the Temple. It had long been found necessary to have a troop of soldiers

[1] "Life and Writings of St Peter," 119, 120.

stationed in the Castle of Antonia (the military fort contiguous to the north side of the Temple), in order to repress these popular riots which so often took place in its courts, specially during the great festivals, when different religious interests were brought into unhappy conflict. It was the same spirit of religious animosity and rancour which still rages so fiercely in Jerusalem at the return of each Easter—the modern battlefield being transferred from the Old Temple to the Holy Sepulchre, requiring the presence of a Turkish Contingent to quell the commotion, and very frequently not without blood. Dr Kitto gives the following interesting account of the famous Tower of Antonia: "It stood at the north-east angle of the wall which parted 'the mountain of the house' (or, the whole site of the Temple) from the city. It was erected by the High Priest Hyrcanus, who made it his residence, and was wont there to lay up the splendid garments of his office, whenever he put them off, after having discharged his duties in the Temple. Herod the Great repaired and strengthened this tower, at a great expense, that it might be a sort of citadel to the Temple; and in honour of his patron Mark Antony, gave it the name of Antonia. As before, the holy robes continued to be laid up in this tower during all the reign of Herod, and that of Archelaus his son. After his removal, the Romans took possession of the tower, and kept a garrison in it, for the guard of the Temple. . . . And although their proximity and supervision appear to have been very unpalatable to the Jews, the Romans seem on most occasions to have acted with temper and moderation, and with very much consideration for the peculiar feelings and customs of the people with whom

X

they had to deal. There was, however, one exception; for the Romans still insisted that the sacred robes should continue to be deposited in the Castle, under their power, until the procurator Vitellius was pleased to perform the popular act of restoring them to their own keeping. There were other companies of Roman soldiers stationed in different barracks about the city; but this one being, as it were, within the verge of the sacred edifice, was most odious to the Jews, as a heathen bridle upon their Temple and service, and the most galling badge of the subjection and servitude to which they were reduced."[1]

From this military Castle there issue forth the Captain of the Guard,—the chief garrison officer, and his band, and apprehend the supposed authors and ringleaders of a religious riot. The narrative leaves no doubt as to the instigators in so sudden an exercise of military authority. "The Priests and Sadducees"—who had either been spectators of the miracle, or who had been otherwise informed of it—saw at a glance that "their craft was in danger." They sped to these guardians of the public peace, and urged them to take the wilful offenders into custody. There are two reasons here specifically given for demanding intervention of the civil power. The first " count in the indictment " of the priestly accusers (if we may use a legal term) was that

---

[1] Pictorial Bible, vol. iv. p. 289. It is only right however to observe, that many able authorities, such as Olshausen, suppose that this Captain of the Guard was not a Roman but a Levite officer, who is called by Jewish writers, the Man of the Mountain of the House. If this were the case, then the band under him would be composed of priests, and not Roman soldiers. But I have preferred following the view of Lightfoot, Calvin, and others.

they "taught the people."[1] This was deemed an odious, unwarrantable assumption of authority on the part of these peasants of the North to put themselves in Moses' seat,—venturing, and that too under the very shadow of the Temple, to propound an ecclesiastical creed :— men, devoid at all events of the higher education, and of intellectual and social influence ; who had never sat at the feet of a Gamaliel ; unskilled in Rabbinical lore, who had never graduated in priestly or prophetic school. How dare they venture to assume functions for which birth and education alike unfit them ? above all, how dare they aver that in another name than that of the Hebrew Jehovah they have wrought a miraculous cure ? They are usurpers of the priestly office, and of those who are the divinely appointed expounders of the law, and "defenders of the faith." Such unofficial functionaries winning their way to popularity by subverting the authorised hierarchy, taking the name of the Lord their God in vain by the substitution of another, cannot for a moment be tolerated.[2] But other informants combined with the incensed and indignant priesthood. The second count in the indictment was preferred by the Sadducees, the dominant religious sect of the hour, specially described by Josephus as being, even when compared with the Pharisees, haughty and cruel. They were more influential than any other in wealth and social station, and in their intellectual opinions, the advanced

---

[1] *Being grieved.*—"The word thus translated occurs but in one other place in the New Testament, Acts xvi. 18. It implies more than simple *sorrow*, it was a mingled emotion of *indignation* and *anger.*"—*Barnes.*

[2] The original appointment by King David of twenty-four courses of Priests — each course having delegated to it the administration of the Temple service for a week—was still in force.

school of the age. The ground of their complaint against
the Apostles was, founding on the alleged miracle,
that they taught the doctrine which of all others
was most obnoxious and hateful to these rationalists
of their day, "They preached through Jesus the *Resurrection from the dead.*" The rejection of this was
the chief and distinguishing tenet of their " negative
theology," along with the denial of a spirit-world,
and a state of rewards and punishments. " Their
God," as it has been well said, " was a God of the
earth, of which it was their happiness and their virtue
to possess a magnificent share. They laughed at all
fables of a life beyond the grave ; deriding the notion
of angels and spirits ; the sole heaven of which they
had any knowledge being about them in the palaces
of Zion, in the Gardens of Ophel, in the fountains of
Siloam."[1] They were the conservative aristocrats of
the age. They had no sympathy with revolutionary
movements, and were jealous of popular power, and
mob supremacy. The bulk of the nation might wince
under the grasp of Cæsar, but they saw in the Roman
supremacy the best security for their own wealth and
ease. If the influence of priest and noble continued
dominant, they did not trouble themselves about
golden shields being suspended in their Temple, as
the symbols of degradation ;—the legions behind these
shields were the safeguards of their own lands and
riches. If credence were now given to the startling
truth, that the crucified Christ who had been buried
in Golgotha a few weeks ago, had actually risen from
His tomb, there was no resisting the logical inference
as to the possibility of others similarly conquering

1 "The Holy Land," p. 171.

the power of death. Allow the truth also of the alleged miracle at the Beautiful Gate, and their favourite doctrine was immediately impugned and confuted. The Sadducees, spurned by the rigid and sanctimonious Pharisee as infidel and sceptic, prided themselves on being the philosophic representatives of the nation. "The honours of the state had for many years past been enjoyed almost exclusively by the Sadducees, not to say by a single family of the Sadducees, viz., by Ananus, or Annas, and his five sons (Eleazar, Jonathan, Theophilus, Matthias, and Ananus), and his son-in-law Joseph or Caiaphas. Annas himself had been in the possession of the high priesthood for a lengthened period, and all his five sons were at different times advanced to the same dignity." [1]

The Apostles then, by the bold preaching of the Resurrection of their Master, attested and verified by so notable a miracle, indirectly poured scorn on the dogmas of this proud, influential sect, and increased against them the hostility of the people. This moreover will account for the silence of the Pharisees on the present occasion, who during the Saviour's ministry formed His most unscrupulous and bitter opponents. Probably not wishing to disturb their good understanding with the populace, among whom they stood high from an affectation of superior sanctity, and seeing their work so thoroughly done by others, they preferred with a prudent policy to abstain from active intervention, and to nurse their hostility for a future occasion. We shall come, by and by, to see that it was opposition, not withdrawn or modified, but simply deferred.

[1] Lewin's Life of St Paul, i. p. 29.

As the evening sacrifice was proceeding, and the shadows lengthening, being somewhere about six o'clock in the afternoon, it was too late formally to secure a full session of the Sanhedrim, so that the Apostles were " put in hold : "—in other words, they had their first experience that night, of those imprisonments, of which, among other trials, their Lord had duly fore-warned them, and which in a few years, under Nero and Domitian, were to leave so many sad blanks and memories among the faithful. We may imagine with what vehemence and intensity the united Sanhedrim nursed their indignation for the morrow. And yet they must have had their own fears and misgivings. A miracle, they dared not deny or attempt to controvert, had been performed,—the popular sympathies had been roused—a wound had been inflicted on their national faith, their judicial authority, their sectarian pride. They must try, at all events, by one bold effort to stamp out the nascent flame.

The Court of the Sanhedrim, the chief ecclesiastical court of the nation, met in the Hall Gazith—the stone or paved chamber. Recalling the Areopagus at Athens, it is designated in the Mishna, as *Beth Din,* " House of Judgment." It was the high court of appeal in all cases, civil, ceremonial, ecclesiastical, and its decisions were long considered absolute and final until its privi-leges in regard to the civil power were abridged by Herod the Great. Still its jurisdiction seems to have been left undisputed regarding doctrine and ritual. " Their edicts went far and wide ; and just as a Papal decree may smite a sinner in either Prague, Dublin, or New York, a word launched from the Lishcath-ha-Gazith would chastise offenders in either Memphis,

Babylon, or Rhodes. They could still condemn a man to death; though they could only proceed to execution after their sentence had been confirmed by a Roman judge."[1] The seventy members of which it was composed were—including the heads of the twenty-four classes of Priests,—the Elders,—reverend Signiors, distinguished for their age, experience, and learning,—and the *Sopherîm*, scribes or lawyers—those thoroughly versed alike in civil and ecclesiastical law. It seems to have been constituted not of Jews resident in Jerusalem only, but to have had delegates also from the lands and cities of their dispersion, Greece, Babylon, and Egypt. The High Priest was not *ex officio* president, but he was by courtesy and usage generally elected to be so. The vice-president, called the "Father of the Council," "Rector of the Great College," sat at the right hand of the chief dignitary,—both in robes of office. Two scribes were seated at the extremities of the semicircle, the one to register the votes for acquittal, the other for condemnation. The rest sat on opposite divans, while "the bar" for the accused, was naturally in the centre where the semicircular seats met. Hence the accuracy of St Luke's description here, when he speaks of the Apostle-prisoners as being "set in the midst."[2] The locality of the Stone Chamber, according to a scholarly and reliable authority on the topography of Jerusalem, was "situated near the spot where the 'First Wall' of Josephus abutted against the western wall of the Temple, with which it was no doubt connected, either by an intervening portico, or by actual junction. We learn from the Talmud that it was built upon piers and arches—in order no doubt to elevate it to the level of

---

[1] Dixon, p. 343.   [2] See Bib. Dict. Art.

the Temple area. The present Mekhemeh or Council Chamber of the Turkish Divan, where the Mejlis or Congress of Jerusalem holds its deliberations, having one entrance directly into the Haram, and another into the elevated causeway street, probably occupies its identical site; and the Sanhedrim like the Mekhemeh may have been built over the pool." [1]

Such was the imposing assembly before which the two Apostles of Jesus were now arraigned. We have even the names of the leaders of these grave counsellors given us by the inspired writer: " And Annas the high priest, and Caiaphas, and John, and Alexander, and as many as were of the kindred of the high priest, were gathered together at Jerusalem " (Acts iv. 6). Annas was till A.D. 24 the ecclesiastical head of the nation ; and though on that year deposed from the high priesthood by Valerius Gratus, from various favourable circumstances he continued to exercise even a greater influence on his countrymen than either his personal qualities or hereditary position would have entitled him. Caiaphas, his son-in-law, was now High Priest *de facto,* although the real power remained in the hands of Annas. There have been various conjectures regarding the two less known names here specified, John and Alexander. The former has been supposed to be the famous priest and rabbi *John Ben Zacchai,* who was said to have witnessed, shortly before this time, the bursting open, of its own accord by some miraculous agency, of another Gate of the Temple which faced " Beautiful," and applied to it on the spot the prophetic words of Zechariah, " Open thy doors, O Lebanon, that the fire may devour thy cedars." The

1 Barclay's " City of the Great King," p. 172.

latter may not improbably be the brother of the Jewish writer Philo, a man of great wealth and distinction—one moreover, who, according to Josephus, must have specially ingratiated himself with all the Temple worshippers, as it was his riches which supplemented the munificent architecture of Herod, and covered these various gates with gold and silver ornament.[1]

It is evident that the members of this assemblage were alive to the seriousness of the crisis. Between the period of the alleged resurrection of Christ and Pentecost, little had been heard of the sect of the Nazarenes. The leaders of the Sanhedrim had therefore probably surmised that, like other bold sectaries who had appealed from time to time for popular support, their little day, with its sudden outburst of zeal, had run its course ;—that the teaching of Jesus would soon be numbered among the things of the past, and that His duped and despondent followers would return back, if they had not already done so, humbled men, to their nets and their fishing-boats. But the gift of tongues on the day of Pentecost had stirred afresh the ashes of the Nazarene heresy, and given proof that the cause was instinct with new life. The miracle of the previous day had given them fresh ground alike for grave alarm and for immediate interference. They could not but remember the gigantic impression made on the multitude by the resurrection of Lazarus. What would be the result of a portent not so stupendous in itself as the other, but performed in a more public place, and capable of the fullest and most irrefragable attestation ?

On the accused taking their places at the bar, the

[1] Ant. xviii. 8. 1 ; xix. 5. 1 ; xx. 5. 2.

judicial interrogatory was put by the president.   It will
recal the similar abrupt method of questioning to which
a greater than Peter was subjected—" By what power or
by what name have ye done this?"   Peter, no less
than his judges, must have realised the gravity of his
position.   Standing in the reputed presence of all that
was venerable and learned in his country's capital, it
would be with no ordinary emotion that he listened to
the words now addressed to him.   There were times of
his former history now well known to us, when, on far
more slender grounds, he would have given way to vacillation and bowed his head before the storm, but now,
reckless of consequences, because strong in the rectitude
of his cause and " full of the Holy Ghost," he held his
ground without flinching.   His feet were not on the
unstable wave of Gennesaret, but on the Rock of
Cesarea Philippi ; he had counted the cost, and deemed
it worthy of all peril, even to martyrdom.   Neither
was there aught of insolent defiance in his look and
mien.   He had been taught by the highest authority to
" render to Cesar the things that are Cesar's ;" and by
an anterior natural law he would instinctively give
honour to those of exalted rank and of reputed wisdom,
to whom honour was due.   Yet neither could he allow
himself to forget that the men whose eyes were now
upon him, flashing the indignation burning in their
hearts, were most of them the very same who had lent
their dominant influence to consummate a crime of the
deepest dye, and most wanton savagery.   Both Annas
and Caiaphas had been personally implicated in the
trial and condemnation of the Divine Prisoner, and
doubtless their most willing accomplices were seated on
the couches by their side.   Peter thus felt constrained

by a divine, overmastering impulse, to bring home to the consciences of his judges the reality and enormity of their guilt. Independent, too, of their hands being stained with the blood of the Innocent, he could not forget that it was these very representatives of reputed sanctity and venerable wisdom who had suborned others to invent and propagate the unscrupulous fabrication, "Say ye that His disciples came by night and stole Him away." He could not, unless false to himself and his Master, with the authors of so infamous a lie gathered around him, have kept silence : had he done so, the very stones would have cried out, and he would have had cause to re-weep that night his old, bitter tears. This suggests yet other and sadder associations, which he could not fail to recal in connection with that place where he now stood. Not only was it there, as we have just noted, though in different circumstances, confronting the same judges, that his divine Master had been sisted before His surrender to the Roman Governor ; not only would the place bring vividly before him "the visage more marred than any man's, and the form more than the sons of men ; " the meekness which no insults could ruffle, the patient endurance which no revilings or insults could shake ;—but surely far more than this, with what still deeper pangs must these walls, and that circle of faces, have summoned before him the unworthy part he himself played in the terrible drama : how there he had probably skulked in cowardly shame from the glance of hostile eyes ;—how, in order to escape detection, he had, by falsehood and oaths and curses, disclaimed all cognisance of the Innocent Sufferer,—refused to raise one note of protest against the cruel wrongs hurled on His guiltless

Master. Might not the thought at the moment, like a lightning-flash, cross his nobler new-born nature, Now is the time and occasion to make all the poor reparation I can, for that base hour of cowardice and denial. I shall vindicate the glories of the name I then forswore, and convert the place of my ignominious defeat, in a strength greater than my own, into a place of conquest and victory.

But to return from the accused to the accusers. Their demand is a peculiar and peremptory one. It is specially to be noted that they do not challenge or impugn the reality of the miracle. *That* it were hopeless to attempt. But they are wishful to know whose *name* the arraigned Apostles have ventured to use in effecting the remedy— was it a power lawful or unlawful? The Jews believed that cures were at times effected through the agency of devils or demons, and such exorcisms were strictly interdicted. The present may have been such a case, which the official obligations of the Sanhedrim will require them peremptorily to prohibit. Hence the summary question, " By what *power*, or by what *name*, have ye done this."[1]

---

[1] The name of all others which the Jews deemed to have most power in working supernatural cures, we need not say, was the sacred incommunicable Name, "*Shem-ham-phorash*," the name of Jehovah (see "Pictorial Bible" *in loco*) ; a name, the very letters of which they imagined to themselves they had consigned to a secrecy that could not be invaded or disclosed. The same authority mentions, that by a base and unworthy fabrication, the Jewish rabbis have for ages attributed the miracles of Christ to a surreptitious possession by Him of that sacred name and secret. The clumsy fable they have invented was to this effect; that a stone found graven with the mystic letters was hidden somewhere within the Holy of Holies ;—that to guard its inviolable sacredness, the wise and pious of the day fashioned two lions of brass, one on each side of the entrance, so that should any one by stealth cross the holy precincts, and venturing to lay unhallowed hands on the stone discover the secreted name, in coming out, the lions would growl upon him so fiercely, as to banish from memory what was thus unlawfully procured.

That proud judicatory, doubtless, assembled under the impression that two timid followers of the Nazarene would crouch panic-stricken under the imposing majesty of law, and volunteer an instant recantation. What must have their feelings been, when, without a glance of timidity or quiver in his voice, in the rough burr and uncourtly patois of Galilee, the accused man replied. Doubtless, as he was about to utter what follows, he would remember the words of his great Lord—"And when they bring you unto the synagogues, and unto magistrates, and powers, take ye no thought how or what thing ye shall answer, or what ye shall say : For the Holy Ghost shall teach you in the same hour what ye ought to say" (Luke xii. 11, 12). The cured cripple, the living trophy of Divine power, the reality of whose miraculous cure could not be gainsayed, was standing evidently in the crowd as his benefactor thus addressed his judges—"Then Peter, filled with the Holy Ghost, said unto them, Ye rulers of the people, and elders of Israel, if we this day be examined of the good deed done to the impotent man, by what means he is made

Jesus, they alleged, by using certain incantations, contrived not only to steal within the forbidden portico, but to discover the stone; and having copied the mystic name on a scrap of parchment, He made an incision in His flesh, and deposited the transcript under His skin—so that though the roar of the lions affrighted Him, He was able thus to recal the priceless secret, and by the utterance of the ineffable Name to work all His miracles. This clumsy and puerile myth is quite unworthy of repetition, except to show, as it does, on what senseless fables the prejudices of the Jew have been based and perpetuated for generations : also to evidence how futile they felt the attempt to deny the reality of Christ's miracles when thus driven to account for them on grounds so utterly frivolous and contemptible. This account is given in the *Sepher Toldoth Jeshu*, or "Book of the Generation of Jesus." "A spurious narrative," says Dr Kitto, to whom we are indebted for the reference, "of Jewish fabrication, from which the Jews have for ages received their impressions concerning the life and character of Jesus Christ. An interesting account of this book may be found in 'Allon's Modern Judaism,' ch. xiv."

whole; be it known unto you all, and to all the people of Israel, that by the name of Jesus Christ of Nazareth, whom ye crucified, whom God raised from the dead, even by Him doth this man stand here before you whole" (Acts iv. 8–10). Every syllable was emphatic. Without attempt at recantation or subterfuge, he repeats even more emphatically the offensive word of the preceding day—"*By the name of Jesus;*" adding to it the more offensive epithet still, that of *Christ* (the Anointed, the MESSIAH); yet, too, "Jesus Christ of NAZARETH," the despised and the lowly; who, though He claimed to be the "Wonderful, the Counsellor, the mighty God," was yet the reputed Son of a craftsman of Galilee, and who chose as His associates and messengers such 'unlearned and ignorant men' as those now prisoners at their bar. "Whom *ye* crucified." These were bold words to hurl at the great religious council of the nation. How they must have winced under them; and more especially if we suppose, as we are warranted to do, that many who had been spectators of the miracle on the previous day, and who by it had been converted to the faith of Jesus, were witnesses and auditors of the present scene. Their presence, while it could not fail to nerve the heart of the speaker, would add to the wrath and consternation of his judges. "Whom ye crucified." As if he said, 'Yes! It is the Man whose blood ye shed, around whose cross ye yelled your fiendish imprecations, that this cripple is now standing here before you whole. God raised His Son Jesus from the dead; and by the power of His resurrection we vindicate the reality of the cure performed at the Beautiful Gate of the Temple.'

Nor is this all. Peter proceeds still farther with his

brief, sententious defence. There was a sentence in the great national Hallel hymn with which each one of these priests and Sadducees must have been familiar from childhood. Often had they sung it at their Paschal season and Feast of Tabernacles. The speaker makes the true Messianic application of it. It was a metaphor, moreover, not unfamiliar in other ways, for it was used by their greatest prophet in predicting the coming of Christ (Isa. xxviii. 16). Nay, further, it had a personal interest in the case of him who now quoted it. For the metaphor was that of a rock or stone. In thus specially selecting it on the present occasion, might not Peter have had indirectly in view the desire of repudiating all claim to any false interpretation that might have been put on his Lord's words, by unequivocally declaring that that Rock—that stone—was Christ? "*This* is the Stone which was set at nought of you builders, which is become the head of the corner. Neither is there salvation in any other; for there is none other name under heaven given among men whereby we must be saved" (Acts iv. 11, 12). Little dreamt these unscrupulous listeners, that in the chanting of that noble psalm, they themselves were the predicted builders who had been guilty of the rejection of this Stone laid in Zion. In common with the vast majority of their countrymen, they had dreamt of the promised Messiah only as the great temporal Avenger of their nation's wrongs, who would tear down the Roman eagles from the palaces on Zion, and reign in a splendour eclipsing that of David and Solomon and Hezekiah. But they could never recognise the fulfilment of that Messiahship in connection with one who lived an unconspicuous life, and died a felon's death.

Yet, says Peter, that rejected Stone, rejected by you, is now the corner-stone of the glorified Temple; and if you and yours seek salvation, that salvation is not to be found in pompous rites, and party shibboleths, and an abrogated ceremonial, but in the name of that once despised but now exalted and glorified Jesus.

These brief words constitute his defence. He need say no more. They form a compendium of Gospel truth, as perfect and beautiful as is to be found in any other portion of sacred Scripture.

We may imagine the momentary hush of the conclave, and then the hum of voices, and the sullen, ill-suppressed indignation. Indeed, we are expressly told the effect the peasant orator produced. Such a bold appeal burst upon them like a thunder-clap. They had come as judges, resolved to proceed against these idle dreamers with severity, and crush at once with menace or punishment, or both, the obnoxious sect. But the tables were turned on them. First, more irresistible than all the logic of the schools, or sophistries of their philosophic thinkers, there stood before them, and before the spectator audience, the living and incontrovertible evidence of miraculous agency; and then, instead of (as they expected) fear, pusillanimity, retractation, they were themselves assailed as the guilty abettors of a foul crime, the murderers of an innocent Man, the crucifiers of the Lord of Glory! Stripped of every plausible pretext to adopt extreme measures against the accused, their recorded emotions proclaimed their own condemnation:—" Now when they saw the boldness of Peter and John, and perceived that they were unlearned and ignorant men, they marvelled; and they took knowledge of them that they had been with Jesus. And, beholding the man which was healed standing with them, they could say nothing against it" (Acts iv. 13, 14.)[1] "The order of things," says a writer, "is reversed. The prisoners at the bar are the accusers, and the judges on the bench are the self-convicted criminals." The court was ordered to be cleared. The Apostles were conducted from it, to allow the members to consult in private, and solve, as they best could, their present perplexity. "What shall we do to these men ?" was the question put by the embarrassed president to his fellow-judges, "for that indeed a notable miracle hath been done by them is manifest to all them that dwell in Jerusalem ; and we cannot deny it. But that it spread no further among the people, let us straitly threaten them, that they speak henceforth to no man in this name" (Acts iv. 16, 17), (lit., "let us threaten them with a threat"). It is possible that some occupying these semicircular benches might have known Peter's recent antecedents—his timidity, and cowardice, and falsehood—and they might be under the impression that little would be required, by maintaining an attitude of firmness, to relieve themselves from their awkward dilemma.

Once more the Apostles were summoned in to hear the sentence. Amid breathless silence the deliverance was given.

"We command you not to speak at all nor to teach in the name of Jesus."

Contenting themselves with a reprimand and caution, without inflicting any penalty, they have little doubt

---

1 The word *boldness* properly denotes *openness* or confidence in speaking. It stands opposed to hesitancy and to equivocation in declaring our sentiments.

that they will manage adroitly to hush the gathering
storm, and deter from any future outbreak ; while at
the same time they will preserve and vindicate their
own dignity, and the majesty of that law of which they
prided themselves to be the interpreters.   But they had
misjudged the temper and character of those with whom
they had to deal. The expedient proved an ignominious
failure.   Peter, once more, rose with the occasion.
Doubtless, his manly soul burned within him to hear
these unworthy and unscrupulous enemies of his Master
pretending to give sentence in the interests of truth,
animated with a pretended zeal for the cause of religion ;
he felt a righteous indignation that they would try to
gag the mouths of those who were the only true expounders of the way of salvation, and bind them down
to ignoble silence.   With a firm remonstrance and protest, which these assembled dignitaries could not gainsay, they refuse to accept liberty manacled and fettered
with such conditions.   "No," is their joint reply,
"Whether it be right in the sight of God to hearken
unto you more than unto God, judge ye.   For we cannot but speak the things which we have seen and heard"
(Acts iv. 19, 20).   It was the first noble assertion which
the Church had made as to the right of private judgment,—the anticipation of that made in the following
chapter—what has been well called "the watchword of
martyrs "—"We ought to obey God rather than men"
(Acts v. 29).   And it would have been strange indeed
if the disciples of Him who came to bear witness to the
truth, had come short of a heathen's maxim : "O ye
men of Athens, I am obliged to you, and thank you,"
said Socrates, "but I must obey God rather than you.
And if you would dismiss me and spare my life, on

condition that I should cease to teach my fellow-citizens, I would rather die a thousand times than accept the proposal." With a mock show of authority, but ill-disguised weakness, the discomfited Sanhedrim deliver once more one of their empty threats. They dared not lay a hand on the prisoners. It would have been more than hazardous, in the temper of the excited multitude, to proceed to the extremities to which their own impotent rage might have urged them ; for the voices of the people, probably in open court, were unmistakably on the side of the prisoners. They were therefore liberated unconditionally. " So when they had further threatened them, they let them go, finding nothing how they might punish them, because of the people : for all men glorified God for that which was done " (Acts iv. 21).

Thus did the purposed measures of violence, threatened by the judges, recoil on themselves. Thus, too, was the bark of the Church, launched on so stormy a sea, enabled by the Great Pilot to weather its first storm. God had given His servant, unskilled though he were in the arts of rhetoric—" the sorcery of eloquence "—a mouth and wisdom which all his adversaries were unable to gainsay or resist. Does not the beautiful combination of courtesy and manly boldness in delivering his testimony, appear yet again, like a personal illustration of that precept of his own, afterwards recorded, " Be ready to give to every man a reason of the hope that is in you with *meekness* and *fear* " (1 Peter iii. 15). By this Christian grace of meek magnanimity he had put to silence the ignorance of foolish men. Had he passively acquiesced without protest in the sentence of the Sanhedrim, he would have betrayed a sacred trust, and compromised himself and his cause. But by his noble adhesion to the right of public testimony and of private judgment, he at once foiled his adversaries, and " strengthened his brethren."

Beautiful and touching is the sequel to the incident just described. The first impulse of Peter and John was naturally to hasten back to the gathered company of believers, who (probably in the same place where they held their Pentecostal meeting) were assembled, waiting with breathless anxiety to learn the result of the Sanhedrim trial. The liberated Apostles gave a rehearsal of the proceedings of the court. " Not for their own glory," is the comment of Chrysostom, " did they tell the tale, but what they displayed were the proofs therein exhibited of the grace of Christ. All that their adversaries had said, this they told : their own part it is likely they omitted." Doubtless, at the same time, would they seek counsel of the brotherhood as to their future attitude and conduct ; whether they should at once leave Jerusalem, where their doings were menaced and their footsteps were dogged, and proclaim the truth elsewhere; or continue where they were, boldly and unswervingly, with a reliance on Divine aid, in the prosecution of their great mission.

We can have no doubt as to the alternative they resolve to adopt. The brief conference is closed and consecrated by the outpouring of united hearts in the following noble prayer and hymn of thanksgiving. In reading it we entertain the strong presumption, alike from the language employed and from the circumstances of the meeting, that the spokesman of these fervid utterances was none other than Peter himself :—" They lifted up their voice to God with one accord, and said,

Lord, Thou art God, which hast made heaven, and earth, and the sea, and all that in them is; Who by the mouth of Thy servant David hast said, Why did the heathen rage, and the people imagine vain things? The kings of the earth stood up, and the rulers were gathered together against the Lord, and against His Christ. For of a truth, against Thy holy child Jesus, whom Thou hast anointed, both Herod, and Pontius Pilate, with the Gentiles, and the people of Israel, were gathered together, for to do whatsoever Thy hand and Thy counsel determined before to be done. And now, Lord, behold their threatenings : and grant unto Thy servants, that with all boldness they may speak Thy word, by stretching forth Thine hand to heal; and that signs and wonders may be done by the name of Thy holy child Jesus." This prayer testifies to the fortitude and unshaken faith which animated the infant Church. It is no wail of the disheartened and disspirited over a hopeless cause ; no bleat of timid sheep when the wolf was prowling close by ; no craven faltering cry of timid mariners when the clouds were gathering in the horizon, and the tempest moaning through the shrouds. It is rather the manifesto of a little band of patriot heroes, who have unsheathed their swords with the resolve to conquer or die ; they merge all thoughts of personal safety in the triumph of the cause so dear to them, and the glory of Him whose they are, and whom they are resolved to serve. They know that He is faithful that promised, " As thy days, so shall thy strength be." Nor, be it further observed, does the prayer contain one imprecation of vengeance —one hard or malicious thought towards their persecutors. They have but one desire—the conquest of truth—the salvation of souls. Peter had been taught, on the most memorable night of his life, to put up the sword of retaliation in its sheath; and others, as well as he, would recall the words of the Lord Jesus, how He said, " Do good to them that hate you, and pray for them that despitefully use you and persecute you."

No sooner were the words of supplication uttered, than He who was thus devoutly invoked, made Himself known, by a renewed outward manifestation, as the Hearer and Answerer of prayer. The place of their assemblage was shaken.[1] The Holy Ghost again descended upon them. His presence was revealed on this occasion in no visible shape or symbol, but by three different moral results, each of which is specifically mentioned—(1.) By imparting to these intrepid witnesses increased fortitude in proclaiming the Gospel message—" They spake the word of God with boldness, and with great power gave the Apostles witness of the resurrection of the Lord Jesus : and great grace was upon them all." (2.) In their disinterested love. Great as as the aggregate of the Church now was, numbering, it has been computed, wellnigh 10,000 souls, the members were linked together by that most excellent gift of charity, which it was said elicited even from heathen lips the exclamation, " See how these Christians love one another !" " They were of one heart and one soul;" no jar or dissension interrupted their spiritual fellowship; fraternal kindness seemed the life and soul of the infant society. " No doubt," says Calvin, " their honesty and temperance, and modesty and

---

1 The word which is translated "was shaken" commonly denotes violent agitation, as the raging of the sea, the convulsion of an earthquake, or trees shaken by the wind. Matt. xi. 7; Acts xvi. 26; Heb. xii. 26.— *Barnes on Acts*, p. 104.

patience, and other virtues, did provoke many to bear them goodwill." (3.) An additional outcome of this fervent brotherhood, was a voluntary assignment made of their property into one common fund. Not many mighty, not many wealthy were as yet called : the vast majority of these followers of the meek and lowly Jesus were doubtless composed of the poor, and those in the humbler ranks of Jewish life. Many, moreover, of the first converts, we may imagine, were Israelites from other countries who had been converted at the Feast of Pentecost. They would naturally be reluctant to leave the company and teaching of the Apostles ; yet, having made no provision for a prolonged absence from their distant homes, they would be as dependent as the permanent poor and indigent on the alms and charity of others ; while, again, many of the natives of Jerusalem, owing to the Jewish hatred of the Nazarene sect, would, by their espousal of the new doctrines, forfeit employment as tradesmen or servants, and be thrown into straits or destitution. But the few exceptional wealthy converts, those who were in affluent circumstances, possessors of lands and houses, came nobly to the aid of their dependent brethren. In an exemplary spirit of self-sacrifice, feeling that they were members of one great spiritual family who had been brought to count their earthly possessions as dross compared to the unsearchable riches of Christ, they realised their property, put the proceeds of sale into a common fund, and made the Apostles its almoners. This fact would almost lead us to conclude that they had by this time surrendered their long, fond dream of the temporal kingdom, otherwise they would not with such alacrity have parted with any portions of that land over which they imagined at one time Jesus was to reign in royal magnificence. Rather anticipating persecution, and the likelihood of being driven from their Judæan homes, those among them who were " owners of the soil " wisely converted their heritable into movable property. The one might be forfeited at any moment by the violence and caprice of their civil rulers ; but the money realised by effecting a sale was a portable commodity, and might be carried with them at any moment of flight to be applied for their common bene- fit. The conquest of what forms with very many the strongest passion of the soul, and one that seems to have been deeply implanted in the Jewish nature, is a pleasing attestation alike to the spirit of faith, and love, and self-sacrifice which animated these single-hearted believers. Those who know what it is to forfeit a patrimonial home and heritage, may gauge the amount of self-devotion and self-denial which prompted these Christian landowners to part with their vineyards and oliveyards, and to esteem the reproach of Christ greater than all other riches. They accepted gladly, in one of its manifold forms, the injunction laid upon them by their great Lord and Master, " If any man will come after Me, let him deny himself, and take up his cross, and follow Me " (Matt. xvi. 24). And yet again, " Whosoever he be of you that forsaketh not all that he hath, he cannot be My disciple " (Luke xiv. 33).

CHAPTER XVI.

Ⱦhe First Case of Discipline.

COMMUNITY OF GOODS.   SIN OF ANANIAS AND SAPPHIRA.   THEIR
  DOOM PRONOUNCED BY PETER.   SPECIAL APOSTOLIC GIFTS.
  THE CHURCH INCREASED.

> " Prophet of God ! arise, and take
>   With thee the words of wrath divine ;
>   The curse of Heaven to shake,
>   O'er yon apostate shrine."

" These things which Luke hath hitherto reported, show that
that company which was gathered together under the name of
Christ was rather a company of angels than men.   But now he
showeth that Satan had invented a shift to get into that holy company, and that under colour of such excellent virtue, for he hath
wonderful wiles of hypocrisy to insinuate himself."—*Calvin.*

" This was doubtless the divine seal and attestation to St Peter's
Apostolic mission and doctrine, and given when the Apostles were
setting up the spiritual kingdom of the Messias.   Like as Korah
and his company were struck dead for their great wickedness,
upon the denunciation of Moses, when he was erecting God's
temporal kingdom over Israel."—*Benson.*

" At the very time when Israel was passing through her first
struggle with the Canaanites, and executing God's judgments on
the abominations of the Amorites, exhibiting themselves as the
holy people of Jehovah, Achan, out of the very midst of Israel, laid
unholy hands on the property.   In the same manner it happened
with the first Church of Christ—the realisation of the idea of the
people of Israel in contrast with a hostile and godless world."
—*Baumgarten.*

ETER is now introduced to us under a new character, as prominent actor and administrator in the first case of discipline which unhappily occurred in the Apostolic Church; a case which stands in Gospel story altogether isolated and unique; tragic in its awfulness; only paralleled by the blighted fig-tree in the Master's allegorical teaching, and reminding more of the wind and the earthquake and the fire, which symbolised the Old Testament dispensation of terror, than "the still, small voice" which was the meet exponent of the New.

We have just been contemplating our Apostle as God's instrument in performing a miracle of healing. We are about to contemplate him as God's agent in a miracle of signal judgment. "As he had first opened the gate to penitents (ii. 37, 38) he now closed it to

hypocrites." [1] "Alas !" as the great German commentator
expresses it, " it is the first trace of a shadow which
falls upon the pure, bright form of the young Church." [2]
The picture of the early Christians, brought before us
at the close of last chapter, was one of unexampled
generosity ; a spontaneous outward expression of the
life and love which pulsed in the hearts of that hallowed brotherhood. The disciples into whose lap the
bounties of providence had been largely poured, were
there represented as bestowing these for the support of
their less favoured brethren. We are not by any
means led to infer that these benefactions resulted
from any apostolic injunction, implying some positive
and authoritative obligation on the part of the early
converts to part with their worldly all for mutual
benefit. It is evident, indeed, from the sad story
itself now to be narrated, that this was not the case.
It is distinctly implied in the charge of Peter to
Ananias, that such renunciation was altogether optional.
It was a voluntary tribute offered by Christian affection
on the part of those who had taken as their motto,
" Ye are not your own, ye are bought with a price."
Even during the period of the Divine Ministry, when it
is evident the wants alike of the disciples and their
Lord were supplied from a common purse, there was
nothing either compulsory or permanent in such an
arrangement. It was one plainly suggested by the
exceptional circumstances of the case, and in carrying
out which they might make what reservations they
deemed proper. Hence we find, after the Resurrection,
that the Apostles, in returning to their old occupations,
had not surrendered their private property. They still

[1] Bib. Dic., art. " Peter."   [2] Olshausen, *in loco.*

had their fishing boats on the Lake of Tiberias; and as has been also noted,[1] John the beloved disciple, in connection with the honoured charge that had been confided to him on the cross, speaks of "his own home;" as if a dwelling-house, wherever it was, had still been retained by him, notwithstanding the temporary agreement for the supply of their common necessities.

Similar seems to have been the arrangement made, not as a matter of obligation and principle, but of expediency, after the Ascension. Indeed this community of goods, though partially appertaining to the Infant Church at Jerusalem, left no trace of its operation in any other of the Apostolic centres of influence. We see subsequently in the Epistles of St Paul, as negativing the theory of a compulsory common store, that the distinctive mutual relations of rich and poor are again and again set forth and defined. We know also that stated collections were made in Macedonia, Achaia, and elsewhere, for the poor saints at Jerusalem, and that for this end the brotherhood and sisterhood were exhorted to set apart so much on the first day of every week; the measure or proportion of the offering being "as God had prospered them;" an injunction which would not have been given had renunciation of property been imperatively required, or had it constituted a condition of membership in the New Society. It would be easy to show that such would not have been among the blessings of Christianity had any such permanent arrangement existed.[2]

And now for the sad story which has led to these

[1] See Dr Kitto.
[2] We have a reference, in Acts xii. 12, to a house belonging to a disciple as a private possession.

preliminary remarks in following the footsteps of St Peter.

Two disciples of the early Church are brought before us. Ananias ("The cloud of the Lord"), a designation not unfamiliar otherwise in Scripture, and Sapphira (or "the beautiful"), a name which, however euphonious in itself and attractive in meaning, has from its bad association perished, ever since, from Christian nomenclature. These wealthy, or at all events independent converts, following the example that had been set by others, sold their possession.[1] As they enjoyed, in the first instance, an absolute control over their own lands, to part with them or no, as they thought fit; so, after the sale was effected, they had a discretionary power to appropriate what portion they pleased of the price procured, to the common fund, stating the amount, and retaining the surplus for their own private use. But the delinquency which brought with it such appalling consequences was, that they made a false representation of the amount of pretended generosity. They alleged that the entire results without reservation were contributed, professing to give all to God; while by a daring insult to His omniscience, they clandestinely entered into a compact to retain for themselves a portion of the price. Their conduct does assuredly seem strange and inexplicable. How, first of all, with natures capable of such baseness, they could be found in a community whose principles and practice had nothing to allure the avaricious and covetous, whose maxim and watchword rather was "Deny yourselves, and take up the cross;" and then,

---

[1] The word rendered in A. V. "possession" is translated in the Syriac, Arabic, and Latin Vulgate, "Land."—*Barnes.* The word used in verse 3 is χωρίον "field." See *Olshausen.*

still stranger, that having accepted these tenets—submitted to that self-renunciation, they could stoop to equivocation and deceit so mean and so unworthy.

"The heart is deceitful above all things, and desperately wicked, who can know it?" After finding among the intimate associates of the gracious and compassionate Jesus one whose inborn avarice could tempt him to plot the murder of the Innocent for the basest of bribes, need we wonder that liars should have crept into the circle of earliest believers?

With no previous data to found upon, we cannot attempt to analyse motive and character. Some have supposed that as moral delinquency often seeks to shelter itself under a pretext of piety and religious zeal, the better to deceive and blindfold a too confiding world;—in the very recklessness of their depravity this guilty pair may have sought to screen their faults and wickedness, by having the reputation of associating with those whose principles were beyond suspicion. But it appears to us unnecessary to resort to any such extreme supposition. They had very probably associated themselves with the new sect, if not from motives as disinterested as those which animated their fellow-disciples, yet at all events which could not be denounced as sinister or unworthy. The two evil spirits, however, Pride and Avarice, which have wrought such havoc in Christian communities, seem still to have survived in the breasts of the unhappy pair after their outward profession of the new creed; and the baneful influence of these twin passions increased, until they came to rule them with demon power. Diotrophes, who loveth to have the pre-eminence, has manifested himself in varied type and phase in every age of the Church. Ananias and Sapphira were, on the one hand, desirous not to be behind any of their fellow-disciples in name and fame for a generosity which would lead to favour and distinction, influence and respect. Perhaps they were well known among the faithful for their ample means; their lands might be familiar to not a few, and they themselves would naturally suppose that by not following the generous example of others, their reputation would suffer. They might be suspected and branded as exceptions to general liberality, and at all events fail of securing general esteem. Barnabas the Levite of Cyprus, as we are informed at the close of the preceding chapter, had realised all his possessions in his native island, and won for himself a conspicuous place in the ranks of disciples by contributing the produce to the common chest. Why may not they follow his example, emulate his generosity, and reap similar approval for kindred gifts? Yet while thus having their names, along with his, among the Church's earliest benefactors, they will take care to purchase reputation on the cheapest terms they can, even though the arts of dissimulation and falsehood be called in as auxiliaries. It might be riskful and injudicious to reduce themselves to straits, when the community they had joined was as yet, as it were, upon its trial, and might be scattered and annihilated like other sects that had arisen before it. They had not the simple, unquestioning faith of their other fellow-disciples, who had cast themselves implicitly on the God they served, and who in surrendering their little all, relied on the injunction of their great Master, "Take no thought for the morrow, for the morrow will take thought for the things of itself." By a prudent, worldly policy they calculated that in this comfortable secret hoard, the residue of their estate, even should the Gospel prove a failure, they would have some reliable provision for the wants of the future. Distrust, worldliness, avarice, thus combined with vanity and ostentation, to make shipwreck of faith and of a good conscience, by tempting to impious prevarication and fraud. "Between the two passions," says a writer, " the dexterity of hypocrisy suggested a compromise. Avarice was contented with the retention of a part, and vanity was gratified by the surrender of the rest under the pretext that it was the whole. . . . They wished to serve two masters, but to appear to serve only one." [1] Their conduct was a spurious imitation, an unworthy counterfeit, of genuine liberality :—base duplicity with a thin veneer of assumed sanctity and generous deed. Nor was the least guilty feature its cool and calculating deliberation. The guilty act was no matter of momentary and reckless impulse, extemporised on their way to the place of meeting; but a carefully matured and concocted plan.

In all these nice and prudential calculations, however, they had omitted the paramount consideration of all, " Neither is there any creature that is not manifest in His sight, but all things are naked and opened unto the eyes of Him with whom we have to do."

Without further attempting to scrutinise their motives, the plot had so far been successfully carried out and consummated. The sale had been effected. The parting with their land had probably been matter of notoriety, as any such occurrence would be among ourselves. Doubtless, they secretly congratulated themselves on the stroke of clever dissimulation. They may

[1] Meyer.

have looked forward to being received by the brethren with flattering encomiums for the substantial proof of their self-denial and generosity. But there was a modern Elijah standing waiting, as of old at the gate of Naboth's vineyard, to unmask and denounce, in stern and awful words, the enormous crime. We gather from the sacred narrative, that Ananias had just entered the congregation of disciples by himself, unaccompanied by the partner of his guilt. Doubtless, he entered the place of meeting with mingled feelings, expecting, on the one hand, as he tendered the produce of the sale, words expressive of grateful commendation that he too "had come behind in no gift," but had, in common with others, provided for the needs of the fatherless and the orphan, and "made the widow's heart to leap for joy." Yet, too, how his unscrupulous deed must have been its own avenger and Nemesis, dogging his footsteps, specially in the presence of the meek servants of Him "who did no sin, neither was *guile* found in His mouth." Peter at once confronts the presumptuous hypocrite with the sin of "lying to the Holy Ghost"—an endeavour to practise deceit on himself and brother-Apostles, in their official character, as the appointed human agents and ministers of that Divine Spirit who had supernaturally endowed and qualified them for their work. Ananias had known—in all probability he had himself seen—the great outpouring at Pentecost, beheld the baptism of fire, and listened to the utterances in varied tongues. All these signs, subsequently followed by miracles, afforded undoubted evidence that the Apostles of the Crucified, in administering the affairs of the Church, were imbued with a heavenly power not their own; in other words, that they had become, in a sense higher than ever before or since, "temples of the Holy Ghost." To attempt upon them, therefore, a scheme of systematic and deliberate deceit, under the mask of distinguished and disinterested goodness, was not only calculated to undermine their own influence, but it was offering an insult to the Divine indwelling Spirit, the Spirit of Truth ; it was a bold and presumptuous trifling with His omniscience, equivalent to a challenge to the Great Heart Searcher to detect the fraud.

But Peter said, "Ananias, why hath Satan filled thine heart to lie to the Holy Ghost, and to keep back part of the price of the land ? Whiles it remained, was it not thine own? and after it was sold, was it not in thine own power ? why hast thou conceived this thing in thine heart ? thou hast not lied unto men, but unto God."

In a moment, as if with a sudden lightning-flash, the convicted man is stretched a corpse on the floor of the assembly, struck down by the judgment of that God he had impiously defied. Death is appalling enough under any circumstances ; but death with a lie in its right hand, hypocrisy unmasked when standing on the borders of eternity, is surely a horror of great darkness. What must have been the feelings of the assembled Christians when they saw one who till now had been a trusted and unsuspected brother ;—who had been wont, doubtless, to join in the hymn of praise and share the memorial feast, arraigned and convicted as a perjured blasphemer ? And no sooner has the dread truth of his flagrant guilt been flashed upon them, than they gaze on livid cheek, and glazed eye, and sealed lips. The trembling culprit has gone to have the sentence, pro-

nounced on earth, ratified at a bar from which there is
no appeal, and to meet a Being who is of purer eyes
than to behold iniquity. "The hope of the hypocrite
shall perish."

Some rationalistic expositors would refer this sudden
doom to purely natural and physical causes; that the
horrors of detection, the fierce tone of Peter's denunciation, the awakened pangs and remorse of conscience,
precipitated some paroxysm or convulsion, destroying
the vital powers, and causing immediate death. God,
indeed, may possibly have thus employed natural means
to effect His own righteous purpose. The sequel of the
story, however, clearly indicates and implies a direct
infliction of Divine retribution.

A few young men of the congregation, probably
" occupying a position similar to that of the acoluthi or
acolytes at a later period," [1] hastened outside to procure
some death-clothes, in order to perform with all celerity
the rites of burial. In Eastern countries the burial
takes place as soon as may be after life is extinct, at all
events, before sunset on the day on which death has
taken place. Instead of coffin or sarcophagus, a linen
garment (sindon) was wound, generally with spices,
around the body. Thus would Ananias, with no wail
of mourners, no tear of affection, be borne by these
youths outside the gates of Jerusalem, probably to some
enclosure or cave in the burying-place of the Jews, on
the slopes of the valley of Jehoshaphat.

A similar awful catastrophe, three hours following,

---

[1] Olshausen. "Certainly," it is added in a note, "there were in the
Church at a very early period persons who were entrusted with the care of
mere external matters, such as the cleaning of the places of meeting, and
the like. These might also take charge of the interment of the dead."—
Ib. vol. iv. p. 412.

was to overtake a guilty accomplice and confederate. She who had shared with her audacious partner in concocting the fraudulent and blasphemous scheme, enters (all in ignorance apparently of his fate), the solemnised and horror-struck assembly. She would do so, expecting perhaps to find her husband the centre of an admiring crowd lauding his beneficence, doubtless hoping too to participate in the ill-deserved approbation. She sees nothing but the mute offering lying neglected where he had laid it at the Apostles' feet, while the significant silence might almost have suggested to her the terrible truth. Peter in a moment charges her with complicity in the dishonourable transaction. We can picture too in thought the feelings and demeanour of the aggrieved Apostle. Though of a different kind, his emotions are probably as profound and thrilling as when he faced the assembled Sanhedrim and braved its fury. Yet doubtless he would feel and act as the representative and vicegerent of Deity, forgetting himself, in the awful message he had to deliver. The sin had indeed in one sense, as we have already said, been against him and his fellow-Apostles, ignoring their Divine credentials, and discrediting their sacred office. But theirs was a subordinate place in the indictment compared to the offence against the great God whose servants they were, and who had vouchsafed them such distinguished proofs of His presence and power. We may therefore well believe, that with deep sorrow of heart, obeying the promptings of the Divine Spirit within him, Peter would deliver, like one of the fiery prophets of old, his burden of woe, "Tell me whether ye sold the land for so much?" The abruptness of the query would have blanched the cheek of most, and covered them with confusion. But in no wise disconcerted, conscience seared as with a hot iron, Sapphira adheres with shameful effrontery resolutely to the bold fabrication, "Yea, for so much ;" intensifying by her obstinacy the baseness of the committed crime, leading some to suppose that like another Eve she was the main instigator in the plot. In her case, at all events, there is no room left for doubt as to the result being a judicial infliction, an immediate judgment of heaven. "Then Peter said unto her, 'How is it that ye have agreed to tempt the Spirit of the Lord? Behold, the feet of them which have buried thy husband are at the door, and shall carry thee out.' "

The same words which announced her widowhood, announced the appalling form in which the first visit would be made to her husband's grave. In the case of Ananias, Peter had pronounced no doom. The miserable man of his own accord, as if struck down by a bolt from heaven, gave up the ghost ; but in the case of Sapphira, he is the medium and mouthpiece of retribution. On listening to the sentence, the infatuated victim of her own sin "fell down," and the newly-dug grave was afresh opened to admit her. The awful dirge and death-knell seems to sound over their common tomb, "Be sure your sin will find you out." "The same unhallowed love of reputation, the same base hypocrisy, the same disregard for the All-seeing Eye of heaven influenced both. They were hateful in their lives, and in their death they were not divided."[1]

It is abundantly manifest from this terrible episode, that special extraordinary gifts were communicated to the Apostles in the first ages of the Church, which have

[1] Professor Dick, p. 81.

been subsequently withdrawn; not only supernatural power to enable them to perform miracles, but also a supernatural insight to "discern spirits," a special power of scrutinising human thoughts, motives, and purposes, so as to render impossible deception and imposture. Nay, farther, that they were invested (according to the only interpretation which the much-disputed words will bear) with "the power of the keys;" authority to bind and to loose; to be the instruments not only of announcing temporal, but of inflicting Divine judgments for spiritual offences. "I write these things," says St Paul, "being absent, lest being present I should use sharpness, according to the power which the Lord hath given me" (2 Cor. xiii. 10). And he previously has defined and signified what that power is, "To deliver such an one unto Satan for the destruction of the flesh, that the spirit may be saved in the day of the Lord Jesus" (1 Cor. v. 5). It has been excellently observed with reference to this by a recent writer, that "the fact should never be overlooked that the men who used this language did so, because they were conscious of an implanted and supernatural might. Peter, like his Lord, could read the heart of Ananias, and could charge him at once with 'lying to the Holy Ghost;' and his accusation was so terrible and so true, that the guilty man fell dead before him. Paul, when withstood by Elymas, could say to him, 'The hand of the Lord is upon thee, and thou shalt be blind, not seeing the sun for a season.' If any men were now to appear among us who could thus take away sight, or even life, by a word, we might listen to their behests as the Christians of Cyprus, or Corinth, or of Jerusalem listened to the command of Paul or of Peter; but if we

see poor ordinary human beings, often destitute of
common sagacity, calling themselves 'successors of the
Apostles,' and assuming, in virtue of that succession,
to determine whether a dying man shall wake up in
heaven or in hell, we feel that such pretensions are not
only sinfully arrogant and false, but that they are also
transparently foolish. The Apostles could show upon
all fitting occasions that they possessed the 'power of
our Lord Jesus Christ' (1 Cor. v. 4). To concede to
them, therefore, some larger authority than belonged to
ordinary human beings was right and proper—it was
obviously reasonable; but to imagine the same prerogatives to exist where no such powers can be discerned, would be wholly contrary to reason. Paul
himself appealed to this test, saying, 'Truly the signs
of an Apostle were wrought among you in signs, and
wonders, and mighty deeds'"[1] (2 Cor. xii. 12).

This lamentable example of insincerity and hypocrisy
we have now considered, inflicting as it did such a scar
on the beauty of the primitive community—enough
to "make devils triumph and angels weep"—was yet
doubtless the means, in consequence of the signal
vengeance it entailed, of protecting the morality of
the infant Church, and vindicating its purity. The
graves of these two hypocrites need no epitaph to read
the perpetual warning, "Verily, there is a God that
judgeth in the earth:" "The candle of the wicked
shall be put out." Moreover, it would tend to confirm
and establish the authority that had been conferred on
the Apostles, and form a new and incontrovertible
credential of their mission. The rumour of such an
appalling visitation must speedily have been carried

[1] Author of "Essays on the Church," p. 125.

throughout the whole city ; and these " terrors of the Lord" would constrain many, hitherto indifferent spectators, to turn with interest and awe towards the followers of the crucified Jesus of Nazareth : " Fear came upon as many as heard these things." None arraigned the rectitude of the judgment, appalling as it was. Indeed, with the large body of the people the event seems to have ingratiated Peter and his colleagues as the bold, heroic, faithful servants of the Most High : " The people magnified them ; and believers were the more added to the Lord, multitudes both of men and women."

CHAPTER XVII.

Peter before the Sanhedrim.

SHADOW OF PETER. IMPRISONED BY THE SANHEDRIM. MIRACU-
LOUS DELIVERANCE. GAMALIEL'S APPEAL. SENTENCE OF
THE COURT. SCOURGING.

> " Nerved is his arm with angel-power,
> He quails not in his trial-hour;
> In face of threat, and scourge, and cell,
> Christ's hero stands invincible."

" As those who occupied the seat of Moses were themselves the murderers of the Son of God, and would not humble themselves before Him to receive even the pardon of their sins which was offered to them by the Apostles preaching in their presence, they fell of consequence into the new sin of seeking to quench the Spirit. Yet their first decided procedure against those who announced the resurrection of the crucified Jesus, plainly evinces that a smitten conscience bore witness to them of their alienation from God and their struggle against the defenders of **true piety**." —*Olshausen.*

" As the influences of transforming, always attaching themselves to the constitutional character of an individual, purify and ennoble it ; so in this instance what Peter became by the power of the Divine life, was in a measure determined by his natural peculiarities. . . A capacity for action, rapid in its movements, seizing with a firm grasp on its object, and carrying on his designs with ardour, was his leading characteristic, by which he effected so much in the service of the Gospel."—*Neander's History of the Planting of Christianity.*

THE reputation of Peter, now more than ever the acknowledged leader of the Apostolic band, was greatly increased by the recent miracle of judgment. "Other signs and wonders," we are told, were at the same time wrought among the people by his hands and those of his coadjutors.

What time elapsed between the death of Ananias and Sapphira and the incident which is now to claim our attention, it is impossible to say. Those best qualified to pronounce on chronological questions are, I think, rightly of opinion, that it may have been a period of years. The inspired Evangelist, we may feel assured, does not bring together in his narrative a succession of events quickly following in consecutive order. Rather he allows considerable gaps and intervals to occur, full doubtless of lights and shadows in the history of the young community, only gleaning here and there points of more salient interest. To have done otherwise would have demanded too wide a canvas. It is not, therefore, at all unlikely, that since we last traced the footsteps of St Peter, a considerable time intervened, during which the new Christian sect was slowly but gradually advancing,—winning its way to reputation and acceptance. If the Church still could claim but few adherents amid the more influential Jewish classes, it was unmistakably gaining favour among the common people. The prejudices of the latter were not so deep-rooted or inveterate as in the case of their ecclesiastical and social superiors. They could not resist the arguments of meekness and love, magnanimity, earnestness, and zeal, displayed amid fierce and unreasoning hostility. They were more open still to the most incontrovertible evidence of all—the possession and exercise of miraculous powers on the part of the Apostles.

A widespread popular enthusiasm, indeed, not unlike that which Peter himself could recall in connection with the great desert preacher on the banks of the Jordan, seems to have spread, with Jerusalem as a centre, to the towns and hamlets round about. The diseased, the sick, the demon-possessed were brought in beds and couches, and lined the streets in hopes of arresting the eye of the wonder-working Apostle. They might not be so fortunate as their mendicant brother at the Beautiful Gate, in obtaining a personal interview, and the crowd would prevent them otherwise approaching; but so great was their confidence in Peter's credentials as a heaven-sent messenger endowed with superhuman power that they would risk hours of exposure to the burning

Eastern sun and to the public gaze, if they could only come within his passing shadow. Nor was it the humbler class of invalids only who solicited his aid. The two words employed in the original ($\chi\lambda\iota\nu\tilde{\omega}\nu$ and $\chi\rho\alpha\beta\beta\acute{\alpha}\tau\omega\nu$) rendered "beds and couches," would indicate that the rich on their soft and costly beds, as well as the poor on their coarse and hard litters, sought these coveted positions.[1] We can imagine the Apostle, as the sun was westering, returning from his teaching in Solomon's Porch, the row of supplicants waiting anxiously for the healing shadow to fall, and still more anxiously for its supposed miraculous influences to follow.

It is unnecessary to remark that restoration was in no way connected with any mysterious influence emanating from the person of Peter; yet, a Greater than he seemed to have owned the simple faith of these helpless invalids, mingled though it was with superstitious feeling; for we gather from the passage that they returned cured to their several homes.[2] But this outburst of popular favour roused to its depths the hostility of the Sanhedrim. The high-priest and his Sadducean councillors were beyond measure exasperated with the new successes. They felt that alike by preaching and miracle these ignorant, and as they doubtless regarded them, vulgar zealots, were supplanting themselves in the affections of the people, undermining their in-

---

[1] See Barnes *in loco*.

[2] "The passage is analogous to what is said of the touching of the hem of Christ's garment"—*Olshausen.* "It might please God to bless such an act of faith in a special manner at that time, in order to give additional authority to the doctrine preached by St Peter and the Apostles, and to show that they were in an extraordinary degree filled with the Holy Ghost, recently poured out upon them on the day of Pentecost."—*Wordsworth on Acts.*

fluence, slighting their authority, and turning the decisions of their ancient tribunal into a derision and laughing-stock. Again they are roused to the necessity of pursuing no longer a policy of silence and inaction, but taking forthwith strenuous measures for stamping out the growing rampant heresy. Once more, too, we have to recognise the preponderating sway of the Sadducees in the Sanhedrim—an influence so strong as to control and dominate its decisions. They were doubtless now peculiarly indignant that their great rivals, the Pharisees, were gaining an accession of strength from that which formed the most distinctive tenet in the teaching of the Apostles—viz., the Resurrection. This dogma had long formed the chief subject of strife and discussion between the two great ecclesiastical parties. The Pharisees could well afford to hold aloof from the "battle of creeds," and preserve a sagacious silence, seeing their own weapons were so ably wielded by those who had ingratiated themselves with the masses of the people.

At the instigation, then, of these leaders of the Sanhedrim, the captain of the guard and his not unwilling band again made forcible seizure of the aggressors, and put them in the prison of Antonia. As on the former occasion, the apprehension seems to have taken place in the afternoon, when it was too late or too inconvenient for the great ecclesiastical councillors to assemble; so that the examination was postponed till next day.

We can picture Peter and his old associate severed from the sympathy of friends, and with the memory in that circular hall of scowling looks and angry words, anticipating their trial on the morrow. Doubtless, as on a future occasion, which we shall come more specially to note, they would lie down in their cell that night with a good conscience. More likely would repose be chased from the uneasy pillows of those who were dogging the footsteps of innocent men, "devising mischief upon their beds, and setting themselves in a way that is not good." But the God whom the persecuted served was "giving His beloved sleep." They are roused; but it is by no unquiet dream of fearful apprehension. At midnight or in the early hours of morning a celestial messenger—one of those angels with whom Peter had recently been familiar on the great Easter-day [1]—effected the escape of the imprisoned Apostles. Conducting them probably to the level platform of the Temple area and pointing to the cloisters, they commanded them there, so soon as the worshippers had begun to gather for the morning sacrifice, to resume their wonted teachings; that, too, with special reference to the new Resurrection-doctrine so obnoxious to the Sadducees, "Go, stand and speak in the Temple to the people all the words of this life" (Acts v. 20). If any remains of a coward, calculating spirit had animated these faithful men, we might expect that on breathing once more the free air of heaven, they would have been tempted to take advantage of the silence and secrecy of early morn, and put themselves beyond the power and oppression of their persecutors. But they were "not disobedient to the heavenly vision." Indeed (Greek) "at the break of day" they addressed themselves to the first straggling groups that had assembled within the sacred precincts, and entered eagerly with them into converse on the one engrossing theme.

[1] It has been suggested that angelic agency was employed in order, by the most irresistible of arguments, to confute the error held by the main instigators in the present persecution—for the Sadducees held that "there was no resurrection, neither *angel* nor spirit" (Acts xxiii. 8).

All in ignorance of the evasion of authority, the high-priest and his civil and ecclesiastical officers had already met in the stone-chamber to put the threatening purposes of past days into execution. Again the services of the guard of Antonia were enlisted to bring the defaulters to the bar. They returned to the assembled court with the startling news, that on going to accomplish their mission, they found to their astonishment the sentinels still faithful at their vigils, unconscious of any unusual occurrence, pacing in front of the well-secured doors ; neither bolt nor lock seemed to have moved : and yet, on entering the cells, the couches of the prisoners were vacant, and the unbound chains lying on the floor. There had been an escape which baffled explanation.

The high-priest and his underlings were filled with amazement. He had summoned for the occasion, not only the usual members of the Sanhedrim, but augmented the number by having also "the Senate" or Presbyters "of the children of Israel," in order to have all the advice and aid possible in so grave an emergency. On hearing the report of the officer on duty, they can think of nothing but some boldly concocted and adroitly executed scheme by the favouring multitude or by some interested accomplice of the Apostles, who had succeeded in bribing the soldiers on guard. Even the supposition of such a plot showed unmistakably the bias of the people. If unchecked in time, there was no calculating to what excesses such craft and artifice might lead. With their sentences thus nullified and their authority defied, "they doubted whereunto this would grow." The captain of the Temple felt that his place and pay and honour were all at stake ; for the possibility could hardly fail of being entertained, that even he and his troop may have connived at their escape—perhaps secretly favouring alike their creed and their safety.

Meanwhile a messenger reaches the court, and announces to the assembled heads of the nation that the incarcerated Galileans are in the most public place of the city pursuing their old vocation, and gathering around them listening crowds in the Temple cloisters. However reluctant these proud authorities would be to believe it, many of them at all events could not help suspecting—dreading—that by a notable miracle the accused had evaded justice and escaped from prison. The Captain and his band are instantly despatched to secure the persons of the troublesome teachers. They perform their errand with as little demonstration as may be; for portent added to portent was intensifying the popular sympathies, and anything like violence or coercion might have precipitated a tumult. The form which reprisals would take is specially noted: "They feared the people lest they should have been stoned." Some fragments of stone would probably be lying about in the uncompleted cloisters, as they were left by the workmen;—similar weapons which a few weeks hence were to be employed in initiating the long roll of the Church's martyrdoms. The Apostles, by resisting the present exercise of authority, might easily have hastened on a riot, and thus effected their own escape or rescue. But unresistingly they obey the summons of the authorities, and in a few minutes find themselves once more in their old position, encountering the gaze of these seventy-two sages in the court of justice. In addition to the company of John, Peter seems now to have had all the Apostles arraigned along with him. It is a new opportunity afforded them to give publicity to the Name and cause they love. Conscious that they have on their side the right though not the might, they would be ready to say in the spirit of the noble words with which Paul, on a future day, braved his unjust judge and accusers in Cæsarea, "If I be an offender, or have committed anything worthy of death, I refuse not to die" (Acts xxv. 11).

The High-priest stood up, and amid the hush of the assembly addressed the inculpated Apostles. In brief but stern words he charged them with contumacy, and the *animus* of the speaker is sufficiently manifested by the unworthy and contemptuous way, as if with a sarcastic sneer, he refers to the Divine Being whose teachings were the cause and occasion of all the present excitement :—"This *Name;*" "this *Man's* blood." He reminds them that the court of which he was president had, under threat of penalties, demanded that they should teach no more in the name of Jesus; adding, that the whole city was ringing with these doctrines. Nor did he conceal what was felt to be the most dangerous of their statements—viz., that in public they had ventured to make the Jewish authorities (himself and his coadjutors) responsible for the blood that was shed on Calvary. The association of their names with a hideous crime might, owing to the growing acceptance of the Christian teaching, draw down upon them at any moment popular vengeance.

Peter was in no wise disconcerted either with the scene in that court-room, nor with the accusation that was hurled against him and his brethren. He uses no exculpatory or apologetic speech; he does not attempt either to modify or to deny the charge laid at their door, or disclaim the strong language in which the accusation against them was couched. In one of those sentences of terse, epigrammatic power so common in his addresses and writings, he utters the great maxim by which his future teaching and conduct were to be regulated—a supreme regard to Divine authority : " We ought to obey God rather than man." And then, the Rock-man, placing his foot on this firm foundation, hurls back the old charge on his persecutors of personal complicity in the guilt of the Crucifixion ;—that they were not only murderers, but had inflicted on their beloved Lord murder in its basest, most ignominious form—"Jesus, whom ye slew and hanged on a tree." He farther refers indirectly to the hated doctrine of his Master's resurrection. Nay, not His resurrection merely, but to the glory which had followed :—that God had exalted Him to the highest heavens "as a Prince and a Saviour, to give repentance to Israel, and forgiveness of sins." Then, with an array of supernatural attestations to point to—from the gift of varied tongues on Pentecost and the crowds of sick that had been healed, to the prison-doors that had been recently thrown open— he can confront his irate judges with the challenge, " And we are His witnesses of these things ; and so is also the Holy Ghost, whom God hath given to them that obey Him " (Acts v. 32). Dean Alford well remarks, regarding the brief reply of the Apostle—" The whole is a perfect model of concise and ready eloquence, and of unanswerable logical coherence, and a notable fulfilment of the promise, 'It shall be given you in that same hour, what ye shall speak' " (Matt. x. 19).

Such bold, persistent words were too much for that

haughty conclave, accustomed as they were to deferential reverence and unquestioned submission. To be charged anew with the blood of the Nazarene! to hear the statement that that Galilean who had lived a peasant's life and died a felon's death, was now enthroned in glory a " Prince and Saviour !" and perhaps, worse than all, to be told that " *Israel*"—the covenant people —to whom pertained such exceptional prerogatives, needed " repentance and forgiveness of sins "—that forgiveness coming from this crucified Man ! What an insult to their self-righteousness and national pride ! It was like the sword-thrust of an assassin : " They were cut to the heart." With an impulse of instantaneous revenge, these inquisitors of the first ages conferred together in subdued tones. One thought takes possession of every heart—"death to the zealots !" Nor would it have been any mere verbal, idle threat. Such was the temper of that unworthy judicature, that the counsel to slay would have been followed by cruel deed, and the death of the protomartyr Stephen would have been anticipated in equally dreadful form by the sword of the executioner, or by the rocky missiles lying ready on the slopes of Jehoshaphat. The averting of the doom, and alteration of verdict, came from a very different quarter from what they might have expected.

Though he had surrendered his place to the high-priest as a matter of official courtesy, the true leader of the Sanhedrim was a man who stood highest of all his contemporaries (and specially in that deliberative assembly), for caution, wisdom, learning, and moderation. Gamaliel, called *Rabban* Gamaliel, the Elder, the highest title of honour amongst the Jews (the same with which Mary Magdalene first hailed her risen Lord), was of distinguished lineage. He was grandson of the great Hillel, and supposed by many, though on doubtful authority, to have been son of the aged father of the Temple who took up the child Jesus in his arms, and sang the " *Nunc dimittis.*" It is the same illustrious personage whose name is farther associated with the early life and training of the future Apostle of the Gentiles. Young Saul was said to sit at the feet of this learned expositor of the law of Moses, and interpreter of its traditions ; and the leading youth of Jerusalem doubtless did the same. His rabbinical learning, his character, birth, and piety, entitled him to wield an enormcus influence in the counsels of the nation. We have no reason to suppose, from what is here recorded (although some of the early Fathers have ventured on the assertion), that though ostensibly a Pharisee and noted expounder of their tenets, he was secretly and in heart a convert to the new faith ; indeed, that he soon openly professed it, and was baptized by Peter and John. Such an idea would seem to be negatived by the fact, that it was under his subsequent teaching that the youthful student of Tarsus had his mind so imbued with hatred of the Christians, that he was said to " breathe out threatenings and slaughter " against them. We have indeed reason rather to adopt an opposite conclusion regarding Gamaliel's final religious views. If we credit the genuineness of the following prayer, which has been attributed to him, for the destruction of heretics, he died a bigoted Pharisee— " Let there be no hope to them who apostatise from the true religion ; and let heretics, how many soever they be, all perish as in a moment. And let the kingdom of pride be speedily rooted out and broken in our days. Blessed art thou,

O Lord God, who destroyest the wicked, and bringest down the proud." [1]

Be this as it may, he was at all events, at present, a singular exception to the intolerance of the sect to which he belonged ;—liberal in his views, rising above party prejudices, and, for the time being, we cannot resist thinking, profoundly staggered, as a man of high principle and dispassionate candour might well be, by all he had seen and heard. On the occasion of which we now speak he rose in his place in the assembly. All the more readily would he command a deferential hearing because, unlike most of his coadjutors, who were detested by the masses, he had conciliated the goodwill and opinion of all outside the Sanhedrim, for he was " had in reputation of all the people." It was customary in this great tribunal, when a case was being adjudicated, that after the parties had been heard and the cause pleaded, the accused were asked to retire, in order to allow the court time to deliberate on the sentence. In the turmoil and confusion this seems at first to have been omitted. But at Gamaliel's suggestion the Apostle-prisoners withdraw. Like the too close proximity of fire with inflammable material, their very look and presence might perhaps have tended to precipitate an extreme issue, making, had they remained, any attempt to act as intercessor unavailing. Gamaliel then proceeds to address his fellow-judges in words of rare wisdom and conciliation. Too plainly did he himself

---

[1] Horne's Introduc. *in loc.* So highly did he stand in the estimation of his countrymen, that the Mishna declares with his death the glory of the law terminated. His funeral was one of imposing and costly splendour, one of his pupils burning on the occasion seventy pounds of frankincense. His death took place eighteen years before the fall of Jerusalem.—*See also Howson and Conybeare*, vol. i., p. 62.

perceive the delicacy and danger of their own position. A rash and violent act might prove, alike politically and ecclesiastically, disastrous. Violence towards the accused, in the present increasingly favourable bias of the people towards them, might lead to riot and bloodshed. With admirable tact and sagacity he counsels to abstain from violent measures, quoting two precedents abundantly familiar to his auditors. It was the case of two zealot upstarts, political fanatics, who, after a brief career of success, in which they succeeded in rallying numbers around their standard, were unmasked as deceivers, and all, as many as obeyed them, were scattered and brought to nought.[1] He grounds on the supposed failure of these insurrectionists a plea for non-interference in the present juncture : " Refrain from these men." He argues that if the doctrine propounded by them, as he would fain wish it to be, were of mere human origin—the work of demagogues or impostors, or shallow and vulgar enthusiasts—it would perish by reason of its own intrinsic weakness, and its adherents would be numbered with other manifold extinct sects which in the course of Jewish history had struggled through a transient life. On the other hand, if the teaching be of Divine origin, authenticated by miracle and portent, no coercive power of Synagogue, or Sanhedrim, or Council could overthrow it. It would outlive all human attempts to doom it to annihilation. It would triumph by virtue of its own inherent strength and vitality:—so much so, that to fight against it would

---

[1] So Gamaliel imagined when he cited the illustration ; but many years afterwards the sect of Judas, as we have noted in Chap. I., which was imagined to be suppressed by the Roman power, renewed the insurrection of former years with the success of desperation, and it was only extinguished by the conquering army of Titus, and the fall of Jerusalem.

be the vain endeavour to "fight against God," and wage
an unequal contest with Omnipotence. Olshausen's remarks are judicious : " He regarded Christianity neither
as a thing plainly objectionable, nor yet as a thing to
be entirely approved of ; he knew not what to think of
this new phenomenon ; and therefore he left the explanation of it to time, which could not fail to develop
fully its true character. Had he perceived it to be
decidedly objectionable, then he would have felt constrained to crush it ; had he perceived it to be decidedly
good, then he would have been obliged to recognise it
openly as such. He had instituted researches, though
without being able to come to a decision." [1]

The appeal of the wise senator was irresistible. The
passions of the assembly are for the moment assuaged.
By the temperate counsels of their sagacious chief the
threatening storm was changed into a calm. The
Apostles were anew summoned to the bar ; and again
the futile order was addressed to them that, while receiving their liberty, they were to refrain from speaking
in the name of Jesus. The sentence, moreover, was
coupled with an act of illegal baseness. The magnanimity displayed by Gamaliel would surely prevent
him, at all events, from being a consenting party. But
the innocent men were ordered to undergo the cruel
and ignominious torture of scourging ; receiving each,
according to the usual Jewish regulation, thirty-nine
stripes. We are almost led to infer from the narrative,
that the sentence was carried out within the precincts
of the court itself ; as if those who saw meet to inflict
it were apprehensive, that if the prisoners once got outside the walls they might escape altogether the penalty.

[1] *Olshausen on the Acts*, pp. 419, 420.

Possibly they dreaded also lest dismissal from the bar, without any mark of disapproval or degradation, might tend to weaken their own authority in the eyes of the people, and leave the impression that victory was on the side of the Apostles; or, if we may venture yet another supposition, they may have entertained the hope that the disgrace associated with scourging would, more than anything else, deter the prisoners persisting for the future in their public teaching.

With trembling limbs and lacerated backs, the victims of impotent rage left the presence of their persecutors. But noble is their mien in the midst of these cruel sufferings and humiliations. Would they not remember Him who, in saying to one had said to all, "Follow thou Me"? Would they not remember Him (they were afterwards Peter's own written w rds) "who, when He was reviled, reviled not again; when He suffered, He threatened not; but committed Himself to Him that judgeth righteously"? (1 Peter ii. 23.) What but fellowship with the Master in His sufferings could have presented to us such a picture and delineation as that with which the narrative closes? No hands lifted in vengeful imprecation; no passionate tears shed; no cowardly resolve for the future. With unabashed countenance, and hymns on their lips, "they departed from the presence of the council, rejoicing that they were counted worthy to suffer shame for His name" (Acts v. 41).

Nor has the threatening charge of the Sanhedrim effected any alteration of heroic purpose. They had obtained that very night a fresh token of encouragement, that "the angel of the Lord encampeth round about them that fear Him, and delivereth them." Nay, that they had One on their side mightier than hosts of angels, " who hath broken the gates of brass, and cut the bars of iron in sunder." The zeal of self-sacrificing love continues unabated, for " daily," we read, " in the Temple, and in every house, they ceased not to teach and preach Jesus Christ."

It was evident now that the Church, and specially its acknowledged valiant leader, occupied a large space in public estimation. The good seed, sown with prayerful hands, had already yielded an abundant reaping in Jerusalem. We shall soon hear of the faithful labourers entering on other and more distant fields, that were white unto harvest.

CHAPTER XVIII.

𝔓eter in 𝔖amaria.

SITUATION OF SAMARIA. PETER'S JOURNEY THITHER. HE ASSISTS
PHILIP THE EVANGELIST. CONFRONTS SIMON THE SORCERER.
DENOUNCES HIS IMPOSTURE. EXHORTS HIM TO REPENTANCE.
LEGEND OF SIMON AND PETER.

> " Seize the banner, spread its fold !
> Seize it with no faltering hold !
> What if to the trumpet's sound
> Voices few come answering round ?
> Scarce a votary swell the burst,
> When the anthem peals at first ?
> God hath sown, and He will reap ;
> Growth is slow when roots are deep."
> —*Keble's Miscellaneous Poems.*

" Hitherto the Church had been crowded up within the city
walls, and the religion had crept up and down in private corners ;
but the professors of it, being now dispersed abroad by the malice
and cruelty of their enemies, carried Christianity along with them,
and propagated it into the neighbour countries, accomplishing
hereby an ancient prophecy, that 'Out of Zion should go forth
the law, and the word of the Lord from Jerusalem.' "—*Dr Cave.*

PON its own isolated summit, the "Watch Tower," or "Watch Mountain," with a girdle of hills around, stood the rebuilt city of Samaria. Even to this day, in its desolation and loneliness, there is beauty and picturesqueness in the site of the old "Crown of Pride." What must it have been, as Peter and his fellow-traveller approached it, when, amid these now silent ruins and broken columns tenanted by the most degraded and poverty-stricken of Syrians, there moved a luxurious population composed of Jew and Gentile — that encirling zone of hills, the setting of this Kingly Crown, covered with gardens and forests, and, through the one break to the east, the waters of the Great Sea gleaming in the distance!

Perhaps of all the cities of the Holy Land which

flourished in the Apostolic age, Samaria, under its changed name of *Sebaste*, was that which, humanly speaking, was least accessible to the new doctrines of the Apostles of Jesus. The simple fact that Jerusalem had become the main focus of the new faith—that the miracles which had recently, at least, attested its truth were performed in the Temple of Zion — would be enough to prejudice the whole system in the eye of a citizen either of Sebaste or of Shechem. The deadly feud which had existed for ages between the rival sects and the rival Temples crowning respectively Mount Moriah and Gerizim, had lost little if any of its virulence. The Jew still avoided the Samaritan, and the Samaritan the Jew, as they would have done a leper's foul touch. They still hesitated to eat from the same platter, or drink from the same vessel, or handle the same staff. The traditional hatred thus expressed by one party in the feud was amply recipro-cated—"There be two manner of nations which my heart abhorreth . . . they that sit on the mountain of Samaria, and they that dwell among the Philistines" (Ecclus. i. 25, 26). [1] The cause of this hatred on the part of the Jews arose mainly from the fact, that those who formed the subject of their inveterate antipathies were, in truth, a half-heathen tribe. A colony of foreigners, at the time of the first captivity, had been sent by the King of Assyria to occupy the province of Samaria. Thither they imported their pagan rites

[1] Possibly the extreme rancour of these malevolent feelings may have been somewhat moderated after the interview of Jesus with the woman of Samaria and its results (John iv. 39, 40), although we cannot fail to recall that on the very last occasion in which Jesus passed through Samaria He was sternly refused the rites of hospitality, "because His face was as though He would go to Jerusalem" (Luke ix. 53).

and manners. This resulted in a strange heterogeneous compound of the worship of Baal and Astarte with the worship of the Jehovah of Israel—a system so debased and corrupt as to draw forth the charge from the lips of the most tolerant of Teachers, " Ye worship ye know not what " (John iv. 22).

Yet, strange to say, despite of these international hates, the persecution in Jerusalem which followed the martyrdom of Stephen, and which resulted in scattering the Hellenistic members [1] of the primitive Church to distant places, found Philip an emissary from Jerusalem in the city of Samaria, " preaching Christ unto them." Perhaps, indeed, this very antagonism of the two peoples may have so far determined the selection of the new sphere of labour. The disciples well knew that the hated power of the Jewish Sanhedrim, from which they had so severely suffered, could not follow them or their Teachers into the territory of the rival race. Any such attempted interference would have been keenly resented. [2] The teaching of this earnest Evangelist was accompanied by miraculous gifts. Truth proved too strong for prejudice, error, or passion. The Samaritans dared not resist the argument of devils exorcised, cripples healed, sick and palsied and fever-stricken restored. The mighty works and the mighty

[1] The Hellenists were converts from among the foreign Jews, or "Jews of the dispersion," and are to be distinguished from the Hebrew Christians, among the latter of whom were the Apostles. The former were more "advanced" in their views as to the "wide embracing scope" of the Gospel, as independent of the Temple ritual; and upon them, therefore, the fury of the first persecution fell. The Hebrew Christians, who were still frequenters of the Temple and its services, were not so obnoxious; hence, when the Hellenists had to flee for their lives, the Apostles remained still in Jerusalem.—*See some thoughtful remarks in Canon Norris' Key,* p 135.

[2] Kitto.

word of God were alike made manifest; while it was
"the name of Jesus Christ" (Acts viii. 12) that formed
at once the key-note of their preaching, and the secret
of their success. "Many, both men and women,"
believed and were baptized; and "there was great joy
in that city."

But in all ages of the Church of Christ, and this
primitive age was not exceptional, there ever have been
tares mingling with the wheat—base and counterfeit
coin amid the true currency of heaven. The cause of
the Master and of His servants was again threatened
to be brought into disrepute, not from the violence of
national and sectarian prejudices, but owing to the
deceit and artifice of a bold impostor.

Simon Magus seems to have been one of those sor-
cerers, magicians, or conjurers of Persian origin, who
have so long wielded a strange fascination over the
credulous of all countries, but more especially over the
more plastic and susceptible Oriental mind. They
wrought themselves and their votaries into the belief
that they held intercourse with spirits and demons,
through whose agency diseases were inflicted or cured.
They pretended to foretell future destiny by the position
of the stars, and to avert impending evils by spells and
incantations. "Half-philosopher, half-charlatan," as
Simon has been called, he had evidently attained a
wonderful notoriety in the city where he had come
to reside. His own birthplace, according to Justin
Martyr, was the village of Gitton, near Shechem;
and, on the authority of Clement, he was educated at
Alexandria,[1] where he was imbued with the dreamy
Gnostic philosophy and theology. By some, indeed,

[1] Olshausen, and Smith's Bib. Dic.

he is deemed to be the founder of that mystic creed.
Samaria, owing to the mixed character of its inhabitants, to which we have just alluded, being largely
imbued with Eastern superstition (belief in necromancy,
and divination, and evil spirits), was the likeliest
ground Simon could have chosen for the exercise and
fascination of his thaumaturgic powers. "From the
least to the greatest," the cultured classes as well as
the poorest, in the city, were under his bewitching spell:
"This man is the great *power* of God" (Acts viii. 10).
"The longing which was everywhere awakened after
something higher, led men to attach themselves to all
such persons as affirmed that they had been favoured
with glimpses of the spiritual world."[1] Sharing in the
universal expectation of a coming Messiah, the dupes
of his artifice may have regarded him as their promised
Divine Deliverer, his magical arts being the apparent
credentials of his mission. Indeed, the full extent of
the man's pretensions are not sufficiently brought out in
our authorised version, where a Greek word (καλουμένη)
has been omitted in the rendering; so that the correct translation ought rather to be, "The power of God
which is called great." The Samaritan recognised
angels as "powers" (δυνάμεις), but theirs was a deri-
vative power from the Supreme Being, emanations from
the eternal first principle of light; whereas the power
ascribed to Simon, and which the impostor himself
claimed, was the power of the great God Himself, of
whom he was regarded as the visible Incarnation. If
we are to credit the account given by Jerome of his self-
assertions, he arrogated the attribute of Omnipotence
("Ego Paracletus; Ego Omnipotens").[2]

[1] Olshausen.
[2] See Smith's Dic., Art. "Simon."

This bold pretender beheld with an envious eye the performance of rival signs, wonders, and well-authenticated miracles on the part of Philip, eclipsing his own. What were the tricks of a conjurer's clever legerdemain compared to deeds of mercy performed over the couch of sufferers, the most appalling mental maladies taking wings and fleeing away?

Artfully feigning to have become a convert (or, as some are inclined to think—better motives mingling with the application—that he was overcome at the moment with the heavenly power of the truth), he received in common with others from the hands of the Evangelist the rite of baptism. He may very possibly have regarded Philip as a worker of miracles like himself, an adept in some new magic art, and saw with a politic glance that to discredit the fact, would have injured and diminished his own popularity with the citizens. He deemed the profession of the new tenets needful, if he were desirous of retaining his influence; moreover that the manifestation of any open hostility to the new sect would be detrimental to him. Either, then, through policy, or through fear, or both combined, he had outwardly attached himself to the followers of Jesus.

It was at this crisis, probably in the year 36 or 37, shortly before Saul's conversion, that Peter appears on the scene. His work at Jerusalem is accomplished. He had laid firm and deep the foundations of the Church in the mother-city despite of all adverse elements. The Sadducees, goaded to madness by the progress of a creed so antagonistic to their own, were still enlisting all the powers of the law for the suppression of the new sect; and more especially that Hellenistic portion most obnoxious to them. Scourge and prison became sadly familiar to the Christians. Even the sacredness of their private homes was violated by unscrupulous inquisitors. Every form of threatening was used to lead them to abjure the sacred Name : neither age nor sex could plead exemption from chain and dungeon. But, despite of these scenes of blood and violence, the Rock-man had the joy of seeing the earliest stone of the great Spiritual Temple laid in Zion ; and he could turn his footsteps elsewhere with the elevating conviction, that even in the very spot where his Divine Master underwent His deep humilia-tion and shameful death, the gates of hell would not prevail against the Church purchased with His blood.

In appropriating to him a new field for his labours, and making selection of Samaria, the Apostolic company had evidently been guided by that same gracious Spirit who had been promised to "lead into all truth ;" and above all, by that unseen but still ever-present Saviour, who was fulfilling in His servants' experience, as in the experience of His Church in all time to come, His own farewell promise, " Lo ! I am with you alway." The Apostles, indeed, could hardly fail to recal the injunction of a former occasion, " Into any city of the Samaritans enter ye not." Yet, too, would they not remember the touching story - parable told by their Master, in which the chief personage was the *Good* Samaritan? Far more, in what an old writer calls " their present marching orders," they must have remembered vividly the very last command which had been laid upon them, " Ye shall be witnesses unto Me both in Jerusalem, and in all Judæa, and in *Samaria*." Peter is left therefore in little doubt, as he passes through the

Northern Gate of Bezetha, and wends his way, along
with his companion John, up the heights of Scopus, that
the highest authority has instigated and ratified the
present appointment of the brethren.   He will at all
events hasten to the scene of Philip's encouraging
labours; and if, in answer to prayer, the Holy Spirit
be visibly imparted as it was at Jerusalem, he and his
fellow-labourer will accept the sign as an indication
from Heaven that they are in the path of duty.   It is
well worthy of note indeed, in passing, that the mission
to Samaria was not a self-selected one on the part of
our Apostle ; neither was the honour of breaking up
the virgin soil claimed as any right by the so-called
" Chief of the Apostles."   As we have already seen,
Philip was the first to carry the good seed to that
unpromising ground.   He was the primary instrument
in the remarkable revival ; his were the miracles and
teaching which had won the city by storm, and led to
so universal a rejoicing.   Peter, so far from occupying a position of precedence and exceptional authority,
was " sent," or deputed along with John, at the special
instigation of the assembled Apostles at Jerusalem
(Acts viii. 14), thereby indicating that he was their messenger, not their leader; acting under their instructions
and jurisdiction ; in other words, homologating the
appointment of his " ecclesiastical superiors."   " He
that is sent," said Christ, " is not greater than he that
sent him."

With a pleasant remembrance of the same route
trodden in recent years, the writer can follow in
imagination, with tolerable accuracy, the track of these
two faithful ambassadors.   The configuration of the
country leaves little, indeed no doubt, that the course

of the great highway between Jerusalem and Samaria
must have been much the same in these days as it is
now; with this only difference, that a well-defined and
oft-traversed road, "doubtless a good specimen of
Roman engineering,"[1] must then have existed, with here
and there artificial fountains for the refreshment alike
of caravans and solitary wayfarers; whereas, at present
in many places there is scarce a bridle path, in others
nothing but the open, unkept fields with their patches
of straggling corn; while in some portions horse and
mule and camel have to grope their way, as best they
can, amid the rough boulders of a winter torrent or
the fragments of former cisterns.

But let us try to sketch more definitely the local
and geographical features.

Every traveller to the Holy Land has one peculiar
association with this very road which our Apostle now
trod—an association which the latter must have experienced in a more intensified form. As at the present
day it is the path by which the tourist takes, with
thrilling emotions, his last farewell look of the City of
God in pursuing his way northwards; so, doubtless,
may Peter, having completed his testimony within these
sacred walls, have taken a backward glance at the
receding Temple and green slopes of its guardian hills,
with the similar impression that he might never again
return to behold a scene so bound up with the dearest
memories of the Lord he loved. There, just vanishing
from sight, was the steep path which in "early morn and
dewy eve" they had oft-times trodden together on their
way to Bethany. There was the cloister of Solomon
abutting on the gorge of the Kedron. There was

[1] Dr Porter.

the grey-green olive-grove which marked the precincts
of Gethsemane, with to him its sadly mingled remembrances ; and there the spur in the Jehoshaphat Valley,
where, contrary to the long-accepted tradition of the
Middle Ages, possibly the closing scene of all in the
awful tragedy was consummated.   The spot itself we
are picturing is that which, in comparatively few years
after Peter left Jerusalem, was to have a very different
association, unknown to him ; as the place whereon the
Roman eagles were gathered and the Roman watch-
fires were lit previous to the destruction of the city,
and from which Titus gazed for the first time on the
splendid edifices which his battering-rams and torches
were to lay in ruins.

But they continue their journey.   The view of the
City of Solemnities is soon hid from sight, and they wend
their way amid valleys many of which were doubtless
then richly cultivated, having terraces planted with fig,
pomegranate, vine, and olive, but whose slopes are now
as bare as the bald limestone which must always have
crowned their unpicturesque summits.   Now and then
as they attained the higher ground, the desolate wilderness of Judæa, with its blighted plateaux and wadys (as
if seamed with crevices like those of an Alpine glacier),
would open in the far distance on the right, hemmed in
by the weird, wall-like mountains of Moab ; while to the
left would rise, most conspicuous among other heights, the
reputed resting-place of Samuel, probably the " Mizpeh
of Benjamin."   They would doubtless pass through the
modern *Wady Suleim*, the traditional if not undoubted
spot in which the interview took place between David
and Jonathan, and where the sacred friendship of these
heart-brothers was renewed and sealed.   There seems a

suggestive coincidence, indeed, in now following the foot-steps of the two Apostles, who in feelings and character were so exactly the counterpart of those noted twin figures in Old Testament story :—Peter, with his impetuous yet noble heart, cast in the same mould as the son of Jesse, while John is in many respects the reproduction of the loving and loveable son of Saul. As the two apostolic friends pursued their way together through that rock-strewn "field," would they not, like the two heroes just mentioned, by mutual encouragement " strengthen one another's hands in God " (1 Sam. xxiii. 18), and " swear both of them in the name of the Lord, saying, The Lord be between thee and me " (1 Sam. xx. 42). Passing by the Hill of Gibeah, the birthplace of Saul, and Ramah of Benjamin, their course would lie amid scenery whose features would not improbably recal the hills around their own native Bethsaida or the rugged " Valley of Doves." They have already entered the tribe of Ephraim, that territory pronounced by their great lawgiver in his farewell benediction, to be " full of the precious fruits brought forth by the sun . . . and the precious things of the lasting hills." Parts of the road, indeed, must necessarily have been then un-clothed and treeless, as they are now. Bare masses of stone and rock still strew the uplands at Bethel, on the borders of the ancient tribe ; apparently left as nature's monument to remind of the olden Patriarch, who on one of these " cairns " pillowed his weary head and dreamed his dream—a dream, whose truest and divinest interpretation these two pilgrim wayfarers now under-stood better than the dreamer. The rounded " Tells," more distinctive of Judah and Benjamin, are varied by valleys of bold outline and crowned with masses of picturesque cliff. Even now, noble groves of olives furrow the mountain sides, natural grey rock in many places dispensing with artificial terraces to support the soil for the growth of fig and vine, as well as patches of grain. If their journey was at the season of the early or latter rain, those loose boulders, along which, in spring, travellers have to pick their way on horseback along the dry bed of a stream, would be washed or submerged by a swift torrent rolling by the side of the highway. That highway, only faintly discernible now, was then one of the many evidences of Roman supremacy and engineering skill, paved like the *Via Sacra*, and similar in character to other imperial roads still familiar in Italy. We have, in a previous chapter incidentally mentioned, in connection with another journey, the well-known fountain under the village of Bethany. These two Apostles could scarcely fail now to pause at a similar spring on the wayside to Samaria, and which, if it corresponded with its modern aspect, would be verdant with bright mosses and festoons of maidenhair and other ferns, called by the rather sinister name of the "Fountain of the Robbers." A discerning traveller thus describes both the fountain and the road beyond. "The water trickles down the side of a cliff amid trails of ferns, into two or three little artificial basins hollowed out near the bottom. Below it is a carpet of green turf, an inviting camping-ground, with the massive remains of a large cistern beside it, now converted into a corn field. It is a strange, wild, lonely spot—not a human habitation is in view, and as the evening closes, not a human footfall breaks the dead silence; yet everywhere around are the marks of industry—olives and fig trees below, and terraces above, leading up the steep hill sides, like stairs to the clouds that rest upon their summits. . . . From the fountain the road winds up the glen, which gradually widens as we advance ; and the sides become lower and less precipitous. The cultivation still continues, and even improves, probably because the hills and glens are less rugged. In fact, the ride through this district in spring is most charming. The terraced hills are so quaint, the winding valleys so picturesque, the wild flowers, anemones, poppies, convolvulus, and hollyhocks so brilliant and so plentiful ; the sombre foliage of the olive, and deep green of the fig, and bright green of the young corn on the terraces, all give such exquisite hues to the landscape. Add to this the grey ruins perched on rocky hilltops, and the peasants in their gay dresses, red, green, and white ; and the strings of mules, and donkeys, and camels defiling along the narrow paths, their bells awakening the echoes ; and the Arab with his tufted spear or brassbound musket, and the shepherd leading his goats along the mountain side." [1]

Such, in its modern dress and aspect, was the mountainous part of the Apostles' present journey.

By and by, emerging from this succession of picturesque "highlands," an altogether new landscape would open before them, as it had once at least previously done, in interesting circumstances (John iv. 5, 6), and doubtless more frequently than once. A break in the hills would disclose, almost instantaneously, the modern *El Mukhna*, Abraham's " Plain of Moreh," seven miles in length, with the Well of Jacob towards its north-west end. The hills of Ebal and Gerizim,

---

[1] See the entire description of this route in Dr Porter's Handbook of Palestine, ii. p. 328.

like lions *couchant,* guard right and left the entrance
to the main outlet, in which the ancient Shechem then
as now nestled.   That ground, as we have just observed, was memorable to these Apostolic Chiefs, on
account of the interview, so strange to them at the
time, between their Master and a female of the hated
sect.   The recollection of that meeting could not fail
surely at present, to be a warrant and encouragement
to proceed boldly on their new mission, in defiance of
the old unworthy prejudice.   As they passed the well-
known spot, and in all probability quenched their thirst
at the same fountain, or as they gazed up to the top
of Gerizim, then crowned with a new temple rebuilt
by Herod, would they not recal vividly the declaration
of Him who in prophetic words had announced the
hour at hand, when they should "neither in that mountain nor yet at Jerusalem worship the Father;" but
when the true worshippers in every land and every
clime, "would worship Him in spirit and in truth."[1]
Or, still more significantly, when the same Divine
Being, as He pointed to the waving corn around, spake
of more glorious spiritual fields "already white to
harvest," and of those who were to "gather fruit unto
life eternal"?[2]   Would not these two devoted husbandmen, going forth bearing precious seed, take comfort in
the promise that they would, "doubtless," in a vast
sense of which they had then no conception, "come
again with rejoicing bringing their sheaves with them?"
How changed the views and sentiments of one of these
missionaries, since the hot words of the zealot would
have lighted up the surrounding valleys with conflagration,—brought down fire from heaven on a churlish

[1] John iv. 23.   [2] John iv. 25, 23.

village of Samaritans (Luke ix. 51) ! The beneficent power of the new faith had broken down the walls of partition, and implanted in his heart the tolerant spirit and love of his Master. He now, at least, remembered his Lord's merited and sharp rebuke, and resolved to act upon it—" Ye know not what spirit ye are of, the Son of Man came not to destroy men's lives, but to save them."

We need not pause to describe the remainder of their journey. If they did not enter, they would, at all events, pass the gates of Shechem, the first camping-place of the patriarchs, and one of the Levitical Cities of Refuge. Then, as now, this narrow valley, part of Ephraim's fruitful heritage, must have been unsurpassed in Palestine for its exuberance, and for the variety of its productions. If they happened to pass at the end of summer, the melon and cucumber, the apricot and orange, familiar to the eye of these natives of tropical Gennesaret, would here greet them, as they do at the present day, in the gardens on the slopes of Gerizim, as well as the less familiar music of running streams in the little " becks " or dells ; while the blue lupin and anemone would carpet the untended wayside. By a Roman road, the remains of which are still visible, the two travellers would continue their journey ; a larger rivulet slowly wending its way close by, and tempering the heat. At the north-western outlet, a lateral valley opens to the right, at " the head of the fat ravines " (Isa. xxviii. 1), and their eyes would rest at once on the ancient and romantically situated city of Samaria, standing in queenly beauty on its own central oval-shaped hill, and sentinelled, as we have already said, with mountains right and left and rearwards.

On reaching its plateau they would enjoy an enchanting prospect. " The view," says the same writer from whom we have last quoted, " is a noble one—embracing the glens and vales round the hill, the circuit of mountains, a section of the plain of Sharon, and the wide expanse of the Mediterranean. No better site for a capital could have been selected in the length and breadth of Palestine—a strong position, rich environs, central situation, and an elevation sufficient to catch untainted the cool healthy breezes from the sea." [1]

The city of Samaria, " the mountain *Shomron*," in which the Kings of Israel so long held their court, was chosen originally by Omri to be his country palace or " Paradise ;" but it subsequently became the capital of the ten tribes who revolted from the house of David. It was subjected, age after age, to the vicissitudes of fortune, often succumbing to the terrors of war and siege. When Peter and John entered its gates, it had risen like the Phœnix from its ashes. Hyrcanus, we are told on the authority of Josephus, had utterly destroyed it. But Herod, the imperial city builder, who recognised its importance as a fortress and place of observation, as well as the singular beauty of its site, had reared on the old foundations an entirely new capital, strongly fortified, which he had called by the Greek translation of the name of his royal master. It has been supposed by antiquarians that the broken marble colonnades and their pillars, still the admiration of travellers, and which have accorded the ruined city the designation of the Palmyra of Palestine, were the results of his munificence. Those who have visited the

spot, and gazed on these noble fragments (between two
and three hundred in number), may picture what the
ancient capital must have appeared, at the time when
the two unlettered Galileans entered it for the purpose
of uprearing a temple not made with hands.   The
cultivated terraces, at present rising tier upon tier on
its hill side, were then probably covered with buildings.
The great central street, along which they passed, would
be flanked with that avenue of columns ; and the apex
or upper terrace of the hill crowned with both a royal
residence, and a magnificent temple dedicated to the
Cæsar.   The whole was surrounded with walls twenty
stadia in length.   To quote the words of another
traveller : "With its circling colonnades and towering temples, it must have looked surpassingly noble.
There is nought like it even in Palestine, whose hills
and valleys seem as if specially laid out as sites
for castles, and palaces, and cities.   It is Ephraim's
'crown' set round with jewels, his 'wreath' all
wrought about with flowers for the head of his
'fruitful valley' (Isa. xxviii. 1). . . . I counted the
mountain tops in this great girdle, and found them
upwards of forty in number . . . though the 'great
joy' is no longer known within the walls of the city,
yet the word fails not, and Samaria awaits the time
allotted to her : 'Thou shalt yet plant vines upon the
mountain of Samaria, O virgin of Israel, the planters
shall plant them, and shall eat them as common
things'" (Jer. xxxi. 5).[1]
     It was, then, this city which Peter and his beloved
associate [2] entered, in order to assist in the great work

---

[1] Dr Bonar's Land of Promise, p. 378, 379, 381.
[2] "This is the last time that John appears in the Acts."—*Alford.*

which had been so successfully initiated by Philip.
" Who, when they were come down, prayed for them,
that they might receive the Holy Ghost : (For as yet
He was fallen upon none of them : only they were
baptized in the name of the Lord Jesus). Then laid
they their hands on them, and they received the Holy
Ghost " (Acts viii. 15–17). It is evident from these
words, that though Philip was a divinely-accredited
evangelist, and had received abundant tokens of the
divine presence and blessing in his labours ; yet
that the extraordinary powers and miraculous gifts of
the Holy Ghost, which had been manifested in the
Pentecostal revival in Jerusalem, were exceptionally
bestowed on the Apostles of Christ alone, the divinely
appointed founders of His Church and ministers of His
kingdom : powers which may have been since profanely
claimed by Papal hierarchs, but which have never really
been wielded. In the present instance, the laying on
of these two Apostles' hands evidently conveyed the
power of working miracles and of imparting special
spiritual blessings. What that " gift of the Holy
Ghost " was, here specially spoken of as having been
imparted, we are not told. It is evident that the communication was made, as at Pentecost, by some external
visible sign or attestation — some outward startling
effect—including, as in the former instance, the speaking with tongues, the working of miracles, and discerning of spirits. This Apostolic power, moreover, was
outwardly conveyed by the imposition of hands, a
universal Eastern practice in the bestowment of benefits.
As at Pentecost, so now, these extraordinary endowments were imparted in answer to prayer. We have
no reason to suppose that they were bestowed upon all,

indiscriminately, or even on the majority of Samaritan believers. The *ordinary* gifts of the Spirit—His saving influences as the Enlightener, Comforter, Sanctifier of His people, were evidently shared by *all* in greater or less degree. As in the subsequent case of Lydia, He had opened each heart to welcome the glad tidings "with joy in the Holy Ghost." But the more striking manifestations of His power had been vouchsafed to a limited and privileged number. "To one was given the working of miracles; to another prophecy; to another discerning of spirits; to another divers kinds of tongues; to another the interpretation of tongues. But all these wrought that one and the selfsame Spirit, dividing to every man severally as He willed" (1 Cor. xii. 10, 11). "It does not appear, that, even in the Church of Jerusalem, which we may conceive to have been, at least, as highly favoured in this respect as any other, there was an indiscriminate distribution of His extraordinary gifts. When an election was to be made of persons to take care of the poor, the Apostles commanded the multitude to look out among them men 'full of the Holy Ghost,' and the command obviously imports, that every man was not so qualified." [1]

"John," observes Stier, "may perhaps have looked back to the days when he desired to call down on the Samaritans another kind of heavenly fire; now at least, he knew what manner of spirit he was of."

Simon Magus had hitherto passed unsuspected among the new company of professing believers. But he now throws off the mask which he had successfully worn, since receiving the outward sign of admission into a

[1] Dick, p. 131.

society to whose spiritual aspirations he was evidently a stranger. And here we cannot resist to note, in passing, how the case of the sorcerer exposes and refutes the figment of what is spoken of as " baptismal regeneration." Had there been any such alleged sacramental virtue or efficacy in the sacred rite, it would have been conferred by an apostolic evangelist, surely. It is abundantly evident, however, that there is no such necessary connection between the sign and the thing signified, seeing that after the sprinkling by the hands of an accredited minister of Christ—one, moreover, ordained, not by " successors of the Apostles," but by Apostles themselves, this outwardly baptized convert was pronounced by Peter to be utterly devoid of inward grace, still " in the gall of bitterness and in the bond of iniquity." " For in Christ Jesus neither circumcision availeth anything nor uncircumcision, but a new creature."

But, to return, the artful magician saw at a glance the double importance, in his own case, of being a sharer in these palpable supernatural gifts. The miracles wrought by Philip had thrown his own spells and incantations into the shade ; for the very spirits from whom, in his diabolical art, he was supposed to derive power, were heard, at the bidding of his Jewish rival, " crying out " as they fled affrighted from the bodies they had victimised. His gains and influence were gone, unless he could augment his former evil reputation, by adding to inferior feats secrets of the invisible world, to which he had not attained. His one thought was to become possessed of the new power wielded by this ambassador of the Christ of Nazareth. " He was convinced, from the works which Philip did, that he

was in league with some powerful spirit. He viewed
baptism as the initiation into communion with that
spirit, and expected that he should be able to make
use of the higher power thus gained for his own purposes, and unite this new magical power to his own." [1]
In a word, he desired to become himself an Apostle—the
more so as he saw that Peter and John possessed the
additional power of conferring a portion of their authority on others. He forthwith makes the proposal of a
money bribe, in order to be invested with similar prerogatives. If in addition to his former achievements,
he could add those of which he had been the covetous
spectator, what a certain passport to fame and gain,
wealth and honour !

Basely imagining that the hearts of these holy men
were instigated by the mean avarice which predomi-
nated in his own, " Give me," said he, " also this power,
that on whomsoever I lay hands he may receive the
Holy Ghost." " Since," in the words of De Wette, " in
external commerce everything may be had for gold, he
wanted to buy it." He had evidently judged these
ambassadors of the cross by the world's conventional
standard ; and that the golden bribe, which to it would
be irresistible, would in their case also conquer all
scruples. He himself was a mere trader in spiritual
power, and he deemed it not unlikely that they too
would be open to a money negotiation. Olshausen
well points out the contrast between the vain ostentation of this pseudo-miracle worker and the perfect
simplicity and humility of the true Apostles, who
" although really replenished with the powers of the
heavenly world, yet most sharply reprehended all

[1] Neander.

undue estimation of their own persons. They desired to be regarded as nothing but weak instruments, and their illustrious works were designed to glorify not themselves, but only the eternal God and His Son Jesus Christ." It is, indeed, truly most notable, that as with their divine Master, so with them, the miraculous powers which scattered blessings on all around and which the sorcerer only coveted for his own aggrandisement, were never employed to increase their own personal wants and comforts, reputation or profit, or preferment. Their disinterestedness and self-abnegation were as remarkable as was his avarice and cupidity. With minds humble and unselfish they ever remembered the words of the Lord Jesus, how He said, " It is more blessed to give than to receive."

Peter feels that the truth he proclaims is degraded and compromised by this arrogant Pretender. The infamous attempt thus to barter and bargain is repellent to a spirit which, with all its natural failings, abhorred covetousness. He repudiates it accordingly. " What communion hath light with darkness, and what concord hath Christ with Belial ? " Again reminding us of the Great Tishbite as he stood in the presence of guilty Ahab, the Rockman-apostle in no measured language hurls back his answer to the nefarious proposal of the mercenary—" Thy money perish with thee, because thou hast thought that the gift of God may be purchased with money." We must not take these words as an imprecation on the head of Simon, as if the speaker " knowing the terrors of the Lord " had denounced him as a castaway ; but simply as an expression of abhorrence at his impious attempt. He farther tells him in this withering rebuke, that his proposal

formed abundant evidence of the insincerity and duplicity of his heart, which could not be "right in the
sight of God." The one utterance of the magician was
criterion enough for Peter to judge his character and
pronounce his profession to be a lie—that he had no
real part or lot in the religion of Jesus, but rather
that he was still the bond-slave of iniquity. The
latter portion of the Apostle's words have been
rendered — "For I perceive that thou art for the
gall of bitterness and the bond of unrighteousness."
"To be for a thing, in Scripture language, is sometimes to be the instrument or cause of it, as when
Simeon says, 'This child is set *for* the fall and rising
again of many in Israel.' There seems thus a prediction of the bitter gall and the unholy fellowship which
Simon would introduce into the Church, a foreboding
afterwards strikingly fulfilled."[1] Sad as was the
Apostle's verdict, yet in beautiful accordance with the
great Pentecostal sermon to Jerusalem sinners, in which
he proclaimed forgiveness even to the very murderers
of his Lord, so now in the same breath in which he
utters the condemning sentence, he urges this Sama
ritan impostor to repentance. Though he too plainly
perceived that, despite of the baptismal rite surrepti-
tiously obtained, Simon was deceiving and self-deceived,
yet he wishes to testify to him that his sin is not included in the awful category of "the unpardonable."
He urges him to resort to penitence and prayer.
"His susceptibility of spiritual impressions," is the
remark of Olshausen, "similar to what we find in the
Old Testament in the case of Balaam, the father of all
false prophets, always left room for hoping that the

[1] Green, p. 88.

truth would gain the victory in his heart, and therefore
Peter preaches repentance to him." " Pray God," are
the remarkable words of the Apostle, " if perhaps the
thought of thine heart may be forgiven thee." Words,
as Dean Alford well observes, " are important, taken in
connection with John xx. 23, as showing how completely the Apostles themselves referred the forgiveness
of sins to, and left it in the sovereign power of God, and
not to their own delegated power of absolution."[1]

The sordid sorcerer, spared a more fearful doom
which might have righteously overtaken him, seemed
for the moment to be covered with confusion and remorse. The rebuke was not without effect : the barbed
dart of the Apostle had reached his guilty heart ; and
smarting under it, perhaps with a knowledge of the
swift and fearful retribution that had been visited on
the other two victims of lying and avarice in Jerusalem,
he importunately entreats his reprover to pray to the
Lord for him, that none of the things spoken might
come upon him. It seems, however, to have been only
a momentary flash of conviction, a momentary slavish
dread of punishment—the cry of terror without the
pang of genuine penitence. Though, according to one
tradition, he broke his magician's wand, and flung his
magical books into the Dead Sea—yet, if we can credit
the mournful sequel as recorded by Irenæus in the
second century, his own seven devils seem to have returned to his swept soul, and his last state to have been
worse than the first. He became the avowed enemy
of the Apostles and of the Christian name. No wonder,
if the account of this ancient father be credited, that
Simon earned the infamous repute of being the first of a

[1] Greek Test., *in loc.*

long progeny of heretics. He came to assert his claim to represent the Trinity ; that by a triple revelation to the Samaritans, the Jews, and then to all the world, he was the incarnation of Father, Son, and Holy Ghost. He added to this profanest of blasphemies the assertion, that a beautiful female from Tyre of the name of Helena, a resuscitation of the famous Helen of Troy, who accompanied him in his journeys as his ἔννοια, or divine intelligence, and was associated with him in his illicit gains, was the mother of all beings, whose first-begotten were angels and archangels. He perverted the Scripture doctrine of grace by encouraging unbounded licence. No wonder when virtue and vice were thus confounded, that many flocked to his standard, and worshipped as a God those who thus pandered to their worst vices. Others of the Fathers relate that, subsequently, he went to Rome, "the rendezvous for all deceivers of this kind," and made himself as conspicuous there as in Samaria ; that a statue was decreed by the Senate and erected to him in the City of the Cæsars on the island in the Tiber, with the dedication " To Simon, the Holy God," " Simoni Deo Sancto." [1] He is, moreover, represented as continuing throughout his later career, the persistent and implacable foe of the Apostle, by whose faithful denunciations he had been so greatly humbled, dogging his footsteps from place to place. Of his end we know nothing,—if we may except the foolish legend, attri-

[1] This statement has been long accepted, but requires to be taken with a qualification. Renan alludes to a remarkable stone, or rather altar, now to be seen in the Vatican of Rome, which was dug out of the island in the middle of the Tiber in 1574, and which has upon it the inscription : " Simoni Deo Sanco—to the God Simo Sancus." There seems a very strong probability that Justin Martyr may have confounded the two names from their similarity, and that his legend about the Samaritan sorcerer is a mistake.

buted to the grave authority of Bishop Ambrose of Milan, of a final meeting having taken place at Rome between him and Peter, and that during the reign of Nero in the year 68, the impostor challenged the Apostle to decide their rival claims by the display of a wild feat of supernatural power : that he rose in the air, in imitation of the ascension of Christ, from the Capitoline Hill, crowned with laurel and supported by demons, intending to alight on the Aventine ; but the prayer of the Apostle caused the demons to let go their hold, and brought him with a crash to the earth, which, though it failed to deprive him of life, drove the deluding and self-deluded man to commit suicide. It is only fair, however, to add, that the genuineness of the passage is also doubted, and so silly a legend certainly seems unlike the wisdom and trustworthiness of this distinguished ecclesiastic.[1] A more evident association with his name, or rather as derived from it, is that to which we have already incidentally referred—the sin of 'Simony'—in other words, the attempt to purchase positions of spiritual influence and responsibility— ecclesiastical preferment—by pecuniary payment,—a traffic in sacred things, " as if the gift of God might be purchased with money." [2]

[1] See the Apocryphal Gospels, &c., in Clark's Anti-Nicene Library, *in loc.*

[2] See Bib. Dict. ; Prof. Dick on Acts ; also Dr Kitto, *in loco*, with quotations in full from Irenæus and Jerome.

CHAPTER XIX.

Peter at Lydda and Joppa.

RETURN TO JERUSALEM. PAUL THE GUEST OF PETER. DESCRIP-
TION OF LYDDA. PETER CURES ENEAS. INVITED TO JOPPA.
MIRACULOUSLY RAISES DORCAS TO LIFE.

> " In the heart no beating, on the cheek no rose ;
> Placid, but rigid, the pale lips close.
>
> No need for hushing her anguish now ;
> No wailings will trouble that placid brow.
>
> No wild lamentings the mourners make ;
> No tumult of minstrels that sleep can break.
>
> .   .   .   .   .
>
> Silence those death-wails of wild despair :
> ' *Not dead, but sleeping ?*' The Life is there !
>
> The gates of Hades, the gates of brass,
> Which through the ages none living pass,
>
> Before those accents quake as with thunder,
> Quiver like aspens, and part asunder."
> —The Three Wakings, &c.

" Like the commander of an army he went about inspecting the
ranks, what part was compact, what was in good order, what
needed his presence."—*Chrysostom, Hom. XXI.*

AVING ministered to the comfort of believers at Samaria, Peter and his coadjutor, in returning to their home in Jerusalem, take the opportunity of scattering in the towns and villages through which they passed, the seed of the kingdom: refreshing the Churches which had already been organised, and planting others. The furrows seem to have been inviting the immortal seed. Everywhere they were hailed as heralds of good tidings. We can picture them, without let or hindrance, traversing these well-known valleys of Ephraim and Benjamin, conscious of their Master's presence and blessing; perhaps remembering the Divine promise spoken by the prophet of Judah, "Again I will build thee, and thou shalt be built, O virgin of Israel: thou shalt again be adorned with thy tabrets, and shalt go forth

in the dances of them that make merry, for I am
a Father to Israel, and Ephraim is my firstborn."
(Jer. xxxi. 4, 5). "How beautiful upon the mountains are the feet of Him that bringeth good tidings,
that publisheth peace ; that bringeth good tidings of
good, that publisheth salvation " (Isa. lii. 7).

One of the most interesting episodes in apostolic
story must find its place shortly after this period.
About the time that Peter and John were sojourning
in Samaria, Saul of Tarsus had been heading the persecutors in the Holy City.   He had stood an onlooker
and ringleader at the death of holy Stephen ; and the
cruel fate of that first martyr was followed, on the
part of this young Pharisee, by indiscriminate cruelties
on the unoffending followers of Jesus.   Neither age
nor sex was respected.   Having vented his fury on the
saints in Judea, he obtained letters from the high
priest (Theophilus the Sadducee, son of Annas) to the
synagogues of distant Damascus, arming him, " as chief
inquisitor," with authority to lay violent hands on those
who had there espoused the Christian creed, and bring
them bound to Jerusalem.   In all likelihood the
fiery zealot had followed the same track we have recently been describing between Jerusalem and Samaria.
When Peter and John were proclaiming the glad tidings
to the Samaritans, a band of horsemen, headed by the
young persecutor of Tarsus, had probably swept along
the narrow valley leading by Samaria to the plain of
Esdraelon,—the old northern highway ; little dreaming
of the momentous incident which would terminate his
week's journey and transform his whole life—changing
the furious bigot and persecutor, with his threatenings

and slaughter, into the meek disciple and Apostle of the Lord Jesus.

It is more than probable that Peter and Saul may have previously met in other circumstances. The latter may have possibly been among the crowd of auditors in the Hall Gazith, and witnessed with suppressed indignation the calm testimony of the Bethsaidan fisherman—the untutored and unsophisticated defender of the faith which he still spurned and scorned. They could not fail, at all events, to be known to one another by public repute—the one as the rising hope of the Pharisaic sect, the other as the reputed leader of the Apostles of a crucified Messiah.

Three years subsequent to that marvellous conversion of Gamaliel's cultured pupil, we find him, strange to say, an inmate and guest in the house of the despised fisherman. Indeed, he tells us that while he was obliged, owing to the machinations of his enemies (suspected by the Christians, and hated by the Jews), to escape from Damascus, he turned his footsteps towards Jerusalem in preference to any other place, specially for the purpose of *seeing* Peter. "After three years (three years after conversion) I went up to Jerusalem to see Peter" (Gal. i. 18). A well-known Father of the Church has noted that there is something peculiarly emphatic in that word " see." It is the same that would be employed in speaking of a pilgrimage to SEE some illustrious city.[1] With the very man he had regarded with such bitter aversion, he now longs to hold confidential intercourse. His cherished wish is at first denied. Even although tidings of his conversion had doubtless reached the Church in Jerusalem

[1] Chrysostom, quoted by Dr Green, *in loco.*

and elsewhere, still, the bold, unscrupulous persecutor was for a time shunned and discredited. They could not fail to recal the dreadful memories that clung to his past history; they had pardonable ground for using, with sarcastic misgiving, the words applied to another of his name—" Is Saul among the prophets ? " The story of his marvellous change would seem too good to be true, and they cautiously waited for it being better authenticated. But a friend in need, unexpectedly but timeously, presented himself. Barnabas, well known for his liberal gifts to the Church, and better known for the loving nature which bestowed them, was said to have been a schoolfellow of the young Tarsian. As on other occasions, so now, he proved his claim to the title, " Son of Consolation." Knowing more accurately the circumstances, and with a deeper and manlier sympathy, he interposed his good offices. When he saw his brethren standing coldly back, and questioning the sincerity of the strange convert, he became sponsor for his old associate. " Cyprus," say the biographers of St Paul, " is within a few hours' sail from Cilicia. The schools of Tarsus may naturally have attracted one who, though a Levite, was a Hellenist; and there the friendship may have begun which lasted through so many vicissitudes, till it was rudely interrupted in the dispute at Antioch. When Barnabas related how the Lord Jesus Christ had personally appeared to Saul, and had even spoken to him, and how he had boldly maintained the Christian cause in the synagogues of Damascus, then the Apostles laid aside their hesitation. Peter's argument must have been, what it was on another occasion : ' Forasmuch as God hath given unto him the like gift as He did unto me, who am I that I should withstand God?' He and James, the Lord's brother, the only other Apostle who was in Jerusalem at the time, gave to him 'the right hand of fellowship.' And he was with them, 'coming in and going out,' more than forgiven for Christ's sake, welcomed and beloved as a friend and a brother."[1]

The distinguished guest of Peter tells us that "he abode with him fifteen days" (Gal. i. 18). Brief and parenthetical as is this statement, yet how profoundly interesting! that for a fortnight these two men were together, holding intimate and endearing fellowship on the great themes which now engrossed the minds of both, to the exclusion of all others. A vain curiosity would seek to pry into these hours of hallowed communion. Next to the great words which fell from the lips of the adorable Head of the Church, would we have prized this " cardiphonia "—these heart utterances of divinest truth on the part of the two chiefest Apostles. They are, however, for wise purposes, denied to us. We can only picture hypothetically what the themes of holy thought and deliberation would be. Doubtless, rising above all, we may place the Person and work, the words and deeds, of the world's Divine Redeemer—His beautiful life, the mystery of His sufferings, and meritorious death. Paul had only heard His voice, " Jesus, whom thou persecutest ;"—but the other had seen Him, talked with Him, listened to His gracious discourses, and beheld His mighty works ;— ay, and better still, had been, as much as the converted persecutor at his side, the subject of pardoning, forgiving love. Can we not imagine him rehearsing, as

[1] Howson and Conybeare's St Paul, vol. i. p. 113.

the other sat with arrested countenance and bated breath, the whole story of that forgiveness? The rash treading of the waters of Tiberias, the broken vows, the Gethsemane slumber, the coward denial, the blasphemous oaths, the base desertion? Yet all forgiven! The tender meeting after the Resurrection, and the public official reponement on the shores of Gennesaret? Then passing from these personal reminiscences to the great official commission, to "Go into all the world and preach the Gospel to every creature." How would Paul's soul kindle afresh at wondrous memories, coming from the lips of one who had himself beheld "the glory as of the only Begotten of the Father full of grace and truth!" May we not imagine with what similar interest would Peter listen to the dramatic tale which the former arch-persecutor had in turn to unfold? Perhaps anticipating Chrysostom's remark of a future age, that the Church owes Saul's conversion to the death of Stephen, might he not tell how the forgiving tones of that voice, and the meek, tender look of that saintly angel-face, had lingered for days and months on his spirit?—the wondrous vision, revealed in the martyr's death-hour, of "Jesus standing at the right hand of God?" Then the mighty crisis of his own spiritual history. He could tell his friend that he had been, though in another manner, similarly favoured as he. He could use to him the words he wrote in subsequent years, "Have not I (too) seen the Lord Jesus?" (1 Cor. ix. 1). He would in all likelihood describe that same Redeemer meeting him by the way, in the blaze of Shekinah glory eclipsing noonday splendour—not in dream, or vision, or trance, or rapture, but truly, as the words seem to imply, in visible manifestation—His glorified human nature (" *appeared* to me ") ;—that it was as really the *form* of the exalted Saviour he beheld, as when he who now listened to that story of grace gazed on the same transfigured Lord on the heights of Mount Hermon — the glorified countenance, the glorified voice, gentle as the murmuring brook, yet " as the sound of many waters"—uttering in that Hebrew tongue, most appropriate to the lips of the divinely exalted Son of David, the expostulation of injured goodness, " Saul, Saul, why persecutest thou Me ?" He would describe the stricken terror of his companions ; the sounds confused and meaningless to them, which were to him so awful and sublime a reality, as they spoke of vain and ineffectual struggles against irresistible grace—" fighting against God ! " Then the groping blindness, the isolation three days in the house of Damascus, " the dark solitary lodging," with its faintness and exhaustion of body and strange inward conflict of soul, the birth-throes of his new being :—the emerging from the horror of great darkness, as humbled and subdued, he fell upon his knees and cried in the agony of despair to the Great Being he had so long persecuted and deemed an impostor ! Then the visit of the devout Damascus Jew,—one of the very converts he had expected to bind, possibly a refugee from Jerusalem,—the ministering angel who delivered him from his remorse and blindness, and welcomed him by the glad name of the heaven-born family —*Brother.* Then the baptism, not in Jordan nor in the waters of Israel, but in one of " the rivers of Damascus ;" not by Peter nor by any Apostle, but by a humble lay member of the Christian brotherhood. Then the great commission,—designated " as a chosen Vessel to bear the name of Jesus before the Gentiles, and kings, and the children of Israel" (Acts ix. 15) : "Unto me, who am less than the least of all saints, is this grace given, that I should preach among the Gentiles the unsearchable riches of Christ" (Ephes. iii. 8). And, last of all, the resolution, in a strength greater than his own, to fight the good fight of faith until he had finished his course with joy. Thus would these two rehearse to one another the common dealings of their common Lord. "Iron sharpeneth iron; so a man sharpeneth the countenance of his friend" (Prov. xxvii. 17). May we not add yet one other touch to the ideal picture, by imagining them commending each other in prayer : in the secrecy of that silent chamber plighting their troth to their beloved Saviour; dwelling on the means and method of best extending His spiritual kingdom; and, amid the certain trials which both had been warned were to overtake them, looking onwards beyond the kingdom of grace, with its "great tribulation," to that better kingdom of glory, where, after heroically sharing in their Lord's cross on earth, they would be admitted to be partakers of His crown? See how these two Christians love one another!

What a vast power, it has been well remarked, must that have been which could have welded together materials so unlike, antagonistic, irreconcilable : that brought the lion to associate with the lamb, the vulture with the dove, the malignant and apparently implacable foe of the meek and lowly Jesus, with his most constant earthly companion; the high-born, cultured young Pharisee, filled with the pride alike of intellect and lineage, to fraternise with the poor boatman of the Sea of Galilee! Each could whisper into the other's ear the mystic secret, " By the grace of God I am what I am." They would attune their lips to the same hymn of praise, " The *Lord* hath done great things for us, whereof we are glad." " The Apostle Peter had witnessed wondrous miracles wrought by his Almighty Saviour. He was himself enabled to work others no less amazing in that Saviour's name. But did ever miracle appear to him so vast and astonishing as the change of Saul the Pharisee into Saul the Christian ? . . . After all that he had witnessed, all that he had experienced of a Saviour's power, must he not still have been ready to exclaim, when exchanging affectionate greetings with his brother Apostle, " What hath God wrought ?" The starting tear in the eye that had once glared so furiously upon the persecuted saint ; the cordial grasp of the hand that had hurled the missile of death at holy Stephen ; the fervent prayer and benediction from lips that had clamoured for the blood of Christ's faithful ones ; these must have thrilled the soul of Peter with emotions that words were inadequate to express."[1]

" Fifteen days," to quote from the same reliable authorities as in the preceding page, " passed away, and the Apostles were compelled to part. The same zeal which had caused his voice to be heard in the Hellenistic synagogues in the persecution against Stephen, now led Saul in the same synagogues to declare fearlessly his adherence to Stephen's cause. The same fury which had caused the murder of Stephen, now brought the murderer of Stephen to the verge of assassination. Once more, as at Damascus, the Jews made a conspiracy to put Saul to death, and once more he was rescued by the anxiety

[1] Lee's Life of St Peter, p. 145, 146.

2 D

of the brethren.   Reluctantly, and not without a direct
intimation from on high, he retired from the work of
preaching the Gospel in Jerusalem.   As he was praying
one day in the Temple, it came to pass that he fell into
a trance, and in his ecstasy he saw Jesus, who spoke to
him and said, " Make haste and get thee quickly out
of Jerusalem, for they will not receive thy testimony
concerning Me."   He hesitated to obey the command,
his desire to do God's will leading him to struggle
against the hindrances of God's providence, and the
memory of Stephen which haunted him even in his
trance furnishing him with an argument.   But the
command was more peremptory than before, " Depart,
for I will send thee far hence unto the Gentiles."   The
scene of his apostolic victories was not to be Jerusalem.
For the third time it was declared to him that the
field of his labours was among the Gentiles.   This
secret revelation to his soul conspired with the outward
difficulties of his situation.   The care of God gave the
highest sanction to the anxiety of the brethren.   And
he suffered himself to be withdrawn from the Holy City.
They brought him down to Cesarea by the sea and
from Cesarea they sent him to Tarsus."[1]

After this, a period of remarkable and exceptional
tranquillity seems to have occurred to the Church of
Christ in Jerusalem.   " Then," we read, " had the
churches rest throughout all Judæa, and Galilee, and
Samaria, and were edified ; and walking in the fear of
the Lord, and in the comfort of the Holy Ghost, were
multiplied " (Acts ix. 31).   Peter employs that season
of calm, and immunity from outward persecution, not

---

[1] Howson and Conybeare, p. 113, 114.

in an intermission of labour, but in an apostolic visitation to these surrounding churches.

Before, however, narrating the details of his pastoral
tour, the question naturally occurs, was there any
reason at this time for so sudden and surprising an
abatement of Jewish and Pharisaic hate? How came
the torch of persecution for the time being to be
apparently quenched, and the disciples allowed a season
of grateful respite, sitting under the Gospel vine and
fig-tree with none to make them afraid? That rest,
we may feel well assured, arose from no diminution in
Jewish prejudice or of aversion to the cause and name of
Jesus. There must surely have occurred one of those
disturbing political crises so common in Hebrew annals,
which diverted their minds from petty warfare with
a religious sect, in order to protect interests of greater
national and social magnitude and importance.

We have not to go far for an explanation in contemporary Roman history.

A large population of Jews mingled with Greeks in
the city of Alexandria, between whom there existed a
deep-seated animosity. The chronic feud in the year
39 was increased, owing to the wanton destruction by
the latter of the Jewish oratories. The exasperated
parties both resolved to appeal to the Emperor, and
appointed accordingly three deputies to plead their
respective causes. Apion, the unscrupulous Gentile
advocate, adroitly succeeded in prejudicing the mind of
Caligula, by representing that the Jews resolutely refused to accord to him divine honours. These, as the
Cæsar, he claimed and demanded. Caligula required
no new arguments to stimulate and embitter his
inveterate hatred for the Hebrew race and name. He

gave immediate orders to Petronius, the new governor of Syria, to have his statue erected within the Courts of the Temple of Jerusalem, accompanying the peremptory command with instructions that any opposition to his decree would be followed by a general massacre and slavery. Petronius, however personally reluctant, had no alternative but to obey the wanton instructions of his royal master; failure on his part would have been resented with swift retribution. With three legions of Roman soldiers he wintered partly at Ptolemais, partly at Tiberias. At both places, crowds of wailing suppliants came from all parts of Palestine to his camp, protesting against the sacrilege. Old, young, and middle-aged, we are told, threw themselves on the ground and implored the Viceroy to use his intercession with the Emperor to avert the awful desecration. Meantime, as we learn from Philo and Josephus, a universal panic or rather paralysis spread over the land. All agricultural work was stopped. Fields were untilled, and vineyards and oliveyards untended. Too well the Jewish population knew that armed resistance would be hopeless against the master of thirty legions. Their tears were their only arguments. These seem still more to have moved the heart of the iron Roman, and with a rare magnanimity he risked his own life by forwarding the appeal. The incensed Emperor, as was to be expected from his imperious nature, pronounced a capital doom on his general, which would have been speedily executed, had not the autocrat's own death in the meantime taken place, and stayed the decree. No wonder that an occasion which goaded the nation to the madness of despair, should have purchased a temporary respite to the Christian Church from the storm which had already burst on her. "Moreover the two great actors in the crime of crucifixion had just been removed ; Pilate banished, Caiaphas deposed. Thus it was that the four years of Caius's reign, miserable as they were to the rest of the world, brought peace to the Christians."[1]

It was then, during this period of rest, that Peter " passed," as it is expressed, "throughout all quarters," making a pastoral round of recently formed churches between Jerusalem and Joppa. On his way by the wild mountainous tract leading past the Bethhorons,[2] he paused by the town of Lydda—the ancient Lud. This town is situated in the tribe of Ephraim on the great plain or " Weald " of Sharon,—that stretch of fertile country extending from the bluff of Carmel to Jaffa, washed by the blue waters of the Mediterranean to the west, and bounded by " the mountain-wall of Ephraim " on the east ; then probably having its rich cornfields interspersed with forests, the remains of which, according to Strabo, existed in the second century. " Eastward, the hills of Ephraim look down upon it—the huge rounded ranges of Ebal and Gerizim towering above the rest ; and at their feet the wooded cone, on the summit of which stood Samaria. But its chief fame then, as now, was for its excellence as a pasture land. Its wide undulations are sprinkled with Bedouin tents and vast flocks of sheep ; the true successors of ' the herds which were fed in Sharon ' in David's reign

---

[1] Canon Norris's Key. p. 49.

[2] All travellers to Palestine who can afford the additional day and undergo the small additional fatigue, should endeavour to approach Jerusalem from Jaffa by this route. The greater proportion adopt the shorter and easier journey by Ramleh ; but they thus forfeit alike interesting scenery and interesting associations ; and above all, lose the impressive first view of Jerusalem from the height of Nebi-Samuel.

under 'Shittrai the Sharonite,' and of 'the fold of flocks' which Isaiah foretold in 'Sharon' as the mark of the restored Israel."[1]   "The whole countryside may be described as an orchard.   Arabs call the plain round Lydda the garden of Palestine, and to distinguish it from the rest of this green district, it is known as the field of Sharon.   Water abounds, and the heat is tropical.   The loam is dark and ruddy, free from the sterile sands of the sea and the not less sterile limestone of the hills.   A hardy and industrious Moslem people till the soil, and gather in the crops of grain.   Few scenes in Palestine have a more perfect Arab character than the gate of Lydda, with its palms and pomegranates, its string of passing camels, its knot of Effendis smoking, and its group of girls gossiping at the well."[2]   We have a peculiarly vivid remembrance of Lydda, being the first place in Palestine where we paused for "rest at noon;" not indeed venturing within its ruined gate, as the modern huts have an evil repute, but gazing under the shade of some trees across to the picturesque ruin of the Church of St George of Cappadocia.[3]   This church is supposed by Pococke to have been the one erected by Justinian to St Peter, and long afterwards (1191) to have been restored by our Richard the First, whose tents were pitched where the Bedaweens are now, and afresh dedicated to England's reputed patron saint, who was said to have been

1 Stanley's Sinai and Palestine, p. 258.

2 Dixon, p. 413.

3 See the heading at the beginning of this chapter sketched on the spot.   It may have been the association with "the Crusaders," but this graceful bit of ruin involuntarily recalled the picturesque nook in the ruins of Dryburgh Abbey which cover the grave of Sir Walter Scott.   A similar thought seems to have occurred to another traveller.   "Yon arch might belong to a part of either Furness or Glastonbury."

martyred on the spot and buried under this shrine.
Indeed the town itself came to be called by the
Crusaders the City of St George. The description which
Volney gives applies to its present condition, " A place
lately ravaged by fire and sword would have precisely
the appearance of this village. From the huts of the
inhabitants of the village to the serai of the Agha is
one vast heap of rubbish and ruins. A weekly market,
however, is held at Ludd, to which the peasants of
the environs bring their spun cotton for sale. The
poor Christians who dwell here, show, with great veneration, the ruins of the Church of St Peter (George ?),
and make strangers sit down on a column which, as
they say, the saint once rested on. They point out
the place where he preached, where he prayed, &c. . . .
The place is now a village of small houses, with nothing
to distinguish it from other Moslem villages, save the
ruins of the celebrated church."[1] Like most other
localities in Palestine, Lydda has undergone many
changes. At the time Peter visited it, there was a
flourishing school under the tuition of Rabbi Gamaliel ;
not the Gamaliel with whom we are already familiar,
but a second of the same name. Shortly after, when
Jerusalem, sacked and ravaged, was rebuilding under
the name of Ælia Capitolina in A.D. 136, the town of
Lydda became known as Diospolis or City of Jupiter—

[1] "Perhaps the most singular event in its strange history was its division by Richard and Saladin into two parts, a Christian side and a
Moslem side, in which it was agreed that under the protection of St
George, the English knight and his Saracenic foe, a foe no longer, should
dwell in peace and charity with each other, the Frank being free to kneel
in his church, the Arab in his mosque. . . . For many years after the last
Crusader had retired from Lydda, the Christian Church was kept in repair
by English funds, and when these moneys ceased to flow into Palestine,
the beautiful remains were protected against waste and theft by the erection
in one corner of a tiny mosque."—*Dixon.*

a temple to the father of heathen gods being erected there. It has later ecclesiastical associations than with the Apostle, for it was raised to be an episcopal see, and here Pelagius was summoned before fourteen bishops to answer on the charge of heresy. Dr Robinson, who gives an interesting and detailed account of the place, mentions, in connection with Peter, that a small stream outside the town still goes by his name, *Abi Butrus*. The Mohammedans have selected Lydda as the supposed scene of conflict between Christ and Antichrist. This Antichrist of fierce countenance is, according to these Moslem traditions, under the name of Al Dajjâb, to become the scourge of the earth, and by fire and sword to attain universal dominion. The Jews of Persia are to be his special retainers ; and after riding triumphant from land to land at the head of his martial hosts, these are to have their rendezvous under the walls of Damascus. The Christ who appeared to St Paul nigh that city, is again to descend near its principal tower or minaret, also in martial array. Rallying His saints around Him, He is to attack the fiendish usurper, scatter His embattled hosts, and drive them across the Hauran and Jordan, till they take refuge on the vast plain of Sharon, around the vast pomegranate and olive groves of Lydda. The gateway of the town is to be the spot where the two opposing leaders are to meet in mortal combat, and where, transfixed by a spear, Antichrist is to be finally destroyed. The victorious Messiah is then to march straight to the Holy City, and Jerusalem, under His benignant sway, is to become the joy of the whole earth.[1]

[1] " He *came down* also to the saints which dwelt at Lydda." The accuracy of the expression "going down" must occur to every traveller, the

A man named Eneas, confined to his couch by palsy, was sought by the Apostle. From his Greek name he would appear to have been a Hellenist—but we may conclude he was among the number of the "Saints" who had solicited a visit from Peter to this lowland town ;—a humble believer in the crucified Jesus of Nazareth, acquainted with the Lord's life of patience and resignation as well as with His death of agony ; perhaps receiving strength and submission under his own affliction, from a knowledge of the meek endurance of the Prince of Sufferers.

For eight long years had this afflicted invalid been bedridden. There had been no mitigation of his symptoms. He and his friends had, doubtless, by this time surrendered all hope of permanent cure. With his faith reposed in Him who was the Conqueror of death, he may have been looking forward to the great change as a happy and joyful release from days of suffering and nights of weariness, when in the morning he said, " Would God it were evening," and in the evening, " Would God it were morning." He longs in his solitary chamber to see the illustrious servant of the Saviour he loved. May he not have heard of those who had, a few years before, been carried powerless as himself to the streets of Jerusalem, and whose faith had been so strong that even the shadow of Peter coming athwart their weary couches had been the signal for gladsome restoration ? Might that same shadow not be blest in his case, in answer to believing prayer ? Peter at all events responds to the longings of the help-

ascent being gradual all the way to the plain or meadow of Sharon from the hilly capitals, alike of Samaria and Judah. See Bib. Dict., art. "Lydda." Also " The Holy Land," p. 416, &c.

less paralytic.   He draws near to the couch and utters
the words, "Eneas, Jesus Christ maketh thee whole,
arise, and make thy bed, and he arose immediately."
Dr Kitto, with his usual discriminating knowledge of
Eastern habits and customs, remarks, "The Orientals
do not leave their beds laid out in the places where
they sleep, except when actually in use.   By day they
are removed, and stowed away in places reserved for
or appropriated to them.   When therefore Peter tells
Eneas to 'make his bed,' he in effect tells him to clear
away his bedding, to fold it up, and take it, together
with the bed itself, from the room, to place it in the
usual repository.   This necessarily involved the lifting
and carrying the bed, though for a shorter distance.   To
understand it of merely readjusting the bed and bedding in the place where it stood, which is what we
mean by 'making' a bed, deprives the passage of the
confirmatory force which properly belongs to it."

We cannot wonder at the result of so signal a
miracle.   As in the former case of the cripple at the
Beautiful Gate of the Temple, there was no possibility
of deception or artifice here.   In a comparatively small
community, Eneas and his ailment would be well known.
"All that dwelt in Lydda and Saron saw him and
turned to the Lord."   It was the remarkable case of a
whole town and district becoming evangelised—a city
like a nation "born in a day."   This spiritual conquest
was, moreover, the more important from the circumstance already mentioned, that Lydda was at that time
a seat of Jewish learning; so that not only the poor and
illiterate, but the educated and cultured, were brought
to embrace Jesus as the Messiah, and in many cases,
doubtless, the learning and endowments of teachers and

taught were laid at the foot of the cross.   The inspired words of the Song of Songs had a significance imparted to them they never had before.   The true " Rose of Sharon" was shedding His spiritual fragrance all around; and the " wilderness and the solitary place was made glad."

The scene is now changed to the great port of Palestine, six miles south-west of Lydda.

As Joppa, the modern Jaffa, seems to have been Peter's headquarters at this time, and has more than one interesting association with his name and doings, it may be well to bestow upon it a brief description. Being the first spot which travellers generally touch on reaching Palestine, it always retains a special place in the memory.   It is, in its own striking situation, a befitting gateway, too, to the " Land of the Morning."   None who have seen it can fail to be struck with its commanding position, built on a bold conical bluff 150 feet high, crowned with a ruined Turkish castle or citadel. The houses rise tier upon tier from the water's edge, with curiously flattened domes,—" a stony hillock," as it has not inappropriately been called,—looking, however, more imposing from the roadstead than when the wretched modern reality comes to be inspected, with its "labyrinths of blind alleys."   Enough, however, remains to show what Joppa may, or must have been, when Solomon's ships rode at anchor outside the dangerous reefs and shoals which guard the landing.   These form a natural harbour or breakwater; yet their dangerous character must always have prevented the town from becoming, in the true sense of the word, an important and available maritime port.   Puteoli and Ostia

have been called the " Liverpools of Italy ; " but Jaffa,
for the above reason, could never to the same degree
have sustained a like relation to Jerusalem. Josephus
more than once refers to this same unsuitability as a
good haven ; so that, unlike other things in Palestine,
it has not been reduced to its present unsafe condition
from neglect. Buckingham, in his travels, thus well
describes its perilous landing, corroborating the testimony of the Jewish historian : " The port is formed by
a ledge running north and south before the promontory,
leaving a confined and narrow space between the rocks
and the town. Here the small trading vessels of the
country find shelter from the south and west winds, and
land their cargoes on narrow wharves running along
before the magazines. When the wind blows strong from
the northward, they are obliged to warp out, and seek
shelter in the small bay to the north-east of the town,
as the sea breaks in here with great violence, and there
is not more than three fathoms of water in the deepest
part of the harbour ; so accurately do the local features
of the place correspond with those given of it by Josephus." [1] Joppa formed a stronghold of the Philistines
on the borders of Dan, who " remained in ships "
(Judges v. 17). The name is taken by some from the
word signifying " beauty," *jafeh*, the same word which
is used in the Psalter and in the Song of Solomon to
describe both Jerusalem and Tirzah. " Beautiful for
situation, the joy of the whole earth, is Mount Zion, on
the sides of the north, the city of the great King "
(Ps. xlviii. 2). " Thou art beautiful, O my love, as
Tirzah, comely as Jerusalem, terrible as an army with

[1] It is a specimen of the wild extravagance of ancient writers, when Strabo
gravely asserts that Jerusalem is visible from the highest part of the town.

banners" (Cant. vi. 4). According to others, Joppa
had a far more ancient than a Philistine pedigree. It
was said by Pliny to have an antediluvian origin, to
have been built by Japhet, the youngest son of Noah,
and from him to have derived its name. So that, as
a writer says, " around it lie the ashes of a hundred
generations of men, Philistines, Hebrews, Macedonians,
Saracens, Franks, and Turks." It was illustrious in
profane history, classical mythology having woven
around it one of its boldest traditions. It was on one
of these reefs of black rock, which guard its entrance,
and are the terror of the mariner, on which, also according to Strabo, Andromeda, the daughter of Cepheus,
was chained, and, when about to be devoured by a sea-
monster, was gallantly rescued by Perseus. Its Scrip-
tural and sacred associations are various. Through
these same reefs, Solomon's workmen towed the vast
floats of cedar trees, hewn by the Sidonians in the
forests of Lebanon for his Temple ; while it was from
the same dangerous harbour the fugitive prophet of
Nineveh embarked in the vessel bound for Tarshish,
when with troubled spirit he fled from the presence of
the Lord. In a later age still, it was the scene of wild
tumults and cruelties during the wars of the Maccabees.
Few cities have been more frequently sacked and pil-
laged, "five times by the Assyrians and Egyptians in
their wars with the Jews, three times by the Romans,
and twice by the Saracens in the wars of the Crusades." [1]
We may only add, that its environs are the most
lovely in Palestine. Indeed, it is matter of disappointment to the traveller that there is not to be found elsewhere, in further traversing the country, a repetition of

1 Dr Kitto.

those 350 gardens,—wondrous hedges of cactus, clusters of date-palm, apricot, pomegranate, citron and orange-groves of delicious fragrance, which greet him on the outskirts of the town, and line his way for several miles on the way to Lydda and Ramleh ; only surpassed, indeed, in Syria by the still more extensive " paradise " of Damascus.[1] On its modern history we need not particularly enlarge. Like its sister town Lydda, it has undergone many changes. Its fortifications, sacked by Saladin, were reconstructed also by Richard, and vastly strengthened and extended by St Louis in the thirteenth century. A part of the walls, fifteen feet high, still remain on the side towards the sea, with towers alternately round and square, on which some old guns are mounted. These, indeed, must have been no mean fortifications, requiring, as they did, batteries to be erected against them by the French in order to be reduced. This recalls its last military memory, in connection with the First Napoleon, whose massacre of the 4000 Albanian prisoners on its sands in 1799 has affixed a lasting stigma to his name. Whatever be the misery and degradation of the modern Jaffa, no one can fail to believe that it will play a conspicuous part in the future destinies of " Palestine restored," and modern science and enterprise may, combined, overcome the difficulties and dangers of its present rock-bound harbour.

When Peter was sojourning at Lydda, two messengers were despatched from Joppa, requesting him with all haste to come to the Jewish seaport, at the urgent desire of the disciples resident there.

---

[1] " About eight millions of oranges are grown every year in the gardens around Jaffa. Several hundreds are borne by a single tree."—*Eastward,* p. 81

A death had occurred, which had plunged the circle of believers into no ordinary grief. A member of their little company, probably one in the upper ranks of life, had fallen a victim to sickness. The deceased lady was one of those attractive specimens of Christian female character, who combined simple faith with boundless deeds of beneficence, the one evidencing the reality and intensity of the other. She was a " disciple ; " and the outcome of her discipleship was " fulness of good works and alms-deeds which she did " (Acts ix. 36). Her name, Tabitha, or Dorcas—the former Syriac, the latter Greek—signified the same thing, " gazelle," " hind," or " antelope." It was a common usage, in former times, to give names to beautiful women from the more graceful of the lower animals. The " eye of the gazelle " was an especially favourite trope in oriental poetry, as descriptive of the same feature in the human countenance. From this we may probably infer, that Dorcas was possessed alike of inner and outer attractiveness ; that her beautiful face was the index and exponent of those lovelier attributes of soul, which had their full expression in her deeds of charity and love.

The account of the cure of Eneas having reached Joppa, the disciples at the latter town were naturally desirous of having God's greatest living minister and Apostle with them in their season of overwhelming bereavement. It has been made a question, whether they could have ventured to entertain any expectation of Peter's miraculous powers being available to raise the *dead*. This mightiest of supernatural wonders had hitherto not been performed by the Apostles ; and hence it has been by most surmised, that the simple object of the mourners at Joppa was to have the comfort of his presence ; that they might have his words to sustain them in their common sorrow, if denied his deeds.   The urgency of the message, however, would seem to indicate that their faith had reached a higher region, and cherished loftier expectations.   The interment of the dead in Eastern countries takes place shortly after the demise ; and the haste requested would almost seem to imply that they *did* entertain some fond hope that, ere earth was returned to earth, the scene which took place of old in the house of Jairus by the Master, might be repeated by His servant.   The loss to the early Church in that Jewish seaport was so great and irreparable, that we cannot be surprised they clung fondly to the hope that "she was not dead but sleepeth."

Peter immediately responded to the summons.   When he reached the shadowed home, he found himself in the midst of a scene of touching sadness.   Some suppose he had been sent for while Dorcas was still alive, and life was "balanced in a breath."   If so, at all events now all was over; the meek spirit had departed; the soft lustre of the gazelle-like eyes had apparently fled for ever.   A group of heart-broken widows were gathered around the bier.   Amid weeping and wailing—the usual loud manifestations of oriental grief—they held up the garments which her hands and her alms had provided for their use, and that of their poorer and more dependent sisters—the dumb, silent tributes to her rare worth and goodness.   It is evidently implied that hers was no mere tossing of redundant ostentatious gifts into the Christian treasury, but that these were hallowed and consecrated by the activities of personal beneficence. Her works and her alms-deeds went hand in hand, the

one the complement of the other. Every tongue had
to tell of some ingenious deed of kindliness in response
to the tale of distress ; the stored gifts were doubly
precious, because her own hands had made them, and
her own hands bestowed them. Her beneficence, too,
was doubtless all the more remarkable and conspicuous
in that age of the world ; for the kindly and generous
developments of a later Christianity were then unknown—those charities which have since taken the very
name of this female of Joppa as their distinctive badge
and description, making her the foster-mother of a thousand gracious agencies, which have put light and hope
and comfort into many a darkened dwelling, many
a stript and desolate heart. Hers was angels' work
indeed. True in her case was the description of the
Patriarch of an earlier age, among his desert tents and
rock cities : " When the ear heard me, then it blessed
me ; and when the eye saw me, it gave witness to me :
because I delivered the poor that cried, and the fatherless, and him that had none to help him. The blessing
of him that was ready to perish came upon me : and I
caused the widow's heart to sing for joy " (Job xxix.
11–13).

But alas ! the eyes that had so often beamed with a
beautiful compassion were now closed—the hands that
had smoothed many a sick pillow were now powerless
—the feet that hastened on many an errand of love had
now sped on the last long journey—the lips that had
so often whispered words of tenderness were still as the
cold marble. Indigence will no longer have its unfail-
ing response ; the widow and fatherless will miss the
look and the tear of sympathy, the warm grasp of the

2 E

hand, the ever new-plenished barrel of meal and cruse of oil.

Deeply mysterious, truly, did such a bereavement appear. Amid the many apparently useless lives around, how strange that the most cherished and valued was the one first taken ! " To what purpose is this waste ? " It was the deep mystery of the sisters of Bethany and their sorrowing friends ; why the flower of fairest promise should be prematurely blighted—why the beauty of Israel should be the first to fall on the high places ! If we could have imagined one home or life in Joppa exempt from the assault of death, and guarded securely by the Lord of Life, it would be hers. But she is cut down, not like a shock of corn in its season, fully ripe, in the time of harvest, but in the midst of summer suns and abounding usefulness. All has in vain been done that skilled and tender watching could do to effect restoration. " How is the staff broken and the BEAU-TIFUL rod ! "

The mourners had apparently finished the last sad offices of affection and respect for the dead. The *Taharah*, or final washing of the body, had taken place ; and over the bier we may imagine the usual words to have been uttered, " May she go to her appointed place in peace ! "[1] But Peter, though he himself at the time knew it not, has been sent by a Greater to awake this loved sister out of sleep. The promise recorded by Israel's Psalmist is about to receive a striking fulfilment in Gospel times : " Blessed is he that considereth the poor : the Lord will deliver him in time of trouble. The Lord will preserve him, and keep him alive, and he shall be blessed upon the earth "

[1] See Kitto's "Daily Readings" *i.. loc*

(Ps. xli. 1, 2). He who perhaps had come with no other thought than to "comfort them concerning their sister," seems all at once to become conscious that he was the subject of an undefined yet divine energy. The mourners are still gathered in the upper chamber. Must not the scene have vividly recalled to the Apostle a kindred impressive spectacle, when he was one of the privileged "three" admitted into the house of Capernaum? There was, however, the notable difference, that while in the case of the latter it was the lugubrious sound of *feigned* minstrels which was heard, here there was no mimic or counterfeit sorrow, but the deep reality of wounded, aching hearts. Notwithstanding this, he follows the example of his Divine Master, in requesting all present to withdraw, that he may be left alone in the presence of death. To secure perfect silence and seclusion for devout prayer, would seem to have been his main object in desiring to be thus alone—a silence which could not be attained amid the distractions of the clamorous crowd. It has been surmised also, that, possibly ignorant as to what the Divine purposes might be, he was desirous of not exciting expectations, by word or deed, that might fail of fulfilment. He followed the example of Elisha in similar circumstances, of whom it was said, "He went in therefore, and shut the door upon them twain, and prayed unto the Lord." "There lies before him the unbreathing form, fast locked in its dreamless slumber. Almost, we think, must a feeling of regret have thrilled his soul at the thought of disturbing that peaceful repose, and calling back the released spirit to the trials and conflicts of this troublous world."[1]

[1] Bishop Lee, 257.

Having risen from his knees in prayer, in the touching simplicity of the sacred narrative, and with a faith
worthy of the Rockman, "turning him to the body, he
said, Tabitha, arise ! "[1]

The effect was instantaneous. The eyes, which had
apparently been closed in their last long sleep, again
awoke, and gazed on the earnest pleader, who had
wrestled like the Patriarch with a mightier than earthly
angel, and, as a Prince, had power with God and prevailed. The shadow of death had been turned into the
morning. The grave-clothes fettered her movements ;
but he gave her his hand, relieved her from her shroud,
and, calling the saints and widows, presented her alive !
" The grave cannot praise thee, death cannot celebrate
thee : they that go down into the pit cannot hope for
thy truth. The living, the living, he shall praise thee,
as I do this day " (Isa. xxxviii. 18, 19). We can only
picture the feelings of that waiting throng ; the burden
unexpectedly lifted off saddened hearts ; the gushing
tears, not of sorrow, but of joy, as the "loved and lost "
had become the lost and loved again. We are told of
the effect that marvellous restoration had, alike on believers and unbelievers, in Joppa and its neighbourhood.
" It was known throughout all Joppa, and many believed in the Lord."

What the future life of the restored one may have
been, we can only conjecture. Can we hesitate in supposing that it was one of loftier consecration and still
nobler energy, " always abounding in the work of the

[1] "This prayer is the essential feature by which the resurrection of
Tabitha is distinguished from that of the daughter of Jairus. Jesus, without any preceding prayer, took the dead child by the hand, and recalled her
to life ; but Peter does not do so, until he had prayed to the Lord for this
miracle."—*Lechler*.

Lord?" "Doubtless," says Wesley, "her remaining days were still more zealously spent in the service of her Saviour and her God. Thus was a richer treasure laid up for her in heaven; and she afterwards returned to a more exceeding weight of glory than that from which so astonishing a providence had recalled her for a season." "O Lord, Thou hast brought up my soul from the grave : Thou hast kept me alive, that I should not go down to the pit. Thou hast turned for me my mourning into dancing : Thou hast put off my sackcloth, and girded me with gladness; to the end that my glory may sing praise to Thee, and not be silent. O Lord, my God, I will give thanks unto Thee for ever" (Ps. xxx. 3, 11, 12).

Neither do we know anything of her second and final falling asleep. Her traditional grave is still shown in the midst of one of the gardens of the city. Nor is her name forgotten in the place of her manifold labours and beneficence. On the 25th of May there is still an anniversary kept, sacred to her memory, by the Christians of Joppa and the neighbourhood. The celebration is observed neither at her reputed house nor grave, but takes the form of a joyous festive gathering of the young, in a long day of early summer, amid the surrounding orange groves, where her virtues are extolled in simple hymns and songs.

I cannot close without referring to the attempts made by German rationalistic writers, in their persistent rejection of the supernatural, to explain away the reality of this great miracle of Peter's. Some consider it an unauthorised and interpolated legend. Some that it amounted to no more than awakening a patient from a long swoon, or temporary suspension of the physical powers ; others that it was a mere accommodation and transposition of the parallel Gospel narrative of Jairus' daughter, in order to give increased notoriety to Peter and his coadjutors. One eminent scholar farther suggests, as giving plausibility to this latter conjecture, the similarity between the words employed on the two similar occasions, *Talitha* and *Tabitha*. The express terms of the narrative forbid any such forced and mythical interpretations. The only fair and consistent explanation is, by giving to the words the Samaritans used regarding the sorcerer Simon a truer meaning as applied to our Apostle, " This man is the power of God, which is called great." [1]

Peter remained in the scene of this his most wondrous miracle for some time. A great and effectual door of utterance had been opened; and momentous events were at hand, for the Church of the future and of the world, in which he was to be the principal actor.

[1] See Dr Gloag's Commentary on the Acts, with references.

CHAPTER XX.

𝔓eter and 𝔠ornelius.

> "Far o'er the glowing western main
> His wistful brow was upward rais'd,
> Where like an Angel's train
> The burnished water blaz'd.
>
> The saint beside the ocean pray'd,
> The soldier in his chosen bower,
> Where all his eye survey'd
> Seem'd sacred in that hour.
>
> To each unknown his brother's prayer,
> Yet brethren true in dearest love
> Were they—and now they share
> Fraternal joys above."

"The accounts which the second part of the Acts embraces
respecting Peter, were not communicated so much to set before
us the ministry of Peter, as to shew in what manner the Gospel
was first carried to the Gentiles. As Luke wrote mainly for Gentile readers, he would naturally feel very solicitous to make it
plain to them that this important event was brought about in
accordance with God's purpose."—*Olshausen on the Acts.*

"By a remarkable coincidence of inward revelation, with a
chain of outward circumstances, the illumination hitherto wanted
was imparted."—*Neander.*

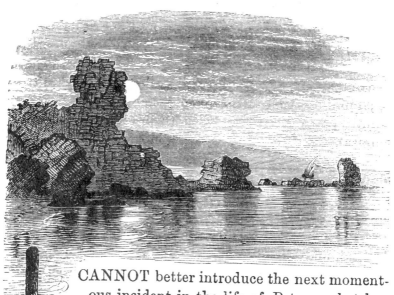

CANNOT better introduce the next momentous incident in the life of Peter—what has
been well called "the crown and consum-
mation of his ministry"—than by quoting
the words of a thoughtful writer.   These
have reference to another important event in the history
of the early Church, but are equally applicable and
appropriate to our Apostle and to the occurrences in
which he had the most important share.

"On One unseen, and on the counsels of His providence, St Luke would fix our attention : *he* can never
forget that this history is but a continuation of that
'former treatise ;' that it is the continued working of the
Lord Jesus that he is inspired to reveal to us.   The
method of that divine working has already been vari-
ously illustrated.   We have seen how their unseen Lord

was ever acting ; guiding the lot, answering the prayer, pouring forth His Spirit in the upper chamber, prompting words that none could withstand, attesting those words with signs of power, touching the hearts of thousands in the Temple, overruling the priests' counsel in the Sanhedrim, baffling their malice in the prison, restraining persecution till the central Church was consolidated ; then, when all was ripe for dispersion, permitting it ; guiding them in this inspiration now by an angel's ministry ; ever working with them (such is St Luke's phrase), with them in the upper chamber, with them in the Temple, with them before rulers, with them in the dungeon, with them in their solitude, with them in the crowd : *such* has been the Lord's method of working hitherto, as revealed in St Luke's narrative—an ever-present power, though unseen. And now a crisis has arrived, and the arm of that Lord whom the heavens had received, must be 'revealed' yet more directly and visibly."[1]

The promise of by-past ages, the longing and burden of prophetic song, is now to be fulfilled. The wild olive is to be grafted. The outlying nations of heathendom are to be brought within the fold of the Church, admitted as participants in those spiritual privileges which had for centuries been the exclusive possession and monopoly of the covenant nation.

How is the vast change to be effected? In a sense greater than any we have yet noted, to the Rockman is to be committed "the keys of the kingdom of heaven." That promised distinction, as we have seen, had its first remarkable realisation on the day of Pentecost, when the door of salvation was thrown open to the Jew—

[1] Canon Norris' "Key to the Acts of the Apostles," p. 42.

Peter preaching "in demonstration of the Spirit and with power," the doctrine of the Resurrection. He is now to be privileged to unlock these same gates to the Gentiles, and by doing so, to introduce a new epoch in the history of the Church and of the world. Christianity, indeed, would have very partially and inadequately fulfilled its great mission, had it merely proved a development or expansion of Judaism—had its Lord and Head reigned in the ancient Zion alone, and His Apostle-band formed the "satraps" of a privileged territory, while the outlying regions of paganism were left to brood in the darkness of former ages, under the undisputed sway of the God of this world or of his vicegerents, ignorance and superstition. In this case the most elevating strains of Hebrew minstrels might have remained unsung, or rather, these strains would have resolved themselves into meaningless, unintelligible flights of hyperbole. But "that which decayeth and waxeth old is ready to vanish away." The irrevocable decree that had gone forth from the lips of Israel's God was, that He would give the promised Messiah "the heathen for His inheritance and the uttermost parts of the earth for His possession."

The importance of the event which is now to claim our thoughts, may be gathered from the narrative of it being twice recorded by the writer of the Acts of the Apostles; and on both these occasions the details are given with unwonted circumstantiality. Like every other great work in God's Church, this ecclesiastical revolution, if I may so term it, required a season of preparation. The rooted prejudices of ages had to be overcome; the light could only gradually disperse the darkness. Although the disciples had been again and again indoctrinated by their Great Master alike in discourse and parable, with the truth "that many would come from the east and the west and sit down with Abraham and Isaac and Jacob in the new kingdom," and although the last supreme commission which had the seal of His living lips upon it, and that, too, as recorded in Peter's own Gospel was, " Go ye into *all the world* and preach the Gospel to every creature," yet still they clung for eight long years with fond tenacity to the lost sheep or the house of Israel alone.   In this, did they not follow, too, their Lord's own example ?   " When He began to teach and preach," says a writer, " He laboured among the Jews and among the Jews only.   His friends were Jews ; His disciples Jews : and like a good Pharisee, like a man set apart, He abstained from entering into the Greek cities and declined an invitation to the Golden House."   Even in the course of their Master's ministry, we find His Apostles ever and anon manifesting a jealousy of their hereditary rights ; they were very far themselves innocent of the pride, illiberality, and prejudice which clung so inveterately to their nation and race.   They little dreamt, therefore, of so mighty a meaning of their Lord's parting command, as that the circle which had Judea for its centre was to have humanity for its circumference.   When He spoke of their carrying the Gospel of the Kingdom to the "uttermost parts of the earth," they might possibly interpret that word, as it might be interpreted, as being synonymous with their own "*land;*" or at the most expect, that any who were to sit down at that spiritual banquet with the patriarchs of the nation, would *come* to Palestine to do so.   If they were to share in Gospel privileges it was to be inside, not outside, the sacred fron-

tier.[1] In a word, unless they received some additional
and very special tokens of Divine authority, it is ques-
tionable if they ever would have ventured, in their apostolic journeys, beyond the borders of Tyre and Sidon or
Cæsarea Philippi. Their Christ was the Shiloh of
Jacob, "the glory of His people *Israel*," no more. The
idea of preaching amid the heathen crowd at Antioch,
or in the theatre of Ephesus, or on the heights of Mars
Hill, or in front of the Temples of Corinth, would have
seemed an innovation alike dangerous and unauthorised.

We observe, however, the initial step in wider and
more comprehensive views of their mission, on occasion
of the first great Pentecostal revival, when the Jews of
the Dispersion to whom they preached, carried the
tidings of the Gospel with them to their distant homes.
Peter's recent pastoral visitation in Samaria, and on the
plain and seaboard of Sharon, had doubtless tended
further to modify old prejudices. The conversion of
the Ethiopian chamberlain, a Jewish proselyte, whose
heathen home was two thousand miles away from the
Covenant land, yet who had received baptism from the
hands of Philip, was an additional startling and significant fact in the development of the Church of the
future. Then that memorable fortnight of holy fellowship with Saul of Tarsus, to which we have recently
adverted, and its earnest conversations, must have still
farther prepared the mind of our Apostle for the startling revolution at hand. The former had such abundantly clear and manifest revelations given to him as
to *his* world-wide commission, "Depart, for I will send

[1] "The conversion of the Gentiles was no new idea to Jews or Christians,
but it had been universally regarded to take place by their reception into
Judaism."—*Alford's Greek Testament.*

thee far hence unto the *Gentiles*," that he could hardly
fail to have indoctrinated his brother, with his own expansive and comprehensive " churchmanship."

While, therefore, " beginning at Jerusalem," and
laying the foundation-stone in Zion, the Supreme Dis-
poser of all events had thus prepared His servants step
by step, for crossing the frontiers of the chosen race,
and bearing the lamp of truth to those sitting in darkness and in the region and shadow of death, Peter is
again made the instrument in this all-momentous
change in the economy of the Church, and in the removing of Gentile disqualifications. His way, moreover, was made so patent, that, with no hesitation or
embarrassment, he is brought to dismiss all hereditary
prejudice, and, with the simplicity of a child, he seems
to say, " I will hear what God the Lord will speak."
In publishing that Gospel to the " alien " Gentiles, it was
only after receiving the most unmistakable of intima-
tions from on high, " THE LORD gave the word." We
may assign approximately the date of the momentous
crisis to the year A.D. 42 or 43.

The city of Cæsarea, with a mingled population of
Jews, Greeks, and Romans, was to have the honour
and privilege of being that wherein the first sheaf of
the Gentile harvest was to be reaped. This city, originally a fishing hamlet, named " Straton's Tower," is
now reduced to a few piles of ruin. The writer has not
personally seen it ; but the most observant of travellers
thus describes it—" On a rocky ledge, somewhat resembling that of Ascalon on the south, and Dor on the
north, rise the ruins of Cæsarea, now the most desolate
site in Palestine. Like the vast fragments of St Andrews, in Scotland, they run out into the waves of the

Mediterranean Sea, which dashes over the prostrate columns and huge masses of masonry; but, unlike St Andrews—unlike in this respect to most Eastern ruins —no sign of human habitation is to be found within the circuit of its deserted walls." [1] At the time of which we write, the cluster of fishing huts were transformed, as with an enchanter's wand, into another of the magnificent monuments of Herod's architectural taste and extravagance. "He built it," says Josephus, "all with white stone, and adorned it with the most splendid palaces." We have recently spoken of the danger and insecurity of Joppa as a harbour, though geographically the natural seaport of Jerusalem. But this imperial builder resolved on an artificial equivalent for the want of natural breakwaters, by erecting a huge harbour, where vessels might take refuge from the unprotected swell of the Mediterranean when roused by the fury of the westerly winds. It consisted of a semicircular mole, equal in dimensions to the Piræus at Athens, and composed of stones 50 feet long, sunk in a depth of 60 feet. At the extremity of the mole was a tower called Drusia, named in honour of the Roman Drusus; while the city itself was called after the Emperor, *Cæsarea Sebaste*. Part of the modern ruins are probably those of the Temple, which crowned the heights of the city and the *Sebasteum*, and which formed a conspicuous object to those afar off upon the sea. "It was to this Temple that the famous shields, the dedication of which at Jerusalem threw the nation into such a ferment in the time of Pontius Pilate, were, by the command of Tiberius, removed." [2] The city became

---

[1] Sinai and Palestine, p. 259. See woodcut at the head of this chapter.
[2] Lewin's St Paul, p. 696.

the official residence of the Roman Procurator, and the Herodian family had here their palatial dwelling. It was thus made, according to Tacitus, the capital of the later Herodian dynasty (*caput Judæae*). It was free of the defect, which attached to the old inland metropolis, as that where there is "no galley with oars, neither gallant ship, to pass thereby" (Isa. xxiii. 21). "From that sea-girt city, Pontius Pilate came yearly across the plain of Sharon, and up the hills, to keep guard on the Festivals at Jerusalem :"[1] it was the Roman amphitheatre of Cæsarea which was the scene of Herod Agrippa's loathsome and appalling death. It would be beyond our purpose to do more than note, that the city has more than one association with the Apostle Paul. The last of these was in the guard-room of the Prætorium, where he was confined by Felix, and where he remained two years in bonds, before his final voyage to Rome. It was also the residence for some years of Philip the Evangelist, whose Christian influence, judging from the fearless zeal with which he prosecuted his mission in the towns of Samaria, could hardly fail to tell with power on its mixed population.[2]

At the time of which we speak, a cohort of 600 soldiers were stationed in the barracks of this garrison town. They were called "the Italian band," because composed entirely of native Romans, the levied or provincial troops not being considered so reliable in case of a revolt in the disturbed state of Palestine. Cæsarea being, as we have just noted, the residence of the Roman Viceroy, it was needful to have a body-guard on whose allegiance and fidelity he could scrupulously

[1] Sinai and Palestine, p. 260.
[2] See Lewin. Also Art. "Cæsarea," Bib. Dict.

depend. "The manner in which the Romans denomi-
nated and distinguished their bands and legions was
very various. Sometimes it was from the order of
places, and so they were called the first and second
band, according to their rank and precedency; sometimes from the commanders they were under, as the
Augustan and Claudian band, &c., because persons of
that name led them; sometimes from their own be-
haviour, as the *Victrix*, the *Ferrea*, the Conquering,
the Iron Band, &c., by reason of the great valour which
in some sharp engagements these had shewn; sometimes from the countries they were chiefly quartered in,
as the German and Panonian band, &c.; and sometimes from the parts from whence they were gathered,
as this is called the Italian band." [1]   The officer at the
head of this Prætorian guard was by name Cornelius.
Loyal in his allegiance to the ruling Cæsar, he was at
the same time the faithful subject of a Greater than
earthly monarch.   He had attained, we know not
through what instrumentality, to a knowledge of the
true God.   He had evidently shared the loftier aspirations of many of his contemporaries, in search of that
summum bonum, which neither their philosophy nor
religion could supply.   Discarding the mythical legends
and childish fables of pagan mythology, which had
lamentably failed to meet and answer " the long-drawn
sigh of humanity," he, and those of similar mould, had
been arrested by the divine simplicity of the Hebrew
faith.   The writings of Moses and the Prophets, the
lofty morality inculcated in psalm and proverb, had
been made accessible and familiar to them through the
wide-spread language of Greece.   The knowledge and

[1] Calmet's Commentary.

worship of the pure and holy God of Israel presented a
calm harbour of refuge amid the widespread atheism,
the restless speculation, the deep and foul corruption of
an exceptionally reprobate age.   Cornelius had accordingly renounced his national idolatry, and had become
a " proselyte of the gate "—worshipping Jehovah, but
as a Gentile, remaining uncircumcised.   We shall presently find Peter, himself a Jew, appropriately located
in the old Jewish port of Joppa.   There was an equal
appropriateness, as it has been well remarked, in laying
the scene of the admission of the Gentiles in a city so
distinctively Roman, with Roman buildings, Roman
name, Roman governor, Roman troops. " No men
could well be more contrasted with each other than
those two, in whom the heathen and Jewish worlds met
and were reconciled.   We know what Peter was—a
Galilean fisherman, brought up in the rudest district of
an obscure province, with no learning but such as he
might have gathered in the synagogue of his native
town.   And now he was at Joppa, lodging in the house
of Simon the tanner, the Apostle of a religion that was
to change the world. . . . No name was more honourable at Rome than that of the *Cornelian House*.   It
was the name borne by the Scipios, and by Sulla, and
the mother of the Gracchi. . . . Cornelius was, no
doubt, a true born Italian.   Educated in Rome, or
some provincial town, he had entered upon a soldier's
life, dreaming perhaps of military glory, but dreaming
as little of that better glory, which now surrounds the
Cornelian name, as Peter dreamt at the Lake of Gennesareth of becoming the chosen companion of the
Messiah of Israel, and of throwing open the doors of
the Catholic Church to the dwellers in Asia and Africa,

to the barbarians on the remote and unvisited shores of Europe, and to the undiscovered countries of the West." [1]

Yet with equal truth has this devout Roman been designated " the Abraham of the New Dispensation," " holding, as the predecessor of the Gentile converts, a relation to us not dissimilar to that of the great Hebrew ancestor to the Jews. Like him, too, who is called ' the Father of the Faithful,' his character is depicted on the inspired page . . . as ' a devout man;' a liberal benefactor of the poor ; a maintainer, like his prototype, of family religion, and a man of prayer." [2] " There was a certain man in Cæsarea called Cornelius, a centurion of the band called the Italian band. A devout man, and one that feared God with all his house, which gave much alms to the people, and prayed to God alway " (Acts x. 1, 2). These prayers were very possibly for an increase of guidance and illumination, specially with reference to the new faith. The supplication of another devout warrior might be his own, " Shew me Thy ways, O Lord ; teach me Thy paths. Lead me in Thy truth, and teach me : for Thou art the God of my salvation ; on Thee do I wait all the day " (Ps. xxv. 4, 5). He was in due time to obtain the realisation of the sure promise, " The Lord is good unto them that wait for Him, to the soul that seeketh Him " (Lam. iii. 25). We have been led

1 Howson and Conybeare, p. 126. It has been often noted that all the four centurions whose names occur in sacred story are favourably mentioned. The centurion of the Gospel, who had his servant cured ; the centurion who, at the crucifixion, recognised the divinity of Christ ; the centurion whose " courteous " conduct to St Paul, on his way a prisoner to Rome, is more than once alluded to in the narrative ; and now this honoured soldier in the barracks of Cæsarea.

2 Bishop Lee on St Peter, p. 264.

recently to admire in the Christian Lady of Joppa a beautiful example of faith working by love—Christianity in one of its most attractive phases, as the handmaid of all generous deeds.   Much more strikingly and impressively are these kindred acts of charity and devotion exemplified, in the case of one surrounded with little calculated to evoke and nurture the tenderer sympathies ; who had been trained in the stern, terrible school of Roman warfare, with its code of cruelty and revenge ; habituated from his infancy, and especially in the dark times in which his lot was cast, to selfishness and oppression ; familiarised in the capital, not with the asylum for the indigent and distressed, the sickly and destitute, but rather with the exhibition of a savage delight in the blood and tortures of Coliseum and amphitheatre.   The law of an exceptional kindness, however, was not only in this man's heart, but it had its outcome in munificent generosity.   Many a poor outcast on the wharves of the gorgeous sea-capital, or amid the slums that were already clustering around its palatial homes, owned him as their benefactor.   Nobler than any warlike insignia that adorned his breast, was the invisible record, engraven on suffering hearts and poverty-stricken dwellings, " He delivered the needy when he cried ; the poor also, and him that hath no helper."

Cornelius could not possibly be in ignorance of the Person, teaching, miracles, and lofty claims of the Christ of Nazareth.   On the contrary, from the circumstances in which he was placed, with these he must have been abundantly conversant.   As a Jewish proselyte, and familiar with the writings of their prophets and psalmists, he must have shared in the ardent longings of the Hebrew people for the advent of the predicted Messiah. The footsteps of Jesus, indeed, had not been nearer Cæsarea than when He visited "the borders of Tyre and Sidon;" but we have reason to believe that, at all events shortly after His ascension, He had disciples and followers in the Roman city. In all probability, too, Philip the Evangelist had been prosecuting his labours in the Herodian capital, and had deepened the already awakened interest of the devout and teachable Roman. In the case of the latter the promise was doubtless realised, "Then shall we know if we follow on to know the Lord:"—"If any man will do His will, he shall know of the doctrine." The "prayers and fastings" of this "seeker after God" would seem to indicate, that with a far deeper meaning than the words conveyed to the Psalmist, he was looking wistfully for those Divine beams to visit his own heart which had already broke over the Hebrew mountains:—"My soul waiteth for the Lord more than they that watch for the morning: I say, more than they that watch for the morning" (Ps. cxxx. 6). "He knew," to quote the words of Lange, "the history of Jesus, so far as it was spread abroad; he knew that no small part of the Jews recognised Him as the Messiah, and that a division upon this question agitated his co-religionists; and probably his own soul was agitated by the same inquiry, and he longed after a true solution from above."

At the same time, however, it must be borne in mind, as that which gives its highest meaning and significance to the whole transaction, that this Roman officer, with all his Messianic aspirations,—his devoutness, and goodness, and noble self-sacrificing generosity,—

was, on the ground of his being a Gentile, looked down upon—to use a Roman term, "ostracised"—by the Jewish race.   They might admire his natural virtues, and strive to emulate his beneficence, but he was debarred from holding equal social intercourse with them.   He could not meet with them at table, eat out of the same platter, or drink from the same vessel.   Being uncircumcised, he was under the ban of separation, and deemed "common and unclean."   If, then, he were desirous, over and above his present acknowledgment of the God of Israel, to enrol himself among the disciples of Jesus—to attach himself to the Founder of that new system which professed itself to be a fulfilling and perfecting of the Jewish dispensation—an all-important question with him must have been, could he do so on the simple footing of being a "proselyte of the gate," or would it be needful so far to surrender his nationality, the proud privileges of a Roman citizen, by submitting to the Abrahamic rite ?   Must he cease to be a Roman, and become a Jew, before he can participate in the blessings of the Gospel ?   Must he put on the galling fetters of the Mosaic law, before he can exult in the liberty and freedom of the Christian ?

One afternoon, at the ninth hour of the day, the hour of evening prayer, when the sun was beginning to decline above " the western wave," while Cornelius was engaged in his wonted devotions, a bright vision appeared to him.   A messenger from the heavenly world addressed him by name.   Brave soldier as he was, accustomed to face serried ranks with unflinching courage, he was for the moment unmanned by the unexpected apparition.

"What is it, sir?" he asked with trembling lip, as he confronted face to face this shining angel.[1]

The rejoinder was, that his prayers and his alms, acting according to the light he possessed, had been accepted at the heavenly mercy-seat:—"Thy prayers and thine alms are come up for a memorial before God." "In the Levitical law, the incense burnt before the Lord, and the handful of fine flour for a sin-offering, which the priests threw into the fire of the altar, are both termed a memorial. By applying the same designation to the prayers and alms of Cornelius, the angel signified that they were spiritual sacrifices, with which God was well pleased. Cornelius believed in the true God, and this faith rendered his religious services acceptable."[2]

The assurance given him by the angel, was followed by the startling and peremptory order to despatch some messengers to the seaport of Joppa, and request the immediate attendance of Peter at Cæsarea, who, on his arrival, would be the medium of some important communication. The specification is most minute as to where the Apostle was sojourning—the city, the house, its locality, its humble owner, and that owner's occupation. "One fact suggested," says Dr Macleod in his "Eastward," "remains for our strength and comfort— that our angel brothers who minister to the heirs of salvation are not strangers to our earth and its inhabitants, nor to the situation of our lowly homes, or the nature of our ' honest trades ;' for the angel who com-

---

[1] Not as in our version, "What is it, *Lord?*" for we have no reason to imagine that he considered the person addressing him as Divine. It was the natural expression of surprise at the unexpected appearance of a mysterious visitor.

[2] Professor Dick on the Acts, p. 166.

manded Cornelius to send for Peter knew this old town
of Jaffa, and knew also the name, the house, and the
trade of Simon."

The angel-visit was brief, but his message was at
once clear and imperative. Accordingly Cornelius, with
military promptitude, summoned two of his household
servants and an attendant soldier; and, after narrating to them the supernatural interview, gave them
orders to hasten to Joppa, and request without delay
the presence of the Jewish Apostle. We may here only
note, in passing, that while the employment of angelic
agency, on the one hand, betokened the momentous
nature of the transaction which was imminent, yet a
signal honour is, at the same time, put upon human
instrumentality. The opening of the gates of the
Gentile world might have been by the " disposition of
angels." This delegate from the ministering seraphim,
who had appeared to the Roman soldier, might at once
have intimated the approaching crisis in God's dealings
with His Church. It might indeed, in one sense, have
given greater impressiveness and solemnity to the incident, and tended more promptly and effectually to disarm all doubt or objection on the part of the Jews.
But the Divine Being here, as elsewhere, desired to
magnify the office of the earthly ambassador. The
great revolution about to be effected was to be entrusted
to an " earthen vessel." And in Peter's subsequent
description of the vision, when he rehearsed the matter
to the Apostles and brethren in Jerusalem, narrating
circumstantially the angelic message, he brings out
more specifically the high honour and prerogatives
conferred on those who have thus committed to them
" the ministry of reconciliation."   " Send men to Joppa,

and call for Simon, whose surname is Peter, who shall tell thee words whereby thou and all thy house shall be saved " (Acts xi. 13, 14).

Nor can the fact be overlooked that, among the varied human instruments who might have been employed in this memorable embassage, special selection was made of Peter. Philip was then, we have every reason to suppose, resident at Cæsarea, a faithful minister and evangelist. John, James, and other distinguished brethren, were at Jerusalem. But it was for him to whom, eight years before, the Lord had given " the keys of the kingdom of heaven," that the privilege and distinction were reserved of first unfolding the charter of Gentile freedom—opening the long-locked gates of the outside world. As in the first, so was he to be chief actor in this second Pentecost—this Gentile Whitsuntide.

The messengers were accordingly despatched probably towards the afternoon, spending the night, it has been surmised, at Appolonia, and completing their journey in the cool of the next morning.

While Cornelius and his household were thus prepared for some communication of extraordinary interest and importance, the Lord of angels and men was preparing His Apostle at Joppa for what, next to companionship with Himself on earth, was the greatest distinction of Peter's life.

The writer of these pages, as in the case of all travellers in the Holy Land, was conducted after landing at Jaffa, to the reputed " house of Simon the Tanner." Whether the dwelling now shewn be the veritable locality or no, the site at all events is appropriate and impressive, and enables one to carry away a

faithful mental picture. On reaching the summit of
the house, you look, as is shewn in the accompanying
engraving, over the flat roofs of the modern city ; and
far as the eye can reach in the northern distance is the
stretch of yellow sand on the way to Cæsarea, the
outer fringe of the plain of Sharon washed by the blue
waves of the Great Sea—the direction certainly, and
probably too the very line of road, by which the three
delegates were now hastening to the temporary home of
the Jewish fisherman.   " The house is close on the seashore ; the waves beat against the low wall of its courtyard.   In the courtyard is a spring of fresh water, such
as must always have been needed for the purposes of
tanning, and which, though no longer so used, is authen-
tically reported to have been so used in a tradition
which describes the premises to have been long employed as a tannery. . . . The rude staircase to the
roof of the modern house, flat now as of old, leads us
to the view which gives all that is needed for the
accompaniments of the hour.   There is the wide noonday heaven above ; in front is the long bright sweep of
the Mediterranean, its nearer waves broken by the reefs
famous in ancient Gentile legends as the rocks of
Andromeda.   Fishermen are standing and wading
amongst them, such as might have been there of old,
recalling to the Apostle his long-forgotten nets by the
lake of Gennesareth, the first promise of his future call
to be ' a fisher of men.' "[1]   Through that same arched
gateway, " the Jerusalem gate," by which the stream
of commerce still surges, and which forms the one
entrance to the town, the Cæsarea messengers probably
passed.   The fountain inside, now adorned with Sara-

[1] Sinai and Palestine, 271-72.

cenic devices and marble trough, determines what must
have been in every age the principal approach. Even
the elders of ancient times, sitting at the gate for judgment, have their modern successors, though of degenerate type and squalid mien.

Although then, we may still be disposed to place
the modern dwelling at Jaffa shewn as Peter's, in the
category of tradition, yet somewhere, doubtless, it must
have been nigh to that very building whither we were led
by our dragoman, that eighteen centuries ago, at the sixth
hour of the day, the sultry hour of noon, the Apostle went
up as was his wont to the roof of Simon's house to perform his devotions. The roofs of the eastern houses were
utilised for a variety of purposes quite unknown to the
western world. "For purposes of exercise, of sleeping in
summer, of conference, of mourning, erecting booths at
the feast of tabernacles, and other religious celebrations;
—for observation, and for any process requiring fresh air
and sun."[1] Morning and evening were the two appointed "canonical" hours for Hebrew prayer; but the
more devout among the nation, as in the case of Daniel
in the city of his exile, added another at the time of
"siesta"—before the mid-day meal. We can even,
without drawing on imagination, picture the very
attitude and position of the apostolic suppliant. As
the Prophet we have just named, when he knelt in his
chamber in Babylon had his face turned towards the
Temple of Jerusalem, so would it be with the "Saint
beside the ocean." With his back to the waters of the
Great Sea—the sea which laved the far-off shores of the
"Isles of Chittim," he would have his eyes directed to-

[1] Alford.

wards the same hallowed spot which had to him mingled, indeed, but still consecrated memories.

It was, then, before the ordinary time of forenoon refreshment, and when the cravings of hunger were upon him, that Peter fell into a trance or reverie. His senses, being abstracted from outward objects and rapt in a supernatural state, a vision was revealed to his inner soul, engrossing and absorbing all his thought and attention. The heavens appeared to be opened; and a great white sheet, knit by the four corners, appeared to be let down from a cleft in the blue sky. Might not this be intended in the first instance to assure him, that whatever truth was about to be revealed, it had its origin in heaven and God? This sheet contained a collection of varied animals, doubtless those most familiar to him in imagination as haunting hill and valley, rock and gorge, reed and sedge, bordering his native lake. Quadrupeds, reptiles, fowls tame and wild, were mingled indiscriminately; both " clean and un- clean." A voice was at the same moment heard issuing the command, " Rise, Peter, kill and eat."

His whole nature seemed fastidiously to rebel against an injunction so repugnant to a Jew. To obey the voice would be to run counter to the express prohibi- tion of the Levitical law, which forbade, on severest penalties, the partaking of the food of animals cere- monially unclean. We see an illustration of how rigid this prohibition was, in Daniel and his companions rather submitting to live on pulse, than to contract defilement by partaking of meat from the royal table (Dan. i. 8); while the uncanonical historical books tell of the dreadful privations to which the Jews submitted in the time of the Maccabees, in preference to polluting themselves with forbidden meats ; accepting slow death rather than violate their law. In obedience, therefore, to the promptings of his Jewish nature, he did not hesitate for a moment to reject the proposal. Indeed, probably imagining at first that it was intended simply as a test of his loyal adhesion to stringent laws which had never been abrogated, he instinctively replies, " Not so, Lord, for I have never eaten anything that is common or unclean." The same mysterious voice conveyed in reply a gentle rebuke ;—at the same time indicating on whose authority and sanction the command had been given. The announcement embodied in brief the whole principle at issue, and formed the groundwork and reason of the new apostolic manifesto—" *What God hath cleansed that call not thou common.*" The revelation was not only repeated, but it occurred three times, in order to make a deeper impression on Peter's mind ; to show that it was no phantom of the brain—no mere ordinary dream destitute of any special significance— but like that of Pharaoh which was " doubled," "because the thing was established by God, and God would shortly bring it to pass." Then the sheet with its multitudinous contents again rose at the bidding of some unseen power to the heaven whence it issued ; and the entranced Apostle woke up to the realities of the scene around him.

He was at first in a state of strange bewilderment. What could this vision mean ? Was he to accept at once its symbolic teaching as a distinct exponent and authentic revelation of the Divine will ? Was he un hesitatingly to accept the lesson of an acted parable, and feel that the distinction between meats and animals, clean and unclean, belonged, not as he had supposed to a permanent, but to a temporary dispensation ; that the Divine legislator had rescinded His own law ; and, as one necessary result, that pollution would no longer be contracted by attending a Gentile banquet, eating with the uncircumcised ? Could he fail to remember, and be staggered at the remembrance of the strong words of his great Master on the one solitary occasion, when, crossing the frontiers of Judæism, He came into actual contact with the Gentile world—"It is not meet to take the children's bread and to cast it to dogs ?"

He was not left long in his perplexity. The providence of God, like another Daniel, was to read the dream and the interpretation thereof. His musings were broken by an announcement made to him "by the Spirit" (in what way we know not), that three men—strangers—one a soldier and the other two civilians, were standing at the humble door of his entertainer wishing to hold audience with him. The Divine voice further enjoined him to go down to those who thus "sought him" without delay or hesitation, and accord with their request whatever it was, for it had the stamp and sanction of Divine authority. "Behold," he said to the three travellers, as descending from the house roof by the outside stair, he stood before them at the gate, "I am he whom ye seek." He requested at the same time to know their errand.

They told, in brief simple words, how their Roman master, "A just man, fearing God" (and adding, to disarm Peter's hesitation), "of good report among the Jews," had been divinely warned "by an holy angel to send for thee into his house and to hear words of thee."

He had no doubt in his mind that the thing,

whatever it was, "proceeded from the Lord." In the four cornered white sheet, as Neander suggests, he may have symbolically seen the intimation that men from north, south, east, and west, were now accounted clean before God and were called to share in His kingdom. With the express injunction received, "Go, nothing doubting," any scruples he might have had were dismissed. He resolved to accompany them in the unprecedented mission. Meanwhile, with wonted Jewish hospitality, he invites the three travellers within. They share his humble fare and lodging for the night; and next morning, joined by other six of his converts in Joppa (Acts xii. 12), the little company proceed along the thirty miles of seaboard to the Roman capital of Palestine. The reason of his taking these six companions with him, though not specified, is made obvious at a subsequent stage. Peter was evidently so far prepared for a new and startling crisis in the Church's "development." Moreover, as his conduct in the sudden emergency might possibly be liable to doubt, misconstruction, it might even be, vehement opposition, with a wise policy and prudent foresight he selects a few reliable Christian brethren who might afterwards be called to give corroborative testimony as to the Divine will and dealings. The long route occupied them more than a day, for it was on the following morning, we are told, they reached the house of Cornelius.

Cornelius, securely calculating on Peter's arrival, was already waiting for him. We might have expected that in the first instance he would have desired and preferred a private audience to reveal his scruples and perplexities. On the contrary, however, he made it the occasion of a public reception ; for his kinsmen and

near friends were also there to welcome the distinguished stranger. Doubtless among that assembly
were many anxious souls, brought together by no mere
vague curiosity, but who, sharing the religious aspirations of Cornelius, were longing to hear with deep
yearning of heart what Divine communication was to be
made to them by Jehovah's accredited messenger.

The first meeting of the Roman soldier and the
Jewish fisherman was remarkable. Cornelius, though
accustomed not to obey but to command, seemed
to be overcome with a feeling of veneration for God's
honoured servant. He probably had heard of the
miracles in the performance of which Peter had been
the main instrument in Jerusalem, and more recently
at Lydda and Joppa. On the impulse of the moment,
as the Apostle entered his house, the centurion fell
down in homage at his feet. This action was not
necessarily, as some think, simply the oriental mode of
showing deference and profound respect to a superior,
but rather the outcome and expression of the religious
faith and habits in which, as a Roman, he had been
from his earliest years moulded. The Jew and the
Pagan were at the opposite poles of thought regarding
the fundamental truth of revealed religion. The former
tenaciously held by the first article of his Covenant
charter, "The Lord our God is one Lord." With him
there were no lords many or gods many. This in startling contradistinction to the polytheism of Greece and
Rome, whose whole mythological system was composed
of groups of divine beings or personages invested with
godlike attributes, most of them too in human shape ;—
from the wielder of Olympian thunderbolts down to
the more familiar deity presiding over wood or cavern or

grove. Accordingly, when the Apostle of Christ on whom his Master had conferred superhuman powers, was announced, it was only obeying a natural and national instinct, even though in his case supplanted by a better creed, that Cornelius flung himself in an act of reverence at Peter's feet. He who, as a soldier and born a heathen Roman, had been in the habit of deifying heroes, was not unlikely to regard as something godlike or divine, the man who had been pointed out to him by an angel. Promptly, however, was the obeisance repudiated. Peter reminded him that he was neither God nor demi-god, but a child of humanity like himself. " Stand up ; I myself also am a man !" (We may say in a parenthesis, How do the indignant words ring in the ears of those who have seen the ignorant crowd in the Great Sanctuary in Rome, touch with their foreheads and lips the foot of the pseudo image, to which, by a strange misnomer, the name of the Apostle has been given ! Equally strange to hear the boasted successor of this "Prince of Apostles" arrogating the title and preroga-tive of the Most High—asserting the claim—not " I also am a man ;" but " I also am as God.")

Peter, with the outspoken and generous manliness of his nature, tells Cornelius what induced him to respond so readily to his solicitation. He alludes in the first instance to the barriers separating Jew from Gentile, which hitherto were deemed insuperable, and specially precluding the former from accepting the hospitality of the latter, on account of the meats proscribed by the Hebrew law. But he now informs him that his scruples had, by the clear voice and intimation of heaven, been removed. Cornelius, in his turn, briefly rehearsed the story of the heavenly visitant, by whose express command it was he had ventured to ask the Apostle to undertake that long journey of thirty miles from Joppa.

If Peter had any wavering or hesitation before, as to the path of duty, he has none now. We may feebly imagine his emotions in that hour of joyous marvel; how his whole soul must have kindled into rapture. No, not even at Pentecost amid its startling supernatural prodigies would he feel so thrilled, as when about to have the privilege of making the glad announcement that the Gentiles were henceforth to become personal recipients of the great salvation. He gives vent at once to a rush of unpremeditated words;—one of those noble epigrammatic addresses or discourses, attempting to paraphrase which, would be to spoil and mutilate— "Of a truth I perceive that God is no respecter of persons: but in every nation he that feareth Him, and worketh righteousness, is accepted with Him. The word which God sent unto the children of Israel, preaching peace by Jesus Christ (He is Lord of all): that word, I say, ye know, which was published throughout all Judæa, and began from Galilee, after the baptism which John preached: how God anointed Jesus of Nazareth with the Holy Ghost and with power: who went about doing good, and healing all that were oppressed of the devil; for God was with Him. And we are witnesses of all things which He did both in the land of the Jews, and in Jerusalem; whom they slew, and hanged on a tree: Him God raised up the third day, and shewed Him openly; not to all the people, but unto witnesses chosen before of God, even to us, who did eat and drink with Him after He rose from the dead. And He commanded us to preach unto the people, and to testify that it is He which was ordained of God to be the Judge of quick and dead. To Him give all the prophets witness, that, through His name, whosoever believeth in Him shall receive remission of sins " (Acts x. 34–43).

While the inspired Preacher was still speaking, the Holy Ghost descended on all present. There was no violent agitation indeed ; none of the bitter tears and self-reproaches which on the former occasion characterised the scene, as the murderers of Calvary were smitten with the awful consciousness of their enormous crime. Cornelius and his family had no such upbraidings, guiltless as they were of the blood of the Prince of Life. But the old and well-remembered symbols of Pentecost were probably both seen and heard—the mighty wind and the tongues of fire—the conjoint evidences of the Divine presence, approval, and blessing. " They of the circumcision " who had accompanied Peter from Joppa, were specially filled with astonishment. They beheld sights strange to Jewish eyes. They listened to sounds strange to Jewish ears. Gentiles, heathens, crowned with Pentecostal flame, speaking with tongues, and in utterances of holy exultation magnifying the God of Israel. What proof more was needed ? " On the Gentiles also was poured out the gift of the Holy Ghost."

Amid that scene of profound interest, Peter's voice again interposed. He saw his way to put still further the seal of Apostleship on the transaction ; and that way surely must have been clearly made plain, when he acted entirely on his own responsibility without asking the advice or co-operation of his colleagues in Jerusalem. With the thing signified so palpably before

him, how could he hesitate for a moment to add the
sign itself? God had baptized with fire, surely he,
His servant, may not be hindered from baptizing with
water? "Can any forbid *the* water" (it is in the original, not simply *water* as in our authorised version). It
is the complement to "the Spirit" in the close of the
sentence—"Can any forbid the water that these should
not be baptized who have received the Spirit?" It is,
moreover, worthy of note, that though the reality was
granted, this did not supersede the employment of the
symbol. It was the reversal indeed of the usual order
and sequence. On other occasions, the rite of baptism
preceded the visible gift of the Spirit. In the present
case, the miraculous token came first. It was probably
so appointed to remove any lingering hesitation in the
mind of Peter, whether baptism could be administered
and Church fellowship enjoyed without first the rite
of circumcision; "teaching us too, that as the Holy
Spirit dispensed, once and for all with the necessity of circumcision in the flesh, so can He also
when it pleases Him, with the necessity of water-
baptism; and warning the Christian Church not to
put baptism itself in the place which circumcision once
held."[1]

Nor is it without significance that the Apostle was
not himself the dispenser of the initiatory rite to Cornelius and his friends. He assigned the duty to others.
"He *commanded* them to be baptized." It is remarkable that such too formed a special characteristic in the
ministry alike of his Divine Lord and of the chiefest of all
the Apostles. "Jesus baptized not." "I baptized," says
Paul, "none of you save Crispus and Gaius. Christ

---

[1] Alford's Greek Test., *in loco.*

sent me not to baptize but to preach the Gospel."
And here, the " Coryphæus of the apostolic choir " delegates the administration of this Christian Sacrament
to the hands of others.   Does not this impressively tell
us—was it not surely designed impressively to tell us,—
that there is no virtue or efficacy in the mere dispenser
of the rite.   Can we forget, as suggested by Peter's
conduct here, that his " beloved brother Paul " was
himself baptized, not by any Apostle either in Damascus
or Jerusalem, but by the hands of a humble unknown
disciple of the faith—" one Ananias ? "

The scene now presented to the eye of Peter, must
have seemed the renewal or rather the fulfilment of
one of the old prophetic voices : " It is a light thing that
thou shouldest be my servant, to raise up the tribes of
Jacob, and to restore the preserved of Israel ; I will
also give thee for a light to the Gentiles, that thou
mayest be my salvation unto the end of the earth "
(Isa. xlix. 6).   Strange and marvellous scene ! the
Gospel of Salvation—the religion of the despised and
rejected Nazarene—proclaimed by a Jew and joyfully
accepted by a representative Gentile !—the first fusion
and amalgamation of the heathen and the Hebrew
elements.   Old things are indeed passing away and all
things are becoming new.

The company assembled in the house of Cornelius
were forthwith baptized in the name of the Lord ; and
as if to strengthen them in their adopted faith, and to
vindicate his own honourable office as through them
the opener of the kingdom of heaven to the Gentile
nations, the Apostle responded to their wish to tarry
with them for some days.

We shall not further linger on this great crisis-hour

in Peter's history, however tempted to do so. The exclusive Jewish ritual with its galling restraints was repealed—the burdensome yoke of the ceremonial law for ever removed—the stranger and foreigner made a fellow-citizen with the " saints and of the household of God." It was, of all incidents in apostolic story, that which was most momentous in its bearing and results to us. It was the birthday of European Christendom. The members of the vast human family, hand linked in hand, could now say, " He is our peace who hath made both one ; and hath broken down the middle wall of partition between us." At that ocean city could the anthem first arise, " He shall have dominion also from sea to sea, and from the river unto the ends of the earth." Peter had the honour and privilege of preparing the way for the world-wide mission of him who, *par excellence*, was " Apostle of the Gentiles." Thus " by revelation God made known the mystery which in other ages was not made known unto the sons of men, as it was now revealed unto His holy Apostles and Prophets by the Spirit, that the Gentiles should be fellow-heirs and of the same body, and partakers of His promise in Christ by the Gospel."

More than one writer has ingeniously pointed out, the close resemblance existing between the cases of the conversion of Paul and the call of Cornelius. Both had been simultaneously prepared by visions for the coming of those who had been instructed to comfort and enlighten them—Ananias in the case of the future Apostle, Peter in the case of Cornelius. Both the divinely-appointed messengers exhibited at first reluctance and hesitation in obeying the call—Ananias pleading the hostile reputation of the persecutor, the " much evil " he had done to the saints ; the other, the stringent ritual obligation and prohibition—"Not so, Lord, for I have never eaten anything that is common or unclean : "—the Divine answer in both cases repelling the objection,—to the one, " Go thy way;" to the other, " What God hath cleansed that call not thou common : " upon this declaration of the Divine will, both giving instant and unhesitating compliance. Farther, in both cases, prayer preceded the blessing. Paul was on his knees when Ananias was sent to him—" Behold, he prayeth." Cornelius was also engaged in his devotions when the angel appeared to him, " Cornelius, thy prayer is heard." Even the minute description of their respective places of abode is remarkable. In the one case " the house of Judas in the street called Straight," the great thoroughfare of the Syrian city. In the other the house of Simon the tanner by the seaside.[1]

We can imagine what surprise, consternation, and at first in some cases, displeasure, these occurrences produced in the Church at Jerusalem. What a shock to their feelings to hear that the alien Gentile had been welcomed into the company of believers, and that, too, by their acknowledged head and leader ;—that Peter had baptized not only Cornelius but his kinsmen, broken bread in their house and thereby contracted defilement ! Some might perhaps recall the impulses of former days, and attribute this rash act to the old ineradicable, impetuous nature—the man of wayward feeling to the last. If so, they did him injustice. The Apostle who walked on the stormy lake, had now, by the grace of God in his soul, lost all the fitful instability of earlier life. The reed shaken by the wind and tossed, had

[1] See Howson and Conybeare *in loco*, also Canon Norris' " Key to Acts."

grown into the cedar of God, its roots moored in the Rock of Ages. And knowing, as his most trusted friends did, the strength of his new-born character—the least likely of any of the Apostolate to be warped and perverted by mere sentiment, they would be the more startled by his prompt and decided action in what was assuredly antagonistic to his traditional predilections. Some influence greatly more than human, must have dominated and determined him to abandon the fondly-clung to idea of national exclusiveness, and use his symbolic "key" to throw open the Temple gates of the spiritual Zion, making it "a house of prayer for all people."

Peter resolves, without delay, to go up to the company of the Faithful in Jerusalem, by whom, as he had every reason to expect, his conduct had been at once arraigned and challenged. And their specific charge demands specially to be noted. The offence is not that he had *preached* the Gospel to the Gentiles in Cæsarea, but "thou wentest in to men uncircumcised and *didst eat* with them." This charge may have included not only associating in their ordinary meals, but possibly partaking with them in the Lord's Supper, the sign and seal of their brotherhood and union. "The Church in Jerusalem," remarks Dean Alford, "seems to have heard the fact, without any circumstantial detail, and from the charge in verse 3—from some reporter, who gave the objectionable part of it, as is common in such cases, all prominence." They were probably moreover in ignorance of the well-known Pentecostal signs which had accompanied and attested the event. Peter's conduct in the trying circumstances in which he was placed, and all the more so, knowing as we do his constitutional frailties, is much to be admired and commended. He might not unnaturally have presumed on his position as ecclesiastical leader ; and standing on his apostolic authority, have repudiated interference on the part of the Jerusalem brethren. Confident of having the Divine sanction on his side, he might even have refused to satisfy the objections and prejudices of others. On the contrary, he seems voluntarily to have undertaken the long journey to remove the not unnatural doubts and scruples of the mother Church, and by a calm statement of facts to have at once disarmed opposition, and for the time at least obtained hearty approval of his procedure. Even anticipating, as has been already noted, thus being called in question, he had prudently taken with him "brethren from Joppa" to Cæsarea, in order that they might be able, as witnesses, to give their independent testimony. Nor can we resist to note in passing, that if the claim set up by the Church of Rome could be substantiated for the primacy and infallibility of "the Prince of the Apostles," never was there a more befitting opportunity than the present for Peter peremptorily declining submission to "Church judicatories"—boldly asserting this alleged pre-eminence his Lord had assigned him. If Christ had given him as His Vicar in the Romanist sense, "the keys of the kingdom," what cause had he voluntarily to sist himself, as he does now, at the bar of his ecclesiastical subordinates, and acknowledge his responsibility by pleading before them in vindication of his conduct ; all the more so, as he had just reason to fear that they would approach the question with minds unreasonably biased and prejudiced? But there are no such prerogatives, no such hierarchal claims preferred. On the contrary, with a spirit of beautiful meekness, gentleness, forbearance, he appears as a brother in the midst of his brethren ; in a simple narration, devoid of all self-assertion, he explains how unmistakably the treasure had been committed to him as an earthen vessel, while he took care to make equally plain, that the excellency and the power were altogether of God.

Thus put on his defence before "the Apostles and elders," Peter frankly and circumstantially related all particulars—unfolded to his hearers the clear and distinct leadings of Providence in the matter, and ended his rehearsal with the words—"Forasmuch then as God gave them the like gift as He did unto us, who believed on the Lord Jesus Christ : what was I, that I could withstand God ?" (Acts xi. 17).

With Christian fairness and magnanimity the assembled council at once withdraw their doubts, and acquiesce in the Divine settlement of the question—"They held their peace, and glorified God, saying, Then hath God also to the Gentiles granted repentance unto life" (Acts xi. 18). The contrast has been noted between the wild tumultuous interruption which assailed the speech of the holy Stephen, when they gnashed upon him with their teeth ; and the outburst of unrestrainable praise—songs of joy and thankfulness, which broke in upon the close of the Apostle's speech, when with kindling eye he uttered the challenge, "What was I that I could withstand God ?" There could not fail to be many in that assembly, composed as it was not of believers in Jerusalem only, but also of the "brethren in Judea" (Acts xi. 1), who with the love of Christ in their hearts and imbued with the unselfish spirit of the new dispensation, must, on the first impulse, have welcomed the intelligence, that the glad tidings which had cheered their own souls, were now to be made the common property of Jew and Greek, Barbarian, Scythian, bond and free. We have said, however, " on the first impulse," for although we need do no more at present than allude to the fact, this catholicity of spirit, genuine as was the expression of its enthusiasm at the time, was destined to be short-lived, and to be succeeded for a while at least, by poorer and narrower views of Christian liberty and brotherhood. We shall come hereafter to find, that years elapsed before the waves raised by this great revolution in the Church's economy rocked themselves to rest. It formed the fertile subject of bitter controversy and contention. Only by a violent struggle would many of the converts to Christianity among the favoured people surrender the old monopoly of spiritual privileges ; and with equal pertinacity the Gentile converts asserted their right of exemption from the demands of an abrogated dispensation.

We are not farther permitted to trace the future career and history of Cornelius. It is possible that when his garrison duties at Cæsarea were over, and he returned with his Italian troops to Rome, he may have prepared the way for a similar welcome to another Apostle who, sixteen years later, arrived a weary prisoner in the capital, and had a little congregation gathered around him in " his own hired house." We might have thought of Cornelius listening to the clank of that chain and helping with his presence and sympathy the illustrious captive. Only had he done so, we cannot suppose that his name would have been omitted in the honoured roll of friends whom Paul mentions in the close of his letters. So that the likelihood is, that the soldier of Cæsarea had either been serving his imperial master in some other post of honour in the vast Roman Empire, or had been called previously to inherit the crown of glory which fadeth not away.[1]

[1] There is every reason to reject the statement of some Latin writers that he was made afterwards Bishop of Cæsarea, and there suffered martyrdom. —*See Whitby's Annotations.*

CHAPTER XXI.

Peter in Prison.

PETER IN JERUSALEM. HEROD AGRIPPA. HIS CHARACTER.
MARTYRDOM OF JAMES. PETER ARRESTED AND IMPRISONED.
PRAYER OF THE CHURCH IN HIS BEHALF. HIS MIRACULOUS
DELIVERANCE. HEROD'S DEATH.

" The Apostle slept,—a light shone in the prison,
    An Angel touched his side ;
  ' Arise,' he said ; and quickly he hath risen,
    His fettered arms untied.

" The watchers saw no light at midnight gleaming,
    They heard no sound of feet ;
  The gates fly open, and the saint, still dreaming,
    Stands free upon the street."—*J. D. Burns.*

" He is not alone who has Christ for his companion."—*Cyprian.*

" This river has been a terror to many ; yea, the thoughts of it
also have often frightened me : but now methinks I stand easy."
—*Bunyan.*

" The walls were never built, the chains never forged, the
guards never breathed that could hold in bondage him whom
God willed to be free. So it proved now."—*Dr Kitto.*

HE Passover Season had brought Peter to Jerusalem.

It was now, as nearly as we can attain chronological accuracy, about the year A.D. 44, when a new occurrence (one of those sudden dramatic incidents we have often had occasion to notice in the history of the Apostle) took place—and which appeared likely at the time to add his name to the glorious army of martyrs. It might be thought indeed not an unbefitting moment for this good and faithful servant to be called to his rest and his crown. He had been spared to nurture, strengthen, and consolidate the infant Church. Might not his natural and official life appropriately close with the last act we have narrated— opening the door of admission to the Gentiles. Having thus successfully used the symbolic " Keys of the King-

dom" with which his Lord had invested him—might
he not have retired from the scene and left others of the
apostolic college to enter into his abundant labours?
His Divine Master, however, had other work for him
still to do. The call was once more to be sounded in
his ears, "Follow thou Me."

Persecution was still dogging the footsteps of the disciples;—indeed ever since the Pharisees had lost their
most promising champion in the "perversion" of Saul
of Tarsus, their hatred to the Christian sect seems to
have increased in intensity. A fresh cause for exaspera-
tion and malevolence was that to which we have just
alluded—the demolition of the old barriers which had
separated Jew from Gentile. Peter was mainly responsible for this aggression on the old monopoly of the
covenant nation, and on him therefore the weight of
their vengeance fell.

The Jewish rulers had a willing accomplice in the
person of him who now sat on the throne of Herod the
Great. This prince inherited his grandfather's name—
as well as his craft and ambition; although combined
with these were features, as described by the partial
pen of the Jewish historian, which certainly redeem his
memory from the blemishes which stain the reputation
of other members of his family. He was the son of
Aristobulus, and nephew of Herod Antipas—the latter
being the cruel debauchee who had imbrued his hands
in the blood of the Baptist, and who had instigated his
brutal soldiery to add insult and ignominy to the last
sufferings of the Innocent Son of God. The previous
life of Herod Agrippa, by which name he is generally
distinguished, had been full of adventure;—a life in
which honour and degradation, extravagance and beggary

had strangely alternated. He had been detected in his earlier years in a conspiracy against Tiberius, for which he had been thrown into prison and bound with chains. The wily Edomite, however, had in youth ingratiated himself with the heir to the Roman purple; and no sooner had Caligula ascended the throne, than, faithful to this early attachment, the newly installed Emperor not only delivered Herod from prison, but—with a strange freak of friendship—presented him with golden chains equivalent in weight to the iron ones he had worn. It is one of the favourable traits in the character of the latter, and which it may well be believed tended to secure the permanent favour of the Jews, that at great personal hazard he used all his influence to dissuade the capricious despot from carrying out his purpose of having a statue of himself erected within the precincts of the Temple. Nor after the brief and inglorious reign of Caligula did he forfeit the imperial smile. Claudius had felt under similar obligations to him; and in addition to the Tetrarchy of Trachonitis, Galilee, and Berea, he added Idumea, Samaria, and Judea; so that his dominion, at the time we speak of, was equal in extent to that of the first Herod. His independence and the splendour of his court may be estimated by the magnificence of his revenue, which, according to Josephus, amounted to twelve millions of drachmæ, or nearly half a million sterling of our money.

His past advancement had been very much the result of cunning and princecraft. He had, by dexterous and unscrupulous time-serving—pandering to the prejudices and vices of others—climbed the ladder of fortune; and his whole policy as ruler of Palestine was formed in accordance with these antecedents. He had won his

2 H

throne by sycophancy, he resolved to keep it by the same. He has been well described as " a supple states-man and a stern Jew." It required, however, all the guile of which he was master, to allay the jealousies of the Jewish leaders, and conciliate their favour. He saw at a glance that he could most successfully attain his ends by two expedients. First, by a hypocritical pro-fession of zeal for the Mosaic law and its requirements —in which law he had himself been early educated. No Pharisee, priest, or zealot was more scrupulous than he in observing ritual punctilio. In the words of Josephus— " he did not allow one day to pass without its appointed sacrifice." His first act two years before, on reaching the capital and assuming the sceptre, was with a parade of religious devotion to hang up the gift of golden chains with which Caligula had signalised his deliver-ance from prison, as a votive offering and memorial in the Temple Treasury. But a second device more ac-ceptable and gratifying still to Jewish hate and fanati-cism, was to let his vengeance fall on the obnoxious ringleaders of the Christian Church. There were not wanting counsellors around Agrippa's throne to whisper in his ear the foul suggestion. What mercy or considera-tion, indeed, could have been expected for the sheep from the hands of those who had smitten the Great and Good Shepherd? Other expedients for the sup-pression of the hated sect had failed,—a war of exter-mination was now instigated ; and the resolution is taken to let loose, in the first instance, the sanguinary edict on those who had "jeoparded their lives in the high places of the field."

James the Greater was the first who succumbed. His early and life-long association with Peter may warrant a few passing words of reference to his history and character. He was the Apostle of whom perhaps we know less than any of the others of the honoured band. It is manifest, however, that he enjoyed peculiar marks of his Lord's favour. He was one of the exceptionally privileged who were admitted on the three special occasions, to which we have previously referred, into nearer fellowship and intimacy with Jesus than the others; viz., at the raising of Jairus' daughter—the scene of the Transfiguration-hill—and at the closing hour of the agony in Gethsemane. We need not add that he was one of the two sons of Zebedee, in whose behalf their mother had preferred the bold request that they should sit the one on the right hand, the other on the left of the Master.

He had now, in a way little dreamt of when the request was made, been brought to drink the same cup, and be baptized in the same bloody baptism. "Christ had named him a 'Son of Thunder;' and this allows us to hazard the conjecture as to the nature of his offence. Gifted with a dauntless spirit, and wielding a powerful eloquence, he was not one to sit quietly by and allow Herod unreproved to lay waste the Church. He took his stand in the tyrant's path; and paying little respect we may well believe to the kingly diadem when it served but to give authority to oppression, he said to Herod, 'Touch not Mine anointed, and do My prophets no harm;' and thundered against him the doom by which every oppressor of the Church of God shall sooner or later be overtaken."[1] His end would seem to have been sudden, as if swift-handed justice had sought to strike signal terror on his fellows, as well as to show the

[1] Dr Wylie's "Scenes from the Bible," p. 324.

irresponsible power of the Jewish ruler.   He seems to
have been sisted before no Sanhedrim, otherwise his
death would probably have been by stoning—the sword
indicated the despotic act of the Roman judge and executioner.   It is somewhat remarkable indeed, that St
Luke, the narrator of this first apostolic martyrdom,
who in all events of interest enters generally into circumstantial detail, should chronicle the death of Peter's
oldest friend and fellow-disciple in one brief sentence
(nay, indeed, in two words—ἀνεῖλεν, μαχαίρῃ.)[1]   Other
writers outside the inspired Canon, in themselves reliable, have supplied us, however, with some attendant
incidents.   Eusebius in his Ecclesiastical History preserves to us one touching anecdote which he gives on the
authority of Clement of Alexandria : that the heroic
testimony borne by the Apostle to his Great Master so
touched the heart of his prosecutor, that the latter not
only professed allegiance to the Christian cause, but was
led along with the martyr to seal his testimony with his
blood.   On their way to the place of execution the
accuser begged forgiveness at the hand of him he had
wronged.   James, after a moment's hesitation, kissed
him, and after giving his loving benediction, "in their
death they were not divided."   Both were beheaded.

This first bloody tragedy is enacted.   But the bold
proceeding was tentative.   It might well form matter
of anxious speculation with the persecutor, as to how
his swift-handed justice, or rather cruelty, might be received by a large party among the Jews.   Stephen, the
proto-martyr, had been judged and condemned by the

---

[1] It has been suggested by Meyer, that Luke may have intended to write
a second and supplementary treatise on the Acts of the Apostles, and that
he had for it reserved the details of James' history and martyrdom, as well
as that of the other Founders of the Christian Church.

Sanhedrim :—the very manner of his death was in accordance with Jewish antecedent and custom. But how
would many—it might even be the majority—of the
subject race be likely to accept of this fresh example
of the arrogance of imperial Rome? Stung as they
were by the growth of the Christian sect, this was but
of yesterday compared to the long-standing humiliation
arising out of servitude to the Cæsars. What would
they say to this new claim to supremacy—the despotical
setting aside of their highest legislative tribunal, and
the precedent which the use of the Roman Sword would
establish for the future. James was a Christian, but
he was by name, birth, and education, a Jew. Would
these proud descendants of Abraham—his brethren according to the flesh—concur in tamely standing by, and
on any pretext submit to this illegal exercise of alien
jurisdiction? It was speedily made manifest, for the
time at least, in the present fever of national passion
and prejudice, that of the two evils—the usurpation of
authority was deemed the least. The major portion
at all events would willingly acquiesce in Cæsar's assumption of supreme prerogative, that Cæsar might be
responsible for the crime they longed to see perpetrated,
but which they had not the courage themselves to commit. The politic Agrippa saw that this opening act of
wanton cruelty " pleased the Jews ; " and that if he
added the murder of the "Rockman" to that of the " Son
of Thunder," it would be like the removal of Jachin and
Boaz from the support of the Christian Temple. Save
Saul of Tarsus, no one of the surviving band of believers
was so obnoxious as the intrepid son of Jonas. Quench
this burning and shining light, and the lesser lights of
the infant community would soon pale. Civil power,

ecclesiastical tyranny, popular fanaticism joined in triple alliance, could hardly fail to accomplish their desired object. Accordingly, the Apostle of the circumcision is arrested and cast into prison.

As Jerusalem was surrounded by three walls, it has been conjectured that the place of confinement (probably the Tower of Antonia) was situated between the outer and middle wall, and that the huge iron door entered from the latter to the street of the city. The walls of a prison, as we now know, were to Peter not strange,—this being the third incarceration to which he had been subjected. It may possibly have been considered by Herod and his abettors that a period of imprisonment, followed by a formal arraignment before a legal tribunal, would tend to strike greater terror into the hearts of his followers. But another and substantial reason is assigned for the postponement of his fate : "Then were the days of unleavened bread." The politic, scrupulous formalist would not connive at so daring a breach of the Mosaic law as to assemble a legal tribunal for a criminal trial during the celebration of the greatest of the Jewish festivals. It would have been deemed an act of profanation at such a time to shed blood.[1] He delayed the tragedy, therefore, till the conclusion of the sacred seven days ;[2] and meanwhile profiting by past experience in the former release of Peter and John, took every precautionary measure by watch and ward to insure the safety of his prisoner, and render escape, whether by personal vigilance or by perfidy and intrigue, impossible.

[1] This rule, it will be remembered, was set aside in the case of Jesus, who was crucified on the week of the Passover.
[2] Intending "after Easter " (xii. 4)—an unhappy rendering for "after the Paschal feast." It was a *Jewish* festival (not the yet unknown *Christian* one) which was referred to.

"In military arrangements, Herod seems to have retained the Roman habits."[1] A picket of soldiers consisting of four quaternions were selected for the critical duty. The quaternion was a body of four, who were by turns told off at each of the Jewish night-watches : thus relieved every three hours. Two were ordered to be with the prisoner in his cell, while the other two were stationed as sentries at the outer gate of the prison. According to Josephus, the usual precaution taken for the custody of a prisoner was to have his left hand chained to the right of the soldier on guard; but in the present case, to make doubly sure, both arms of the Apostle were fastened to the soldiers on either side of him.

These custodiers were doubtless made well aware of the momentous trust confided to their vigilance, and the certain penalty that would ensue did they prove unfaithful. Truly in one sense there was little need of all these military precautions. Those who had a tender and loving concern for their incarcerated chief were in themselves powerless either to concoct or effect a rescue. They had no sword to measure with these sentinels of imperial Rome. To attempt deliverance would only be an act of rash folly, that would furnish a pretext to the tyrant for an indiscriminate massacre. Destitute of carnal weapons, they were equally powerless in respect of other means. No friend or intercessor had they at court to plead for leniency, or to urge postponement of the sentence. James had been murdered in cold blood without giving time for any such intervention. Was there any likelihood that one more hated still — the chief abettor and propagator of these strange doc-

[1] Alford.

trines—would have extended to him respite or mercy?
So far as human instrumentality was concerned, "no
hope" must have been the words quivering on every
lip. They had only one gleam in the cloud. But as
the gloom gathered more ominously around, that ray of
comfort and promise shone the more brightly. Could
not He who, in answer to prayer, had delivered Daniel
from his den of lions, and Hezekiah and his people from
the hosts of Sennacherib, interpose in this hour of extremity? Could not some of them remember (he in the
prison at all events could) how at another " fourth watch
of the night," when the darkness was deepest, ONE appeared to the perishing crew walking on the crest of the
waves and changing the storm into a calm? "The
Lord's hand is not shortened that it cannot save, the
Lord's ear is not heavy that it cannot hear." They
will, as aforetime, carry their trouble to Heaven's "Court
of last appeal." They will use an invisible power stronger
than Roman legion—a power that can defy key and
lock, bolt and bar, chain and sentinel: " With God all
things are possible." " Peter therefore was kept in prison : but prayer was made without ceasing of the Church
unto God for him " (Acts xii. 5). Doubtless as day by
day crept on, these intercessions became more fervent :
prayer mainly and chiefly that God would interpose to
soften the heart of the persecutor and those who had a
guiltier complicity in the crime,—loose His servant's
chains and set him free; and on the other hand, if
death were inevitable, that He would vouchsafe the
martyr grace and strength to witness a good confession,
strong in faith to give glory to God, enabling him in
the last hour to add the noblest testimony to his previous avowal—" Thou knowest that I love Thee." Words

spoken years before by Divine lips, would doubtless linger in the ears of some : " Again I say unto you, that if two of you shall agree on earth as touching anything that they shall ask, it shall be done for them of My Father which is in heaven. For where two or three are gathered together in My name, there am I in the midst of them " (Matt. xviii. 19, 20). The expression, moreover, in the narrative would lead us to conclude that it was no ordinary season of intercession. " Prayer was made *without ceasing ;* " the same emphatic word— indicative of deepest earnestness—which is employed with reference to the Saviour's supplications in Gethsemane, when, " being in an agony, He prayed *the more earnestly.*"[1] How intense must have been those wrestlings of the Church at that time, when they can be compared to the " supplication with strong crying and tears " of the Divine Victim " unto Him that was able to save from death ! "

The conjecture has been made by some commentators, that among the suffering, sympathising group which constituted that " prayer meeting," it is not improbable may be included the names of Barnabas and Paul, recently come from Antioch. It is impossible with any certainty to pronounce on this. But even the possibility of the " son of consolation " and " the chiefest of Apostles " aiding with their presence and devotions, their prayers and tears, that little gathering of the faithful, lends a new interest to the scene.

It was now the last night of that solemn time. The sun had set on the mountains of Bether, and the clear

---

[1] The Greek is ἐκτενής. Peter uses it in one of his own Epistles in a different sense, but also to indicate intense fervour ; "have *fervent* charity among yourselves " (1 Pet. iv. 8).

Passover moon was again looking down from the silent depths of heaven. Others may have gone to slumber ; the hum of the busy city was hushed ; but here and there, unseen and unheard, were gathered anxious groups of the followers of Jesus " preventing the dawning of the morning " with their fervent cries, more fervent and importunate as the fatal moment was approaching.

Still there is no response. The heavens seem as brass and the earth as iron. A few hours more, and if no answer be vouchsafed, then ere the orb of day has climbed the meridian, a bereavement will be theirs second only to that when their Great Master Himself vanished from sight on the heights of Olivet.

Others too were, doubtless, that night sleepless from a different cause. The priests and Pharisees would, with the first dawn of morn, anticipate with cruel satisfaction the triumph of their malevolence. The toils are gathering surely around their victim. Probably also the main figure in this complicated tragedy had similar sad forebodings. Yet it forms one of the most beautiful and affecting touches in the dramatic tale, that Peter " was *sleeping.*" He had but a few hours to live—a few hours ere he were led forth to a cruel death—these cruelties intensified by scoff and ridicule and buffeting—nevertheless, he " sleeps " on his litter of straw with the tramp of the sentinels in his ears, the heavy breathings of the soldiers by his side, and the occasional clank of the chain with which he was himself bound. What his dreams were we know not. As the scenes and associations of early life come often clustering around the last moments, his miagination may have been wandering around the shores of Gennesaret ; to childhood's home at Bethsaida, or

youth's adventurous first hours out on the moonlit lake.
Likelier still, if his thoughts reverted to distant Galilee,
would Diviner forms and themes take shape and substance in these closing slumbers.   The august Being
that stilled the midnight tempest may have been seen
yet again approaching, breathing His own sweet
requiem " Peace be still," " Fear not, it is I, be not
afraid."   Be this as it may, " Peter was sleeping " calmly
as a little child on its mother's bosom !   A noble and
glorious testimony to that peace of God which " keeps
the heart."   It shows how his moral heroism had grown
since we first knew him.   He who showed a coward's
pusillanimity once, not far from the place where he at
present lay, was now hushed in tranquil repose.   " So He
giveth His beloved sleep."   Doubtless he was prepared for
whatever the will of his Lord might be ; able to say in
the words of his beloved brother Paul, " To me to live
is Christ, and to die is gain."   The dungeon where he
lies is hallowed to him as the last abode of his now
sainted fellow-apostle.   James would seem to whisper in
his ear that " Courage, brother," which was handed down
afterwards as a sacred watchword from age to age, and
by which many a hero in the noble army braced others
for witnessing a " good confession."

We feel it only right to add, that although not in
any way detracting from the strength of his *faith*, this
representation of the Apostle's feelings on the approach
of death may be somewhat modified by the conjecture,
that he had some strong ground for expecting, even to the
last, that Divine succour would be extended to him.   His
Lord had distinctly told him in that same remarkable
interview on the shores of Gennesaret, " that when he
was old he would *stretch forth his hands,* and another

would gird him and carry him whither he would not."
He was still in his mid-day career, by no means yet a
veteran in the battle. May he not, therefore, as he lay
powerless in his cell, have had the thought vividly impressed upon him, that the Lord he loved would in
some unknown way yet come to his rescue, strike these
fetters off, and send him forth once more, like his own
healed cripple, " walking and leaping and praising God,"
only nerved and strengthened for fresh spiritual conquests ? We may, however, feel assured that whatever
were his thoughts and expectations, whether prolonged
work on earth or an early martyr's crown, the words
of the prophet were abundantly realised in his experience, " Thou wilt keep him in perfect peace whose
mind is stayed on Thee." He was at all events
readier far now, than when he originally uttered the
words, to say, " I will even lay down my life for Thy
sake."

But once more, as in manifold instances in the records
of the Church in every age, man's " extremity was to be
made God's opportunity." It was now, as is supposed by
Wieseler, the last watch of the night, and being at the
vernal equinox considerably before sunrise. The slumbers of the prisoner are suddenly broken by a heavenly apparition. One of those bright inhabitants of the upper
sanctuary, whose office it is to minister to them who are
heirs of salvation, appears standing before him. A bright
light, we are specially told, illuminated the cell ; but at
first neither the angel's footsteps nor the glow which
encircled the sleeper disturbed his repose. The celestial
visitant had to " touch his side " in order to rouse him.
" Arise up quickly," were the words which fell on his
ear. As he obeyed the summons, the chains dropt from

his hands and he felt himself free.[1] There was no undue haste or precipitation, however. As was the wont among the Jews in taking rest, he had loosed his upper cloak, ungirded the cincture which fastened his inner garment, and taken off the sandals from his feet. The angel tells him deliberately to replace all these; and Peter feeling himself in safe custody, complied in each particular with the messenger's direction. The last injunction to " put on his sandals " was a distinct indication that he was about to leave the cell.[2] As the words sounded in his ears, he must have felt that mightier than Herod's mailed bands was the arm now stretched out visibly for his rescue. The words of the Great Prophet may have been recalled by him, " Ye shall not go out with haste, nor go by flight : for the Lord will go before you, and the God of Israel will be your rereward" (Isaiah lii. 12). The God he served had sealed the eyes of his watchers, and under the guidance of the heavenly attendant he leaves the soldiers sleeping at

1 Some of my readers may doubtless have visited the well-known church in Rome, St Pietro in Vincoli, on the Esquiline, built in the fifth century by the Queen of Valentinian III., for the alleged purpose of enshrining the chains which bound St Peter. These are still annually exhibited from the 1st to the 8th of August, but at other times are concealed from public view in a bronze tabernacle in the sacristy. The mythical story of these chains is thus well described and commented upon : " That some of these soldiers who guarded Peter, converted to the Christian faith, should mark and take away these chains, and give them to the Bishop of Jerusalem ; and that they should be kept as a treasure, not only through all the Jewish wars, but about four hundred years after, until Juvenal, Bishop of Jerusalem, gave them to Eudoxia, wife to Theodosius the younger, who gave one of them to the Church of St Peter in Constantinople, and sent the other to Rome, is a legend that smells too rank of superstition to deserve the least credit."— *Whitby's Annotations.* It may be noted that the beautiful chapel in our own Tower of London is dedicated to St Peter *ad vincula.*

2 " *Gird* thyself (*i.e.,* gird up thy tunic or χιτῶνα), and bind on thy *sandals* and cast thy *gaberdine* ('Ιμάτιον) about thee and follow me."— *Lewin.*

their post with the loosened chains dangling at their sides.[1] At first the whole thing appears unreal. Peter's first thought was that he saw only a feverish vision, which the morning light would dispel. In this state of half unconsciousness he follows the angel's footsteps. The silence is unbroken. No word is exchanged between guide and follower. They have gone through both first and second ward, and in doing so have probably passed also the other two sleeping sentinels. They have reached the ponderous gate in the prison wall, which for security had been plated and rivetted with iron. This opened of its own accord. They are now standing outside the prison; and after one other street is traversed, the angel speeds away and leaves the wondering Apostle to himself.

How strange and bewildered he must have felt in that lone, dark hour; and yet not dark, for as we have already noted, the Passover moon enabled him without difficulty to thread his way through these familiar wind-

----

[1] I have alluded in the preface to Raphael's picture of the subject now treated, "St Peter in prison," the centre of which is engraved in the title page, while one of the side compartments, "the sleeping soldiers," forms the heading of this chapter. In refinement and finish it is doubtless far inferior to many of the great painter's other and better known works, and the colouring through age has suffered. We doubt, however, if in any of his pictures he has displayed greater grandeur of conception and more original power of treatment. It has thus been well described :—"He has seized on the obvious point of effect both as to light and grouping ; and we have three separate moments of the same incident, which yet combine most happily into one grand scene. Thus in the centre, over the window, we see through a grating the interior of the prison, where St Peter is sleeping between two guards, who, leaning on their weapons, are sunk in a deep charmed slumber ; an angel, whose celestial radiance fills the dungeon with a flood of light, is in the act of waking the Apostle. On the right of the spectator, the angel leads the Apostle out of the prison, two guards are sleeping on the steps. On the left, the soldiers are roused from sleep, and one with a lighted torch appears to be giving the alarm ; the crescent moon faintly illumines the background."—*Sacred and Legendary Art*, p. 202.

ings. The full truth gradually burst upon him. The refreshing air of that spring morning, so grateful after the stifling damps of his cell, wakes him to the consciousness that it was no mere vision he had seen, but a glad and wondrous reality. The Lord had sent His succouring angel to deliver him from the plot of wicked rulers and exasperated citizens.

> "Touch'd, he upstarts—his chains unbind—
> Through darksome vault, up massy stair,
> His dizzy, doubting footsteps wind
> To freedom and cool moonlight air.

> "Then all himself, all joy and calm,
> Though for a while his hand forego,
> Just as it touched, the martyr's palm,
> He turns him to his task below."[1]

He pauses for a moment, and then resolves to hasten to the house of an eminent female disciple and

[1] St Peter's Day, "Christian Year." Strange and persistent are the efforts of many of the German exegetical scholars to get rid here as elsewhere of the supernatural. But in the words of a recent writer, "All rationalistic explanations to account for this deliverance of Peter are in direct opposition to the narrative. According to Hezel, a flash of lightning shone into the prison, and loosened the chains of Peter. According to Eichhorn and Heinrichs, the jailor, or others with his knowledge, delivered Peter, without the Apostle being conscious to whom he owed his freedom ; and as the soldiers are a difficulty in the way of this explanation, they suppose that a sleeping draught was administered to them. All this is mere trifling. Others endeavour to get rid of the miraculous by questioning the correctness of the narrative. Meyer and De Wette think that the truth is so mixed up with the mythical element that it is impossible to affirm what actually took place. Baur supposes that Herod himself delivered the Apostle, as he found in the interval that the people were not gratified by the death of James, but that on the contrary that proceeding had made him unpopular. Neander passes over the narrative with the remark, 'By the special providence of God, Peter was delivered from prison.' When once the miraculous in the narrative is given up, the only resource is the mythical theory —to call in question the truth of the history—as all natural explanations are wholly unavailing. The narrative here, however, has no semblance to a myth ; there is a naturalness and freshness about it which remove it from all legends of a mythical description." See Dr Gloag's excellent Commentary on the Acts, p. 418. Edinburgh: Clark. 1870.

friend, " Mary the mother of John whose surname was Mark." She was the sister of Barnabas ; and this connection, if the conjecture be correct, that Barnabas and Paul were then in Jerusalem, renders it the more probable that the former would be present in the house of his own sister rather than at any of the other similar meetings convened on that anxious occasion. Hers, at all events, was one of several households in Jerusalem which that night had been sleepless, and whose chambers had been converted into oratories. "Many were gathered together praying."[1] While probably in the very act of supplication, the service is interrupted by a knocking at the door of the outer porch or vestibule (in our version spoken of as "the gate"). A young woman of the name of Rhoda, or Rose, perhaps the servant of the household, went out to ascertain the cause. Doubtless some present would not unnaturally surmise that Herod's myrmidons had been despatched at that early hour to effect new captures. It would sound to many as a death-knell.

On listening, Rhoda imagines that she recognises the voice of the imprisoned Apostle. But refusing to credit the testimony of her own senses, or rather deeming the news too good to be true, she rushes back in an ecstacy of emotion to tell the company the startling intelligence. Strange that though the prisoner's deliverance had been forming the subject of their earnest prayers day after day and hour after hour, yet when the wonderful answer really came, their weak faith

---

1 The traditional house of Mary the mother of Mark in Jerusalem, is pointed out in the Armenian Quarter, and is now the "Syrian Convent." " Though Luke writes that Rhoda ' hearkened only,' the monks do, or did show at Jerusalem, the very window through which Rhoda looked and saw Peter."—See Maundrell's Travels *in loco.*

failed to credit the reality. They imputed the story to the girl's heated imagination, which had got the better of her sober reason. "Thou art mad," was the hasty and incredulous verdict on her tumult of joy. But as she earnestly reiterated her statement, they qualified their first incredulous denial, by saying, "It is hi angel." The Jews had a beautiful legend or dogma, that every good man of their nation was attended from birth to death by a guardian angel. The friends gathered in Mary's house accordingly concluded, either that this was Peter's tutelary angel who had assumed the tones of his voice: or we may give the alternative supposition: they may have imagined that at that instant the terrible doom had been consummated, and that the released spirit of the martyred Apostle had come thither on its way to the unseen world with the tidings they had so much dreaded.

The knocking continued; and when the door was opened and they saw the veritable head of their Apostolic Teacher standing before them, they were for the moment panic-stricken, astonished, speechless. Like the recorded feelings on the occasion of a greater restoration, "they believed not for joy, and wondered" (Luke xxiv. 41).

It would appear from the narrative that Peter did not enter the room where they had been assembled. He was fully alive to his present danger. The morning light may already have been streaking the east, and he knew too well every hour increased the peril of his position. The Man of the Rock, whatever he may have been formerly, was now at least no coward; and we may well believe he would never have connived at au ignominious flight. Seeing, however, that a special heavenly messenger had been delegated to unloose his chains and open his prison-doors, it would have been ungrateful to contravene a higher will, had he lingered in the place of danger and failed to use every means to save his life for that farther duty and service which his Lord evidently had signified were in store for him. Accordingly, we are told, when the little band of praying followers were gathered in the outer porch of Mary's house, and perhaps, now fully alive to the reality of the deliverance, were giving too audible expression to their joy, " he beckoned unto them with the hand to hold their peace." Even a few hurried interchanges of sympathy and congratulation would have been perilous. After briefly narrating his miraculous rescue, and enjoining them to go and acquaint James and the rest of the brethren with the circumstance, he abruptly leaves them, and sets out, we know not where, on his solitary way. "He went into another place." The Roman Catholic Church, on no conceivable or feasible ground, assigns to the City of Rome this temporary refuge. We have much stronger reason to believe that he had gone no further than Lydda or Joppa, where he might enjoy a brief exemption from the plots of the capital, the intrigues of Herod and his satellites, and still be employed in acceptable ministrations to the recent converts.[1] The Apostle at all events is safe. Effectual fervent prayer in his behalf has availed much. We can only farther

---

[1] Dean Alford remarks on the Greek words (εἰς ἕτερον τόπον), "I see in these words, a minute mark of truth in our narrative. Under the circumstances the place of Peter's retreat would very naturally at the time be kept secret. . . . We find him again at Jerusalem in ch. xv. Whether he left it or not on this occasion is uncertain. It is not asserted in ἐξελθών, which only implies that he left the *house*."

imagine how the supplications of these various assemblies
of Christians in Jerusalem would be turned into praises.
" This poor man cried, and the Lord heard him, and
saved him out of all his troubles. The angel of the
Lord encampeth round about them that fear Him, and
delivereth them. O taste and see that the Lord is good:
blessed is the man that trusteth in Him " (Ps. xxxiv.
6–8). " Then they cried unto the Lord in their trouble,
and He saved them out of their distresses. He brought
them out of darkness and the shadow of death, and
brake their bands in sunder. Oh that men would praise
the Lord for His goodness, and for His wonderful works
to the children of men ! For He hath broken the gates
of brass, and cut the bars of iron in sunder " (Ps. cvii.
13–16). Their experience has left as a precious legacy
to the Church of the future, alike collectively and individually, not only that " The Lord is good unto them
that wait for Him, unto the soul that seeketh Him,"
but that in the midst of environing perils, when all
seems humanly speaking at the last extremity, there
is ONE on high, " mighty to save," who " neither
slumbers nor sleeps," and who makes the wrath of
man to praise Him.

Meanwhile the wildest consternation must have seized
the sentinels, who knew well what they had to expect
from the too palpable evidences of dereliction of duty.
When the day had dawned and the full revelation of
the escape was known, we can feebly imagine the
inflated rage of the baffled Inquisitor. An instant
examination takes place. Assuming that the guard
had either slept at their posts, or had connived at the
escape of their prisoner, they are consigned to pay the
last ignominious penalty of the Roman law.

Though not properly forming a part of our narrative, we cannot resist in a few sentences referring to the swift doom which overtook Peter's kingly oppressor. His day of retribution was at hand.[1] It would seem almost immediately after this averted crisis, that Herod, perhaps moping in impotent wrath at his frustrated scheme against the Christian leader, proceeded to Cæsarea. In that city, as we have previously noted, there was a large theatre erected by the elder Herod. One day about the beginning of the month of August, this building was crowded with people. The cause of the immense assemblage is to us an interesting one. The Emperor Claudius had gone to join his armies in Great Britain, and remained there for sixteen days. During this time he obtained several victories, and took, among others, the city of Colchester, which was then, what London is now, the capital of the Empire. On returning to Rome there was universal rejoicing; he was called "Brittanicus," after our island; he had a naval crown put above his palace; and an annual celebration of the event was instituted at Rome, consisting of the usual barbarous sports of fighting wild beasts, with war dances, and chariot racing. Herod Agrippa, who was both much indebted to Claudius, and desirous of retaining his favour, resolved to keep the festival also in imposing splendour in the theatre at Cæsarea. The stone seats, which rose one above another, were a moving mass of human beings. On

[1] This persecution of the unoffending Christians was only in harmony with other acts of cruelty which disgraced Herod's reign. To give one example: "At Berytus, a city which he highly favoured, he built a splendid theatre, where the most costly musical exhibitions were displayed; and in an amphitheatre in the same city, two troops of gladiators, malefactors, of 700 each, were let loose upon each other; and thus horribly fulfilled the sentence of the law."—*Milman's History of the Jews*, ii. 159.

the second morning all faces were turned towards a private portico, through which, in great pomp, Herod entered, clad in sparkling robes of silver. He took his seat on a purple throne. When the people saw him, they shouted and cried, "Behold, a god !" adding, according to Josephus, "Be thou merciful unto us ; for although we have hitherto reverenced thee only as a king, yet shall we henceforth own thee as superior to mortals." The same writer, in his account of it, also relates that at that moment the unhappy being they were thus worshipping, looked up and saw an owl (a bird of " evil omen ") perched on a rope above his head. He was immediately filled with dread. The great God of Heaven, who will not give His glory to another, made him to be " eaten of worms !" He was carried away to his palace in the agonies of a dreadful death. Josephus adds, that the assembled multitudes fled from the theatre, and, as was the custom with the Jews, rent their clothes and sat in ashes, making a great lamentation. " And the king being laid in a high chamber, and looking down on the people prostrate on the ground, could not himself forbear weeping. And having continued in agony five days . . . he departed this life." What a contrast between the calm Apostle (the apparently doomed man), and his tyrant oppressor, with apparently a demigod's power and a monarch's splendour ! " I have seen the wicked in great power, and spreading himself like a green bay-tree. Yet he passed away, and, lo, he was not : yea, I sought him, but he could not be found. Mark the perfect man, and behold the upright : for the end of that man is peace " (Ps. xxxvii. 35–37). " Verily there is a God that judgeth in the earth."

With this dramatic tale of deliverance and retributive reckoning, closes what may be called the continuous history of Peter in the Acts of the Apostles. Cuspius Fadus had been appointed in Herod's place—a ruler whose name is happily unfamiliar, testifying, as the silence of the historic record does, to the toleration that was accorded to the Christian sect during his peaceful and uneventful sway. Perhaps, however, there may have been another reason for this unfamiliarity. The Christians in Jerusalem, justly alarmed at Herod's high-handed tyranny, may have fled in a body from the capital, in obedience to their Lord's own command, "When they persecute you in one city, flee ye to another."

CHAPTER XXII.

Peter and Antioch.

INTERVAL OF FIVE YEARS IN PETER'S LIFE. THE CITY OF ANTIOCH. ITS SPLENDOUR. GROWTH OF THE CHURCH WITHIN ITS WALLS. THREATENED SCHISM. PETER AT THE COUNCIL OF JERUSALEM. HIS RETURN TO ANTIOCH AND UNWORTHY VACILLATION.

" Climbing up high, its hills are battlements
The work of Titans "————.

" The Apostles did not cease, even after they received the Holy Ghost, to be sinful men; along with the new man the old man too still lived in them; as sinful men therefore they remained subject to the possibility of error. . . . . They were distinguished from the world not by this, that they never went wrong, but by this, that when they did go wrong, they were sufficiently humble to acknowledge their mistake and immediately to correct it."— *Olshausen.*

" In the person of Paul, the Lord once more ' turned and looked on Peter;' and the erring disciple was again awakened, and checked, and finally delivered."—*Archbishop Whately.*

" He had before defended himself almost with rudeness, when his Divine Master had predicted his denial and desertion. In after ages, he humbly and silently permitted Paul to withstand him to the face."—*Blunt on St Peter.*

FTER the memorable escape from his Jerusalem prison, there occurs a blank of five or six years in the life of Peter. Not, we may feel well assured, that there had been any intermission in his active work, but the peculiar scene of his labours is left unchronicled. Some traditions represent him, as we have noted in last chapter, engaged during this interval in ministering to believers among the coast towns on the western shore of Palestine; while, as also already referred to, Cardinal Bellarmine and other Papal controversialists allege that he had taken up his residence in Rome, and as his Lord's Vicar had there laid the foundation of the future Mother Church of Christendom.

While there is no reliable positive evidence to support such an assertion,[1] there is much to militate against the assumption. Whatever probabilities there may be in favour of a later visit, which we shall come in due time to consider, not a tittle of proof can be adduced as to his having been in the Roman metropolis at this particular time. Such a residence indeed would have been chronologically impossible, and involves an unscrupulous perversion of facts to suit a purpose.

First of all, is it at all likely that his faithful biographer would have left entirely unnoted a sojourn of such importance and interest to the whole Church? Is it likely that if Peter had gone, as we shall find him presently doing, to the Council of Jerusalem, as " Bishop of Rome and Metropolitan," that such a fact would have been passed in silence? Moreover, if Rome were the centre of his diocese, how came he, at the close of the council, to make the detour to Antioch in North Syria, which we shall also presently find him doing, and to maintain for a considerable time intercourse with the converts there, with all his urgent work on hand in the Roman capital? Then, on the supposition that a permanent residence from this date in the city of the Cæsars had actually taken place, how can we account for Paul's studied silence regarding it in his letter to the Romans? While the author of that Epistle, with a remarkable profuseness, occupies a whole chapter in sending greetings to other members of the Roman Church (embracing no less than twenty-six different persons whom he designates as "his helpers in Christ,") how comes it that the name of the most illustrious of all

[1] Eusebius and Jerome, and from an incidental allusion we may add Irenæus, are the only authorities that can be quoted in favour of such a theory. Their statements have again and again been refuted as having arisen from a confusion of names and dates.

never once occurs ? Moreover, had the " Rockman "—
he to whom the Keys of the kingdom of Heaven were
metaphorically committed—been then in the capital,
how can we account for Paul's strong language when he
speaks of his own anxiety to visit his Roman converts
personally, that as an Apostle he might impart unto
them spiritual gifts ? " If we should say St Peter was
absent, we cannot escape the difficulty ; for not only
does St Paul abstain from saluting Peter, but he writes
positively to this flock as to a flock which had never yet
seen an Apostle. ' I am ready,' he says, ' to preach the
Gospel to you that are at Rome also ; ' that is, to preach
the Gospel to the Christians of Rome,—the flock of
another, and that other the Prince of Apostles, established as their Bishop for years." [1] How utterly unlike
him to employ what we would not unnaturally designate as insulting language : ignoring the presence, and
gifts, and labours of one so distinguished. On the
supposition of Peter having founded the greatest of the
Gentile Churches in the World's Metropolis, strange and
inappropriate surely would be similar expressions of
his brother Apostle in addressing the Galatians :—" He
that wrought effectually in Peter to the Apostleship of
the circumcision, the same was mighty in me toward
the Gentiles." Could he thus speak of himself as the
specially accredited messenger to the Gentiles, and associate Peter with the Jewish element alone, if the
latter had been then installed as Bishop of Rome, and
had entered on his twenty-five years' alleged Episcopate ? [2]
When Paul was on his way a prisoner to Rome A.D. 60,
a number of sympathising brethren came to give him a

---

[1] Dr Scheler quoted by West. Also Canon Norris *in loc.*
[2] See this well stated by Bishop Lee *in loc.*

kindly welcome at Appii Forum and the Three Taverns.
There is not a syllable said regarding Peter being among
them. When the former reached the capital of the Cæsars,
we read that the chief of the Jews came to his lodging,
and with eager curiosity poured in their questions regarding the origin, doctrines, and practice of the new
sect—which they had " heard of " as everywhere spoken
against :—" We desire to hear of thee what thou
thinkest ? " What a strange query to put to this
prisoner in chains, if, on the Romanist supposition,
Peter had for sixteen years been occupying the Episcopal
chair : and yet here are the members of his flock desiring instruction in the elements of Christianity ! Could
he who preached so nobly at Pentecost, and from whose
Episcopate we might well expect such great results,
have lived for years the nominal head of the Church :
but so complete a cypher—in a state of such inaction,
that these his own countrymen were glad to appoint a
day to go to the lodging of a chained prisoner—for what
purpose ? To hear of his own personal grievances ? No :
to get information about the Religion of Jesus. " To
whom he expounded and testified the kingdom of God,
persuading them concerning Jesus, both out of the law
of Moses, and out of the prophets, from morning till
evening " (Acts xxviii. 23). For two whole years Paul
lived in this hired house, " receiving all who came to
him." Strange that among the sympathising visitors
the name of Peter is never mentioned. Paul must also
at this time have written from Rome his Epistles to the
Philippians, Colossians, Ephesians, Philemon, and
Timothy, but there is the same absence in them all
of any reference to Peter. It is inconceivable that such
a ministry as his would never have been so much as

alluded to, nor an apostolic salutation sent. Once more, when the same great Apostle was confined in the Mamertine dungeon, how he yearns for Christian sympathy! How he loves to enumerate the few names of those who had not been ashamed of his chain, but who had cheered him in his solitude, such as Luke and Onesiphorus. Peter, had he been in Rome, would surely have received special mention; he is again conspicuous only by his omission.

In the absence then of all evidence in support of the Roman theory, we may much more reasonably conclude that during this gap in his history with which in the present chapter we are concerned, Peter was either engaged in the discharge of pastoral duty in some outlying districts of Palestine, or possibly among his countrymen ("they of the circumcision") in the provinces and towns of Asia Minor.

At the close of that interval, however (about A.D. 50 or 51), the Apostle's name re-appears as one of the speakers in what is familiarly known as "the FIRST COUNCIL OF JERUSALEM." The purport of his utterances there, will be best understood by transferring our thoughts, in the first instance, to another noted locality on the eastern shores of the Mediterranean, with which he is specially identified.

A magnificent city of that era was Antioch in Syria. It was picturesquely situated on the river Orontes, twenty miles from the sea, and three hundred miles from Jerusalem. It formed, with its half a million inhabitants, the great emporium of Eastern luxury; and, from its central position, commanded the whole trade of the Mediterranean by means of its port Seleucia. It was the outlet for merchants and caravans who travelled from the banks of the Tigris and Euphrates, and ranked third (after Rome and Alexandria) among the capitals of the Roman empire. In the stately language of the historian of the "Decline and Fall," "Antioch and Alexandria looked down with disdain on a crowd of dependent cities, and yielded with reluctance to the majesty of Rome alone." It was built by Seleucus Nicator, B.C. 301,—the site being selected, as was often the case with Greek and Roman towns, by an eagle's flight, after sacrifice, on Mount Silpius. It stood in a spacious hollow or plain, into which the Orontes flowed after cleaving its way between the mountain ranges of Casius and Amanus: while, through a second defile guarded by lofty precipices, the same river, after leaving the city, found its way to the sea. Owing to its isolated and remote position, Seleucus granted the newly-built capital exceptional privileges. Jews had the same political rights accorded to them as the Greeks, and were governed by their own Ethnarch. Hence a great influx of the Hebrew race. A strong temptation for Greek settlers and for thousands of annual pilgrims arose from its proximity to the famous Temple and Groves of Daphne. Here the Pythian Apollo had his renowned sanctuary; enriched inside with gold, and gems, and art,—surrounded with bewitching scenery of rock, and glen, and rushing stream, and wealth of vegetation— thickets of bay and sacred cypresses. Add to this, what was more to these dissolute citizens of the gay capital— it was "a Sensual Paradise"—enjoying a base repute for the most licentious orgies—deeds of darkness perpetrated under the sanction of the "God of Light." In the words of a writer to whom we are indebted, "under

the glorious sun of Syria and the patronage of Imperial
Rome, all that was beautiful in nature and art had created a sanctuary for a perpetual festival of vice."[1] The
town of Antioch itself was nearly five miles long, and
lay on the northern slope of Mount Silpius. Walls of
enormous heights and thickness (fifty feet high, and
fifteen wide) spanning in many places the deep ravines
of the mountain, were miracles of art and labour. A
remarkable island was formed in the centre of the city,
on which stood the palace of the Seleucidæ, with a
bridge connecting it with the northern portion. The
crags of the mountain just mentioned were all of them
bold and rugged. One remarkable column of rock over-
hung the town, which the arts of the Greeks had formed
into an immense head with a crown upon it, and which
they called "the Head of Charon." A spacious colon-
nade in the central street had been erected at enormous
cost by Herod the Great, running eastwards towards
Aleppo, where the citizens could assemble for business
or pleasure, and be protected either from rain or heat.
Strange and motley must have been the crowds which
there gathered—Roman soldiers, servants from the prefect's palace, gay and pleasure-seeking Greeks, Israelites
with their keen dark eyes, not arrayed in the poor garb
in which they were often found in other cities, but bearing the evidences of wealth and prosperity, and worshipping the God of their fathers in handsome synagogues. From all this it will be seen that Antioch was
well entitled to the name it bore, "the Queen of the
East:" and it long maintained its name and reputation.[2]

---

[1] Dr Porter.

[2] See also "Footsteps of St Paul," with authorities there quoted.

But this city was invested with a deeper interest than that which gathers around towers and temples, villas and gardens, baths and theatres. Some Hellenists from the Island of Cyprus and the city of Cyrene in Africa,[1] who had been scattered on the death of Stephen, had crossed a year before from their native shores and preached in this mighty mart. It was in the Hebrew synagogues in the first instance that the religion of Jesus was proclaimed. But these Hellenists of the Dispersion ventured to unfold the glad tidings also to the numerous Gentile population. The new faith, comparatively slow in combating the ancestral pride and prejudices of the children of Abraham, told with greater power on the susceptible Greeks—perhaps all the more so, as they listened to the new and strange tale, not from the lips of pronounced Jewish Evangelists or ordained propagandists, who might have had a purpose to serve in their proselytising, but from lay converts of their own blood and kindred; probably men engaged like many among themselves in ordinary commercial business—the battle of life. And more than all, some of these may have even been at one time also like them, the devotees of Apollo, and yet had been willing to renounce the bewitching dreams and fascinations of their mythology for the doctrines and worship of a peasant of Galilee. Nothing short, surely was it, of that Pentecostal baptism of fire, which gave potency to the word of these Cyprus Hellenists, and diverted their voluptuous and demoralised countrymen, votaries of pleasure and vice, from the licentious rites of the Sun-God, to sit at the feet of Jesus of Nazareth.

---

[1] It will be remembered that the Jews from Cyrene are specially mentioned as being present on the day of Pentecost.

The tidings of this remarkable movement in one of the great mercantile centres of the empire, had created naturally alike interest and anxiety among the members of the mother Church in Jerusalem; and desirous of ascertaining the true state of matters, they resolved to delegate one of their own number, on whose prudence and wisdom they could rely, to visit the scene and report on the rumoured revival. Barnabas, "the son of consolation," whose name is already familiar to us, was selected for this delicate mission. His character, "a good man, full of the Holy Ghost and of faith," was guarantee sufficient for its faithful discharge. Being himself a Cyprian and Jewish Hellenist, he was specially calculated to judge of the novelty of the situation without bias or prejudice, while his personal qualities would render him acceptable to all parties. On reaching Antioch he seems to have entertained no doubt as to the reality of the work. His first favourable impressions received growing confirmation. He recognised in all he saw the indubitable tokens of the grace of God: and the pleasing outcome of his mission was not rebuke but encouragement and consolation. "He was glad; and exhorted them all that with purpose of heart they would cleave unto the Lord" (Acts xi. 23). The scenes witnessed now on the banks of the Orontes would take his mind back to the marvels of those days of first Whitsuntide, when he himself had felt the kindlings of a new and nobler life. Even the novel and interesting scene we recently contemplated in the barracks of Cæsarea was dwarfed in impressiveness by these vast accessions from the ranks of Gentile and heathenism.

Barnabas seems soon to have felt the responsibility too onerous of working there alone, and sought the co-

2 K

operation of some one better able than himself to cope
with Jewish prejudices, Greek learning, and false philosophy, and to combat the subtleties of human wisdom
by the wisdom of God. He secured such a fellow-
worker in the great Apostle of the Gentiles. He was
personally acquainted with his friend's exceptional
ability, as well as with his future appointed work among
the Gentiles. Perhaps it was with unfeigned sorrow
that he was aware of Saul's present constrained domi-
cile in his native Cilicia, whither he had retired owing
to attempts made on his life. It was a waste and
neglect of much needed power : and to make all the
more certain of securing his invaluable services and co-
operation, he resolves, long as the journey was, to lay
the urgent case before him by a personal visit. Accordingly we may think of the good Cyprian setting out
from the mountain-girded city—travelling across the
ridge of Amanus by what is known as "the Iron Gate
of Syria," and round the head of the Gulf of Issus, to
the city of Tarsus. "He departed to Tarsus to seek
Saul, and when he had found him, he brought him to
Antioch." His illustrious colleague and he continued
probably for a year their abundant labours. The cause
nearest and dearest to their hearts abundantly prospered.
Jews and Gentiles in vast numbers believed in Jesus as
the Son of God and the Saviour of the world. Indeed
beyond Judea, Antioch soon came to contain numeri-
cally the largest community of the faithful. The once
insignificant sect of believers within its walls gradually
developed itself into a "*Church*," and the name was
there assumed which has survived to this day—"The
disciples were called CHRISTIANS first in Antioch" (Acts
xi. 26). It has been well observed, that as Jerusalem

was the natural head of *Hebrew*, so was Antioch that of *Gentile* Christianity. It was the scene of the first conse-cration of Christian missionaries ; the centre of Church life and Church operations ; the spiritual Pharos of that earliest age. Nor, it is interesting further to note, was that light soon dimmed or extinguished. In the age of Chrysostom we find the Christians numbering one hundred thousand, and supporting no less than three thousand poor, besides relieving many more. It became —along with Rome, Alexandria, Constantinople, and Jerusalem—one of the five patriarchates, for centuries continuing the capital of Christendom, and called by the name of Theopolis ("the City of God.")[1]

But to return from this somewhat lengthened but needful introduction, to the connection of this " Mother City " with the Apostle Peter.

Not many years had passed, we cannot be far wrong in speaking of it as A.D. 49 or 50, when a new subject of alarm and anxiety occurred with reference to the now consolidated Church in Antioch—a momentous dis-cussion arose on a question which threatened to rend the spiritual community in twain, and Peter was one of

[1] It was as Bishop of Antioch that Ignatius was summoned by Trajan to Rome in the year A.D. 115, and thrown to the lions in the Coliseum ; while in the fourth century it was the home of the " golden-mouthed Chrysostom." It may not be out of place to refer also in this note to the present condition of the illustrious city. Dr Porter, who visited it personally, speaks specially of the magnificence of the ruined walls and towers on the dizzy heights of Mount Silpius, carried in some places along the edge of precipices,—" tri-umphs of mural architecture." An old gate where this gigantic wall crosses the Aleppo road still bears the name, not of Peter, but of his distinguished brother, *Bab Bûlus,* "Paul's Gate." Another traveller speaks of the re-mains of a church on the top of Mount Silpius conjointly dedicated to St Peter and St Paul. Antioch still boasts of a Patriarch, though its degraded Christian population only number a few hundreds. "The spirit of Apos-tolical Christianity has long since deserted it. Nothing in fact seems to re-main of the Antioch of olden times, but . . . the name in its Arabic form— Antâkieh."—*Ib.*

those, as we shall presently see, who was in the first instance at least instrumental in healing the threatened
breach.

The question was the old one which appeared to have
been finally settled on the admission of Cornelius to the
Christian brotherhood, but which we then stated was
likely at a future time to imperil the Church's peace
and safety. That time had now arrived. Nor is it
difficult to account for the fact of how a debateable
point which seemed to have been definitely adjusted
should have been afresh raised. The signal revelation
that had been made to Peter at Joppa, followed by the
judicial decision of the elders and brethren at Jerusalem, had, for the time being, allayed the scruples and
smoothed the prejudices of the conservative party among
the Jews : they had tacitly accepted the admission of
Cornelius and his friends within the circle of believers,
ratified as it had been by the united voice of the
Church. Since then, however, converts had been
announced from the most distant and unlikely quarters.
As the result of the first great missionary journey of
Paul and Barnabas, even the mountaineers from the
half civilised regions of Upper Asia were reported to
have embraced the religion of Jesus. The smouldering
fires of Jewish exclusiveness again burst into a flame,
and the old complaints were vehemently renewed that
Ichabod had been written on the cherished Mosaic dispensation. Judaism sought once more loudly to assert
its prerogatives ; the Hebrew converts resented the
thought of an abrogated ritual. They would make
their rites and ceremonies a preliminary to Christianity
—they would conserve their ancient polity by having
every convert to the new doctrines become in the first

instance a Jew. They were willing to accept the new faith as an advanced Judaism ; but they were unwilling to accept it if it were designed to absorb the Jewish element altogether. This would be " a rebellion against all they had been taught to hold inviolably sacred. . . Many of the Pharisees, after the example of St Paul, had believed that Jesus was Christ ; but they had not followed the example of their school-companion in the surrender of Jewish bigotry." [1] We must not, indeed, judge these children of Abraham harshly for such fond adherence to the old observances of their law. Had not the Christ whom they had been brought to acknowledge as their Saviour—Himself a Jew—submitted to the initiatory rite ? Had He not in His opening sermon proclaimed, that He had not come to destroy their law but to fulfil it ? Nay, had not those who had instructed them in the doctrines of the new faith—the Apostles of Christianity—themselves clung lovingly to their ancient Temple, to its hours of prayer, its morning and evening sacrifices? Was it unreasonable, then, that Hebrews who had become Christians, should make an effort to combine both systems, and specially endeavour to make the rite of circumcision obligatory on all Gentile converts ?

Matters were brought to a crisis by some professing Christians—zealots belonging to the sect of the Pharisees, but who had entertained these scruples and prejudices in their extremest form—having gone down clandestinely from Jerusalem to Antioch. They evidently claimed to be representatives of the opinions of the Mother Church, and openly inculcated that Christian baptism would be of no avail, unless accompanied with

---

[1] See Howson and Conybeare *in loc.*

circumcision. "It is very important to observe the
exact form which their teaching assumed. They did
not merely recommend or enjoin, for prudential reasons,
the continuance of certain ceremonies in themselves
indifferent; but they said, "Except ye be circumcised
after the manner of Moses, *ye cannot be saved.*"[1] In
one word, these emissaries, whom Paul does not scruple
to call "false brethren," wished to incorporate Christianity with Judaism, and make the rites and duties of
the latter, ceremonial and moral, "a conjunct cause of
justification." It is well indeed also carefully to note
that it is to *Gentile converts* these strong dissuasives are
addressed. The Apostles, as "Jews by nature," did
not, as we have more than once noted, lay aside the
observances of the old dispensation (see Acts xviii. 18
and xxi. 24). To have done so would have implied that
the law was contrary to Christianity, which it was not.
"Paul himself," to quote the words of Archbishop
Whately "(like the other Apostles), always continued
to observe the Mosaic law, as national customs . . . lest
he should seem to cast any slight on the institutions of
his nation, as in themselves adverse to Christianity;
while, on the very same principle he declared to the
Galatians, that if they embraced the Mosaic law 'Christ
profited them nothing,' since *that* would have implied
their trusting in those observances for salvation under
the Gospel."[2] In matters of mere ritual he was never
unreasonable or intolerant; indeed, on the principle of
doing all things to all men, and not unnecessarily to
wound Jewish prejudices, it will be remembered that he
afterwards, "with a prudential accommodation to circum-

1 " Howson and Conybeare's St Paul," p. 225.
2 Whately's " Lectures on the Apostles," p. 184.

stances, without endangering the faith of the Gospel," performed the rite of circumcision on Timothy. He ever sought to illustrate in practice his own great principle and maxim, " If it be possible, inasmuch as lieth in you, live peaceably with all men." At present, however, he saw with eagle eye the danger that would inevitably result if these false teachings were suffered to go uncontradicted and unopposed. He refused to compromise truth by silent acquiescence, and by any connivance at principles so diametrically opposed to the whole spirit of the religion of Jesus. He tells us " he could not give place by subjection, no, not for an hour." This doctrine of ceremonial justification must be dealt with as with a spirit of evil, and at all hazards be exorcised and cast out; since whatever was thus put upon an equality with the Great Sacrifice of our Lord, would dim the glory of His work, and render His cross of none effect. It would be tantamount to declaring that the One only Foundation of a sinner's hope was insufficient, or at all events that that Foundation would be rendered broader and more secure, by buttressing it with the forms and ceremonies of Judaism. How strongly Paul himself felt, is evidenced by the vehemence of his protestation to the Galatians against these troublers in Israel: " Stand fast therefore in the liberty wherewith Christ hath made us free, and be not entangled again with the yoke of bondage. Behold, I Paul say unto you, that if ye be circumcised, Christ shall profit you nothing. For I testify again to every man that is circumcised, that he is a debtor to do the whole law. Christ is become of no effect unto you, whosoever of you are justified by the law; ye are fallen from grace " (Gal. v. 1–4).

This unfortunate dissension continued to vex and disturb the minds of the Gentile converts in Antioch; and as the violence of party feeling prevented an amicable settlement there, Paul and Barnabas were requested to go up to Jerusalem again to submit the question to the Apostles and brethren; and by obtaining in the stronghold of Jewish nationality an authoritative deliverance, silence the agitators, and restore tranquillity. He had a higher authority in undertaking the journey. God Himself had commissioned him to proceed. He mentions expressly in his Epistle to the Galatians that he went "by revelation." "Besides, it was not a local, but a general question, which might be agitated in any other part of the world; so that it was necessary to obtain a final sentence which should be alike respected in Antioch and in all the cities of the Gentiles."[1]

Paul's two companions were well selected. Barnabas was himself a Jew and a Levite. Titus, his other fellow-traveller, was a young uncircumcised Greek, and therefore a good sample of a heathen convert. They journeyed along the coast-road through Phenicia, thence to Samaria. It would seem they were not travelling among strangers to the Gospel; for we are told, that "as they passed through, declaring the conversion of the Gentiles, they caused great joy to all the brethren."[2]

On reaching Jerusalem, the great Apostle, sensible of the intrigues of his adversaries, determined, before holding a conference in public, to see Peter, James, and John in private. After consulting with these "pillars of the Church," a meeting or synod was convened for a full hearing and decision.[3] "It must have been," says

---

[1] Prof. Dick, *in loco.*   [2] Acts xv. 3.   [3] Gal. ii. 2.

a thoughtful writer, "a most interesting assembly. From different regions were gathered the Apostles and Evangelists, the standard-bearers and leaders of the sacramental host. There were to be seen a number of those venerable men, the chosen attendants of our Lord while He was upon earth, who had now for twenty years, since His ascension, been fighting manfully under His banner. Time must have traced its furrows on their brows, and the burden of constant labour and care must have bent their frames ; but their hearts were as full of fervour, zeal, and love, as when they beheld their risen Saviour on the first memorable Easter. There were many others, who, on their testimony, had believed in a Saviour unseen by the bodily eye. There were laborious missionaries, like Paul and Barnabas, who had travelled many a weary mile to spread abroad the glad tidings of salvation. Men who had never before met face to face, but well known to each other by reputation, and loved as well as known, now first exchanged fraternal greetings. Truly must such a meeting have presented to the observer a most impressive scene, and have proved to those gathered there a most affecting and refreshing season, a lively emblem of the blessed assemblage of all God's dispersed children in His Kingdom of Glory."[1]

There seems to have been at first a keen discussion, "much disputing" on the question. The Pharisees, who believed, strongly held to the views already stated. "They professedly embraced the Gospel, but . . . baptized Pharisaism proved as dangerous and hostile to the Gospel of Jesus, as ever did Jewish Pharisaism to Jesus Himself."[2] Of the speeches which were delivered

[1] Bishop Lee, p. 309. [2] Ib., p. 308.

we have only four mentioned, and these probably no more than outlines—those of Peter, Paul, Barnabas, and James. They all advocated the same ground, and claimed the same deliverance. Peter rose first to address. He was heard with that marked attention, due alike to his own character, and his special connection with the subject under debate. He declared again what had been revealed to him years before by means of the vision at Joppa, that he had been divinely authorised and commanded to preach the gospel to the Gentiles. He reminded his hearers that the Holy Spirit had on that memorable occasion been poured out upon the uncircumcised Cornelius and his household; thereby unequivocally testifying God's acceptance of the believer independent of ceremonial rites, and that any attempt to impose such a burden on the Gentile converts would be in direct opposition to the Divine will and purpose, as then and there made known. It would, in his own words, be "a tempting of God." It were strange, moreover, he adds, if those who now listened to him, Hebrews by birth, professing their entire dependence on Christ and on the all-sufficiency of His atoning Sacrifice, and who rejoiced at their own deliverance from legal bondage, should dream of assenting to the imposition of a ceremonial yoke on the necks of their Gentile brethren. Let his own calm, sententious utterances be given in full : " And when there had been much disputing, Peter rose up, and said unto them, Men and brethren, ye know how that a good while ago God made choice among us, that the Gentiles by my mouth should hear the word of the gospel, and believe. And God, which knoweth the hearts, bare them witness, giving them the Holy Ghost, even as He did unto us ;

and put no difference between us and them, purifying their hearts by faith. Now therefore why tempt ye God, to put a yoke upon the neck of the disciples, which neither our fathers nor we were able to bear. But we believe that through the grace of the Lord Jesus Christ, we shall be saved, even as they" (Acts xv. 7–11).

After a few moments' silence, Paul and Barnabas followed. The concluding speaker was James the Just. Founding on the statement made by Peter (Symeon),[1] he adverted to a passage in the prophecies of Amos, wherein God announces beforehand His purpose of mercy in the formation of a Gentile Church, figuratively there spoken of as " the restoration of the tabernacle of David." He argued that it would be equivalent to an attempt to frustrate the Divine purposes, were the Jewish converts to insist on making conformity on the part of their Gentile brethren to a partial and local ritual, a condition of membership in the new dispensation. His opinion could not fail to carry great weight, not only from his reputed sanctity, but from his Hebrew sympathies. The Judaising party may have entertained strong hopes of support from one they had supposed with some reason to be of their " school of thought." But when his sentiments endorsed those of the preceding speakers, and upheld and vindicated Gentile freedom, they could do nothing but acquiesce. As "Moderator" or President, he pronounced the deliverance : " Wherefore my sentence is, that we trouble not them, which from among the Gentiles are

[1] " It is worth noting how James, in his final speech, speaks of his brother Apostle under the Hebrew form of his name, 'Symeon,' as if to suggest to the Jewish multitude that the great Apostle was truly one of themselves."— *Dr Green, p.* 107.

turned to God. But that we write unto them, that
they abstain from pollutions of idols, and from fornication, and from things strangled, and from blood" (Acts
xv. 19, 20).

We have already, in an earlier chapter, adverted to
the incidental but cogent refutation which is here given
us of the alleged primacy of Peter. We may repeat
the reference. Had he been invested with the precedence, which the Church of Rome claims for him, as
representative of his Lord, the authorised Prince of the
Apostles, his judgment infallible in the settlement of
controversies,—what an opportunity was now presented
for exercising his prerogative, as ecclesiastical umpire
and arbiter ! But it is evident he claims and arrogates
no such distinction. He states his view of the case,
calmly and clearly, as a member of the court, placed on
a parity with Paul and Barnabas ; and the decree
issued was the result of their united deliberation. If
any one member in that sacred conclave seems to
claim priority of official rank, it is rather, as we also
previously noted, the venerable James, who, in a tone
of greater authority, as the mouthpiece of the Assembly,
thus formulates and announces its decision, " My sentence is." It has been well remarked that "if these
few words had fallen from the mouth of Peter, rather
than of James, they would have constituted a far
stronger argument for the former's supremacy than all
besides that is to be found in the New Testament."
But " he did not preside at the meeting ; for he neither
summoned nor dismissed it, he neither collected the
suffrages, nor pronounced the decision."[1] " Had Peter
been Pope," is the quaint remark of Mr Lewin, " the

[1] Bib. Dic., Art. " Peter."

appeal would have been to him personally, and he would have issued his Bull; whereas the appeal was to the Council, and the decree was issued by James."[1]

The glorious truth was then finally and for ever proclaimed, that the Gentiles were released from the yoke of the ceremonial law ; that henceforth there was to be neither " Jew nor Greek, circumcision nor uncircumcision, barbarian, Scythian, bond nor free, but Christ was all and in all."

A letter was drawn up in the name of the Assembly, to be conveyed by the hands of confidential messengers to the Gentile brethren at Antioch. It is short, but of much interest ; being the first missive of the kind we possess as given forth by a Church Court. " This remarkable and interesting document seems to bear the mark of James' own hand in the form of salutation— ' greeting ' (Acts xv. 23), which occurs nowhere else but here, and in the salutation of his own Epistle (James i. 1)." [2] We may picture a crowded gathering in the great Syrian city, where the following communication was read amid breathless silence : " The Apostles and Presbyters, brethren,[3] send greeting unto the brethren which are of the Gentiles in Antioch and Syria and Cilicia : forasmuch as we have heard that certain which went out from us have troubled you with words, subverting your souls, saying, Ye must be circumcised, and keep the law ; to whom we gave no such commandment : it seemed good unto us, being assembled

---

[1] *Lewin's Life of St Paul, vol. i. p.* 159. [2] Kitto, 236.

[3] So in the most approved MSS., probably indicating the unanimity of the decision. " How needful it was thus to assert the perfect accord of the elder Apostles with Paul and Barnabas, appears only too plainly from the Epistles of St Paul, in which he is ever alluding to the wicked attempts of the Judaisers to represent them as heads of opposite factions."—*Canon Norris, p.* 74.

with one accord, to send chosen men unto you with our
beloved Barnabas and Paul. Men that have hazarded
their lives for the name of our Lord Jesus Christ. We
have sent therefore Judas and Silas, who shall also tell
you the same things by mouth. For it seemed good to
the Holy Ghost, and to us, to lay upon you no greater
burden than these necessary things : That ye abstain
from meats offered unto idols, and from blood, and from
things strangled, and from fornication ; from which if
ye keep yourselves, ye shall do well. Fare ye well "
(Acts xv. 23–29).

Judas and Silas still further explained the scope and
contents of the letter by word of mouth. The result
was a happy one. The storm was immediately changed
into a calm. The Gentile Christians would hail with
satisfaction, and the Jewish converts would gladly
acquiesce in, what came with the stamp of unquestionable authority. Agitated minds were soothed, and the
danger of future disturbance averted.

Not long subsequent to this, however, an occurrence
took place at Antioch, which has a peculiar and painful connection with our Apostle. It forms the last
exceptionable incident in his life.[1] Ever since the

[1] Both Neander and Lange suppose the meeting to have taken place some
years later, and Wieseler at great length supports the view, that it must
have occurred after Paul's second missionary journey. But though we have
nothing definitely to fix the time, by far the preponderance of reliable
authorities are in favour of its immediate sequence to the events just
described. Dr Howson, in supporting the latter hypothesis, remarks in a
note : " From the order of narration in the Epistle to the Galatians, it is
most natural to infer that the meeting at Antioch took place soon after the
Council at Jerusalem. Some writers wish to make it anterior to the Council,
from an unwillingness to believe that Peter would have acted thus after the
decree. But it is a sufficient answer to this objection to say, that his conduct
was equally inconsistent with his own previous conduct in the case of
Cornelius."

Lord's Ascension, a period of seventeen or eighteen years, his path which we have been endeavouring to trace has been that of the just, " as the shining light," "shining more and more." One transient cloud dims the lustre of the sky. Unmistakable symptoms of the old pusillanimity betray themselves. He had now come to Antioch, to prosecute from thence a missionary journey in Asia Minor, entertaining no design save to strengthen the hands of his fellow-workmen, Paul and Barnabas, and to see that the decree of the Council of Jerusalem, which he had so vigorously supported, was carried into full effect. In accordance with that public and manly declaration, he was in the habit of mingling freely and without scruple with the Gentile converts in the Syrian capital, partaking of their meals, and sharing with them their " Agape," or love feasts ; owning them in every way indeed as " one in Christ Jesus." But, ere long, some of the Judaisers, inspired by the lingering jealousies of their party, came down from Jerusalem, evidently to ascertain for themselves the precise relation which existed socially between the Gentile and the Hebrew converts. They expressed their displeasure at finding the Apostle holding with the former unrestrained intercourse, and, by sitting with them at the same tables, contracting ceremonial uncleanness. Peter began to waver ; his manner was suddenly changed towards the Gentile believers ; and though we have no ground to infer that he carried matters so far as entirely to cease holding communion with them, all social fellowship was at least suspended. The wall of separation was once more raised.

He performed in this a double part. It was the same lamentable weakness which we found led him, at one of the great crises of his former history, to quail in the presence of the portress in the High Priest's hall, and after the loudest protestation of his fidelity, three times to deny his Lord and Master.   It was an unworthy repudiating of what he had done so much by word and personal influence to settle at the Jerusalem Council, " contradicting his own principles, and giving the sanction of his example to the introduction of *caste* into the Church of Christ."[1]   The perils likely to result from his conduct were manifest.   The fear and threat of forfeiting such social fellowship would inevitably have tended to Judaise the Gentile converts.   It would have induced many of them at least to submit to circumcision, in order thereby to avoid exclusion from the intimate society of the Apostles of the Church.

Paul was roused to a holy indignation against his erring brother, thus seduced into abandonment of his own avowed principles, and to an unwarrantable and indefensible compliance with the prejudices of the weak.   He " withstood him to the face, because he was to be blamed."[2]   His conduct, indeed, had already produced much mischief, as even Barnabas, who had gone as his colleague to Jerusalem for the settlement of this very question, was carried away with his dissimulation;[3] and as Dr Lightfoot well remarks, " This incident, by producing a temporary feeling of distrust, may have prepared the way for the dissension between Paul and Barnabas, which shortly afterwards led to their separa-

---

[1] Howson and Conybeare, p. 239, vol. i. p. 212.

[2] "' Because he was self-condemned,' would perhaps be the more exact rendering : that is, he was acting in contradiction to his own avowed principles, and exhibiting a complete inconsistency." — *Archbishop Whately*, p. 186.

[3] Gal. ii. 13.

tion." We cannot wonder, however, that Paul was obliged to do, what must have cost him a painful effort, " to rebuke Peter before all." These were the words which doubtless with a heavy heart he uttered; I give them as paraphrased by one of the ablest of his biographers:—" If thou, who art a *Jew*, didst before, as it were, go over to the *Gentiles* by living with them, why now, by a contrary example, dost thou countenance the doctrine of these Judaisers, that the *Gentiles* should come over to the *Jews?*"[1] " The reproof of Peter," continues the same writer, " in the face of the Antiochian Church, is one of the most remarkable incidents in the New Testament. Both Paul and he were inspired; and yet one of them was in the wrong. But the question at issue, it will be observed, was one not of *doctrine* but of *conduct*. Both were agreed as to the article of faith, viz., that henceforth the Jew was not bound by the law of Moses; but what called the vehement spirit of Paul into action, was the duplicity of Peter, in at one time associating with the Gentiles, and at another avoiding the contamination of their company."

All thanks to the heroic fidelity displayed by the great Apostle on this occasion. But for his prompt intervention, there is no predicting what would have been the result, had this refluent wave of Judaism and Hebrew exclusiveness again swept through the recently erected barriers. He may well have had transferred to him the title which his unstable brother had, for the time being at all events, forfeited,—as the true " Rockman " who broke the force of that threatening wave and averted the disaster of a lamentable schism. But for his brave policy of " no surrender " (not in all cir-

[1] Lewin's " Life and Letters of St Paul," vol. i. p. 339.

cumstances the wise one, but certainly so in the present case), there might have been a formidable disruption among the Faithful, dividing them into rival organisations of Jew and Gentile. He saved the Church from being narrowed into an insignificant sect. The victory he achieved vindicated its God-given destiny and comprehension as the Spiritual Temple of the whole human race.[1]

We believe that, sharp as the rebuke was, it was given and received in love. Nor can we fail to note the beautiful lesson of humility the conduct of our Apostle conveys. One in his dignified position might have resented the wrong sought to be inflicted. So long the acknowledged leader of the Apostolic band, he might have felt stung to the quick by the interference of a younger brother, who, moreover, was not satisfied with a private remonstrance, but must needs sist his senior before a public tribunal. But Peter gives no acrimonious retort as he once might, as he once *would have* done. He modestly submits, without even an attempt to extenuate his fault or to justify himself. He manifests no false shame in owning and confessing his inconsistency. He felt that "faithful were the rebukes of a friend." "His mind was easily susceptible of quick and sudden changes; his disposition was loving and generous, and we should expect his contrition, as well as his weakness, at Antioch, to be what it was in the High Priest's house at Jerusalem."[2]   At all events,

---

[1] At a later period, indeed (in the course of the second century), these old Jewish prejudices once more strove to reassert their claims. The Church had, however, by this time, become too strong to be imperilled by the schismatics, who, under the name of Ebionites, separated themselves on this very question from their brethren.

[2] Howson.

he died twenty years after, loving his rebuker, and speaking of him to all the churches, as a "beloved brother;"[1] while Paul amply reciprocates, more than once, by an honourable reference to Cephas. We should have been sorry to have been without this short clause in the end of one of Peter's letters :—"*Our beloved brother Paul.*" We might have been apt otherwise to fear that the reprimand had created a misunderstanding and estrangement, which they had carried to the grave. No such thing. Grace brought about what nature might not have done. Nor is it the least beautiful attestation to Peter's complete forgiveness, his penitence, his humility, his noble-hearted, magnanimous unselfishness, that he could thus in one of his own letters direct public attention to "all the Epistles" of his brother Apostle, when, as it has been remarked, one of these very writings contained the circumstantial account of the rebuke which had been administered to him by their author. "It is pleasing to trace the traditionary confirmations of their entire unity—the unity which joins St Peter to St Paul, rather than to his own early friend St John, the legends which represent them as joint rulers of Antioch,[2] Corinth, and Rome, . . . and in all the early works of Christian art, both ever exhibited side by side, the one with his inverted cross, the other with the executioner's sword."[3] These vague traditions are sufficient at least to show what the impression of the early age of the Church was, as to the sacred harmony existing between these two truly great

---

[1] 2 Peter iii. 15, 16.

[2] An utterly unsupported tradition, in contradiction to others already referred to, represents Peter as being Bishop of Antioch for seven years before he was elevated to the See of Rome.

[3] Stanley's "Sermons on the Apostolic Age," p. 101.

men ; that they died faithful to their Blessed Master's last bequest, " This is My commandment, that ye love one another."

We close this chapter with the happy thought in regard to the one with whom we are most concerned, that the transient moral cowardice displayed at Antioch in carrying out his professed convictions, forms the last recorded blemish in a noble life. The God he served seemed to have signally answered the prayer which has grown familiar to worshipping millions : " Strengthen such as do stand : comfort and help the weak-hearted : raise up them that fall, and finally beat down Satan under our feet."

CHAPTER XXIII.

***

𝕱𝖎𝖓𝖆𝖑 𝕾𝖕𝖍𝖊𝖗𝖊 𝖔𝖋 𝕷𝖆𝖇𝖔𝖚𝖗.

PETER'S OUTWARD APPEARANCE. HIS VAST SPHERE AS THE
APOSTLE OF THE CIRCUMCISION. ASSOCIATED WITH JOHN.
ASIA MINOR. BABYLONIA. EXTENT OF THE DISPERSION.
SCENE OF PETER'S FINAL LABOURS. EVIDENCES OF HIS SUC-
CESS. "THE CHURCH THAT IS AT BABYLON.'

> " The clarion calls ; away ! to take
> Thy station in God's hosts.
> And with His mitred watchmen wake ;
> And in meek silence, for His sake,
> Endure what scornful music earth can make
> When holy ground seems lost."
> —*Keble's Miscellaneous Poems.*

"Hitherto in drawing up the life of this great Apostle, we
have had an infallible guide to conduct and lead us ; but the
sacred Story breaking off here, forces us to look abroad, and to
pick up what memoirs the ancients have left us in this matter."
—*Dr Cave, p.* 136.

"It is remarkable that Galilee is the scene of none of those
transactions which are related in the Acts. The blue waters of
Tiberias, with their fishing-boats, and towns on the brink of the
shore, are consecrated to the Gospels. . . . When we come to the
travels of the Apostles, the scenery is no longer limited and
Jewish, but Catholic and widely extended, like the gospel which
they preached."—*Howson and Congbeare's St Paul.*

"There remaineth yet very much land to be possessed " (Joshua
xiii. 1).

HIS may not be an unbefitting place to endeavour to give the reader, from a few scattered notices which have come down to us from the Apostolic era, an impression of the outward appearance of Peter, now that he was approaching the confines of old age.

Nicephorus, to whose account of him we have already incidentally referred, probably speaks of his early life, when he describes him as " slender in person, inclining to tallness, and of pallid complexion." St Jerome, on the other hand, quoting from the " Periodoi " of Clemens, apparently refers to a more advanced period —when the head, once covered with " black and crisp hair," had become bald. Baronius notes that with a dark Jewish eye, he had a redness in the eyelids, which, by a freak of imagination, he alleges to have arisen from the frequent tears the Apostle-penitent was known to shed, caused by the torturing memory of his fall and denial ; while the broad nose and distended nostril were the indication of that strength and vigour of character which enabled him to rise superior to his weaknesses. We may farther be permitted to add to these brief notices, which I need not say have little more than a legendary value, the remarks of one to whose Art volume we have been indebted more than once in the preceding pages :—" The ancient Greek type of the head of St Peter is so strongly characterised as to have the air of a portrait. . . . He is a robust old man, with a broad forehead, and rather coarse features; an open undaunted countenance, short grey hair, and short thick beard, curled, and of a silvery white. . . . In some early pictures, he is bald on the top of the head, and the hair grows thick around in a circle, somewhat like the priestly tonsure. . . . It is a tradition that the Gentiles shaved the head of St Peter, in order to make him an object of derision, and that this is the origin of the tonsure. . . . On the early sarcophagi, and in the most ancient church mosaics, he bears a scroll or book. . . . A little later, we find him with the cross in one hand and the Gospel in the other." The same writer adds, what is worthy of note, that " the keys in his hand, appear as his peculiar attribute about the eighth century (not earlier). . . . In general he carries two keys, one of gold and one of silver, to absolve and to bind."[1]

We enter from this date on a new and interesting portion of the Apostle's life.

[1] "Sacred and Legendary Art," pp. 187, 188.

It is true we have no longer inspired data for our guidance; but there are sufficient hints in his own Epistles and in those of Paul, along with corroborative statements of contemporary writers, coupled with the vaguer and less reliable source of ecclesiastical tradition, to enable us to form a tolerably coherent narrative.

He was probably about the age of sixty-one, in the full maturity of his powers, when called to make other, perhaps we may even be warranted to say, more wondrous use of the symbolic "keys." On the occasion of the same meeting of the Council of Jerusalem, at which the decree was issued as to the parity of Jew and Gentile in respect of Christian privilege, another decision and arrangement was made of vast moment for the extension of Christ's kingdom at that era, as well as for the Church of the future.[1] Under the distinct guidance and direction of the Holy Ghost, a partition of work in the evangelisation of the human race was then and there resolved upon between the Apostolic leaders. To Paul was committed " the heathen "—the vast Gentile world, with Rome as its acknowledged centre. His Lord's words at the hour of his conversion were to receive their amplest fulfilment: " Depart; for I will send thee far hence unto the Gentiles ;" while Peter was commissioned to go to " the Circumcision." His appropriated sphere was " the lost sheep of the house of

[1] There is a legend regarding Peter at this time, whose beauty redeems it from the puerility which characterises the majority of these. It is to the following effect:—That the Apostles, before finally separating, resolved to construct a creed for behoof of the Church universal, to be called, as it still is, "The Apostolic Creed;" and they agreed that each of them would contribute a sentence or article. To Peter was intrusted the opening one. He gave the grand foundation truth so familiar to the bygone centuries of Christendom : " *Credo in Deum Patrem omnipotentem, Creatorem cœli et terræ.*"

Israel." That phrase was not by any means restricted to his brethren in Palestine. Hitherto his work lay exclusively there. For twenty years he had remained in his native country as a faithful Evangelist; but from this time these labours were to take a wider sweep, and include all the bordering lands where thousands on thousands of Israelites were to be found—specially the towns and cities of Asia Minor and the countries watered by the Tigris and Euphrates. It is well for us to note this distinct transition-page in his history. In former years, from the time in which as a boy he mended his father's nets on the shores of Gennesaret, we have followed his footsteps in Capernaum, Jerusalem, Samaria, Lydda, Joppa, Cæsarea. In none of these from this date are his footsteps to be traced. He is a voluntary exile for ever from the favoured territory which he doubtless loved so well. In neither case, indeed, were these two illustrious men debarred from scattering the precious seed wherever it was likely to take root. Hence we find Paul making his first missionary tours, and distributing the bread of life among the countries of Syria and Asia Minor, Cilicia, and Pamphylia, and the half-heathen tribes of Pisidia and Lycaonia, previous to his spreading the greater Gentile feast in Western Europe. He remained for a considerable time detained by illness in Galatia, and continued to have a very special interest in the church which he had founded there. We know the length and value of his labours at Ephesus in after years. Moreover, wherever he went, it was "to the Jew first." This is specially mentioned in each entry of his journeyings in the Acts of the Apostles. At Berea, at Antioch of Pisidia, at Iconium, at Salamis, at Corinth, at

Ephesus, he and his fellow-travellers invariably first opened their lips in the sanctuaries of their Hebrew countrymen. On the other hand, Peter, though thus the appointed Apostle of the Circumcision, we have seen was honoured to be the first to open the kingdom of heaven to the Gentiles, and to vindicate their freedom from the observances of the Mosaic law. In his Epistles he addresses Gentiles as well as Jews on the obligations of their common faith—those who were "once not a people, but are now the people of God" (ii. 10); and who were formerly involved in the practice of "abominable idolatries" (iv. 3). We have strong reason also to conjecture that he was associated with Paul and Apollos for some time at Corinth. His name occurs several times in the First Epistle to the Corinthians as the head or reputed leader of one of the religious parties; "I am of Paul, and I of Apollos, and I of *Cephas;*"— engaged, with the two former, in a common work among its mixed population of Jew and Greek. We are led also distinctly to infer such a temporary residence, from the epistle which Clement of Rome sent to the Corinthian Church; and his assertion is further confirmed by Dionysius, Bishop of Corinth, A.D. 180: "a man of excellent judgment, who was not likely to be misinformed nor to make such an assertion lightly, in an epistle addressed to the Bishop and Church of Rome."[1]   It is interesting thus to think of the Fisherman of Bethsaida coming in contact with another of the vast Pagan centres of mercantile and intellectual life in Europe, as he had already done in Asia;—the

---

[1] Bib. Dic., Art. "Peter." His words are: "Thus likewise you have mingled the flourishing seed that had been planted by Peter and Paul at Rome and Corinth. For both of these having planted us at Corinth, likewise instructed us."

city which at that day, in the words of Dean Milman, "was the emporium of the eastern and western divisions of the Roman Empire, the Venice of the old world, in whose streets the continued stream of commerce, either flowing from or towards the great capital of the world, out of all the eastern territories, met and crossed." Peter would here be brought too into conflict with darker phases of life to which in Palestine he had been comparatively a stranger. For even in that polluted age, when the demoralising influence of Greek and Roman vice and luxury was universally felt, the citizens of Corinth obtained the reputation of a bad preeminence.

It will be remembered, at the same time, how Paul was suddenly arrested in his missionary labours in the populous Asiatic provinces of which we have spoken. He was "forbidden of the Holy Ghost to preach the Word in Asia." He "assayed to go into Bithynia, but the Spirit suffered him not ;" while a voice, that could not be mistaken, came from the shores of Greece, reminding him that his appointed field was the Great West—not Asia but Europe. Obedient to the heavenly vision, he at once quitted Troas, and began his labours in Greece. It was a similar divine monition, doubtless, which farther dictated the resolve, "I must see Rome also ;" and which in a subsequent year led him to the extremest bounds of the West by a journey into Spain. And why, may we ask, did the Divine Monitor thus interpose to divert his labours from Oriental lands? Other reasons in the all-wise providence of God there may have been ; but we have no hesitation in saying, that that diversion was mainly intended emphatically to point to the allotted sphere of Peter's ministry, as well as to indicate Paul's own peculiar mission to Europe. The latter was to storm the great capitals of Pagan civilisation—Rome, Athens, Corinth, Philippi. Peter and John were to devote the main energies of their future lives to the "DIASPORA" (the Dispersion) ;[1] in other words, to the Jewish brethren scattered among the cities and provinces of Syria, Asia Minor, Mesopotamia, Babylonia, and Egypt. To quote again the language of the modern historian of the Jews in confirmation of this view : "In no part of the authentic Scripture, occurs the slightest allusion to the personal history of St Peter as connected with the Western Churches. At all events, the conversion of the Gentile world was the acknowledged province of St Paul. In that partition-treaty in which these two moral invaders divided the yet unconquered world, the more civilised province of Greek and Roman heathenism was assigned to him who was emphatically called the Apostle of the Gentiles ; while the Jewish population fell under the particular care of the Galilean Peter."

Independent altogether of the claims of the "Children of God scattered abroad," one very sufficient obstacle prevented the Apostles of the Circumcision tarrying longer in Palestine, and making Jerusalem their headquarters. A horde of bloodthirsty fanatics, instigated by the priesthood, had spread consternation through the entire country, although mustering in chief force under the shadow of the Jewish Temple. By the robbery and murder of the Christian sect, they imagined, as one better known had done not long before, that they were

[1] That word, erroneously rendered "scattered abroad" in our authorised version, is only found once in the Gospels (John vii. 35), when the Jews said among themselves of Jesus, "Whither will He go? Will He go unto the *diaspora* among the Greeks" (*marg*).

doing God service. Not a few had already fallen victims to the daggers of these *Sicarii* as they were called. If the life even of the Jewish High Priest was taken by them while performing his most sacred duties at the altar of Jehovah, what security would there be for the safety of the Christian ringleaders? Accordingly, it was alike obeying the dictates of a wise prudence, as well as the express command of their Great Master to His servants, to evade the sword of persecution in one city and country by fleeing to another. James alone remained in Jerusalem to brave the storm. As the head of the Church there, he accepted the post of great and increasing danger, animated doubtless by a heroic sense of duty. The other two Apostles, hitherto so closely associated with him, took their journey north and east of Palestine. It is pleasant to think of Peter as again joined in sacred fellowship and labour with his earliest friend John. We have already traced them together as playmates on the beach at Gennesaret; together in the earliest developments of a new and higher life at the Jordan; together in the most momentous incidents of the Master's ministry from which the others were excluded; together on the Mount of glory; together in the Garden of suffering; together in the awful interval of suspense; together at the Tomb; together at the two final meetings at Tiberias and Olivet; together at Pentecost and its subsequent miracles. And now, at another great crisis in their history which was to apportion and determine the work of future years, how appropriate that the two faithful brothers should blend yet once more their counsels and prayers, and share the perils and rewards of the new gigantic mission-enterprise.

In the first remarkable sermon at Pentecost which Peter preached, we may recall, that among the multitudes gathered at the Feast and who were numbered among his auditory, are specially mentioned " Parthians, and Medes, and Elamites, and dwellers in Mesopotamia . . . Cappadocia, in Pontus, and Asia, Phrygia, and Pamphylia." It is surely interesting to think that we have the strongest grounds (amounting indeed to certainty) for supposing that the Apostle's final sphere of labour lay among these very peoples ; that among the Paschal Pilgrims, to whom in A.D. 33 he addressed his stirring words, he spent from fifteen to seventeen of his latter years, journeying during the earlier and longer portion of that time from place to place along with his wife, who would seem to have accompanied him in his mission tours ; that to these same " strangers of the Dispersion " in Asia Minor, as we shall come more particularly to observe, he wrote his two Epistles. And we may here so far anticipate by remarking, that it is impossible to read these two inspired letters without feeling that the writer must have been personally conversant with his correspondents. The mere fact of such communications, indeed, does not necessarily imply that he had enjoyed previous intercourse and fellowship with them ; for more than one of Paul's noblest Epistles (such as the Romans), were written to those with whom he had never come in contact. But in perusing Peter's words, with their affectionate and tender messages of paternal counsel and consolation, it is obvious that he writes to those who had " seen his face in the flesh," and in whom he felt a sacred personal interest and responsibility. His references in his First Epistle imply that he was well acquainted with their "manifold temptations" (i. 6) ; that he had a thorough appreciation of their fervent strivings in the midst of their "suffering for righteousness" (iii. 14), and a knowledge of the shameful excesses of the Gentile population among whom their lot was cast (iv. 3, 4). This personal connection is perhaps more apparent still in his Second Epistle—where, as we shall find, he speaks of intimate knowledge of their condition, stating that he writes the letter not as embodying new information or new truths, but to "stir them up by putting them in remembrance;" so that after he was gone, they might have his writings as a *souvenir* of oral instructions (i. 12, 13 ; iii. 1, 2).

He probably entered at first, on quitting the shores of Palestine, on St Paul's labours in Galatia ; and when we read afterwards the impressive Epistles sent by the Exile of Patmos to the Seven Churches of Asia, may we not warrantably entertain the thought, that these communities of the Faithful had in many cases been planted, in all cases watered, by Peter ? In the partition of labour to which we have alluded, John probably had assigned to himself the spiritual oversight of the cities and provinces occupying the west of Asia Minor, making Ephesus his principal place of residence. Peter's dutiful son, Mark, had, if we may follow a very probable tradition, the charge given him of the Dispersion in Egypt, fixing his abode in populous Alexandria. Jewish settlements had been established there by Alexander and Ptolemy I., and members of the Hebrew race were scattered all through North Africa extending to distant Abyssinia inland,[1] while still one other "companion in labour," Jude (Thaddeus), seems

[1] Art. "Peter," Bib. Dic.

to have had assigned to him the region of Mesopotamia, with Edessa for its capital.

While all these countries and districts appear to have enjoyed the Evangelistic labours of Peter, there is a brief statement made at the end of his First Epistle which seems to point to one particular place as forming, in latter years at all events, his headquarters, or if we may so call it, the seat of his Episcopate : "The Church that is at BABYLON, elected together with you, saluteth you" (1 Pet. v. 13). We are led to suppose that when exceeding the allotted threescore and ten — the infirmities of advancing age no longer permitting the untiring energies and activities of former years, he delegated the missionary work in the more distant provinces to his juniors, making Babylonia the principal sphere of his ministrations, and Babylon his principal dwelling-place.

It may be something new and startling to many readers the thought of the Apostle—whose name and labours we are in the habit of associating with Galilee, Judea, and Samaria—thus spending the ripest fifteen years of his life in countries, some of which we scarcely hear of in Sacred Story ; and, above all, making the place of his final abode the old decaying capital of the Euphrates, whose latest connection with Scripture narrative is with the Jewish captives seated by its willowed streams and weaving their mournful elegy over Jerusalem and Zion. Indeed some may be apt incredulously to say, "Can it really be so?" What could induce Peter to fix his abode in these far-off lands, where we can hardly imagine the harvest he sought to have been plenteous? If Palestine itself, as we have seen, had become a perilous mission field, would not, at all events, the districts contiguous to it be a more appropriate and fruitful sphere for the designated " Apostle of the Circumcision ?"

When we come, however, to examine the question in the light of contemporary history, our impressions are rectified, and we shall find that it is no such strange or incredulous tale as may at first be supposed. If not to us, at all events to Peter's contemporaries, the idea associated with the term " Dispersion" was not a limited but a vast one. So far from its being descriptive of a mere handful of Jews who had strayed beyond their native land, and settled down in groups in the thinly-peopled districts of Asia, the truth was, that the Hebrew population in the countries bordering on Palestine, including Egypt and the islands of the Mediterranean, was something enormous—in some cities and provinces even outnumbering the native races. " Jerusalem," says Agrippa in a letter to the Emperor Caligula, " is indeed my country, but it is the metropolis not of one region but of many,—of Egypt, Phœnicia, Syria, Pamphylia, Cilicia, and the chief parts of Asia as far as Bithynia and the most remote shores of the Euxine." In Alexandria, as the capital city, and including the country south of it stretching to Ethiopia—of which we have just spoken—there were, according to Philo, about a million of Jews.[1] " The persecutions of Antiochus Epiphanes," says Canon Westcott, " only served to push forward the Jewish emigration to the remote districts of his empire. In Armenia the Jews arrived at the greatest dignities, and Nisibus became a new centre of colonisation. The Jews of Cappadocia (1 Pet. i. 1) are

[1] See Norris' Key, p. 133.

casually mentioned in the Mishna, and a prince and princess Adiâbene adopted the Jewish faith only thirty years before the destruction of the Temple. Large settlements of Jews were established in Cyprus, in the islands of the Ægean, and on the western coast of Asia Minor (Ephesus, Miletus, Pergamos, Halicarnassus, Sardis). The Romans confirmed to them the privileges which they had obtained from the Syrian kings, and though they were exposed to sudden outbursts of popular violence, the Jews of the Syrian provinces gradually formed a close connection with their new homes, and, together with the Greek language, adopted in many respects Greek ideas;" [1] and although it scarcely concerns us in this place to trace the ramifications of this "*diaspora*" further, we may only observe, that in Rome itself, the Transtiberine quarter, allocated by Pompey to the Jewish settlers, had enormously increased in the reign of Augustus: so much so, as to lead Horace in one of his Satires playfully to dread lest the population of the city be outnumbered by the alien race (Sat. i. 70). It has been noted that in no city of Greece or Asia Minor, Athens alone excepted, did Paul not find either a synagogue or proseucha. [2]

As to Babylonia, we know that at the return from the exile in the time of Ezra, very many Israelites who had it in their power to retrace their steps from the land of captivity, preferred remaining and settling in the country of their adoption. Much as they treasured the memories of their youth, and proud as they were of their nationality, yet that beautiful poetical figure of a contemporary Psalmist, to which we have already referred,

---

[1] Bib. Dic., Art. "Dispersion," p. 441.
[2] "Sermons on the Apostolic Age," p. 204.

was true only of a portion, and that too the minority, whom he described as "hanging their harps on the willows of the Euphrates," as they longed for the banks of the Kedron, the groves of Olivet, and the altars of Zion. Of the twenty-four courses of priests, only four followed their head into Palestine. To quote the language of a modern writer : "The rich, the learned, the high-born among them, declined to go back into the bleak mountain-wastes of Judah ; and even the masons and dyers, the weavers and tinkers, whom Cyrus had sent away to rebuild Jerusalem, sighed over the country they were leaving as a Paradise on earth ; a land of plenty, a land of great rivers and a bounteous soil, a land of pleasure, in which the seasons came and went with an indolent beauty unknown among their own barren ravines and rugged bluffs."[1] "The successive deportations," says Dr Kitto, " of the people of Judea by the Chaldeans, comprised the princes, the nobles, the priests, the warriors, the skilled artisans, leaving nothing but the unskilled labourers, ' the poor of the land, to be husbandmen and vine-dressers.' In the lands to which they were taken, they were not slaves or captives, but free colonists,—free to follow their several pursuits, and to enrich themselves by their exertions. . . . . . Of all people that ever lived, the Jews were adapted to thrive under such circumstances. If they have thriven in modern times, in all the countries of their dispersion, in spite of the dislike and abhorrence with which they have been regarded by those among whom they dwelt, how much more must they have thriven among a people who had no strong hatred against them, and under a government which had a due sense of their value as

[1] " The Holy Land," p. 48.

useful citizens and servants of the State, and which, therefore, sought rather to encourage than to depress them ! No doubt, there were exceptions. We know historically of some. But that, upon the whole, the Jews did not eventually find themselves in an evil case, is shown by the fact of their general backwardness to return to their own land, when the decree of Cyrus left them free to do so ; and by the acknowledged fact, that as it was the flower of the nation which had been taken into exile, so it was the flower of the nation which chose to remain in the land to which it had been exiled." [1] The words of Josephus writing of the apostolic era are, " There were tens of thousands of the people that had been carried captive and dwelt about Babylonia." Generally credited to indulge in exaggeration, the old Jewish historian would seem in the present case to have fallen beneath the reality—the estimated amount of Israelites in this large province being upwards of two millions. To other inducements for these numerous Jewish settlers may be added the famous seats of Hebrew learning, Neharda and Susa, which attracted many aspirants after Rabbinical lore and intellectual culture.

Regarding Babylon itself, although its citizens had recently suffered severe persecution under the reign of Caligula, yet (Jerusalem excepted) it contained within its gates the largest Hebrew population in the cities of that era. They continued there as they do at this hour in Frankfort and the Ghetto of Rome, a separate com-

---

[1] Dr Kitto's Daily Readings *in loc.* Other authorities to the same effect might be quoted. " Under the Parthian kings," says Dean Milman, " they lived in peace, unmolested in their religion, sometimes making proselytes of the highest rank—in the case of Izates, even of kings ; and they were oppressed by no exclusive taxation. The Jews of Africa and Syria might have looked with repining envy on their more prosperous brethren in Babylonia."—*History of the Jews, vol. ii. p.* 422.

munity, refusing to commingle with the Gentile inhabitants. Philo estimates their number at two hundred and fifty thousand ; and as fortifying the correctness of his statement it may be added, that as every faithful Jew living in foreign lands contributed annually his half-shekel for the expenses of the Temple at Jerusalem, Josephus speaks of the very escort which accompanied the yearly tribute from the capital, alone as consisting of several thousands. The former indeed of these historians (also a contemporary of the Apostles) farther mentions, that such was the preponderance of Jews in the province, that when the Emperor Caligula demanded that one-half of his troops stationed in Babylonia should march to Palestine, in order to enforce his insulting decree as to having his statue placed in the Temple, Petronius, the proconsul of Syria, used his influence to retain them, fearing a successful rising of the Jewish inhabitants,—adding, that had they obeyed his mandate during the war, so formidable were their numbers that they might have driven out the invaders.

As may be gathered from what we have described, the multitudes in this vast " diaspora," notwithstanding the lapse of successive generations, never forgot in these lands of their adoption their nationality, or merged their religion in that of the Pagan kingdoms where they dwelt. The loyalty and allegiance of the modern "colonists" to the "mother country" is as nothing compared to the devotion with which these foreign Israelites regarded the name of Zion, and the rites and solemnities performed within her gates. The authority of the Sanhedrim was faithfully acknowledged, respected, obeyed. Their " ecclesiastical calendar was fixed at Jerusalem." Great as was the distance between the latter and Babylon, the new moons were regularly signalled by the only "telegraph" then known. A beacon-fire first lighted on Mount Olivet—was repeated on Bethaccerem—and onwards thence, on every available mountain-top in Moab and the Hauran, till it reached its destination in the far East. As the most indubitable proof of the strength of the link which bound every absent child of Abraham to the City of the Great King, we are informed in the Talmud that each of these distant provinces and cities maintained at their own expense a separate synagogue at Jerusalem, in which their representative pilgrims were enabled annually to worship when attending the great festive celebrations :—this, independent of the half-shekel contribution already alluded to for maintaining the services of the Temple. The Babylonish Jews indeed would seem to have been Hebrews of the Hebrews. Peter nowhere else out of Palestine could have cherished so much of a home feeling. It was a proverbial saying, " Whoever dwells in Babylon is as though he dwelt in the land of Israel." " Their language, probably a mixture of Hebrew and Nabatean, must have borne a near affinity to the Galilean dialect." [1] In a word, with the one exception of the sacred territory which was virtually closed against him, he would be as truly doing duty among his own nation in these diverse cities and provinces of the old plain of Shinar, as if he were still under the shadow of Gerizim or Zion.

As we have endeavoured in an early chapter of this volume to picture the surroundings of Peter's boyhood and youth on the shores of the Galilean Lake, it may not be without interest to bring before us the scene of his last

[1] Bib. Dic.

years;—we may hope years of comparative calm, after a
manhood of struggle and toil. Babylon,[1] however shorn
of its pristine splendour, occupied the same vast area
of two hundred square miles, fifty-six in circumference.
Adhering to its original construction, it was not, like
other cities, formed of contiguous houses, but rather an
assemblage of Parks or " Paradises "—more resembling
our modern villas :—so that the dwellings really occupied only a twentieth part of the ground included
within the walls. We can think of our Apostle surrounded in that vast plain with very much the same
wealth of vegetation as that on which his eye fell in
the " Land of Gennesaret " and around " the spring of
the fig-tree ;" while the magnificent palace erected by
Herod in the midst of his old familiar Tiberias had its
counterpart in the Paradise of the King of Parthia—
under whose sceptre the province was then placed. Of
the home of Peter in this " palm country " of course we
know nothing, save that we are warranted to infer it
was gladdened by the society of her who had faithfully
shared with him his labours and anxieties; " like
himself no longer young, and unequal, we may well
believe, to the more perilous and laborious journeys
which marked the activity of St Paul." " May we not
trace," the same writer adds, " an unconscious embodi-
ment of his own experience, in the words which bid
husbands to ' give honour unto the wife as unto *the
weaker vessel*' ? " (1 Pet. iii. 7 ; comp. 1 Cor. ix. 5).[2] On

1 Some writers have advocated that the Babylon here spoken of is not the
ancient capital, but another city of the same name built on the Tigris by
Seleucus Nicator. We see, however, no good reason to support the trans-
ference ; still less admissible is the suggestion of others, that Babylon near
Memphis in Egypt is intended ; for the latter at this time, according to
Strabo, was only a fort for a Roman garrison. (Strabo xvii. 1.)
2 Dr Plumptre's Biblical Studies.

the authority of Metaphrastes, she was the daughter of Aristobulus, brother to Barnabas the Apostle, of whom more hereafter. Clement of Alexandria—reliable as an ecclesiastical historian—mentions Peter and Philip as the two Apostles "who had children ; and that both took about their wives, who acted as their coadjutors in ministering to women at their own homes. By their means, the doctrine of the Lord penetrated without scandal into the privacy of women's apartments." 1

But to return. An interesting and important question remains to be considered and answered. Granted that such was the wide field of Peter's final ministry, have we any historical proof that these Evangelistic efforts, extending over fifteen long years, were crowned with success ? We have *a priori* reason to expect that he who, filled with the Spirit of God, had been the means of leading many thousands by one sermon preached at Pentecost to a saving acceptance of the great salvation,—to whom moreover his Lord had three years previously by the visible symbol of the miraculous draught of fishes given promise of vast results—would not be left to tell the discouraging experience, "I have toiled all night and caught nothing." We are enabled, however, to gather ample evidence that that success *was* great ;—that his was the blessedness of those who had "turned many unto righteousness," and who will at last have the glorious testimony that they "have not run in vain, neither laboured in vain." Jesus had assuredly not sent forth His chief under-shepherd to " feed His sheep " on barren pasture.

St Luke indeed is silent on these interesting facts. That sacred penman leaves us in no doubt as to the

1 Bib. Dic. *in loco.*

other great Apostle's triumphs in the vast missionary field of the West. We have entry after entry in the Acts as to the formation by St Paul of churches in the great capitals of Europe ;—and doubtless the pen of the Evangelist would not have been reluctant to trace also the footsteps of St Peter, but for the valid reason, that he was separated by half a continent from him. It has even been surmised, that having broken off suddenly the story of the one Apostle in the midst of his history, the threads of that story would have been gathered up again by the narrator, had he not himself been called to lay down his life for the Saviour he had served so well. The testimony, however, on which we are compelled to fall back is all the more valuable and convincing, coming as it does not from friends but foes. The evidence of Peter's Apostolic labours and triumphs is substantiated not by converted Jew or Christian Evangelist, but by Pagan proconsul and Roman historian.

Forty years after the death of Peter—about the beginning of the second century, the younger Pliny had been appointed by the Emperor Trajan governor of two of the provinces which had specially come under the Apostle's ministrations,—viz., Pontus and Bithynia. A letter, well known in ecclesiastical history, was sent by the propraetor to the Emperor, describing the religious condition in which he had found these provinces. The letter was one of perplexity, anxiety, complaint. And what was the cause? He writes, earnestly desirous to receive instructions from his imperial master, as to what measures he is to adopt in order to arrest the rapidly-growing apostacy from the national faith. In vivid language, he represents that the Temples of the gods are shut, and the sacrifices intended for the altar left without purchasers:—that the desertion was universal. Men and women of all ranks and ages—not excepting the young—were flocking to the churches of the Christians. He speaks of the "pestilent heresy" spreading like a contagion from city to city, and that the villages and country places had caught the infection as well as the populous centres. It is evident, moreover, from the tenor of his epistle, that he was deeply impressed with the purity and blamelessness of the Christians' lives,—the oaths they had voluntarily taken to abstain from sin,—not only from sensuality—but from the sins of violence—such as theft and murder, which seemed to have been prevalent. "We see," says the author of "Sermons on the Apostolic Age"—referring to this very letter, and comparing it with some of Peter's own utterances in writing to his converts— "how by 'their well-doing they put to silence the ignorance of foolish men':—how by their universal practice 'not to be thieves, or murderers, or evil-doers,' they disarmed the suspicions alike of the proconsul and of his imperial master" (p. 99). Pliny was himself a humane man, and he served under the least tyrannical of the Cæsars; yet he mentions, in the same document, that he had attempted coercive measures which had been attended with a very partial success. He gives indeed the most indubitable evidence, that in less than half a century the temples of Jupiter and Mars were deserted, and the religion of the crucified Jesus—which he branded by the name of "an absurd superstition"— had taken their place, and that scourge and prison had failed to shake the faith of the votaries. We have no "roll-call" given us of the names of this noble army of martyrs. The only illustrious exception, in the same place and era, was the aged Ignatius, whose fidelity had exacted the penalty of a savage death in the Roman amphitheatre. But doubtless there were not a few who had testified with unshaken confidence to the faith of Christ: and the famous saying of Tertullian had proved true in these Asiatic provinces as elsewhere, " The more you mow us down, the more do we increase. The blood of Christians is their seed."

Nor does the testimony of Pliny stand alone. Those who have fully investigated this subject have been able to sist other corroborative witnesses.[1] Among these is the Greek satirist Lucian—who speaks of *" Pontus "* " being full of atheists and Christians." " It is incredible," are his words, " with what alacrity these people support and defend their cause; they spare nothing in short to promote it: they had been taught that they were all brethren, and that, quitting our Grecian gods, they must worship their own sophist, who was crucified, and live in obedience to His laws. These poor creatures are firmly persuaded they shall one day enjoy eternal life; therefore they despise death with wonderful courage, and offer themselves voluntarily to punishment. They looked with contempt on all worldly treasures, and held everything in common; a maxim which they had most irrationally taken up." We pass on a few centuries later, and " the pestilent heresy " has reached still more gigantic proportions. The Bishop's Sees in Asia Minor alone, equalled in number those in Italy, Spain, and France combined. In the fifth century there were 388 dioceses. At the second general

[1] The reader is referred to the chapter by author of "Essays on the Church," where the story of Peter's latter days, as the Apostle of the Circumcision, is vividly narrated; indeed forming the most valuable portion of a volume of unusual interest.

council of Constantinople, held A.D. 381, while the
European Bishops numbered less than ten, the Eastern
ones present amounted to a hundred.[1]   From all this it
is evident, alike how vast was Peter's field of labour,
extending from the banks of the Euphrates to the shores
of the Ægean Sea ; and how great, under God, was the
harvest which he, and those who followed him, were instrumental in gathering in.   It was truly a gigantic task
—when he and his handful of coadjutors issued forth
from the gates of Antioch bearing the keys of the kingdom.
In the midst of his arduous and often cheerless labours,
the words of his Master—whose significancy were not
understood at the time—would frequently be recalled,
" Have faith in God."   Among the varied auxiliaries
which had aided him and those associated with him in
his work, opening the way for the proclamation of the
truth among Jew and Gentile, there was one that demands special reference and acknowledgment—viz., the
wide diffusion, through the Asiatic cities, of the Septuagint translation of the Old Testament Scriptures, made
at Alexandria.   Greek was then—more than French is
at the present day—the universal language spoken.
The translation of the sacred books into that " tongue
of many nations " was the ploughshare which prepared
the furrow for the reception of the immortal seed.   The
Holy Record was no longer a sealed volume to the thousands who were longing for something better than their
own effete creeds and systems could supply.   Seeking
after the true God " if haply they might find Him,"
the Greeks—so numerous in these cities of the Dispersion—were freely admitted into the synagogues of their
Jewish brethren, and there heard the Hebrew Scriptures

[1] Ib. : quoting from Bingham's Antiquities, *in loc.*

read and expounded in their own unrivalled tongue. "Under the influence of this wider instruction, a Greek body grew up around the Synagogue, not admitted into the Jewish Church, and yet holding a recognised position with regard to it, which was able to apprehend the Apostolic teaching, and ready to receive it."[1]

Here would seem to be the befitting time and place to refer to the arbitrary assumption made by Romanists regarding Peter's residence in "Babylon"—founded on the innocent closing reference in the postscript to his First Epistle. The strange thing is, that the belief seems to have remained for centuries undisturbed, and is still clung to pertinaciously by the adherents of the Papacy: not only so, but it has enlisted in its favour not a few names of eminence and repute among Protestant divines, such as Grotius, Macknight, Lardner, Schaff and Wieseler; viz., that the BABYLON there mentioned was a figurative name or metonomy for RCME, from which place the Prince of the Apostles wrote, and where he had been established in his Episcopate for twenty-five years. One ancient authority of note can alone be quoted in support of the claim. Eusebius, A.D. 325, Bishop of Cæsarea, on the alleged authority of Papias and Clement of Alexandria, accepts this non-natural interpretation. But it will be observed that he only asserts the fact from hearsay. His words are: "Peter mentions Mark in his First Epistle, which, *they say*, he wrote in Rome itself—and that he signifies this by calling that city figuratively 'Babylon.'" In this view Eusebius is supported by Æcumenius, Jerome, and Isidore of Seville.[2]

---

[1] Canon Westcott.   [2] See Alford, Proleg.

This perversion of a simple name seems obviously to have arisen from what we have previously stated,—the apparent improbability of the Apostle fixing his residence and exercising his ministrations in a place which prophecy had described as the tenantless haunt of the owl, the dragon, and the satyr.

We have sufficiently, we trust, met this objection. Moreover—as it has again and again been noted, who would ever have dreamt of a plain, unsophisticated man going out of his way to use a trope—a poetical simile —when a prosaic one suited him and his Epistle so much better? Torquay has been called the Montpelier of England :—who, in writing a letter to a distant friend, unless in a very facetious mood, would date his epistle not Torquay but "Montpelier?" London is not unfrequently called "the modern Babylon." Strange, if the Archbishop of Canterbury were to pen a pastoral from his palace at Lambeth to the clergy of his archiepiscopal diocese, and date it, not "London," but "Babylon!" In the words of the learned Michaelis, making analogous suppositions, such "would be a greater piece of pedantry than ever was laid to the charge of the learned."[1] It is well known that those who defend so forced a nomenclature, appeal to a similar use of the word in the Apocalypse of St John, where Rome the city of the seven hills is spoken of as "the Great Babylon." But the two cases can bear no comparison. Peter's letter, first of all, was written thirty-five years before that of John. He was a stranger alike to

[1] It is strange that even so safe and reliable a guide as Dr Cave is disposed to reject the literal Babylon and accept the metaphorical reference to *Jerusalem,* "no longer now the Holy City, but a kind of spiritual Babylon, in which the Church of Christ did at this time groan, under great servitude and captivity."

the words and the style of that divine allegory. Besides,
the Book of the Revelation, after the opening, is a sustained metaphor throughout,—composed of tropes;
whereas Peter's is a plain, simple, earnest, hortatory,
matter-of-fact Epistle; where anything poetical or
figurative would be utterly out of place.[1]

As an additional confirmation of the Assyrian Babylon and not Rome being referred to—it has been noted
by Niebuhr, that the order of the provinces quoted in
his First Epistle is what would have suggested itself to
one describing them who was situated *in Babylon*. The
enumeration begins nearest hand, with the province in
the east,—thence west, and terminating with the south
and most distant. Dean Alford gives this farther corroboration of the natural interpretation, that "Cosmas
Indicopleustes, in the sixth century, quotes the conclusion of the Epistle as a proof of the early progress of
the Christian religion, without the bounds of the Roman
Empire: by which therefore we perceive that by Babylon he did not understand Rome." [2]

It is evident, indeed, unless there had been this theory
to maintain, that so gratuitous and unnatural an assumption would never have been propounded. Babylon
with its thronging Jewish and Gentile population has
now passed away, and only heaps of ruin remain to
memorialise its greatness. Had this old capital of the
Euphrates survived, as the capital of the Tiber has done,
perchance among its literary treasures and traditions

---

[1] Cardinal Baronius is driven to the disingenuous reason in accounting for
the writer resorting to the metaphorical name,—that he did so in order the more
successfully to evade detection after his escape from prison in Jerusalem—
a surmise at once to be dismissed as imputing to the prince of the Apostles
a worldly policy and pusillanimity unworthy of his better and manlier days.

[2] Alford, Proleg. 1st Peter, p. 246.

might have been found some interesting and valuable mementoes of Peter's labours, more reliable far than the legends and relics with which his name is associated in Rome. But the besom of destruction has dealt impartially with the records alike of Chaldean art and Greek and Christian literature. Who can tell, but possibly the patient excavator may yet exhume from these desolate mounds some papyrus roll that may tend to throw valuable light on this debated point, or rather may substantiate what all dispassionate minds can have little reason to doubt or question, that not the least busy or eventful of Peter's years, though his closing ones, were spent in the ancient " beauty of the Chaldee's excellency ; " and that from his home in Babylon—in no forced metaphorical sense—those two great letters of his were written which we shall consider in next chapter.

CHAPTER XXIV.

Peter's Catholic Epistles.

> 'These are the tones to brace and cheer
> The lonely watcher of the fold,
> When nights are dark and foemen near,
> When visions fade and hearts grow cold."

"Peter also sounded with the two trumpets of his Epistles."—
Origen.

" Wonderful is the gravity and alacrity of Peter's discourse, most agreeably holding the reader's attention."—*Bengel.*

"This Epistle is full of apostolic dignity and authority, and worthy of the Prince of the Apostles."—*Erasmus.*

" Every part of Peter's writings indicates a mind that felt the power of the doctrines he delivered, and a soul that glowed with the most ardent zeal for the spread of the Gospel."—*Horne's Introduction.*

IT was then, probably after eleven or twelve years of arduous labour in the five great provinces of Lesser Asia, that Peter took up his head-quarters at Babylon. The allotted threescore and ten must now have furrowed his brow with wrinkles and dimmed the lustre of his eye. But he is still strong in faith, giving glory to God.

These previous years, we have every reason to believe, had been spent in continuous Evangelistic ministration : moreover, that these labours did not consist in the mere hurried visits of the itinerant preacher—the wayfaring man that turneth aside to tarry for a night. We seem warranted to infer that he remained sufficiently long in each place to consolidate the Churches which he reared, and to form intimate and endearing fellowships—fellowships and friendships

which he not only retained but strengthened when
settled down in the comparative leisure of his final
home.

Here also, with the true sympathy of the pastor who
" knows his sheep," he wrote his two comforting and
consoling letters, of which we shall now endeavour in
succession to give a brief account. As containing the
latest product of his mind—his most matured sentiments on Christian ethics and doctrine, they cannot
fail to be specially interesting. They give evidence,
patent to the observation of the most superficial reader,
that a vast transformation had taken place in the entire
nature of the man who writes them. We fail to discover
any trace of the once proud, reliant disciple, who lorded
it over his fellows, and indulged in boastful protestations; who often, in his moments of rash and unguarded
impulse, " wist not what he said." The passion of
youth, the impetuosity and arrogance of manhood, the
earthquake, the wind, the tempest, and the fire, are all
over. There is nothing heard but the " still small
voice." Paul was no egotist; yet even in his Epistles
there are many personal references and " boastings,"
from which these letters of Peter are free. In the case
of the latter, the boisterous day subsides into the
calmest of sunsets, where all is love, gentleness, meekness, peace. Even the more venial early fault of
Jewish prejudice and intolerance had merged into
catholic, expansive, universal charity. There is a total
abnegation of self, and a sole glorifying of his Great
Lord. The star loses its own lustre the nearer it
comes to the glory of the central sun. A beautiful
testimony to the power of the grace of Him who, in
the words of an old divine, " from the roughest of

materials, fashions stones for the high palace of His glory."

But these remarks will be best substantiated as we examine the Epistles in detail.

The First was written probably in the year 63, immediately before Nero's persecution, which commenced in A.D. 64.

As is the case in the Epistle of St James, he sends it to the "*diaspora*," with this difference, that the former was a general or circular letter addressed to the dispersed Jewish settlers in all the provinces—European, African, and Asiatic—whereas that of Peter is limited to the latter, " the elect sojourners of the dispersion of Pontus, Galatia, Cappadocia, Asia (proconsular), and Bithynia." [1] Not that we are by this to restrict it exclusively to Jewish converts, for we have reason to suppose that the Churches Peter founded were largely

---

[1] "The Church," which in our authorised version conveys the salutation from Babylon," is not in the original. " She that is elected together with you." Dean Alford, in common with others, supports very strongly the theory that the salutation is conveyed by Peter's wife (1 Cor. ix. 5) ; and more especially as the Epistle is addressed not to the *Churches* of the Dispersion, but to *the elect sojourners* of the Dispersion. The salutation is to individuals, not a collective body,—" To the Elect Christians," and greetings are sent from an elect Christian sister in Babylon. " She, her husband's companion in travel," says Dr Plumptre, " might well send a salutation to those whom she had known, whose wives and daughters she had probably taught to aspire after a higher and purer life, to whom she had presented a type of womanhood as yet new and strange to them." (See *Biblical Studies.*) Nor shall I venture any opinion on a disputed point with regard to another reference to " Marcus my son," in the same verse. I give the words of a note in " Sermons and Essays on the Apostolic Age," with the opinion which the author seems to share with many others : " 1 Pet. v. 13. It is difficult to resist the conclusion that the ἡ συνεκλέτη is the wife of Peter, and if so, that ὁ υἱός μου is not metaphorically (in which case τέκνον would be the natural word, as in 1 Tim. i. 2), but literally " his son."

made up of the Gentile element,—those who had "turned from idols to serve the living God." [1]

A few preliminary remarks may be made regarding this cluster of provinces (in the order in which they are here given), which formed his vast diocese—the sheep-fold for which he, along with the Beloved Apostle John, were responsible to the Chief Shepherd. We say advisedly "vast diocese," for it had a superficial area almost equal to the entire of France, with, generally speaking, not a scattered but a dense population. "The 500 cities of Asia Minor," spoken of by Josephus, give us a glimpse of the numbers with whom he held epistolary converse.

Pontus formed the north-east province, having for its northern boundary the shores of the Black Sea. It was the native country of the Christian Jew Aquila, and became a kingdom of celebrity under the sceptre of Mithridates the Great, who was engaged in a protracted war with the Romans, but on being defeated the greater portion of his dominions were annexed by Pompey to the Roman Empire. Its principal town, Amasia, gave birth to the geographer Strabo. It was distinguished alike for fertility of soil and abundance of inhabitants.

[1] Dr Plumptre, who traces with great ingenuity subtle references and deductions which escape alike the ordinary reader and ordinary scholar, remarks of those to whom this Epistle was sent:—"We may infer from St Peter's warnings against the luxury that showed itself in 'the plaiting of hair, and the wearing of gold, and putting on of apparel,' that the new faith numbered some at least of the 'honourable women' of the wealthier classes among its disciples ; and from his desire that the believers should be able to give an answer (literally an *apology*), to every man that asked them a reason of the hope that was in them, that there were men among them with sufficient culture to venture on such a vindication."—*The Bible Educator*, p. 130.

Galatia (Gaulatia), the country made familiar to us by St Paul's Epistle, lay to the west of Pontus and east of Phrygia and Bithynia. Ancyra, where the main thoroughfares converged, was its ecclesiastical metropolis. It was originally colonised by some Gallic or Celtic tribes who, three centuries before Christ, had made an irruption into Macedonia and Thrace, and were invited by Nicomedes, King of Bithynia, to cross the Hellespont and help him to subdue his brother. After acceding to his request, they made good their own settlement in the country, and lived predatory lives, till Attalus, King of Pergamus, succeeded in curbing them and restricting them within a certain territory. Their independence, for a time regained, was finally lost ; and Galatia became a Roman province sixty years before our Apostle set foot on its soil.

Cappadocia formed the largest province in Asia Minor. It was bounded by Galatia on the west, and by the Euphrates on the east, with Mount Taurus on the south. It also for long enjoyed its own tributary kings ; but at the time Peter was spending his early manhood at Bethsaida, it was absorbed by the Roman power. From Acts ii. 9, we find Jews from Cappadocia coming up to Jerusalem to attend the Feast of Passover and Pentecost. These probably carried back to their own country the first intimation of Messiah's Resurrection, and the fulfilment of Joel's prophecy as to the outpouring of the Spirit. It became the birthplace of Gregory and Basil of a future age.

Still further south and west we have proconsular "*Asia ;*" not Asia Minor, but that portion of it lying along the shores of the Ægean which formed a special Roman province, bequeathed as such by Attalus, King

of Pergamus.   Here were the scenes of Paul's earliest
labours and triumphs.   Lystra, the birthplace of
Timothy ; Iconium, Derbe, and Antioch in Pisidia.   It
included also the well-known towns, Philadelphia,
Sardis, Thyatira, Laodicea, Hierapolis, and Colossæ, the
latter doubly associated by us with Paul's Epistle and
with his friend Onesimus.   Ephesus, the capital and
seat of government, "the emporium of Asia Minor,
with its schools of magic and its magnificent Temple,"
recalls the names of Aquila, Priscilla, Apollos, and their
great master and teacher.   Smyrna, identified in an
after age with "the blessed Polycarp," who shed his
blood as a martyr for the truth in the Stadium, and
whose reputed tomb, which we have visited with interest, still crowns the heights above the city ; and Alex-
andria-Troas, from which the Apostle of the Gentiles
received his call to the great mission-field of the West :
leaving the vast domain east of the shores of the Ægean
to the Rockman and the Son of Thunder.

Bithynia was situated to the west of Galatia,
bounded by the Euxine on the north and the snowy
range of Mount Olympus in the south.   Its chief
ecclesiastical interest was in times subsequent to the
life of Peter.   It is associated with that remarkable
letter of the younger Pliny to which we have already
referred ; also with the memorable first Council of Nice.
It was into this province the Apostle of the Gentiles
sought to enter, but was deterred by some divine
Providential intimation, "the Spirit suffered him
not."

Such, then, was the wide auditory to which Peter
spoke by means of his First Epistle.   Silvanus, probably
the Silas of the Acts, was the bearer of it.   It is sur-

mised that, possibly at the instigation of Paul, he may have been sent on a tour of visitation to these Asiatic Churches, some of which had been founded by the illustrious Roman prisoner, and that subsequently visiting Peter in Babylon and reporting on their condition and circumstances, the Apostle of the Circumcision may have resolved to send back, by this faithful minister of Christ, words of needed counsel, comfort, and exhortation. At its close, he specifies the particular object and motive he had in writing it, "Exhorting and testifying that this is the true grace of God wherein ye stand." From sundry allusions, too, it would appear probable that Mark was with Peter at the time of its composition—some have supposed while St Paul had left Rome on a distant missionary expedition. As Mark, we know, was with the latter in his first imprisonment, it has been surmised that he may have been, during the great Apostle's absence, the bearer of the encyclical letter to the Ephesians, and proceeded at the same time further east to visit Peter in Babylon. The writer of the Epistle evidently refers in that closing verse, just quoted, to some body of doctrine which his readers had previously received (" the grace of God wherein ye stand "); and again "Stir up your pure minds by way of remembrance;" indicating, what we have already noted, that he himself previously, by faithful ministerial labour, had a personal connection with these churches which he now sought to build up and establish, not by oral word, but by Epistle.

One very essential part obviously of this First Epistle, and admirably adapted for the purpose, was to comfort his converts and sustain them in their constancy. "It is the following out of our Lord's command to its writer,

'when thou art converted, strengthen thy brethren.'" [1]
"It was at a time, apparently," says Professor
Plumptre, "when they needed counsel, when no
other teacher of equal authority was at hand to comfort
them; when St Paul, who had founded so many churches
in those regions, had been cut off from them, possibly
after that last visit of his, subsequent to the first imprisonment at Rome, of which we read that it was a time
of trial and persecution, which led all in Asia 'to turn
away from him'" (2 Tim. i. 15).[2] "The trial of
their faith" (i. 7), was the key-note of the letter. Nor
was it an ordinary trial which they were thus either
enduring or anticipating—it was a "trial by *fire*"
(7)—the emblem of suffering and endurance for the
sake of Jesus :—"reproached for the name of Christ"
(iv. 14). "The answer for the reason of the hope that
was in them" would be demanded, if it had not been
already extorted, by threats and penalties. But they
were not to be "ashamed" when called thus to "suffer
for the will of God" (iv. 19), and "for righteousness'
sake;" but to seek to confront the "evil-doers" (persecutors) with "a good conscience" (iii. 16);—"suffering as Christians," and "glorifying God on this behalf"
(iv. 16). Above all, does he counsel his beloved converts in the midst of these "fiery trials" (iv. 12) to look
to the exalted and holy example of their divine Saviour,
who "suffered for us, leaving us an example, that ye
should follow His steps" (ii. 21). How he repeats and
reiterates this one encouraging thought, to disarm the
sting of their own persecutions: "because Christ also
suffered for us" (ii. 21). "For Christ also hath once
suffered" (iii. 18). "Forasmuch then as Christ hath

1 Alford.   2 The Bible Educator, p. 130.

suffered . . . . arm yourselves likewise with the same mind " (iv. 1). " Rejoice, inasmuch as ye are partakers of Christ's *sufferings*" (iv. 13). " He who dated his own faith," says Wiesinger, " from the sufferings of his Master, is never weary in holding up the suffering form of the Lord before the eyes of his readers to comfort and stimulate them ; he before whom the death of a martyr is in assured expectation, is the man who most thoroughly, and in the greatest variety of aspects, sets forth the duty and the power,—as well as the consolation, of suffering for Christ. If we had not known from whom the Epistle comes, we must have said it must be a rock of the Church who thus writes : a man whose own soul rests on the living Rock, and who here, with the strength of his testimony, takes in hand to secure the souls of others against the harassing storm of present tribulation, and to ground them on the true Rock of Ages." [1] He further quickens his converts by the elevating thought of " the glory to be revealed " (iv. 13), that that God, who had made them " *suffer* awhile," had " called them unto His eternal glory by Christ Jesus" (v. 10). Not only is the frequent reference to this future glory another distinguishing characteristic, but it is a glory, moreover, not distant, but near and imminent :—so much so, as to have led a well-known German commentator to give to Peter the appellation, " the Apostle of Hope." " While St Paul dwells with most earnestness upon justification by our Lord's death and merits, and concentrates his energies upon the Christian's present struggles, St Peter fixes his eye constantly upon the future coming of Christ, the fulfilment of prophecy, the manifestation of the promised kingdom. In

[1] Quoted by Alford, p. 255.

this he is the true representative of Israel, moved by those feelings which were best calculated to enable him to do his work as the Apostle of the Circumcision." [1] With such comforting and elevating themes, we may safely aver that there is no portion of Scripture which has proved a greater help to the tried believer, whether these trials be from sin or sorrow. It is full of strong consolation ; with its representations of God as a Father, preparing His children by His own loving discipline for their eternal home—the inheritance "incorruptible, and undefiled, and that fadeth not away" (i. 4).

Its doctrinal statements are very pronounced and decided, leaving little room for the " negative theology" of recent times. The precious sacrifice of the Redeemer— "the sprinkling of the blood of Jesus Christ" (i. 2), takes its central place in Peter's teaching. He reminds his readers of the great procuring cause of liberty, peace, salvation ;—they were "redeemed with the precious blood of Christ, as of a lamb without blemish and without spot " (i. 19) ; words which perhaps vividly recalled —or rather were themselves suggested by—the never-to-be-forgotten exclamation which had revolutionised his thoughts, and transfigured his whole life—" Behold the Lamb of God, that taketh away the sin of the world !" They were pointed by the Rockman " to the chief corner Stone laid in Zion, elect, precious" (ii. 6)—to the Great Surety-Substitute and Propitiation " who His own self bare our sins in His own body on the tree" (ii. 24) ; and as if to leave no manner of doubt as to this foundation truth of his belief, he recurs to it in still more emphatic words in the third chapter, " Christ also hath once suffered for sins, the Just for the unjust, that

1 Art. "Peter," Bib. Dic.

He might bring us to God." "The most salient characteristic of this writing," says a French divine—
"that which from the commencement strikes the attention and touches the heart—are the transports with which the Apostle sets forth the Redemption. His opening (i. 2) is a cry of acknowledgment and joy. The idea of the salvation brought by Jesus Christ, the recollection of His promises and His example, dominates over all his thoughts, is found at the basis of all his instructions, and recurs as the motive of even his smallest precepts. . . . . There is here, moreover, a profound feeling of the price which the reconciliation of man cost,—the blood shed upon the cross (i. 2, 18, 19 ; ii. 24, &c.), as well as of the danger of neglecting this great salvation, and the folly of confronting the judgment of Him—who after having here acted as a Father (i. 15, 17), will judge without respect of persons hereafter." [1]

Nor is there any trace or support of Antinomianism in his creed ;—the great practical lesson he enforces is "holiness." Called by Him who is holy, they were bound to be " holy in all manner of conversation " (i. 15). He reminds them of their high prerogatives—" a chosen generation, a royal priesthood, an *holy* nation, a peculiar people ;" invested with these high privileges in order to " show forth the praises of Him who had called them out of darkness into His marvellous light " (ii. 9). They are the professing followers of One " who did no sin, neither was guile found in His mouth " (ii. 22).

But he is not content with mere general exhortations on the subject of sanctification. He enters with singular minuteness of detail into practical duties arising out of

---

[1] Cellérier, quoted by Dr Kitto.

the relationships of common life; addressing pastors and people, rulers and subjects, masters and servants, husbands and wives;—descending to a special enumeration of the sins of the heart and the tongue and the life: "malice, guile, hypocrisy, envy, evil-speaking" (ii. 1); "fleshly lusts which war against the soul" (ii. 11). Recalling one of the painful incidents of a hallowed past, he remembers how his Lord had forewarned him of the subtle power of the great Tempter; and how, true to the monition, Satan had "sifted him as wheat." With that sad experience in view, he can, with all the deeper solemnity and earnestness, warn them of "their adversary the devil, who as a roaring lion goeth about seeking whom he may devour" (1 Pet. v. 8.)

It is also worthy of note (distinctly appearing throughout all the Epistle), his demonstration to his Jewish brethren, that in accepting the doctrines of the Gospel, they were in truth not renouncing their ancient distinctive privileges; they retained these on a higher platform and under an advanced dispensation. He beautifully spiritualises Judaism. They are still a "peculiar people," but holding a grander charter of election. Their fathers were encouraged to "hope in God," but they are "begotten again unto a *lively* hope by the resurrection of Jesus Christ from the dead" (i. 3). Their ritual of sacrifice had culminated in the death of the great Antitype—"the Lamb without blemish and without spot" (i. 19). They enjoyed a better than the royal Levitical priesthood: for they were themselves priests;—each individual believer a "king and priest unto God" (ii. 9). A nobler land was theirs than Palestine—they were the living stones of a more enduring Temple than that which crowned the summits of Moriah" (ii. 5).

"Do you not believe," says Van Oosterzee, "that in the hearing of such language, the hearts of the strangers in the Dispersion beat with more joyous exultation?"

Nor can the reader fail to trace, in the perusal of this beautiful letter, what might be called the inverted personality of the writer. It is not the letter we should have expected from him in his earlier days;—but it is quite the ideal pastoral we should look for, after tracing his future history in the Acts of the Apostles;—written by the man whom the grace of God had softened and saddened, subdued and transformed. "The quick, impetuous Peter is heard admonishing with a mildness and serenity of argument which might only have been looked for from the most gentle of human spirits. . . . . We are enabled to contemplate his completed character. We find it retaining all the elements which gave it a degree of rude grandeur even at the commencement of his course; which made us feel when he first pronounced his most sublime confession, 'Thou art the Christ, the Son of God!' and when he dared to attempt a pathway over the angry sea, because it led to his Lord."[1] We almost trace the thoughts welling up in his bosom as memory carried him back to the former days of pride, waywardness, arrogance, and vain-boasting, as he dictated the words which spoke by implication of his own besetting sin and the change grace had effected—"Be ye clothed with humility: for God resisteth the proud, and giveth grace to the humble." Who can fail to be struck with the rebuke which the reputed Prince of Apostles conveys to those who would arrogate for him a precedence so strangely at variance with his own words? Assuredly that man claimed no infallible

[1] Cave's "Lives of the Apostles," p. 17.

lordship over his fellows who penned the exhortation:
" The elders which are among you I exhort, who am
also an elder, and a witness of the sufferings of Christ,
and also a partaker of the glory that shall be revealed :
Feed the flock of God which is among you, taking the
oversight thereof, not by constraint, but willingly ; not
for filthy lucre, but of a ready mind; neither as being
lords over God's heritage, but being ensamples to the
flock.   And when the chief Shepherd shall appear, ye
shall receive a crown of glory that fadeth not away "
(1 Pet. v. 1-4).   What a travesty of these noble and
beautiful sentiments (a brother speaking to brothers—
co-ordinate in rank and service) is the proud assumption
of Roman decretals, and hierarchal pomp and splendour ! [1]

The authenticity of the Epistle, which it would be
out of place to examine here, is undoubted.   Few
portions of the Sacred Canon rest on more irrefragable
evidence, both external and internal.   It was universally
accepted by the Church of the first centuries, and all
the more reliable scholars of recent times have accorded
with the verdict of antiquity.   The style of the Epistle
is peculiarly Peter's own.   It lacks the system and
logical sequences of St Paul.   One topic, or even word,
seems suddenly to suggest another, and he indulges in
those rapid transitions characteristic of his whole mind
and nature.   The reiteration of thought also is remarkable.   " In this Epistle," says Dr Hartwell Horne, " he
writes with such energy and rapidity of style, that we
can scarcely perceive the pauses of his discourse, or the

[1] " That Apostle, after whom the Church of Rome ever by preference calls
herself ; but whose First Epistle, in itself, suffices to make manifest her de-
Parture in many respects from the truth."—*Van Oosterzee.*

distinction of his periods. Little solicitous about the choice or harmonious disposition of words, his thoughts and his heart were absorbed with the grand truths which he was divinely commissioned to proclaim."[1] "A few great facts, broad solid principles, on which faith and hope may rest securely with a spirit of patience, confidence, and love, suffice for his unspeculative mind."[2] It is evident from some peculiar expressions which he has appropriated, that he must have been familiar with Paul's writings. Indeed this is only in accordance with the latter's own declaration, that he had communicated the Gospel, which he preached among the Gentiles, "*privately to those of repute*," including doubtless Peter among these.[3] A careful reader of this Epistle, comparing it with those which Paul addressed to the Romans, Ephesians, Colossians, Galatians, Thessalonians, and 1st Corinthians, will detect the use of identical words and turns of phrases, which give unmistakable proof that the elder Apostle had drunk deep into the spirit, and not unwittingly adopted the very phraseology, of his distinguished and honoured brother in Christ.[4] We may take, as an illustration, one of these similarities, which is worthy of note in connection with the scene at Antioch, when the two Apostles were brought into collision. Whatever were their variances then, on the very subject of that variance they are at one now. Paul thus writes to the Galatians regarding the rights and responsibilities of Christian liberty : "Brethren, ye have been called unto liberty ; only

[1] Horne's Introduction, *in loco.*
[2] Art. "Epistles of Peter," Bib. Dic.
[3] On these affinities and coincidences see Alford's "Prolegomena."
[4] See these compared passages given in full in Kitto's Cyclopædia, Art. "Peter."

use not liberty for an occasion to the flesh, but by love serve one another" (Gal. v. 13.) Peter echoes back the sentiment of his brother in a kindred strain: "As free, and not using your liberty for a cloak of maliciousness, but as the servants of God" (1 Peter ii. 16). "St Peter, therefore, we see," remarks Bishop Wordsworth, "did not manifest any resentment towards St Paul for the rebuke given at Antioch, and for the publication of its history to the world. He frankly comes forward and adopts *St Paul's own language on that very question* which had been the subject of their dispute. Here is a noble specimen of victory over self, and of generous confession of error; here is a beautiful practical application of his own precepts concerning Christian humility, meekness, and gentleness, and of love for the sheep whom Christ purchased with His blood." Indeed, by sending this First Epistle by the hand of Paul's friend and companion Silvanus (v. 12), and in the second one making such marked allusions to the "wisdom" displayed by the great Apostle in his writings (2 Pet. iii. 15, 16), he would seem desirous of repudiating and rebuking the unseemly partisanships which would make those two ministers of Christ, who were so essentially one, the heads or leaders of opposing parties in the Church. "At the close of his life," it has been justly said, "he appears not glorying in his early fame, as leader of the first Apostles, not entrenching himself within the sphere of his natural Jewish prepossessions, but striving to merge his own individual character and existence in the career of him whom his own followers would fain represent as his rival and his enemy. . . . It may well be taken as the pledge of the last work of St Peter, in crushing absolutely and for ever this fatal schism, which would have divided the two great Fathers of our faith—him who gave it its first outward form, and him who proclaimed its deep inward spirit."[1]

A like similarity to that between the writings of Peter and Paul, cannot fail to be noted between many expressions in the encyclical Epistle of James, with those in this First Epistle of his early friend. These are not to be considered as "plagiarisms," but rather the identical expression of two minds that had been often in the past brought together ; each writer gives, in his own way, the outcome of his private cogitations. Yet even the phraseology in which their thoughts are reproduced, has been noted to be characteristic of the two men. The sentences of James are cast in sterner moulds ; while in Peter's there is that mellowed gentleness and tenderness of later years to which we have previously alluded. "Whether through natural disposition, discipline, or circumstance, there is far more of softness and gentleness to be discerned in St Peter, by the witness of his Epistle, than we find in St James. 'Ye adulterers and adulteresses.' 'Go to now, ye rich men, weep and howl.' 'Wilt thou know, O vain man, that faith without works is dead?' It is in this form of stern and point blank address, that St James would arouse some readers of his epistle ; to whom, if St Peter were speaking, we should judge that he would rather say, as in a similar case we find he does say, 'Dearly beloved, I beseech you, as strangers and pilgrims, abstain from fleshly lusts, which war against the soul.' "[2]

---

1 " Sermons on the Apostolic Age."
2 " Waiting for the Light," p. 185.

We cannot better close these observations on this First Epistle of our Apostle, than in the words of the saintly Leighton : " It forms a brief yet very clear summary both of the consolations and instructions needful for the encouragement and direction of a Christian in his journey to heaven, elevating his thoughts and desires to that happiness, and strengthening him against all opposition in the way, both that of corruption within, and temptations and afflictions from without. The heads of doctrine contained in it are many, but the main that are insisted on are these three : *faith, obedience,* and *patience ;* to establish them in believing, to direct them in doing, and to comfort them in suffering." [1]

If the genuineness and authenticity of Peter's First Epistle, as we have seen, are incontested, securing from Apostolic times a rare unanimity in its favour, it is not to be denied that his Second Epistle has not enjoyed the same ; although we shall endeavour to show that the main grounds on which these doubts of its canonicity have been founded are insufficient and untenable.

It would exceed the limits of this volume, and be foreign to its object, to enter exhaustively upon this question. Those who may desire to prosecute the investigation will find the arguments for and against its reception fully stated by all the best known exegetical

---

[1] I have deemed it unnecessary to add to the bulk of this volume by inserting the text of the Epistles, alike so familiar and accessible to the reader. The more so, as the alterations from the authorised version are, generally speaking, unimportant ; tending in this instance, as, indeed, in the rendering of the entire English Bible, to confirm our faith in the accuracy of our excellent translators.

commentators.[1]   We shall endeavour, throwing ourselves on the forbearance of our readers, to present a
resumé of the *pros* and *cons*, with the results in favour
of the retention of the Epistle in its place among the
sacred writings.

With the single exception of the ancient fragment
known as the Muratorian Canon, it was, after the fourth
century, embodied in all the catalogues, and incorporated
in the Canon of Holy Scripture.   It was received by
Athanasius, Cyril, Jerome, Epiphanius, Augustine,
Rufinus.   It is enumerated in the Canon of Laodicea
(*circa* 360 A.D.)   It was adopted by the Council of
Carthage A.D. 393 ; in later times by the Council of
Trent, and since acknowledged and recognised by all
reformed confessions.[2]   Accepted, too, by such authoritative names as Michaelis, Lardner, Olshausen, and the
more reliable and scholarly of modern English theo-
logians.

And now for a few of the reasons which have gene-
rated doubts regarding its reception.

Origen, in the third century, is the earliest to express
hesitation.   While cordially admitting the authority of
the First Epistle, he puts the Second into the category
of " doubtful."   His expression is, " Peter has left one
acknowledged Epistle, *perhaps* a second, for this is
contested."   Yet in other places (as in one of the
mottoes which head this chapter, taken from his
" Homily on Joshua "), he evidently recognises   its

---

[1] None will be found to do so with greater fairness than Dean Alford,
who in his *Prolegomena* to 2d Peter gives, without the feelings or bias of a
partisan, and with the minute accuracy of a scholar, full details.   See also
an elaborate article in Kitto's Bible Cyclopædia.

[2] It was received by Luther, but placed by him among what he called
" The Apocrypha of the New Testament."

genuineness, and, as one of "two trumpets," puts it on a par with the first. Yet again, on Numbers, " as *Scripture* saith in a certain place (2 Peter ii. 16), ' The dumb animal, speaking with human voice, convicted the madness of the prophet.' "[1]

Eusebius, by whom the statements of Origen are preserved, and referring to these doubts which had been insinuated, relegates it among the *Antilegomena,* or books whose authority had been disputed. His words are : " As to Peter's letters, one Epistle—that which is called the first—is received as genuine, because this the ancient Fathers use as undoubted in their writings; but that which we have called the second, we have not understood to be included among the New Testament Scriptures. Yet, as it appeared useful to many, it has come to be reverenced with the other sacred books."

It is not found in the Peschito or ancient Syriac version of the New Testament Scriptures : at all events, it occupies a subordinate place among the Apocryphal books of the Syriac Church. " It is not directly quoted by any writer before the latter part of the third century, though phrases occur in some earlier writers, that seem, as it were, echoes of its language, or of that of some writing closely resembling it."[2] It will be sufficient, however, here to note in passing, that we may accept as a tolerably sufficient and satisfactory explanation of this unfamiliarity, as compared at all events with the Pauline Epistles, that these latter were written to churches occupying a prominent place in

---

[1] See Alford, *in loco,* who, however, states at the same time that the Epistle is not quoted in Origen's extant *Greek* works, but only those in a Latin version.

[2] Bible Educator, p. 133.

the eye of the world; while those of Peter were sent to Asiatic communities, many of which in these earlier centuries were comparatively unknown, or at least restricted in their intercourse with the rest of Christendom. In the words of Dean Alford, both Epistles are among "those latter fruits of the great outpouring of the Spirit on the Apostles, which, not being entrusted to the custody of any one church or individual, required some considerable time to be generally known; which *when* known were suspected, bearing, as they necessarily did, traces of their late origin and notes of polemical argument; but of which, as apostolic and inspired writings, there never was, when once they became known, any general doubt" (p. 273).

The earliest argument we find seriously urged against the genuineness of Peter's Second Epistle, that which is mentioned indeed by Jerome as being the specific reason for its rejection, is the discrepancy in style and language with the first. The words of that ancient Father are: " He (Peter) wrote two Epistles which are named catholic, of which the second is by most denied to be his, *because of the variation of its style from the former Epistle.*" The objection was resumed at the era of the Reformation, and supported then and since, among others, by Erasmus, Calvin,[1] De Wette, Reuss, Neander. Granting, which we do not, that the objection is a serious one, even Jerome himself, while stating it, is the first to suggest a probable explanation. It is

---

1 Calvin's verdict is peculiar: " If the Epistle be regarded as unworthy of credit that it came from Peter, not that he himself wrote it, but some one of his disciples in obedience to his orders. He was then, as is probable, in extreme old age and near death. It is possible that at the request of the disciples he suffered the Epistle to go forth as his dying testimony."
—*Commentary, in loc.*

to the following effect :—That as Peter was evidently in
the habit of employing an amanuensis, he may possibly
have dictated his two Epistles to different transcribers
(probably Mark and Silvanus), leaving to them the
clothing of his thoughts and ideas in their own phraseology.[1]   As we have quoted the language in which this
old writer couches his objection, we may add the precise words of his refutation : — " The two Epistles
which are ascribed to Peter are discrepant in style and
character and structure of words ; by which we understand that, from straits of circumstances, he used
different interpreters."   Nor is this the only cause to
account for discrepancy.   Although it is impossible to
arrive even approximately at the extent of the interval,
some years at all events must have elapsed between
the writing of the two Epistles.   The one was probably composed during the Apostle's residence in
Babylon, when he had no immediate apprehension of
suffering and death ; the other when on the threshold
of his martyrdom, possibly during the agitation of his
last journey, when summoned, as we shall in next
chapter describe, to take his stand at Cæsar's judgment-
seat in the imperial capital.[2]   The innocent Christians
had recently been accused as the incendiaries of Rome.
There is every probability that a summary mandate
had gone forth from the exasperated authorities in the
metropolis to seize the chiefs and ringleaders of the
obnoxious sect in east and west, and that Peter, accord-

---

[1] " The Fathers supposed that such of the sacred writers as did not
understand Greek (among whom they reckoned St Peter) dictated in their
native language to an amanuensis, who wrote down in Greek what they
uttered in Hebrew."—*Kitto's Bible Cyclopedia*, art., *Epistles of St Peter.*

[2] Bishop Sherlock supposes five years to intervene between the writing
of the two Epistles.

ing to the true rendering of the words, had "suddenly"
(not "shortly," as in A. V.) received tidings in Babylon
that he must prepare for the "putting off of his tabernacle" (2 Peter i. 14).   Much, we repeat, there would
surely be in the circumstances of the Apostle to account
for this want of similarity between a letter written at
such a crisis and an older Epistle.   Even in ordinary
compositions, there are few authors unconscious of their
style undergoing material alteration by the lapse of
years, by outward influences and impressions, and
specially by the fellowships with which at the time
of writing they may be surrounded.   "Who sees not,"
to quote the words of Dr Cave, "the vast difference
of Jeremiah's writing in his Prophecy and in his Book
of Lamentations? between St John in his Gospel, his
Epistles, and Apocalypse?   How oft does St Paul alter
his style in several of his Epistles—in some more lofty
and elegant, in others more rough and harsh? besides
hundreds of instances that might be given, both in
ecclesiastical and foreign writers, too obvious to need
insisting on in this place."   In these early days of the
Church, when all was in a state of chaos and unsettle-
ment, when revealed truth had not yet been formulated
into the creeds and confessions of later years, and
when the doubts and heresies of to-day were succeeded
by new phases of error to-morrow, a writer's weapons
had to be changed and modified to adapt themselves
to shifting exigencies.   A single year might be enough
to alter his whole cast of thought, and to mould his
very language into new shape and form.   Accordingly
we may readily imagine that Peter, either in the comparative seclusion of his Babylon home or the active
occupations of his Babylon ministry, would pen a very

different letter from what he would compose as the
old man, accompanied and watched by a Roman guard,
who had heard his earthly knell too surely rung ; who
wrote under that most solemnising of human influences,
that he was bidding farewell for ever to the home of
his manhood and age, and being hurried to a violent
death. Bishop Wordsworth thus repels the objection
to the genuineness of the Epistle, founded on the force
and energy of style being out of harmony with the
advanced age of the writer :—" The force of the Holy
Spirit stirring within him vents itself in bold com-
parisons and imaginative metaphors, and in an impetuous flood of words. Nor was his old age any bar
to this poetic outpouring of his soul. What Moses
was in his old age when he sang his last song ; what
David was in his old age when he chanted his last
psalm, full of ardour and energy imparted by the
Holy Ghost, who inspired him ; such was the aged
Apostle St Peter when he wrote his Second Epistle
before his martyrdom for Christ." We at once reject
the escape from the difficulty of a divergence in style
suggested by Grotius, that the " Symeon," who in the
opening sentence of the Epistle announces himself the
author, was St James' successor in the bishopric of
Jerusalem, and that the name Peter had been interpolated in a later age. The supposition is at once
refuted by the writer declaring himself the author
of the former Epistle (iii. 1), by his specific reference
to being personally known to Jesus (i. 14), to his
enjoying the peerless privilege of having been one of
the spectators of the glory on " the Holy Mount," and
to have heard the voice which came from the Excellent
Glory attesting his Lord's Messiahship (i. 16–18). Still

more unwarrantable and unworthy seems to be the view
of Neander, who construes that very avowal of authorship into a proof of the apocryphal character of the
Epistle—indicating, he alleges, an attempt at deception
by this obtrusive introduction of an incident in Peter's
history. Such an inference to any candid reader is
surely inadmissible. If valid, it would impair the
genuineness of some of the Pauline Epistles, specially
those which most correspond with the object Peter had
in view when he denounces false teachers, and brings
into prominence his own Apostolic authority in rebuking error and vindicating truth. Neander's objection ought rather in all fairness to be enlisted as an
argument in support of genuineness.

We have alluded to the main ground of doubt and
rejection arising from the difference of style in the two
Epistles. It may be well, however, to state more
particularly in what this discrepancy is alleged to
consist.

Some hostile critics have dwelt on what they assert
to be the total omission of quotations from the Old
Testament which abound in the First Epistle : that
in the second, the thoughts and sentences follow in
much more regular order and sequence than in the
earlier one, where they are more desultory, taking the
shape generally of isolated utterances and propositions.
That there is a diversity, too, in the name or title given
to the Saviour in the two Epistles. In the first, it is
simply " Christ " or " Jesus Christ ;" in the second, it
is " *our Lord* Jesus Christ," " Jesus, our Lord," but
never " Christ " only. " The revelation of Jesus
Christ " in the First Epistle, as descriptive of His second
coming, is altered into " Day of God," " Day of Judg-

ment," in the second. The general tone of the latter is alleged to be more in harmony with the vivid and graphic picturing of the Apocalypse of St John, than with the earlier writing of his more prosaic friend; while the taunt of the scoffer at the long delay of the expected coming of Christ, would seem to point to a date later than that of the age of Peter. A sufficient time would not otherwise elapse to make the phrase applicable, " Our fathers fell asleep."

Granting that there is a certain force in one or more of these minute criticisms, it is only right to inquire if there does exist, after all, so remarkable a discrepancy as has been alleged between the two Epistles; also, on the other hand, if there are no points of resemblance that may be traced between the two, that would lead us to infer identity of authorship.

It forms, indeed, a curious illustration of diversity in opinion and conflict of judgment, when we find such an acute and able critic as Michaelis basing his *defence* of the genuineness of the Epistle on its *similarity* of sentiment and language with those of its predecessor! Nor do we think the impartial student will fail to recognise the justice of the verdict of this distinguished commentator. All the more satisfactory are these resemblances which he and others have traced, that they are in themselves comparatively insignificant, and therefore undesigned, not bearing the marks of systematic forgery.

Let us present a few specimens.

The salutation in both Epistles has a remarkable identity in one word there employed. The verb occurs in these two Epistles alone, and in no others, " Grace and peace *be multiplied*." There is a similar correspondence in the writer's view of ancient prophecy (compare 1 Peter i. 10–12 with 2 Peter i. 19–21, and iii. 2).—*Alford.* The same retributive judgment is foretold in 1 Peter iv. 17, and 2 Peter ii. 3. The expression, or rather combination, of two words (ἀμώμου καὶ ἀσπίλου), "without blemish and without spot," of 1 Peter i. 19 is repeated, though with a different application, in 2 Peter iii. 14, "without spot and blameless." One of these words, as noted by Dr Plumptre, does not occur elsewhere in the New Testament. The same accurate scholar points out the employment in each Epistle of the rarely used word—also occurring nowhere else in the New Testament—the "behold" of 1 Peter ii. 12, iii. 2, and the "eye-witnesses" of 2 Peter i. 16 (ἐποπτεύειν and ἐπόπται). There is in both not only a reference to the Deluge, but the number of persons saved — viz., eight — is specified (1 Peter iii. 20, 2 Peter ii. 5). "As free, and not using your liberty for a cloak of maliciousness" (1 Peter ii. 16). "While they promise them liberty, they themselves are the servants of corruption" (2 Peter ii. 19). The inculcation of humility and the condemnation of pride (1 Peter v. 5–8) has its parallel in 2 Peter ii. 18 in the condemnation of those who "speak great swelling words of vanity." The writer's partiality is remarkable for the use of the word "precious" in both Epistles—in the one as applied to the trial of faith and the blood of Christ (1 Peter i. 7, 19), and to faith itself and the promises of the Gospel in the other (2 Peter i. 1–4).[1] Even the objection to which we have alluded, of a diversity in the name and title given to the Redeemer, is thus disposed of by Dean Alford:—

[1] See entire article in Bible Educator, p. 134.

" This, which has been also alleged as against the identity of writers, is, I submit, strikingly characteristic of
the different realms of thought of the two Epistles.
In the first it is community of suffering and glorification with Him which is to give encouragement; His
lordly and glorious titles are dropped, and His office
(' *Christ* '), or combined Person and office (' *Jesus Christ* '
or ' Christ Jesus ') is ever brought forward. But in
this second, where warning and caution against rebellion
are mainly in view, we are ever reminded of His lordship, by ' *Lord*,' and of what He did for us, by ' *Saviour ;* '
and without the former, or both titles, He never appears " (p. 269).   Farther, as pointed out by the same
writer, the alleged absence of reference to the Old
Testament Scriptures is simply unfair and untrue, as
the reader will judge for himself by referring to 2 Peter
i. 19-21 ; ii. 1, 5-7, 15, 22 ; iii. 2, 4-5, 8, 13.[1]

On the above and other grounds, impossible to state
in so brief a compass (among these, very chiefly the
subjective one—its internal structure), we may with

---

[1] Dean Alford has added several other ingenious, undesigned coincidences, alike from Peter's 1st Epistle and from his sayings in the Gospels
and the Acts. (See p. 372.)

To examine the question of the similarity between a portion of the
Second Epistle of Peter and the Epistle of Jude (Lebbæus) would
occupy more space than can be allowed. St Jude, by a reliable tradition
on the authority of Hippolytus, had the country of Mesopotamia, with its
capital Edessa, appropriated to him. Is it unreasonable to surmise that,
bordering as it did on the Babylonia of Peter, the two faithful ambassadors
of Christ had at times met together to discuss the prevalent heresies and
dangers to which the Church was subjected, and that each gave in his own
phraseology the thoughts which had occurred at these brotherly con-
ferences ; specially the warnings and denunciations they had, by mutual
compact, deemed it well to commit to "pen and ink," and circulate far
and wide among the flocks committed to their charge? Or we have the
alternative theory, that both may have drawn from some other authoritative document unknown to us, and which has perished. The former
view seems the more likely and natural.

strong confidence retain our faith in this precious letter, as being part and parcel of the "all Scripture which is given by inspiration of God;" invested to the Church with the greater interest and solemnity, as having been written by Peter at the time when the note of preparation had been sounded for the violent "departure" of which his Lord had forewarned him. It would be passing strange if, after all, one of the most touchingly beautiful and powerful of the Apostolic writings had turned out to be a literary artifice, a base deliberate forgery, opening with the assumption of an Apostolic name and title, and closing by an affectionate entreaty to "grow in grace." The spurious writings of the earlier centuries, even the best of them, are very different — puerile, mystical, and fanciful, compared with this;—coin which betray their counterfeit beside the true ring of this currency of heaven. We might possibly have been staggered—there would have been some plausibility, at least, for caution and hesitation— had the letter in question abounded in hierarchal pretensions, the assertion on the part of Peter of the bold claims of future centuries. But it maintains the same singular reticence as regards the author, which is characteristic of the First Epistle : no lording it over God's heritage; on the contrary, its tone throughout is humble, self-forgetting, affectionate. In fact, as Calvin says, "If it is to be received as canonical, Peter must have been its author. . . . For any other one to have personated the Apostle would have been a deception unworthy the Christian name." "The Church," says Canon Cook in his able article, " which for more than fourteen centuries has received it, has either been imposed upon by what must in that case be regarded as a Satanic device, or derived from it spiritual instruction of the highest importance.   If received, it bears attestation to some of the most important facts in our Lord's history, casts light upon the feelings of the Apostolic body in relation to the elder Church and to each other, and, while it confirms many doctrines generally inculcated, is the chief, if not the only voucher for eschatological views touching the destruction of the framework of creation which from an early period have been prevalent in the Church."[1]

For our own part we accept it reverentially, as in all respects worthy of him who made the noble confession of his Master's Messiahship, who enjoyed such pre-eminent tokens of that Master's tenderness and love, and to whom in a deep spiritual sense, as the leader in subsequent Apostolic thought and action, the keys of the kingdom had been committed.   It is in keeping with his fervid zeal; worthy of the heart that had been quickened by a generous restoration, of the tongue which had been touched with living fire on the day of Pentecost, of the brave soul whose heroism in many a trying hour was to culminate soon in a cruel martyrdom.   We could not afford to defraud our Bibles of so precious a compendium of the mysteries of spiritual religion; and if a man's last recorded words are regarded with special sacred interest, it is remarkable that he who was the first to testify to the divinity of his Lord, after a lapse of twenty years leaves this as his last known bequest to the Church of the future, with the light of eternity shining upon his soul.   It is an echo of the testimony of Cæsarea Philippi embodied in a doxology—" Our Lord and

1 Smith's Bib. Dic., Art. "Peter," p. 809.

Saviour Jesus Christ. To Him be glory both now and for ever. Amen."

And now as to the subject-matter and design of the Epistle.

Without any formal dedication, we infer from iii. 1 that it was addressed to "them that have obtained like precious faith with us;"—the same individuals or communities to whom his First Epistle was sent— "This Second Epistle, beloved, I now write unto you; in both which I stir up your pure minds by way of remembrance" (2 Peter iii. 1); though there is reason to believe (i. 1) that he designed the second letter for a wider and more general auditory than the other. He adopts in his Apostolic superscription, not the ordinary name Simon, but the Hebrew, or rather Aramaic form of Symeon. The letter would seem to have been mainly prompted in order to counteract the spread of some dangerous errors alike in doctrine and practice—errors which he evidently regarded with more serious apprehension than the "fiery trials" which had formed the burden of the earlier communication. Obnoxious teachers and teaching, "lawless men," had crept into the Church. He remembered the words of the Lord Jesus how He said—and he counselled his flock accordingly—"Beware of false prophets, which come to you in sheep's clothing, but inwardly they are ravening wolves. Ye shall know them by their fruits. Do men gather grapes of thorns, or figs of thistles?" (Matt. vii. 15, 16). It is evident that the blight of Antinomianism is that to which he specially alludes as spreading far and wide its withering influence. What Paul mourned over in Europe, had become a still more

2 P

formidable adversary in the more effeminate and sensuous Asiatic nature :—"For many walk, of whom I have told you often, and now tell you even weeping, that they are the enemies of the cross of Christ : whose end is destruction, whose God is their belly, and whose glory is in their shame, who mind earthly things" (Phil. iii. 18, 19). Bishop Wordsworth, while he allows for the very considerable diversity of feeling and style to which we have alluded, observes that "there were good reasons for the difference. St Peter had a twofold work to do : first, to *declare the truth ;* next, *to refute error.* He had executed the first of these two tasks in his former Epistle : he performs the second in the latter. . . . If the Church of Christ had not had any enemies who assailed her doctrinal foundations, St Peter might have been contented with the work of *building up* the fabric of Christian life grounded on Christian faith ; but his position was like that of the wise and valiant leader of God's ancient people, Nehemiah, in building up the Holy City after the Babylonish captivity. He and his associates were encountered by Sanballats and Ammonites, who interrupted the labour, and were ready to overthrow it. They had, therefore, a double work to do : they must fight as well as build. . . . In the First Epistle, St Peter had been, like a faithful and affectionate shepherd, feeding and tending Christ's sheep and lambs ; but in the Second Epistle he is like the same shepherd driving away the wolves, who were ready to tear and devour those sheep and lambs which Christ had purchased with His own blood, and had specially committed to his care." These false teachers seem specially to have made the second coming of the Lord the subject of their profane derision, making light of the warnings concerning the day of approaching reckoning —a day which the description of the writer invests with an awe and solemnity paralleled in no other part of Scripture, unless in those final discourses of his Master, to which he himself listened, regarding the same subject, on the Mount of Olives. He speaks of the delay of the advent which had emboldened this scoffing of the atheist, as a token of God's long-suffering mercy and forbearance—a mercy, however, which would have its limits. Not perhaps when Peter wrote had these heretical teachers developed their assaults against the truth into any distinctive systems of error such as that of the Gnostics and Nicolaitanes of subsequent years, but he too surely foresaw "where-unto these things would grow,"—the too certain germ of future apostacies. He brings prominently forward the great topic of his ministry—the passport alike to the kingdom of grace here, and the kingdom of glory hereafter. Four times in the Epistle is the same car-dinal saying repeated unchanged — " The knowledge of the Lord and Saviour Jesus Christ." And as having been himself an eye-witness of the words and deeds of Jesus, he is the more competent to be their instructor in the true way of salvation. He exhorts his faith-ful converts to seek advancement in the divine life, that so an entrance might at last be ministered unto them abundantly into Christ's everlasting king-dom (i. 10, 11). Still more than in the First Epistle, does he dwell on the " Parousia "—its joy to those who are " looking for and hasting unto it " (2 Peter iii. 12), and who shall then " be found of Him in peace, without spot and blameless " (iii. 14); while, on the other hand, awful are the denunciations he utters against the above false teachers we have just referred to, terrible the doom of hypocrites and apostates. He closes with the solemn warning — "Ye therefore, beloved, seeing ye know these things before, beware lest ye also, being led away with the error of the wicked, fall from your own stedfastness" (2 Peter iii. 17). But he who on the day of Pentecost called on the weeping, stricken multitudes to "repent," points even the guiltiest to that same Lord who is "long-suffering, not willing that any should perish, but that all should come to repentance" (iii. 9).

There is an association of an interesting kind, peculiar to itself, suggested by Peter's Second Epistle, which cannot be passed in silence, viz., his reference to the writings of the great Apostle of the Gentiles. These two great chiefs of the ancient Church had been for long years separated by long distance. For a quarter of a century—save once at Jerusalem, once also at Antioch, and possibly at Corinth—they had never met. The meeting at these two latter cities, moreover, had doubtless regretful memories. The one was the scene of a merited public rebuke; the other, though we have no reason to infer the existence of personal animosity or alienation, was where the names of the two Apostles had become, on the lips of bigots, wild party watch-words antagonistic to true brotherhood. Peter, however, was now unexpectedly cheered and comforted by fellowship with his illustrious friend in another form. This we gather from the special mention of the name of Silvanus at the close of his First Epistle (v. 12). Silvanus had been long the companion of St Paul. He is mentioned by him among the salutations in his Epistles to the Thessalonians; by some, though this is doubtful, he is supposed to be the amanuensis (Tertius) who wrote the Epistle to the Romans. He appears, in coming to visit the Apostle of the Circumcision in Babylon, to have brought along with him the priceless gift of Paul's letters—those of them, at all events, that were already written.[1] Some have contended, from the peculiarity of the expression " written unto *you*," that very specially was reference made to the great Epistle whose authorship is so uncertain—the Epistle to the Hebrews,—an Epistle which, from its whole scope and contents, would have a peculiar value and interest to the Apostle of the Circumcision as well as the Christianised Hebrews of the Dispersion, for whose behoof it seems mainly to have been intended. What a gush of feeling must have thrilled the old man's heart, as he bent over these inspired guiding lights for the Church of his age, as well as for the Church of future Christendom! How rejoiced would he be to find, that whatever may have been former divergencies, or even threatened estrangements, Paul and he were now essentially at one in the great cardinal articles of that faith for which both were ready to die!—both actuated by the same loyal love and allegiance to their great Master — both alive to the hydra-headed foe imperilling the truth alike dear to them—both with equal earnestness contending for the purity of the faith delivered unto the saints! " Hard to be understood " as some things were in these Epistles of his " beloved brother," they would come to him in his old

---

[1] " All his Epistles " must be taken in a relative sense, as referring to his more important writings,—those which Peter had seen. The collection of his entire Epistles was not made before the second century.

age as ministering angels.   He gratefully recognises
for himself, as well as for others, "the wisdom given"
unto the writer (2 Peter iii. 15); and doubtless their
perusal, while awaking grateful and hallowed remembrances of the past, would tend to cheer and brace the
"lonely watcher in the fold," when his ear caught
only too surely the mutterings of that coming storm
of which a Divine Monitor had long ago forewarned
him.[1]

In closing this chapter it may not be out of place to
mention, that—although utterly unreliable, and bearing
in their whole style and matter the refutation of their
genuineness—the Apostle was credited in later centuries
with being the author of other books and treatises.   We
cannot do better than give the condensed account of
these apocryphal compositions furnished by Dr Cave:—
"Besides his Divine Epistles, there were other supposi-
titious writings which, in the first ages, were fathered
upon St Peter.   Such was the book called his Acts,
mentioned by Origen, Eusebius, and others; but rejected by them.   Such was his Gospel, which probably at first was nothing else but the Gospel written
by St Mark, dictated to him (as is generally thought)
by St Peter; and therefore, as St Jerome tells us, said
to be his; though in the next age there appeared a book
under that title, mentioned by Serapion, Bishop of
Antioch, and by him at first suffered to be read in the
Church; but afterwards, upon a more careful perusal of
it, he rejected it as apocryphal, as it was by others
after him.   Another was the book styled his Preaching,
mentioned and quoted by Clemens Alexandrinus and

1 See some interesting remarks of Professor Plumptre in "Biblical
Studies."

by Origen, but not acknowledged by them to be genuine, nay, expressly said to have been forged by heretics, by an ancient author contemporary with St Cyprian. The next was his Apocalypse, or Revelation; rejected, as Sozomen tells us, by the ancients as spurious, but yet read in some churches in Palestine in his time. The last book was his Judgment, which probably was the same with that called Hermes, or Pastor—a book of good use and esteem in the first times of Christianity, and which, as Eusebius tells us, was not only frequently cited by the ancients, but also publicly read in churches."[1]

While these writings are at once dismissed as spurious and unauthentic, we gladly fall back on the two priceless inspired legacies he has bequeathed to us in the encyclical Epistles which have formed the subject of this chapter,—writings, which, in the words of the commentator to whom we are largely indebted in the preceding pages, "as the Sacred Canon became fixed, acquired, and have since maintained, their due and providential place among the books of the New Testament."[2]

[1] Cave's "Lives of the Apostles," pp. 159, 160.
[2] Alford, p. 273.

CHAPTER XXV.

𝕿𝖍𝖊 𝕮𝖑𝖔𝖘𝖊 𝖔𝖋 𝕻𝖊𝖙𝖊𝖗'𝖘 𝕷𝖎𝖋𝖊.

MUCH THAT IS CONJECTURAL. HIS PROBABLE AGE. GROUNDS FOR BELIEVING THAT HE WAS TAKEN A PRISONER TO ROME. NERO AND THE CONFLAGRATION OF THE CITY. THE MAMERTINE. "DOMINE QUO VADIS?" HIS TRIAL AND CRUCIFIXION. SAN PIETRO IN MONTORIO. HIS PLACE OF SEPULTURE. CONCLUSION.

> " The time for toil is past, and night has come,
>   The last and closing of the harvest eves :
> Worn out with labour long and wearisome,
> Drooping and faint the reapers hasten home,
>   Each laden with his sheaves."

" Let us come to the champions of our times ; . . . Peter having suffered martyrdom went to his deserved place of glory." —*Clement.*

" Peter appears to have preached in Pontus and Galatia and Bithynia, Cappadocia and Asia, to the Jews in the Dispersion. He also in the end being at Rome was crucified."—*Origen.*

" What a happy Church is that on which the Apostles poured out all their doctrine with their blood! where Peter had a like Passion with the Lord."—*Tertullian.*

" It may be permitted us, until the day when all shall be known, to follow the cherished associations of all Christendom,—to trace still in the Mamertine prison and the Vatican the last days on earth of him to whom was committed especially the feeding of the flock of God."—*Dean Alford.*

THE concluding chapter of our Apostle's history is involved in great uncertainty. Deeply interesting would it have been to us to be able to follow under inspired guidance, as in the case of his illustrious contemporary, the final stages of his memorable career. What Irenæus says of Paul is more true still of Peter, "Luke at the close of his story leaves us thirsting for more." The Acts of the Apostles are here as silent as on the previous twenty years of his life;—and we are compelled to weave together as best we can,—partly from scattered notices in the New Testament, and partly from uncanonical authorities, the account of the closing scene. In much it must at the best be conjecture; and yet, there are many broken links in various ways supplied, which enable us to claim a strong probability, at all events, for the accuracy of the narration.

He must now, as previously noted, have exceeded three-score and ten. The infirmities of age must alone have read to him the monition that soon he must " put off his tabernacle." Though his spirit may have been vigorous as ever, there were rents and chinks doubtless in the decaying earthly tent. The Apostle of the Gentiles bespeaks the sympathy of Philemon as being " such an one as Paul the aged ;" and if Peter, as we have reason to believe, was considerably the senior of the two, we can confidently think of him with " the hoary head;" —" the crown of glory " when found, as in his case, " in the way of righteousness."

We have so far prepared our readers for what our own theory is, in this disputed story of Peter's concluding years ; viz., that we reject the supposition—so strongly advocated by Romanists—of his having lived for a quarter of a century as Bishop of Rome and founder of its Church. We shall not recapitulate the grounds on which we consider such a belief to be utterly untenable ; indeed only an ecclesiastical myth. On the other hand, we are not of those who repudiate, *in toto*, the idea of his ever having been in the city of the Tiber,—who hold that as he spent his latter years, so he also died in the Eastern Babylon. On the contrary, we are very strongly of opinion (as we have incidentally indicated in the previous chapter, and which we shall presently speak of at greater length), that after living for many years as the Apostle of the Circumcision in the city of the Euphrates, he was summarily arrested by order of the tyrant Nero, taken a prisoner to Rome (which he could have reached only shortly before his death), and that there he obtained his martyr's crown.

While the early Fathers give no support whatever to the conjecture of Peter's long residence in the latter city, and of his being placed there as head of the Church, there is a remarkable unanimity among them as to the fact of his death occurring in the world's metropolis. Clement, Ignatius, Papias, Dionysius of Corinth, Irenæus, Origen, Tertullian, and others, all testify to it. It is only the more zealous Protestant partisans who dispute his being in Rome at all; deeming that such a position, could it be established, would prove the most effectual means of demolishing the Romanists' assertion of his primacy. We need not say, however, that the mere fact of ending his life in the city of the Cæsars is altogether apart and distinct from his claim to "St Peter's chair." The evidence supporting his martyrdom there is ample, while that supporting his alleged primacy is capable of easy and satisfactory refutation from the incidents of apostolic history. The one affords no necessary proof or corroboration of the other.[1]

Is there no higher authority still that may be quoted, as indirectly confirming these conclusions; and at all events negativing the idea of the venerable Apostle dying a natural death in the Eastern city of his adoption?

[1] One among many other testimonies to his Roman martyrdom is that of Lactantius—"When Nero found that not only at Rome, but everywhere, multitudes were daily falling off from the worship of idols, and going over to the new religion in contempt of antiquity: execrable and noxious tyrant as he was, he determined to destroy the heavenly Church and to abolish righteousness: and first of all men, becoming persecutor of God's servants, he crucified Peter and slew Paul."—*Quoted by Dean Alford, Proleg.*, p. 238.

What did our Lord say to Peter on that memorable occasion we have dwelt upon in a previous chapter, when, on the shores of Gennesaret, the Master contrasted the freedom of the fisherman's younger days with the restraints to which alien hands would subject him in old age ? " When thou shalt be old thou shalt stretch forth thy hands, and *another shall gird thee*, AND CARRY THEE WHITHER THOU WOULDEST NOT. This spake He, signifying by what death he should glorify God " (John xxi. 18). Here we have, not only the prediction of the certainty of his martyrdom, and that too by crucifixion— " the stretching forth of his hands ; "—but there is with equal specialty foretold a peculiarity in the manner of his death and the place of it. He was to be suddenly seized and bound ; and they who were thus violently to " lay hold on him " and " gird him," were also " *to carry him whither he would not.*"

How exactly does the Saviour's prediction accord with what we accept as the fulfilment ! It is well worthy of being noted, that the Gospel of St John, in which this statement occurs, was written, as is generally believed, not earlier than A.D. 97, and at all events many years subsequent to Peter's death. The 21st chapter, moreover, has all the appearance of a postscript, or supplement, added after the previous portion had been completed ; in which the writer, by detailing the description which his Lord had given of the Apostle's end, is evidently desirous, among other things, of bearing testimony to the prescience of his Divine Master. He refers to the well-known fulfilment of a prediction uttered, more than a quarter of a century before, on the shore of a Syrian lake, and which had now circumstantially come true. " There is implied in it this remark :—' The Lord told

Peter, more than thirty years before the event, that, at the close of his life " when he should be old," he should be bound as a captive, and be carried away to be put to death in some other place. And so ye know, it fell out.' This is evidently the drift of those words of Christ, which ' the beloved disciple' so particularly notes down and preserves. We accept the Apostle John's testimony, therefore, to this fact, that at the close of Peter's life and labours, he was seized and bound, and carried off to be executed. If he was found in Babylon, as we suppose, then he was carried away *from* Babylon. But whither? He might be ordered to be put to death in Antioch, or in Jerusalem : but no reason appears for his conveyance to either of these places. If he was not to be put to death in Babylon, then it seems most probable that the order was, ' Bring him to Rome, that he and the other chief of the sect, Paul, may be executed together.' This same course was taken, fifty years after, with Ignatius, who was carried prisoner from Antioch to Rome, there to be thrown to the lions. In Pliny's letter, too, we find a reference to the same practice in other cases. He says, ' Others were brought before me possessed with the same infatuation, but being citizens of Rome I directed that they should be conveyed thither.' " [1]

An occurrence of savage import in the imperial city, to which casual allusion has already been made, precipitated the catastrophe. The guilty perpetrator and his acts demand more special description, from their intimate connection with the fate of our Apostle.

Nero was now sovereign of the Roman world. He was still only a youth of twenty-one ; but his life of guilt and infamy had already begun. There is scarce

[1] " Life and Writings of St Peter," p. 263.

the crime that can be named into which he had not already plunged. He had murdered many courtiers in cold blood ; and Octavia, his beautiful and noble-minded queen, was living in exile. The infamous Poppæa was residing with him as his unlawful wife in his palace on the Palatine. Shortly after, he not only gave orders for Octavia's murder, but for his cruel satisfaction had her head brought to Rome ! A few weeks later he committed the most enormous of his many unnatural deeds, in the assassination of his own mother. His first purpose was to loosen the rafters of her bed-chamber, and to bury her as she was asleep under the ruins of the ceiling. This failing, he next arranged to drown her on her way to her villa on the Lucrine Lake, when on board an ornamental yacht, so contrived as, on a given signal, to fall to pieces. This also having failed, she was despatched the same night with daggers. It gives a mournful picture of his hardened levity, that, a short time after, he was singing to the guitar, and acting in presence of crowds of Romans ; the nobler of whom shed tears when they saw the imperial honour so tarnished. When the tidings of revolt among his subjects came to his ears, he threatened to poison the whole Senate, consume the city by fire, and let loose wild beasts among the people in the streets. No wonder Paul speaks of him as a " lion," and thanks his God who had rescued him from his jaws.

On the night of the 19th of July A.D. 64, a fire broke out in the Circus Maximus, between the Palatine and Aventine Mount. It raged fiercely for six days and seven nights, spreading with amazing rapidity, the people being forced to seek for shelter among the monuments and tombs of the dead. No besieging army could have so effected the work of destruction. The citizens saw, with bitter sorrow, their homes and noble buildings becoming a prey to the furious element; and it must have added much to their indignation to find (what it is to be feared was too true) that Nero was the cause of this fearful calamity. " He was offended," says Suetonius, " with the deformity of the ancient buildings, and the narrow passages and turnings of the streets. . . . Besides the vast number of ordinary houses, the palaces of the great captains of former ages, adorned with the spoils of former conquests, were all consumed to ashes, together with the temples of the gods, which the ancient kings of Rome had raised, and had afterwards been consecrated to the memory of the Roman victories." The unfeeling tyrant soon came to find that so wanton and cruel an outrage had roused, as it might justly have done, the anger of the Romans. What is he to do? The base expedient occurs to fasten the guilt of the burning on the innocent *Christians*, whose purity he hated, because it condemned his own vices. The plot answered too successfully. He succeeded, by this malicious lie, in rousing the popular feeling against the followers of Jesus; saving himself by involving the innocent. Cruelties beyond description followed. The sufferers were besmeared with pitch, and then set fire to at night to lighten the darkness; others were sewn up in the skins of beasts, hunted down by dogs, and torn to pieces. Nero exulted personally in this spectacle. He moved about, as Tacitus tells us, in a circus erected in his own gardens, " in the dress of a charioteer, sometimes on foot, and sometimes viewing the spectacle from his car." [1]

[1] See " Footsteps of St Paul," pp. 376, 408, 409.

We may imagine what the feelings of the mob were likely to be towards the reputed heads of the hated sect of the Nazarenes.

Paul, as their chief representative in the West, was immediately seized. But there was another propagandist in the far East, well known at least to prætors and proconsuls, who had been founding communities of these same obnoxious religionists, who, in the words of Tacitus, "were convicted on account of their sullen hatred of mankind." [1]

That Peter could have been at Rome only a very short time before Paul's death, is evident, independently of other reasons, from the fact we have noted in a previous chapter, of no mention having been made of him in the last Epistle of the great Apostle to his son Timothy. In that letter the doomed prisoner makes affecting allusion to the old friends who had forsaken him, and denied him their sympathy and solace. We cannot for a moment believe that Peter would have stood aloof from his noble-minded brother in such a crisis, had he then been resident in the same city. The likeliest conjecture we can form is, that his violent seizure by the myrmidons of Nero had taken place immediately after the writing of that touching Epistle. Perhaps Paul had little expected such a response to his pathetic appeal as the appearance of his honoured "fellow-soldier" from distant Asia ; and it would add a tinge, if we may so call it, of sacred romance to that unexpected answer, if we can credit the legend so universally received in the ancient Church, that the two

[1] It is noteworthy that Peter, in one of his Epistles, uses the corresponding word in Greek to that which, in Latin, Tacitus employs regarding the Christians. They were punished as "evil doers ;" "*Malefici*" is the term of the Roman historian, "κακοποιοί" that of our Apostle (1 Pet. ii. 12).

prisoners were together immured in the same dungeon
of the Mamertine. That prison is still pointed out as
the scene of Peter's incarceration. Its position is adjoining the Forum, at the foot of the descent from the
Capitol, and beside the arch of Septimius Severus.
It is considered the oldest relic of Etruscan architecture
in the city, deriving its name from Ancus Martius, the
fourth king of ancient Rome, and enlarged by Servius
Tullius. It is reached, in the present day, by a vault
under the church of St Giuseppe dei Falegnami, where
the visitor finds himself in two dismal cells ; the lower
is only six-and-a-half feet in height, and the huge blocks
of tufa of which it is built are united by cramps of
iron. There is a circular opening or aperture above,
through which prisoners, on their condemnation, were
said to have been lowered either to starve or be
strangled to death. Jugurtha suffered the former of
these cruelties within these terrible walls. No wonder
Paul wrote so anxiously for his winter cloak to protect
him from the pestilential damps and cold of such a
place. The ecclesiastical officials who to this day conduct strangers to these dungeons, retail the baseless
traditions given by Baronius of the impress of Peter's
head on the wall, the pillar to which he and Paul were
bound for the space of nine months, and the fountain
which miraculously burst forth to supply water for the
baptisms of the two centurions Processus and Martianus,
with forty-seven other converted fellow-captives. In
commemoration of the imprisonment of the two Apostles,
deputies from all the churches in Rome assemble by
torchlight on the night of the 4th of July, and in
solemn silence kneel in front of the traditional pillar.[1]

[1] See " Footsteps of St Paul," p. 407. Also " St Paul in Rome," p. 75. The

If we can accept even the reasonable probability of so strange a reunion, in so strange a place, between these two doomed and devoted chiefs, imagination may be left to picture it. It would vividly recall to both the never-to-be-forgotten fourteen days when they had met, long years ago, under the same roof in Jerusalem. On that former occasion they were only girding on their armour :—now the fight had been wellnigh fought, and the garlands of victory were in view. The Roman *Via Sacra* and *Via Triumphalis* were close by their prison. But theirs was a nobler triumph and nobler trophies than those associated with conquering chariot and blare of martial trumpet.

We shall accept, then, the general patristic testimonies on this point, as these are expressed in the words of so reliable an authority as Dionysius of Corinth, who asserts that Peter arrived in Rome in A.D. 66, and that he was not longer there than one year.[1] Our own belief indeed is, that the period of his residence was considerably shorter. The way was long, and the facilities for locomotion limited between the Euphrates and the Tiber. It is supposed the order for his seizure was given in the opening year of Nero's persecution, A.D. 64. "It would be the spring of A.D. 65 before it could reach Babylon. Preparations for the journey would then have to be made; and it might be nearly A.D. 66 before he reached Rome."[2]

writer may be allowed to refer the reader to a preliminary dissertation in the latter volume, where there are details given regarding some recent interesting light thrown by archæological research on the ancient Mamertine prisons.

[1] See "Bibliotheca Sacra," January 1859. Nero died June 9th A.D. 68.

[2] "Life and Writings of St Peter," p. 268.

All that follows is still more matter of conjecture.[1] What treatment he received when he reached the great capital, we cannot tell. One of the most beautiful of ancient legends regarding him (if legend indeed we may call an incident which has been narrated both by Ambrose and Origen, and which may perhaps here find the most appropriate place), would seem to indicate that he was not altogether bereft of friends. The well-known story they have left is this :—

At the instigation of some of the faithful, Peter was urged to flee for his life. At first, the proposal was met by him with a decided negative, justly fearing reflections on his courage and constancy,—that friends and foes might alike accuse him of shrinking from those sufferings for his dear Lord, to the endurance of which he had exhorted others. But the appeal of their prayers and tears as to the value of his life to them and the infant Church, fortified too as the recommendation was by Christ's own injunction (Matt. x. 23), for the moment overcame his scruples. With reluctance he acceded : and by night was assisted over the prison wall. He betook himself along that same Appian Way, by which probably, as in the case of Paul, he had entered the city. He succeeded in getting two miles beyond the Porta Capena, and was nigh the spot, bordering on the wide Campagna, which was soon after sacred as the place of repose for Christian dead. The same Lord, whom last he saw in the ascension-cloud, appeared to him hasten-

[1] The strangest and most incredible of the many legends regarding Peter is that given by Eusebius on the authority of Metaphrastes, that he not only had a lengthened sojourn in Europe, but visited for a considerable period the British Isles, "where he converted many nations to the faith." As Dr Cave, however, who finds a place in his pages for the legend, quaintly remarks, "We had better be without the honour of St Peter's company, than build the story on so sandy a foundation."

ing in the direction of the city. The fugitive Apostle immediately recognises the Divine Master. The same penetrating look, doubtless, was cast upon him, with which he had once been confronted in the palace-court of the High Priest—a look of sadness and gentle reproach. Peter was the first to break silence with the question—"Lord, whither goest Thou?"[1] The answer was immediately returned, "I go again to be crucified."

The interrogator continued—"Lord, wast Thou not crucified once for all?"

"Yes," was the reply, "but I saw thy flight from death, and I go to be crucified in thy stead."

"Lord," was the immediate answer of Peter, "I go to obey Thy command."

"Fear not," was the Master's farewell word as He vanished from sight, "for I am with thee."

The Apostle at once retraced his steps, returned to his cell, and surrendered himself to his keepers.

The above story we are aware is by many rejected; —classed among the "*apocryphal writings*," and deemed only another of the many similar inventions of a credulous age. It may be so: but we see nothing in the narrative itself to relegate it to the category of the purely mythical and legendary. True, it is not recorded in Scripture. It has no shadow of an inspired basis. But the answer to this is—that the whole narrative of Peter's latter life is

---

1 "*Domine quo vadis?*" The words which have given name to the well-known church erected on the reputed spot. In accordance with the usual childish superstitions, there is shown a fac-simile of the stone on which Christ stood while He talked with Peter, and on which He left the impression of His feet: the original being alleged to be preserved in the neighbouring church of St Sebastian. Michael Angelo's statue in the Church of Sta Maria Sopra Minerva, is supposed to represent the Saviour as He appeared to Peter on this occasion.

left unchronicled by inspired pens : so that such omission is not by any means fatal to its credibility. Similar divine appearances of the Lord Jesus were, moreover, by no means uncommon in the life and experience of St Paul. The revelation of Christ to him on the way to Damascus did not stand alone. In Corinth, when oppressed in spirit by the obstinate rejection of the gospel message by his fellow-countrymen, that same Lord appeared to him " in a vision by night," with words of encouragement—words proceeding from the lips of a glorified *Person*—" I am with thee, and no man shall set on thee to hurt thee : for I have much people in this city " (Acts xviii. 9, 10). When apprehended at Jerusalem, and called upon to make his defence on the stairs of Antonia, he narrates a similar appearance of his Lord while he was praying in the Temple : " And it came to pass, that, when I was come again to Jerusalem, even while I prayed in the Temple, I was in a trance ; and saw Him saying unto me, Make haste, and get thee quickly out of Jerusalem : for they will not receive thy testimony concerning Me. And I said, Lord, they know that I imprisoned and beat in every synagogue them that believed on Thee : and when the blood of Thy martyr Stephen was shed, I also was standing by, and consenting unto his death, and kept the raiment of them that slew him. And He said unto me, Depart : for I will send thee far hence unto the Gentiles " (Acts xxii. 17-21). Yet again, when he was put in safe ward by the captain of the guard who had generously rescued him from the violence of the Sanhedrim : " The night following the Lord stood by him, and said, Be of good cheer, Paul ; for as thou hast testified of Me in Jerusalem, so must thou bear witness at Rome" (Acts xxiii. 11). Nor need we remind our readers of an instance still later than the closing years of Peter; when the same heavenly Redeemer appeared to the last of His living Apostles in the isle of Patmos; He revealed Himself in the lustres of His glorified humanity, with the circlet of stars in His right hand, and speaks as a divine, glorified *Person.* "And when I saw Him, I fell at His feet as dead. And He laid His right hand upon me, saying unto me, Fear not; I am the first and the last : I am He that liveth and was dead; and, behold, I am alive for evermore, Amen; and have the keys of hell and of death" (Rev. i. 17, 18). We can substantiate with no proofs this alleged analogous appearance of the Lord to Peter; but we have said enough to show from the experience of his most like-minded and like-privileged brothers, that such an appearance was not impossible in itself,—that it was by no means novel or exceptional in apostolical story; and the details of the narration as regards Peter himself are certainly in remarkable keeping with his character and antecedents.[1]

He had at all events now resigned himself to his fate, —and the end was drawing near. Like a brave general he had cut down the bridge behind him, so that escape or retreat was rendered impossible. His fellow-prisoner's words might with truth be adopted as his own —"I am now ready to be offered, and the time of my departure is at hand."

It is not at all probable that, like Paul, he would be summoned for trial before the Emperor personally in his imperial palace on the Palatine Hill. In the case of the former, a free - born Roman "appealing

[1] See note in Professor Plumptre's "Biblical Studies."

to Cæsar," we have every ground to picture him
standing either before Nero or his consular legate in
the pillared hall of Justice—the Basilica, which the
spade of the antiquary has lately laid bare—surrounded
with his twelve lictors, courtiers, and assessors. With
Peter, in all likelihood, it would be different. He had
no diploma of Roman citizenship to give him claim to
an imperial hearing. A mere hated and despised
member of the Jewish race, his case would be dealt
with summarily and arbitrarily, and his doom would
be swift; although, doubtless, some form of trial would
be gone through by an imperial subordinate—perhaps
the prefect of the city, who had supreme authority
over criminal suits. He would, at all events, have no
Burrhus or Seneca at his side, such as the other Apostle
had, to speak a kindly word for him. ONE only,
Mightier than earth's mightiest, would be faithful
to him in that hour. The appearance, be it myth or
reality, we have described on the Appian Way, would
be a sublime verity now. He could doubtless say
with his devoted brother-captive, "Notwithstanding,
THE LORD stood with me and strengthened me."

Nor are we allowed to picture him in his prison
life. We can only conjecture, and no more, the earthly
friends who possibly may have visited him, or of whose
presence in the city or nearness to his cell he may have
been cognisant. We know the devoted band who
were faithful to the last in brightening the closing
hours of Paul's life. Could Peter, too, have seen the
beloved Luke—his own future biographer? or Onesiphorus, who had come all the way from Asia, forgetful
of danger, to see his venerated father, and cheer the
gloom of the Mamertine? "He sought him out dili-

gently, and found him." Or Linus, or Pudens and his wife Claudia? or Timothy, who had hastened, at the urgent solicitation of his best friend, to give and receive a parting blessing? Perhaps with greater probability than those now named, would be Clement, who seems to speak from personal knowledge, when he writes of "Peter having borne testimony unto death." All, however, is uncertainty. If any of these were seen, it may have only been at best a passing glimpse, giving perhaps, by look and silent expression, the sympathy which they dared not embody in words. We have the authority, at all events, of ancient tradition in mentioning the name of *one* specially dear to him. It was she whom he had "led about" in his missionary journeyings; who had been the companion of many hours, or rather busy and eventful years of anxiety and labour, and to whom he now addressed words of heart-cheer when he saw her on her way to martyrdom. To Clement of Alexandria we are indebted for the following affecting story regarding her: —"They say that St Peter, beholding his wife led out to death, was rejoiced at her calling of the Lord and her conveyance to her heavenly home, and cried out encouragingly and comfortingly, addressing her by name, 'Oh, remember thou the Lord!' Such was the marriage of that blessed pair, and the perfect agreement in those things that were dearest to them."[1]

---

[1] I may here venture, without comment, to insert "the legend" (for legend we can only call it) "of St Petronilla," the alleged daughter of the Apostle Peter. In doing so, I shall avail myself, in the first instance, of the words in which it is given in the pages of "Sacred and Legendary Art":—

"The Apostle Peter had a daughter who accompanied him in his journey from the East. Being at Rome with him, she fell sick of a grievous infirmity which deprived her of the use of her limbs. And it happened that

It is a question in the case of Paul whether his Roman citizenship shielded him from the cruel custom of scourging the condemned before death. It is not likely that even he evaded the humiliation. " Baronius tells us that in the Church of St Mary, beyond the Bridge in Rome, the pillars are yet extant to which he is said

as the disciples were at meat with him in his house, one said to him, 'Master, how is it that thou who healest the infirmities of others, dost not heal thy daughter Petronilla?' And St Peter answered, 'It is good for her to remain sick.' But that they might see the power that was in the Word of God, he commanded her to get up and serve them at table, which she did ; and having done so, she lay down as helpless as before. But many years afterwards, being perfected by her long suffering, and praying fervently, she was healed. Petronilla was wonderfully fair, and Valerius Flaccus, a young and noble Roman, who was a heathen, became enamoured of her beauty, and sought her for his wife ; and he being very powerful, she feared to refuse him. She therefore desired him to return in three days, and promised that he should carry her home. But she prayed earnestly to be delivered from this peril ; and when Flaccus returned in three days, with great pomp, to celebrate the marriage, he found her dead. The company of nobles who attended him carried her to the grave, in which they laid her crowned with roses ; and Flaccus lamented greatly."

The legend places her death in the year 98—that is, thirty-two years after the death of St Peter. But it would be in vain to attempt to reconcile the dates and improbabilities of this story.

St Peter raising Petronilla from her sick-bed, is one of the subjects by Masaccio in the Brancacci Chapel. The scene of her entombment is the subject of a once celebrated and colossal picture by Guercino. The copy, in mosaic, is over the altar dedicated to her in St Peter's. In front, and in the lower part of the picture, she is just seen as they are letting her down into the grave crowned with roses. Behind stands Flaccus with a handkerchief in his hand, and a crowd of spectators. In the upper part of the picture Petronilla is already in Paradise, kneeling in a rich dress before the feet of Christ, having exchanged an earthly for a heavenly Bridegroom.—*Sacred and Legendary Art,* p. 210.

I cannot resist further referring the reader to an interesting paper on the same subject, contributed to *Good Words* in November 1874, by the eminent Roman archæologist Mr Shakspere Wood, whose personal kindness when in Rome I have, in common with others, gratefully to acknowledge. The article referred to is a description of the discovery of the Basilica of Santa Petronilla at a farm on the Campagna, called Tor Marancia, and not far from the church *Domine quo Vadis.* The discovery is one of the many successful explorations which have been made by Signor de Rossi. In digging into the catacombs known to be in this place, he came, as long ago as the year 1854, on a crypt of considerable size. Three marble columns,

to have been bound and scourged."[1]   To Peter we may
well believe there was no such clemency shown.   Even
his venerable years would insure no exemption from
the lacerations of the rod.   Neither would the reason
which spared Paul the agonies of crucifixion operate
in saving him from that cruel lingering death—the
death, indeed, which Christ had specially indicated—
" Thou shalt stretch forth thy hands : " " the hands
extended upon either side on the transverse bar of
the cross."—*Trench*.   The legend was commonly accepted in the ancient Church that they both suffered

also two sarcophagi ornamented with lions' heads, rewarded his labour;
but circumstances, detailed by Mr Wood, necessitated his abandoning
farther investigations at that time.   Recently, under the new *régime*, the
explorations were renewed, and rewarded by the discovery of the long-lost
Basilica, " with its walls and apse standing to the height of some 12 or
14 feet," exactly in the locality where the ancient Itineraries placed it
(*Ecclesia Sanctæ Petronillæ*).   Mr Wood mentions that after the siege of
Rome by the Lombard king in the eighth century, the remains of Petronilla,
with her sarcophagus, were taken to St Peter's ; after which the original
Basilica was abandoned.   As to the question of Petronilla being the veritable
daughter of the Apostle, the writer of the article wisely does not commit
himself.   Signor de Rossi's opinion, on grounds there stated, is rather
unfavourable to her being so in any other sense than that of the spirit.
We may append the words of the great archæologist of the seventeenth
century, Bosio, as given by Mr Wood.   He thus speaks of this catacomb
before any explorations had been made :—" We may enumerate this among
the most ancient of the cemeteries in Rome, for it had its beginning about
the time of the holy Apostles ; and in it was buried Petronilla, *santissima
Virgine*, who is commonly called the daughter of St Peter, either because,
as some will, she was really his daughter, inasmuch as we read in Clement
of Alexandria, St John Chrysostom, and Nicephorus, that St Peter had a
wife who became a martyr ; or because, as others will, this holy virgin was
baptized by St Peter, and therefore called his daughter. . . . It was
then with the sepulture of Santa Petronilla that this cemetery had its beginning, distant a mile and a half from the walls of Rome, in a sandy
grotto which was on the Via Ardientina, at a farm belonging to Santa
Flavia Domitilla, *illustrissima Virgine*, niece, on the sister's side, of Flavius
Clemens, consul. . . . And in this cemetery were also buried the bodies
of the holy martyrs Nereus and Achilleus, chamberlains to the same Santa
Domitilla."

[1] Cave.

martyrdom the same day. The one was led out to
Aqua Salvia, like his Lord, " without the gate," on the
road to Ostia, one of the Tyburns of ancient Rome ;
and, where stands the church familiar to travellers as
the Tre Fontane, suffered death by the sword of the
Roman executioner. The other, if we follow tradition,
after saluting his brethren, and having taken his last
farewell of Paul, was led across one of the bridges of
the Tiber to those heights on the Vatican Mount—the
ancient Janiculum—now well known by their association with the Basilica which bears his name—*San Pietro
in Montorio.* There, in the courtyard of a barrack
or military station, he is said to have undergone the
punishment from which Roman citizens were exempted,
but which was reserved for malefactors.[1]

1 The Church of St Pietro in Montorio is reputed to have been built by
the Emperor Constantine. Having fallen into decay, it was restored by
Ferdinand and Isabella of Spain at the close of the fifteenth century. I
remember in visiting it being much impressed with the beauty of the
adjoining chapel of Bramante, certainly more so than with the cluster
of monkish relics and legends which have gathered around it. "It
is a small circular building, having on the outside a corridor sustained
by sixteen columns of the Doric order in grey granite. . . . In its
upper chapel, before the altar, is a sitting statue of St Peter ; and in
the crypt below, richly decorated with stucco reliefs, is shown the hole
into which was stuck the cross upon which the Prince of the Apostles was
crucified."—*Murray's Handbook to Rome,* p. 189.

Giotto's well-known picture in the Sacristy of the Vatican, represents the
crucifixion, in accordance with a rival legend, as having taken place
between the two *metœ* or goals of a circus close by, round which the chariots
turned.

If we are correct in assigning the Vatican Mount as the scene of Peter's
martyrdom, it is plain that the old tradition is a baseless one of the final
meeting which took place between him and Paul outside the Ostian Gate,
and which I have thus elsewhere described :—"In passing along the straight
road (probably, too, unchanged since the first century), and which still
conducts to Ostia, the student interested in tracing the footsteps of the
great Apostle cannot resist pausing for a moment by the small inconspicuous
chapel on the wayside to mark one of the scenes which tradition, although
without any authority, has grafted on this memorable last journey. In the
rude bas-relief above the door is a slab containing a representation of the

On the horrors of the final scene we need not dwell.
These to him would be disarmed of their terrors by " the
vision and fruition," with the assurance of which he had
supported other sufferers in his earlier Epistle—" the
glory to be revealed "—and which, even in the midst
of their " fiery trials," would enable them " to be glad
also with exceeding joy" (1 Peter iv. 12, 13). The

supposed parting which here took place between St Peter and St Paul.
The words alleged to have been spoken have as singular a quaintness about
them as the sculptures they illustrate :—And St Paul said to St Peter,
'Peace be with thee, Foundation of the Church, Shepherd of the flock of
Christ.' And Peter said to Paul, 'Go in peace, Preacher of good tidings
and Guide of the salvation of the just.'" We may adopt the safe verdict of
Dr Cave, "That however fictitious may be this and other recorded incidents, the best is, which of them soever started first, they both came at last
to the same end of the race, to those palms and crowns which are reserved
for all good men in heaven."

> " Oh, then the glory and the bliss,
>   When all that pained or seemed amiss
>   Shall melt with earth and sin away !
>   When saints, beneath their Saviour's eye,
>   Filled with each other's company,
>   Shall spend in love the eternal day ! "
>   —*Christian Year*, p. 321.

It may only farther be added, that the two Apostles continued in all
subsequent centuries to be associated with one another in ecclesiastical art
alike in pictures, statues, and medallions.

"In former years, among the ecclesiastical pageants which attracted
multitudes at Easter to St Peter's, was one at the close of Vespers on Monday.
A canon appeared on a balcony underneath the vast dome, and in sonorous
voice announced that what were now exposed to the view of the faithful
were the famous portraits possessed by Pope Sylvester—portraits which,
when shown by him to Constantine, were called by the Emperor 'those
gods named Peter and Paul.'"—*See Heman's "Christian Rome,"* p. 158.
A copy of a valuable bronze medallion, three inches in diameter, of St
Paul and St Peter, also in the Vatican, will be found carefully rendered in
one of the engravings of Mrs Jamieson's " Sacred and Legendary Art." It
is considered the earliest known representation of the Apostles—probably
in the time of the Flavian Emperors. It was discovered by Boldetti in
St Domitilla's Cemetery in the catacombs of St Calixtus, and is artistically
and classically executed; but it is at present in a portion of the Museum
to which, when I was in Rome, the public were forbidden access. See
" St Paul in Rome," pp. 96, 98.

latest scenes of his life in distant Babylon may have mingled with older, and still more sacred reminiscences; and all with bright anticipations of the heavenly future. The words of an excellent poet may be put into his lips as possibly descriptive of the emotions of the hour :—

" But on before me swept the moonlit stream,
    That had entranced me with its memories—
    A thousand battles and one burst of psalms—
    Rolling its waters to the Indian sea
    Beyond Balsara and Elana far,
    Nigh to two thousand miles from Ararat.
    But its full music took a finer tone,
    And sang me something of a gentler stream
    That rolls for ever to another shore,
    Whereof our God Himself is the sole Sea,
    And Christ's dear love the pulsing of the tide.

.   .   .   .   .   .

    And then I thought I knelt, and kneeling heard
    Nothing—save only the long wash of waves,
    And one sweet psalm that sobbed for evermore."
                                    —*Waters of Babylon.*

It would only be in harmony with his character, if yet another widely-known tradition be accepted—that he refused to be placed on the cross in the ordinary manner; or rather, feeling unworthy of suffering in the same posture as his great Lord, that he expressed a desire to be crucified with his head downwards. The words of Jerome are—" By this Emperor (Nero) he was crucified and crowned with martyrdom, his head being turned towards the earth and his feet in the air, protesting that he was unworthy to be crucified as his Lord was." Some authorities are disposed to deny the truth of this tradition, as dating no earlier than a disputed reference of Origen, and the above more pronounced affirmation of Jerome. But it was doubtless credited by the early Church ; and, as a writer remarks, besides being in keeping with the " fervent temperament and deep humility of the Apostle, it was a death not unlikely to have been inflicted in mockery by the instruments of Nero's wanton and ingenious cruelty."[1] " Happy man ! " is the exclamation of Chrysostom, who accepted the truth of the legend, " to be set in the readiest posture of travelling from earth to heaven." Crucifixion, in any form, was a death of intense anguish. Nor can we resist the remark, in passing, that doubtless, though not fully cognisant of all the terrible accessories, yet knowing from lips which could not err that he was to suffer martyrdom in this way, what a sublime superiority was manifested to the pangs of dissolution, when in his last letter he could calmly compare his departure, as the words may mean, to the laying aside of an old cloak or garment—" I must put off this my tabernacle" (2 Peter i. 14).

We have spoken of the friends who may possibly have ministered to him with their sympathy in his closing days. Many more there would be amid " the children of God scattered abroad," especially among his Asiatic converts, who would bewail the loss of their spiritual father. While these, however, are unknown to us,

[1] Bib. Dic., art. "Peter." "Seneca mentions that the Romans sometimes crucified men with their heads downwards ; and Eusebius testifies that several martyrs were put to that cruel death (adding that smoking wood was sometimes placed immediately under the victim's head, either to add to his tortures or to hasten his death). Accordingly the executioners easily granted the Apostle his extraordinary request. St Chrysostom, St Augustine, and St Austerius say that he was nailed to the cross : Tertullian mentions that he was tied with cords. He was probably both nailed and bound with ropes."—Butler, quoted in Hare's Walks in Rome, p. 450. Those who have been in Cologne will remember Rubens' great painting of St Peter's crucifixion, and which the artist considered his own masterpiece. It is treated in accordance with the above tradition.

there is one, whose name has been pre-eminently familiar in the preceding narrative, who surely could not fail to be numbered among "the chiefest mourners;" one whose hallowed love and friendship, strong in life, would be stronger still in death. Peter's friendship even with Paul was but of yesterday compared to that of the play-mate of his youth, and the true yoke-fellow of his riper years. We may realise for a moment the feelings of the beloved and tender-hearted John, when he had learnt, as soon he must, that his oldest, dearest friend—the friend linked to him with devout memories never shared before or since on earth—had been called to his martyr's crown. We know indeed from the last chapter of the fourth Evangelist's Gospel, how sacred and imperishable these memories were;—how fondly and lovingly he cherished the worth of the departed. Let another in his graphic sentences express what these feelings must have been :—" The very writing of this chapter, it would almost seem, is to be regarded as a tribute of friendship, on the part of John, to the memory of his beloved com-rade Peter. It was, as is generally believed, the last task on earth of 'the disciple whom Jesus loved' to prepare his Gospel. Moved and inspired by the Holy Ghost, he gave to this work the latest days of his lengthened life. And what more congenial occupation could he have had assigned to him ! He had addressed to the Church at large, as well as to individuals, letters of warning, affectionate and faithful, against the deadly errors of that time, when men were already beginning to deny or explain away the reality of the atonement made by Christ, and the renewal wrought by the Spirit. He had put on record the revelation of all things about to happen on the earth, down to the era of the Lord's appearing in glory, and the establishment of His glorious kingdom. And now, on the near verge of the grave, with his foot on the very confines of the eternal world, he is summoned to live over again, in inspired recollection and in minute detail, those three youthful years of his personal fellowship with the Lord, which to him are worth uncounted ages.

"Blessed toil! nay, rather rapturous enjoyment! How does he throw his whole soul into it, and linger over it, feeling as if he never could have done!

". . . Plainly the venerable writer was then laying down his pen. It is the formal finishing of the book. But he cannot tear himself away : he cannot bring himself to say 'Farewell.' There are more last words to utter ; there is a postscript—an appendix to add. . . . He has to rear a monument more durable than brass, not only to his Master, but to his Master's friend and his own.

"For who can doubt that it is partly, at least, as a memorial of Peter that this extra matter in the 21st chapter is given? The whole chapter is about Peter. And with what exquisite tact and taste—with what tenderness and what truth—is Peter sketched to us in this affecting picture!"[1]

We return from this digression to the scene of the crucifixion on the Janiculum. The mere accessories and surroundings of that scene may be of little moment ; and yet it may not be out of place for readers who have never visited Rome to remark, that in striking contrast with the dreary and desolate locality in the Campagna which witnessed the martyrdom of Paul, there is perhaps no spot in or around the city which lingers longer

[1] Dr Candlish's "Scripture Reminiscences," pp. 271–273.

in the "mind's eye" for its unparalleled view, than the traditional scene of Peter's martyrdom, and specially when beheld under the cloudless blue of an Italian sky. At the time of which we speak, far to the right, stretching a long way beyond the Forum and Mamertine prisons, would be seen the now treeless Campagna, which girdles the modern Rome as with a zone of death, but which then would be studded with patrician villas and palatial residences. The range of Alban and Sabine hills would appear in the extreme distance. On their nearer slopes would be discerned Frascati, on its gentle eminence, enshrined in olive groves; Tivoli, nestling in its purple shadows. Snowy Soracte would form the solitary guardian of the northern landscape. In the middle distance outside the city would rise those enormous aqueducts, then in their completed vastness, whose weird colossal fragments, still spanning the naked "Prairie," form the most picturesque of all the relics of Rome's ancient splendour; while nearer would be the yellow Tiber winding its serpentine way from the Flaminian Gate through the Pons Triumphalis, and sweeping along the base of the Aventine Mount. Yet what was the grandeur of earth's greatest Capital, with so beautiful a setting, to him who was on the threshold of "the building of God, an house not made with hands, eternal in the heavens!" "And then, said they, We will show you the Delectable Mountains. So he looked, and, behold, at a great distance he saw a most pleasant mountainous country, very delectable to behold. . . . And when thou comest there, from thence thou mayest see to the gate of the Celestial city."

"And o'er his features poured a ray
Of glory, not to pass away;

2 R

> One to sublimer worlds allied,
> One from all passions purified,—
> Even now half mingled with the sky,
> And all prepared, oh, not to die,
> But, like the prophet, to aspire
> To heaven's triumphal car of fire."
>
> —*Hemans.*

We mention, however, the impressiveness of the modern view from the church of Montorio, more on account of one feature in it which was totally wanting on the occasion of that crucifixion scene. To the left of the panorama the spectator is now mainly arrested by a building which dwarfs and overpowers all its compeers; the first to be seen in the far-distant view of Rome,—the last to linger on the horizon as he leaves the old plains of Latium. It is the reputed spot where the remains of our Apostle are said to repose—the Cathedral Church bearing his name — the colossal monument which hierarchal pride has reared to the memory of the alleged Vicar of Christ.[1] "He was buried at Rome, in the Vatican," are the words of Jerome, "by the side of the Triumphal Way; it is honoured with the veneration of the whole city." "I am able," says Caius, the learned Roman Presbyter, who lived in the third century, "to show the very tombs of the Apostles: for whether you go to the Vatican or the Ostian road, you will find the sepulchres of those who founded this church." Whatever were the superstitious abuses to which the custom led, it was, we know, the habit of the primitive Christians most sacredly to guard the localities where martyr-blood was shed. St Cyprian is the interpreter in a single sentence of the sentiment

---

[1] His body being taken from the cross is said to have been embalmed by Marcellinus, the Presbyter, after the Jewish manner.

of the faithful in these ages : " To the bodies of those who depart by the outlet of a glorious death, let a more zealous watchfulness be given." [1] The first memorial to the Apostle of the Circumcision was a humble one, in the shape of a small oratory, erected over the place where he was supposed to be buried, at or nigh the site of the present Basilica. It was built in A.D. 90 by Anacletus, Bishop of Rome, who was said to have been ordained by Peter himself. This, however, was destroyed by Heliogobalus, and the body was removed in the first instance, along with that of Paul, to the Catacombs in the Appian Way, where it rested till the popedom of Cornelius, who in the fourth century transferred it once more from the subterranean crypt of St Sebastian to the vicinity of the scene of martyrdom on the Janiculum. The Emperor Constantine, digging with his own hands part of the foundation, and removing twelve loads of earth, reared a new and more befitting shrine for the Prince of Apostles. According to Anastasius, this shrine was of silver, enclosed in a sarcophagus of gilt bronze. It was erected on the very spot where in an after age the prodigal munificence of Leo X., assisted by the genius of Michael Angelo, reared the modern fabric. Immediately under the vast cupola stands the high altar ; and on a sunk circular balustrade of marble, surrounding the reputed relics, are a gleaming circlet of lamps, ninety-three in number, which are kept burning night and day.

The martyrdom and burial of Peter in Rome, at the same time with the Apostle of the Gentiles, seems to have been universally accepted by the ancient Church. Dionysius, Bishop of Corinth, who lived in the second

[1] "St Paul in Rome," p. 86.

century, states in his Epistle to the Romans, that Peter
and Paul suffered martyrdom in Rome at the same time
(—κατὰ τὸν αὐτὸν καιρόν Euseb. ii. 25.)   St Jerome mentions the same thing.   " Oh, consider with trembling,"
exclaims Chrysostom, "that which Rome will behold,
when Paul suddenly rises with Peter from this sepulchre, and is carried up into the air to meet the Lord." [1]
Thus, then, amid manifold uncertainties which encom-
pass the closing page in our Apostle's history, it may
still be allowed us, with reasonable certainty, in the
words of an eloquent writer, " to trace his footsteps by
the banks of the Tiber—to witness beside the Appian
Way the scene of the most beautiful of ecclesiastical
legends, which records his last vision of his crucified
Lord—to overlook from the supposed spot of his death
the city of the seven hills—to believe that his last remains repose under the glory of St Peter's dome." [2]   But
a nobler than the noblest of earthly shrines is his ; in
the memories of the millions who have pondered the
mighty deeds and mighty words of this Luther of the
apostolic age ; who *have* listened or who *are* listening to
the echoes of his undying voice ; receiving still his

[1] Chrys. " Hom. on Ep. to Rom."   It was supposed by some that for a
time at least the hallowed dust of the two Apostles was actually mingled.
There is a feast in the Roman calendar celebrated on the fifteenth of July
called "The Feast of the Division of the Apostles."   The legend to which this
refers is as follows :—" The remains of St Peter and St Paul were placed together after their martyrdom, and when Pope Sylvester, at the consecration
of the great church of St Peter, desired to place the sacred remains of the
patron saint in an altar, it was found impossible to distinguish them from
those of St Paul ; but after fasting and prayer, a divine voice revealed that
the larger bones were those of the preacher, the smaller of the fisherman (?),
and they were consequently placed in the churches of St Peter and St Paul
respectively."—Smith's "Dic. Christian Antiquities," p. 109.   A portion of
the relics of Peter are now claimed to rest in the Roman Basilica of St John
Lateran.
[2] "Sermons and Essays on the Apostolic Age," p. 96.

apostolic benediction ; and who feel that to him, in nobler than any poor meaning attached to it by superstition, have been given " the keys of the kingdom of heaven." " On the early sarcophagus St Peter bears a cross, and is generally on the left hand of Christ. The cross, often set with jewels, is supposed to refer to the passage in St John xxi. 19, ' Signifying by what death he should die ; ' but it may surely bear another interpretation, *i.e.*, the spirit of Christianity transmitted to all nations by the first and greatest of the Apostles." [1] Apart altogether from his apostolic gifts, as a mere human study, he was a beautiful example, if we may yet again, ere we close, repeat the remark made in a previous chapter, of the transforming, refining power of divine grace. The weakness and impetuosity of youth —the rashness and the prejudices of manhood passed away ;—his growing years only ripening him for his crown. Like the divine vision beheld on the " holy mount," he was transfigured before he was glorified : till at last a brighter than any halo with which the painter's art in after ages surrounded him, encircled his white hairs and furrowed brow. It was of himself he was unconsciously writing in the closing sentence of his First Epistle : " But the God of all grace, who hath called us unto His eternal glory by Christ Jesus, after that ye have suffered a while, make you perfect, stablish, strengthen, settle you " (1 Pet. v. 10). However different it might have been at one time, the Rockman could in the last hour of all make the avowal with unfaltering voice, " Why cannot I follow Thee now ? I will lay down my life for Thy sake." That life, with its strangely varying moods, its not unfrequent deflections

[1] " Sacred and Legendary Art." p. 190.

from duty, rash impulses, and grievous falls, was like
the mountain which, to the near view, is torn and splin-
tered,—ploughed up with unsightly scars by spring
floods and winter storms.   But as we recede, and the
soft autumn evening light falls upon it, the jagged outline is lost; there is seen only a mass of mellowed
lustre.

We need not follow him "within the gate into the
city."   While we reject its superstitious surroundings,
we may feel certified of the accuracy of Giotto's great
picture in the sacristy of St Peter, where angels are represented as bearing the soul of the martyred Saint and
Apostle in a bright cloud to heaven.   Or the still more
beautiful conception of the Florentine "Memmi," who
depicts him in his fresco standing along with two angels
at the portal of Paradise, putting garlands on the heads
of the many he 'had turned to righteousness' as they
enter hand in hand the New Jerusalem.   With equal
truth may the words be applied to him which Chrysostom
employs regarding St Paul: "If we listen to him here,
we shall certainly see him hereafter; if not as standing
near him, yet see him we certainly shall, glistening
near the throne of the King, where the cherubim sing
the glory, where the seraphim are flying.   There we
shall see him as a chief and leader of the choir of the
saints, and shall enjoy his generous love."

> " Nobly thy course is run,
>   Splendour is round it ;
> Bravely thy fight is won,
>   Martyrdom crowned it.
> In the high warfare
>   Of heaven grown hoary,
> Thou'rt gone, like the summer sun,
>   Shrouded in glory."

APPENDIX.

SITE OF "BETHABARA."

SINCE the preceding pages were printed, I have received the Report of the recent identifications made by the "Palestine Exploration Society." Among the most interesting of these, is the alleged discovery of the true position of *Bethabara* referred to in page 47 of this volume,—the scene of Peter's first introduction to the Messiah. I give, in the words of the Report, the objection to the traditional site, and the grounds for supporting a more northerly one :—

"There is a serious objection to placing Bethabara so far south. Our Lord descended from Galilee to Jordan, and to Galilee he returned after the baptism and temptation. In the chapter which relates the testimony of John the Baptist to Christ, and which contains the passage, 'these things were done in Bethabara, beyond Jordan, where John was baptizing,' we learn, in continuation (ver. 43), 'the day following Jesus would go forth into Galilee,' and the next chapter commences, 'and on the third day there was a marriage in Cana of Galilee,' at which Christ was present (John ii. 1)."

On instituting a search for a more appropriate site within thirty miles of Cana of Galilee (the present Khirbet Kana), the explorers came upon the name, at one of the Fords of the Jordan, one mile north of the mouth of Wady Jalúd, and not more than twenty-five from Nazareth and Cana.

"The ford in question is called Makhádhet 'Abára, or the 'Ford of the Crossing Over,' for the name is derived from the Arabic root, 'Abr, having the meaning of crossing. . . .

"Makhádhet 'Abára is one of the principal northern fords; the great road descending Wady Jalúd on its northern side, and leading to Gilead and the south of the Hauran, passes over by it. The situation is well fitted for the site of the baptism, not only on account of its nearness to Galilee and Nazareth, but also because the river bed is here more open, the steep banks of the upper valley or ghor lesser and farther retired, thus leaving a broader space for the collection of the great crowd which had followed John the Baptist into the wilderness."

The above must be accepted with all the deference due to the reliable and indefatigable labourers engaged in this noble mission. The point which seems least satisfactory in transferring the site from the traditional one, is the greater accessibility of the latter to the multitudes who flocked to the preaching of the Baptist "from Jerusalem and all Judea, and all the region round about Jordan" (περιχωρος : most probably the wide plain, or lower valley around Jericho) (Matt. iii. 5). Moreover, the mere name 'Abára cannot, of itself, in the present case, authoritatively fix the site, as the word Bethabara—meaning "the House of the Crossing," or "the Ford"—is allowed by the explorers in their Report "to be applicable to many points on the course of the Jordan." Meanwhile, at all events, the question must remain an open one.

1982-83 TITLES

0203	Dolman, Dirk H.	The Tabernacle	19.75
0603	Lang, John M.	Studies in the Book of Judges	17.75
0701	Cox, S. & Fuller, T.	The Book of Ruth	14.75
0902	Deane, W. J. & Kirk, T.	Studies in the First Book of Samuel	19.00
1301	Kirk, T. & Rawlinson, G.	Studies in the Books of Kings	20.75
2102	Wardlaw, Ralph	Exposition of Ecclesiastes	16.25
4603	Jones, John Daniel	Exposition of First Corinthians 13	9.50
4902	Pattison, R. & Moule, H.	Exposition of Ephesians: Lessons in Grace and Godliness	14.75
5104	Daille, Jean	Exposition of Colossians	24.95
5803	Edwards, Thomas C.	The Epistle to the Hebrews	13.00
5903	Stier, Rudolf E.	Commentary on the Epistle of James	10.25
6202	Morgan, J. & Cox, S.	The Epistles of John	22.95
7000	Tatford, Frederick Albert	The Minor Prophets(3 vol.)	44.95
7107	Cox, S. & Drysdale, A. H.	The Epistle to Philemon	9.25
8403	Jones, John Daniel	The Apostles of Christ	10.00
8404	Krummacher, Frederick W.	David, King of Israel	20.50
8405	MacDuff, John Ross	Elijah, the Prophet of Fire	13.75
8406	MacDuff, John Ross	The Footsteps of St. Peter	24.25
8801	Lidgett, John Scott	The Biblical Doctrine of the Atonement	19.50
8802	Laidlaw, John	The Biblical Doctrine of Man	14.00
9513	Innes, A. T. & Powell, F. J.	The Trial of Christ	10.75
9514	Gloag, P. J. & Delitzsch, F.	The Messiahship of Christ	23.50
9515	Blaikie, W. G. & Law, R.	The Inner Life of Christ	17.25
9806	Ironside, H. A. & Ottman, F.	Studies in Biblical Eschatology	16.00

TITLES CURRENTLY AVAILABLE

0101	Delitzsch, Franz	A New Commentary on Genesis (2 vol.)	30.50
0102	Blaikie, W. G.	Heroes of Israel	19.50
0103	Bush, George	Genesis (2 vol.)	29.95
0201	Murphy, James G.	Commentary on the Book of Exodus	12.75
0202	Bush, George	Exodus	22.50
0301	Kellogg, Samuel H.	The Book of Leviticus	21.00
0302	Bush, George	Leviticus	10.50
0401	Bush, George	Numbers	17.75
0501	Cumming, John	The Book of Deuteronomy	16.00
0602	Bush, George	Joshua & Judges (2 vol. in 1)	17.95
1101	Farrar, F. W.	The First Book of Kings	19.00
1201	Farrar, F. W.	The Second Book of Kings	19.00
1701	Raleigh, Alexander	The Book of Esther	9.75
1802	Green, William H.	The Argument of the Book of Job Unfolded	13.50
1901	Dickson, David	A Commentary on the Psalms (2 vol.)	32.50
1902	MacLaren, Alexander	The Psalms (3 vol.)	45.00
2001	Wardlaw, Ralph	Book of Proverbs (3 vol.)	45.00
2101	MacDonald, James M.	The Book of Ecclesiastes	15.50
2201	Durham, James	An Exposition on the Song of Solomon	17.25
2301	Kelly, William	An Exposition of the Book of Isaiah	15.25
2302	Alexander, Joseph	Isaiah (2 vol.)	29.95
2401	Orelli, Hans C. von	The Prophecies of Jeremiah	15.25
2601	Fairbairn, Patrick	An Exposition of Ezekiel	18.50
2701	Pusey, Edward B.	Daniel the Prophet	19.50
2702	Tatford, Frederick Albert	Daniel and His Prophecy	9.25
3001	Cripps, Richard S.	A Commentary on the Book of Amos	13.50
3201	Burn, Samuel C.	The Prophet Jonah	11.25
3801	Wright, Charles H. H.	Zechariah and His Prophecies	24.95
4001	Morison, James	The Gospel According to Matthew	24.95
4101	Alexander, Joseph	Commentary on the Gospel of Mark	16.75

TITLES CURRENTLY AVAILABLE